THE CONSTRUCTION OF NEGOTIATED MEANING

A Social Cognitive Theory of Writing

Linda Flower

Southern Illinois University Press

CARBONDALE AND EDWARDSVILLE

Printed in the United States of America
Designed by Edward D. King
Production supervised by Natalia Nadraga
97 96 95 94 4 3 2 1

Library of Congress Cataloging-in-Publication Data

Flower, Linda.
The construction of negotiated meaning : a social
cognitive theory of writing / Linda Flower.
p. cm.
Includes bibliographical references and index.
1. Rhetoric—Study and teaching (Higher)
2. Meaning (Psychology)
3. Authorship. I. Title.
P301.F58 1994
808'.042'0711—dc20
ISBN 0-8093-1900-4 93-26585
ISBN 0-8093-1901-2 pbk. CIP

The paper used in this publication meets the minimum requirements of American National Standard for Information Sciences—Permanence of Paper for Printed Library Materials, ANSI Z39.48-1984. ∞

Contents

Figures and Tables

Figures

Tables

Acknowledgments

Since much of this book grew out of our work with collaborative planning and with what planners have told us, it is a happy occasion for me to acknowledge my own collaborators and colleagues who have had a valued role in developing these ideas. Lorraine Higgins and Joseph Petraglia were my partners in the study of freshman collaborative planners (chaps. 6 and 7), supported by the National Center for the Study of Writing and Literacy at the University of California, Berkeley and Carnegie Mellon University. As we tried to translate the theoretical categories of the Planner's Blackboard into a coding scheme that responded to the data, we not only expanded the theory, but in our own generative disagreements over how to interpret these students, we saw the need for a more complex strategic analysis that might capture more of students' own complex motivations and awarenesses. Lorraine took the lead in extending our analysis of reflection, and her continued conversation and balanced judgments are an important part of the argument offered here.

Barbara Sitko was my collaborator in the classroom inquiry of chapter 8, with support from the Howard Heinz Endowment, Superintendent Richard Wallace, and the Pittsburgh Board of Public Education. Barbara's presence in the classroom made Freire come alive and made us see collaboration as a gift writers give one another. Her own work on metacognition not only stimulated my thinking but helped focus our analysis on the links between awareness and action.

The support of both the National Center for the Study of Writing and Literacy and the Howard Heinz Endowment allowed me to start this book in Berkeley in the fall of 1990, welcomed by Sarah Freedman and the NCSWL team. Much of the research for this book was supported by a grant from the Office of Educational Research and Improvement, Department of Education (OERI/ED) for the National Center for the Study of Writing and Literacy. However, the opinions expressed here do not necessarily reflect the position or policy of the OERI/ED, and no official endorsement of the OERI/ED should be inferred.

Various parts of this book are really transplanted conversations or attempts, in the afterlight of a good discussion, to build a better response. I am especially grateful to Stuart Greene and John Ackerman for talking construction over dinner, over texts, and on horseback, and to Glynda Hull, who, as we were packing the car to leave Berkeley, asked, "What are you really doing for education?" Her question and the answer that became chapter 1 pursued me from California to Iowa. Thanks to Stephen Witte, Susan Florio-Ruane, David Kaufer, Barbara Walvoord, and especially David Wallace whose insights and generous engagement reshaped my understanding, and to Martin Nystrand and Deborah Brandt who tell the story a little differently. Thanks, too, to my undergraduate students who became coauthors in a classroom inquiry, especially Jennifer Severa, Gina Marsala, Cheryl Montgomery, Martha Vockley, and Laura Ann Lemay.

I also want to thank people who not only inspired me with their work but who graciously read parts of this manuscript: Charles Bazerman, Rebecca Burnett, Mike Carter, Courtney Cazden, Peter Elbow, Dick Hayes, Karen Harris, Janice Lauer, Sarah Freedman, Kathleen McCormick, Annmarie Palincsar, Louise Phelps, Mike Rose, Melanie Sperling, John Trimbur, David Russell, and John Willinsky.

My gratitude goes to Kathy Meinzer, who put her expert hand to creating this manuscript and is my valued advisor.

And most of all, I am delightedly grateful to my primary collaborator and best reader, Tim Flower. I want to thank him for making my ideal of collaborative planning real: long days of sunshine and writing in our single-room sabbatical looking over San Francisco Bay, breaking for morning buns to talk each other through our stories about the aesthetics of precision watch design and the negotiation of meaning.

THE CONSTRUCTION OF NEGOTIATED MEANING

I

Literate Acts

I. Conversations about Literacy

The public discussion of literacy in crisis is like a long-running soap opera that continues to ask: Why can't Johnny read, write, or think? In this ritual tale, test scores and literacy rates reappear as shocking evidence of a decline from better days. But defining the "basics" to which schools should return as well as the "basics" that must be taught first is also a chief source of conflict among the players in this drama. For some of them, written literacy is equated with error-free, standard written English. For others, "basic" is equated with a more elite set of conventions—the ability to write an essay or five-paragraph theme associated with the belletristic essay tradition in English studies. (Each group assumes that its valued skills constitute the basic building blocks with which instruction must start.) For still other voices in this discussion, literacy, true literacy, does not merit the name until one can read, write, and talk about some valued body of knowledge such as the traditional literary canon of middle-class, male-authored works taught in English departments. But whatever the definition, when talk turns to "Is it true high school students can't read and/or college students can't write?," the discussion will echo with the language of deficits—deficits in students' cultural backgrounds, the embarrassing gaps in their knowledge, and their measured failure to achieve (and teachers to impart) some aspect of either functional, essayistic, or cultural literacy.

The public talk of literacy has become a ritual discourse defined by a powerful set of commonplaces and concepts. However, because it has so clearly failed to account for both the personal and social practice of literacy, it is being challenged by a new conversation in social, cognitive, and rhetorical theory. At issue is a focus on literate actions rather than on texts alone. In this conversation, the concept of literacy has been exploded into *literacies*, defined as *diverse discourse practices* that grow out of the needs and values of different communities. That community may be academic literacy theorists, African farmers, or cognitive anthropologists who, like Scribner and Cole (1981), interpret the practices of the first two groups using the discourse strategies of the third. Gee describes a capital *D* "Discourse"

> as a sort of "identity kit" which comes complete with the appropriate costume and instructions on how to act, talk, and often write, so as to take on a particular role that others will recognize. Being "trained" as a linguist meant that I learned to speak, think, and act like a linguist, and to recognize others when they do so. Some other examples of Discourses: (enacting) being an American or a Russian, a man or a woman, a member of a certain socioeconomic class, a factory worker or boardroom executive, doctor or a hospital patient . . . a student of physics or a student of literature, a member of a sewing circle, a club, street gang, lunchtime social gathering, or a regular at a local bar. We all have many Discourses. (1989, p. 7)

That was a linguist speaking. Other voices that we will hear in this social cognitive conversation shift attention from the features of a discourse to the *practice* of literacy. Described from this angle, literate action is a socially situated *problem-solving process* shaped not only by available language, practices, partners, and texts, but by the ways people interpret the rhetorical situation they find themselves in, the goals they set, and the strategies they control. When the discussion turns from the conventions of discourse to the practice of readers and writers within it, it becomes clear that literate acts are also moments of making meaning. Literate actions emerge out of a *constructive* cognitive process that transforms knowledge in purposeful ways. And at critical moments, this constructive literate act may also become a process of *negotiation* in which individual readers and writers must juggle conflicting demands and chart a path among alternative goals, constraints, and possibilities.

This more expansive view of literacy is both the foundation for and, in the long run, the justification for this book and its study of how meaning is constructed. In place of a literature review (which academic "Discourse" might suggest here), I would like to ground this alternative view of literacy in some cognitive and social specifics by sketching four distinctive but everyday constructive acts as cases in point. From this basis, we will explore how a social cognitive perspective on literacy not only challenges our public, textual view with some strong claims about what is basic, but may also force us to deal with a potentially generative conflict that is at its own center.

Oren: Constructing a Life

I am sitting at the kitchen table with Oren, who at 82 is gazing out the window but is in actuality looking back over years, marshaling what he sees into a finely forged chain of events. Like Studs Terkel and his interviewee rolled into one, he is constructing the story of his working life. This is a selective account that links and transforms telling bits of information, building a meaning out of facts. It starts with the year he spent reading water meters to get enough money to attend a local college, which led the water company—an unlikely first mentor—to create the part-time job platting city mains that allows him to stay in school. His goal was engineering and Iowa State, but the depression and tales of 400 unemployed graduates cancel the dream. A local minister helps him land work in the Kansas wheat harvest. Adventure and a Colorado uncle keep him working in the Rockies through fall roundup. His Model A repaired with baling wire barely makes it back to Iowa, but he has heard that Chillicothe Business College in Missouri can guarantee a job for its graduates. He works for his board and room; Grandmother sends him money from selling her cinnamon rolls. The road of this working story leads through Chillicothe, Ottumwa, Chicago, Wichita; each chapter is a job won in hard times, an achievement always connected in some way to friends, teachers, or bosses who find him a place, and put in a word and also to effort and persistence that sometimes pay off. These three themes—an inescapable social context, interpersonal support, and personal initiative—are sources of coherence and significance in this constructed life.

Events often hinge on persuasion. It was 1941. Germany had invaded the Netherlands and the British were building tanks in a plant outside of Chicago where the factory was on three shifts and the staff worked 12-hour days. It is clear the general manager on the other side of the desk needs to hire a buyer: a pile of unfilled requisitions are stacked in front of him. For Oren this job could mean staying in Chicago, near Peggy. But the interview is not going well.

> I could see we weren't getting anywhere. So I got up, took off my jacket, hung it on the back of the chair, and then pulled it around to his side of the desk. "Let's look at these requisitions," I say. "Oil cans. You need oil cans. O.K., I can help you here; I know where to find these. [Oren is at that point a hardware buyer for the Montgomery Ward Company.] I have been getting these for two years from Eagle Oil. Let's see what else is here." We began to work down through the stack. When we were done, he asked me to report tomorrow or as soon as I could leave Ward's. You see, what they needed was someone who was willing to roll up his sleeves and pitch in.

Oren, my father, is constructing the story or rather a story that makes meaning out of a part of his life. This constructed meaning is framed and shaped by both conventions and personal themes—hard work, persistence, reading a situation, seeking and making opportunities and always the mentor, manager, friend, or contact who helps you out, gives you a chance. Each new episode is an oral paragraph with a topic sentence that picks up this thematic thread as he recovers from brief tangents. The conventions of narrative, the tricks for achieving focus, give structure to this gaze into the past, as do other conventions of depression discourse. I hear, for instance, the optimistic echos of Horatio Alger simultaneously undercut by a sense of the tremendous vulnerability and interdependence of all the characters in his story—like the college friend fed with rolls smuggled in baggy sweaters from the dining hall after his college savings disappeared overnight in a bank failure, the boy that might have been anyone of them.

If we step back slightly to regard this as a literate act, we see the familiar threads of other literate practices like autobiography and documentary. A variety of local discourse conventions like repetition, thematization, parallelism, and chronology based on critical incidents give this meditation coherence and direction, while other moves, such as shifting perspective and pausing for commentary, create a space for reflection and wonder at it all; they allow a kind of eloquence. But *meditation* is the wrong word, for this literate act is also driven by a desire to communicate, to bring the daughter and son-in-law at the kitchen table into his life and into the experience of a distant time. When we reach Wichita, his asides show he is anticipating places I would remember and thinking where he needs to fill Tim in on background. But for my father himself, this account is at its heart a constructive act, an attempt on this November afternoon to construct a meaning out of experience, perhaps to explore the comment he had made about his working life the night before: "I have been lucky. I may not have accomplished something great, but what I have done has been satisfying to me."

This account of a working life is not only a constructive, literate act itself, it creates a meaning for these events in which literate practices play a distinctive role. Working in Chicago begins with the challenge of taking legal dictation (accurately interpolating the gaps in your shorthand), followed by writing and filling requisitions in tight times as a buyer for Ward's, crafting imaginative sales letters and job applications, like the one that convinced Mrs. Beach to make him the wartime buyer for Beach Aircraft in Wichita and, of course, the love letters that brought Peggy to Kansas. The love letters aside, Oren talks about each of these practices as distinctive abilities, often associated with classes at Chillicothe and Northwestern University. These skilled literate acts—as performances and challenges to meet—are central to the dramatic logic of his account.

Thinking back over this twilight account as an educator, I saw in it an interesting touchstone for literacy, not because we could point to its blurring of oral and written discourse or because of the commonplaces and conventions of autobiography, reflection, and argument that give it structure, but because all of these features are being woven into a highly meaningful, but everyday literate act that was functioning in its different ways for the three people at that table. As an educator, it is this action, this constructive process—the radical selecting, organizing, and connecting of ideas and language for personal and social purposes—that I want to keep in the picture as I envision student literacy. Let me be clear that by *constructive process* I mean something a good deal more precise, robust, effortful, and strategic than just personally meaningful recollection. Meaning construction involves at least three active, often time-consuming processes (Spivey, 1990): *selecting* information (the relevant events and details from a working life); *organizing* it at all levels, from making local transitions to imposing a larger, organizing discourse structure, like a reflective autobiography (though note how the principle of organization may in fact anticipate and guide the process of generating and selecting ideas); and *connecting*, which ranges from seeing and verbalizing parallels in events, to drawing inferences that create a pattern of cause and effect, to explicitly locating one's own ideas in the context of larger issues, other readers, other texts.

This constructive literate act is a social, cognitive, and rhetorical process. And it leads me to ask, Does the literacy we teach and measure support the capacities dramatized here? How well does the development that students *do* undergo, as writers and rhetors in school, fit into their larger history? Does it help them construct meanings that are at once personal, communicable, and useful? Consider another literate act closer to school.

Ron: Constructing a Discourse

At Northwestern, my father studied the art of writing personal sales letters from a celebrated Mr. Crane. The course that impressed him so is probably no longer in the university catalog, its discourse practice replaced by the telephone. But no matter, for what remains vivid from that experience is not a template for texts, but the social and rhetorical practice of persuasion he encountered there. Fifty years later, Ron, a freshman I am interviewing for the Reading-to-Write research project, sees writing through a similar wide lens, as a practice that extends beyond text features. At six weeks into the semester, Ron is trying to construct a workable image of what literate practice in college entails. He sees his writing assignments in English and history as specialized and mysterious but ultimately as rule-governed kinds of discourse—it is his job to figure out the rules of the game (Flower et al., 1990).

Ron: I try to write it as soon as I can and let them look at it. Even take it right to the teacher, and say, "Look at this. Am I going in the right direction or not?"

Interviewer: That's a kind of expensive way to do it, isn't it?

Ron: You pick up things. You pick up good things. It's expensive in terms of that paper, but it's not expensive in terms of putting that away for future reference for the rest of the course. Really, it's pretty practical if you think about it. Rather than going about it and getting two, three C's on a paper.

Learning to be literate in school, constructing a theory of the discourse at hand, is itself a constructive act that does not end with soliciting feedback. It depends on savvy and critical intelligence, selecting the details and cues that matter, organizing and connecting information or, more accurately, transforming it into a plan for future action. Ron is adept at reading a situation and using his audience to figure out ways to think, goals to set: "It's not really a conscious process that I go through. You just got to listen. I don't know if it sounds weird or what. But I sit there and I watch them during the lecture. I listen to key words that they use. They register."

For Ron, constructing meaning (i.e., both propositions in a text and the meaning or rules of a new discourse) is an intensely rhetorical act. The cognition and the social relations he describes are based on strategic decisions, guided by goals and strategies of which he is highly conscious. Perhaps it is no surprise that Ron is not eighteen, that he has come to college after 10 years rising from stock boy to assistant manager in a large store. The constructive process he describes is the strategic construction of negotiated meaning.

> And to be honest with you, I think it has a lot to do with my being . . . I've been out for 10 years, and I came back. And this is more related to real-world experiences. How it goes. I mean, you can go out and you can tell your boss, "Well, I think we could do it this way." And you have a real good idea. And he just says, "Get outa here." Meanwhile, if you really think it's a good idea you can twist it around and maintain the gist of the whole thing and maybe get it pushed through. Mutually beneficial: it's gonna help him and help you.

For Ron, learning to write in college is not upgrading skills; it is learning how to operate within a new discourse. Moreover, to construct a successful text a student must first construct (and test) his or her own theory of that discourse. Ron's ten years of "being out" also taught him that entering a literate practice is a political act; it depends on reading a situation and reading the audience as well as reading texts and having good ideas.

Heidi: Constructing a Meaning from Text

Reading research and most tests measure comprehension by the reader's ability to recall the author's main points and the structure of the text. Heidi, who is thinking aloud as she reads an article by Stephen J. Gould, is a cooperative research subject/student who knows what is expected (Flower, 1987). Throughout her reading, she dutifully rehearses those key points, struggling to construct a representation of the author's main point (i.e., why people have had so much difficulty accepting three claims in Darwin's theory). However, side by side with this process, the transcript reveals another constructive act going on, one that is building a quite different, even more significant political reading in the mind of this reader. "Now what I've done is, I've lost track of the sort of—highest-level—point of this—this article, which is why [there is] the difficulty in accepting Darwin's theory, because I've been trying so hard to remember what the damn theory was. Ok. What I—I can't wait to hear about [is] the radical philosophical content [just alluded to in Gould's text]. . . . Good . . . Oh, I'm really—I love this."

In tandem with her repeated attempts to construct and rehearse a main point reading about difficulties with Darwin's theory, Heidi, a dedicated social activist, ended up creating another well-developed "radical reading" with its own hierarchy and set of gists. (She was even more effective at recalling this than the main point construction she labored over.) What stands out in this vignette is a reader who is not simply comprehending a text, but is actively constructing multiple coherent meanings, guided by both her "good reader" strategies and her personal goals for reading.

Dawnise: Constructing a Text

Dawnise is an at-risk teenager from an inner city housing project on Pittsburgh's North Side, but at the Community Literacy Center she is a writer working with a group of other young writers to investigate the story of teen pregnancy from the little-heard side of the teen. The text Dawnise is reading to the group is based directly on her interview with Mary who is 14 and pregnant. It is disappointing: Mary's thoughts about getting pregnant, continuing school, financial planning, and raising a baby, all seemed minimal; the text is offering a flat, two-dimensional portrait of this teenager. However, when Dawnise begins to talk about the silent dialogue that had been in her own mind as she talked with Mary, another meaning begins to form around the text.

> I was thinking, did she really know what I was talking about, so I tried to explain a little bit more. . . . Or maybe she was sort of avoiding

> it. It was like something you could tell that she wanted to talk about, then when you get more into it she just blanked out. . . .
>
> She really didn't feel [having a baby] would jeopardize her life. And I was thinking, maybe. . . . [pause] I thought she wouldn't make it. Cause it's like she just knew these things would happen and she really didn't sit down and talk to anyone about it. And it was just, like well, it was like a fantasy, because you always wish for the good things to happen. . . .
>
> I felt sort of sad when I was interviewing her. I felt why would a person want to jeopardize their life like this. Why would they really want to want this for themselves. I thought maybe if someone could talk to her a little bit more and tell her about it, you know, try to make her understand then maybe it could work.

In a short conversation afterwards, Dawnise added a final, tentative, but it seemed strongly felt, thought: "And I wondered if maybe she just didn't want some love. I also wondered was it because her mother and father have an alcohol and drug problem. If maybe that had something to do with it."

The compelling meaning of this interview was not on the tape; it was in the interplay between Mary's words and Dawnise's empathetic reading of what they and the situation could mean. The problem this writing group had to face was, How does someone represent such meaning in a text? Should Dawnise use *I*? Should she even bring her own response into the text? And if so, what conventions or strategies let writers integrate multiple voices or weave their interpretation of a scene while still trying to document it and let these teens speak for themselves? Constructing this text was, in part, a matter of knowing some writerly conventions, yet even simple moves in the text, like using *I*, were contingent on larger rhetorical decisions and would send the group back to questions about what they wanted this text to do, for whom.

II. Competing Images of Literacy

Vignettes of constructive processes like these challenge our public discourse about literacy and urge us to examine what our discourse values and what it has failed to see. Looking at literacy as part of a social action puts text features like grammar, spelling, topic sentences, and transitions in perspective. Correctness and convention, those easy-to-spot text features that stir the blood of the public press, move out of the spotlight. However, when that happens, what moves in? Our popular discussion lacks a vocabulary for going beyond the borders of a text, for naming the basics that support genuine literate action or for judging success (Hull, 1991).

By contrast, the image of literacy emerging out of the new social cognitive conversation starts with an event that is at once public and personal. A literate act, like those in our vignettes, is an attempt to create meaning, and in doing so, it reflects—is itself shaped by—literate, social, and cultural practices that existed long before the writer. At the same time, literacy is also a personal, intentional action, an attempt to understand, express, explore, communicate, or influence. This image of literacy also highlights the real diversity of social practices and cognitive processes carried on under the blanket name of literacy. For example, the person who is an expert or insider in one discourse community is likely to be a novice or outsider in another, whether that community is one that trades business letters, produces rap songs, understands budgets, constructs academic arguments, or engages in community advocacy at city council. Learning these practices and moving among them as a reader and writer calls for strategic knowledge, for understanding the conventions of *that* discourse and how they are used to carry out people's intentions. A conceptual pocket guide to the vocabulary of this new conversation, then, would include partially overlapping notions such as discourse communities, social practices, discourse conventions, and literacy events that would be, in turn, linked to discussions of situated cognition, constructive processes, strategic thinking, and rhetorical awareness.

To draw attention to the "vocabulary" used for literacy may seem like a peculiarly academic exercise in the face of a crisis, but in dealing with the kaleidoscopic nature of literacy, the elements of that process that we talk about are the ones we reify and make real. The features that we make explicit, understandable, and operational are the ones that shape our educational vision (Hull & Rose, 1989). The features we name become the elements that instructors try to teach, that administrators and policymakers support, and that the evaluation industry tries to measure. The politics of literacy are inextricably tied to how we define and measure it. But both definitions and measurement have a troubled history.

Let us consider for a moment how competing images of literacy figure in three important sites of conflict: in the ways we measure and define literacy, in decisions about what to teach, and in the ways we theorize about a discourse.

Measuring and Defining Literacy: Problems with a History

The ground for conflict begins with the troubling fact that our methods of measurement cannot always tell us who is literate and who is not. In current public discussions of the rise (and/or decline) of literacy, being literate usually means the ability to decode and comprehend written language at a rudimentary level. But even with this definition, there is an uncertain relationship between what the standard tests measure and what people do. For periods before the 1850s, literacy rates were measured by evidence such as signatures on marriage registers, army rolls, wills, and other public records; for later periods by multiple choice tests like the SAT and the Armed Forces Qualifying Tests. Although "most historians of the subject have this crude literacy skill in mind when they estimate literacy rates," recent studies have shifted attention from "nominal possession of literacy" to "the uses of literacy among those who are literate and how those uses change over time" (Kaestle, 1988, pp. 96–97). This may be an overdue move (1) if Graff is right that "qualitative abilities cannot be deduced *simply* or *directly* from the quantitative levels of literacy's diffusion" and (2) if there is indeed a "significant disparity between high levels of the possession of literacy [as measured by some limited means] and the usefulness of those skills (1985, p. 81). In other words, the aspects we can measure may not capture performances that matter.

The argument about literacy goes deeper than problems of measurement; it is over what this social construct, this historical chameleon, literacy, means. Tracing the history of these definitions, Resnick and Resnick conclude that our current national literacy crisis was not brought on by a decline in skills but by a dramatic rise in our expectations since the mid-nineteenth century. In 1820, signing one's name would have identified a person as literate (unlike the majority of people even in the developed countries of Europe). A dramatic escalation of literacy (and its definition) had occurred earlier in Sweden when the Lutheran church made reading (to answer questions) and memorizing portions of the catechism and prayer book a requirement for marriage. But both of these skills represent a limited literacy if people want or need to read unfamiliar texts to glean new information, including information that is not directly stated and must be inferred. And what if that knowledge needs to be related sensibly to other texts (1988, p. 191)? Or what if people need to communicate the fruits of their thinking to others?

In our technological society, the demand for literacy goes beyond the receptive capacities of reading to the productive literacies of writing. The National Assessment of Educational Progress view of the workplace calls for a written literacy that does not simply reproduce information but that transforms it: "Skills in reducing data, interpreting it, packaging it effectively, documenting decisions, explaining complex matter in simple terms, and persuading are highly prized in business, education, and the military and will become more so as the information explosion continues (1981, p. 5). And in a competitive, pluralistic society struggling to be democratic, written literacy is a critical way for voices to be heard—even if those voices do not speak in a prestige dialect or do not use the patterns of discourse taught in school. In both the technology and democracy scenarios, the literacy in question appears to be a purposeful and constructive performance with text.

Teaching a Limited Literacy

In contrast to these demands for strategic literate acts, much of our public discourse talks about literacy as if it were a single, generalizable ability and tells schools to make students attain it by teaching grammatical correctness and one or two privileged literate practices. For instance, Hull's "critical assessment of popular views on literacy and work," reviews the popular images of workplace illiteracy that chalk up economic loss to skill deficits while ignoring the more powerful disincentives for literate or productive action that surround these supposedly "illiterate" workers (1991). The equation of literacy with correctness has a long and tenacious history in American schools. As Rose notes, under the influence of Edward Thorndike and turn-of-the-century behaviorist educational theory, correctness (i.e., the particulars of usage, grammar, and mechanics) became the era's "most significant measure of accomplished prose" (1985, p. 343). That focus continues in both remedial and freshman composition programs despite attacks from progressive, liberal, and now process-centered theory. "It is somewhat curious, then, that a behaviorist approach to writing, one that took fullest shape in the 1930's and has been variously and severely challenged by the movements that followed it, remains with us as vigorously as it does. It is atomistic, focusing on isolated bits of discourse, error centered, and linguistically reductive" (p. 343). The legacy of this approach is apparent in the writing currently done in high schools: in Applebee's (1981) study only 3% of high school writing assignments elicited more than a paragraph of text.

The pedagogy of correctness has another quality that may contribute to its staying power. Its drills and exercises, workbooks, texts, and potential for nationwide testing are efficient ways to manage, market, and deliver education. Correctness is big business. Despite 50 years of research demonstrating that teaching grammar does not improve writing (Baron, 1982), teachers at even progressive public schools are still accountable to tests like the California Achievement Test that measure students' writing ability with 55 multiple-choice questions that ask them to distinguish correct words, correct grammatical constructions, and correct sentences from incorrect ones. Middle-class Standard English speakers can even find it fun to play this game with artificial language and test logic: "I am ______ preparing to accept responsibility for the project." Choose among: quick, quicker, quickly, or quickest. But the literacy of conventions and rules is a disempowering game for many who are forced to play it.

Educators make another simplifying move when they identify literacy instruction with instruction in a given privileged practice, such as the essay. Like good grammar, essay writing has many virtues. The problem is letting the part stand for the whole. Essayistic definitions of literacy do indeed have a long history in education, based on the comfortable association between belles lettres, the transmission of culture, and the development of a cultivated mind (deCastell & Luke, 1988). Even in its homely schoolroom incarnation (e.g., the five-paragraph theme), essayistic literacy is venerated as the way young minds acquire skills such as logic, analysis, development, and generalization. Patterns of development in a text are not only equated with patterns of thought, they are the way to teach such intellectual skills—or so the assumption goes (DeAngelo, 1975). Teaching a given textual convention is justified by equating that convention with literate thinking. One radical version of this association is found in the Great Divide theories that see the move from orality to literacy as not only a great watershed in human culture but "claim that mastery of a written language affects not only the content of thought but also the processes of thinking—*how* we classify, reason, remember" (Scribner & Cole, 1981, p. 5).

Some devastating challenges to these assumptions have come, however, from cross cultural, cognitive, and linguistic research. Abstract, rational, and critical thought regularly appears in "unlettered" societies in the absence of both formal education and literacy, although Western intelligence tests have an embarrassing record of unreliable, ethnocentric attempts to measure it (Goodnow, 1976). As Scribner and Cole (1981) showed with their comparisons of Vai, Arabic, and English literacies in a single Liberian society, people do indeed differ in the specialized thinking skills they develop, such as the tendency to use functional versus categorical methods of classification. But these differences are not the result of literacy per se, but a function of urban life, Western schooling, and the specific discourse practices used in one's community. Practice in writing "themes," this work suggests, will enable you to write themes; it will not make you a literate thinker for all occasions. Closer to home, the "myth that middle-class language [i.e., Standard English] is in itself better suited to dealing with abstract, logically complex, or hypothetical questions" has been forcefully undercut by Labov's linguistic research. It shows such thinking where it was least predicted—in the definitely nonstandard, decidedly anti-academic street talk of adolescent members of a Harlem gang (1972, p. 220).

The decision about what to teach in the name of literacy has also depended, in the public discussion, on the assumption that literacy is a unified, stable entity, a generalized ability a person can acquire in one setting and transfer to all others. This monolithic concept, too, is being redefined by richly documented analyses of "literacy transactions" (Resnick & Resnick, 1989), "literacy events" (Heath, 1983), and "literate situations" (Anderson & Stokes, 1984). In these ethnographic, historical, and rhetorical studies, the literacies people practice range from reading sacred texts in expected ways, to "sounding" to gain prestige, to keeping agricultural and family records, to collaborative reading, writing, and problem solving in response to newspapers, official documents, and academic assignments. The literate acts uncovered here are not limited to schoolwork or a schooled elite. They are performed by preschoolers, school dropouts, parents, workers, and they show literacies that are woven into the lives of Americans regardless of age, class, ethnic background, education, or job. Literacy becomes "a complex of actions that take place inside a web of social relationships and social assumptions. . . . If we want to know how literate we are, therefore, we must ask how much and how well people use the printed word, to carry out each kind of social transaction we consider important. . . . Instruments such as the NAEP literacy examination, although they go farther than most standard tests . . . are not geared to this situational analysis" (Resnick & Resnick, 1989, p. 193).

The public discourse of literacy and its assumptions about how to define, measure, and teach literacy are coming under fire (Hull, 1991; Lunsford, Moglen, & Slevin, 1990), but the problem is not a simple one. On the one hand, who would deny the practical and social significance of being able to use Standard English or dismiss the rich history and value of essayistic and academic conventions (on which the present text, for instance, depends). Even the maligned five-paragraph theme is a useful simplification for teaching key skills. True, we are beginning to discover "hidden literacies" in high school dropouts and "print awareness" in preschoolers, but is this any reason to sit back, celebrate, and let natural development replace teaching? If anything, these challenges to the meaning of literacy problematize the question of what is "basic," which practices to privilege, and how to teach genuine literate acts.

On the other hand, it is becoming clear that we need a new conceptual vocabulary for talking about being literate that does not shrink our image down to a limited Literacy defined solely by text features. Popular references to Literacy are, I would argue, often references not to the sweep of literate performance but to a particular and far more convenient construct I am calling a limited Literacy. This construct does two things. First, it identifies literacy with some privileged set of text features or conventions (whether it is a comparison/contrast theme or an error-free paragraph) that are indeed significant in some settings, but not in all. (Such literacy is rather like the fluency in Pig Latin that was admired by many, but possessed by few, in my grade school—a practice with local prestige and limited transfer.) These prized literate practices are often the familiar genres, text conventions, or patterns of development taught in school, or they are identified with knowledge (e.g., of spelling or grammar) that can be reliably measured by tests. By this definition, any given practice would qualify as a limited instance of literacy. However, limited literacies aspire to the status of a generic term. Not satisfied with promoting their chosen set of conventions or text-based skills as a valuable tool or a desirable ability, they begin to masquerade in public discourse as the essential, necessary, or defining elements of literacy. They claim the status of a synecdoche as when essayistic literacy comes to stand for the whole. And even more problematic, limited literacies, like the pedagogy of correctness, solidify their position by posing as a necessary foundation, the basic skills, which must be in place before other literacies can develop. They pass themselves off as the entry point to literacy when they are merely a part; they pose as a defining practice and aggressive stand-in for the whole when they are neither.

The ritual public discourse of literacy, a discourse that habitually links correctness and essayistic expectations with student failure, has failed to put these limited literacies in perspective. In confusing parts with the whole, it has dictated ways to teach literacy that routinely fail to develop the genuine literate capacities students already possess (Dyson, 1986; Heath, 1983). Perhaps even more ironically, it has also failed to teach the limited literacies it set up as the goal and the yardstick for instruction. A cultural critique of this situation might not even find this failure unexpected, since these limited literacies often function as powerful social gatekeepers. They call for a special performance that minority and poor students are not likely to have acquired.

Theorizing about a Literate Practice

Different images of literacy can lead us literally to see different parts of this process: to construct different stories about what happened and to see different parts as the essential features. The debate over the scientific essay is a case in point. The rise of the analytic and scientific essay is a milestone in the history of Western literacy. But is it the success story of a textual convention or the outcome of a strategic and ongoing social/intellectual event? And what difference would either view make?

Olson uses this genre to make a strong case for an exclusively textual conception of literacy; he sees the history of the essay as a slow climb out of situated, oral utterances—statements that depend on their context to make sense—moving towards what he calls autonomous text. Such texts, loosed from the mooring of context and speaker/listener relations, create knowledge through "the repeated application in a single coherent text of the technique of examining an assertion to determine all of its implications" (1988, p. 182). This process "of formulating statements, deriving their implications, testing the truth of those implications, and using the results to revise or generalize from the original statement characterized not only empiricist philosophy," but the practice of science mirrored in the developing Royal Society (p. 183). The result of this textual practice, Olson goes on to argue, was "the formulation of a small set of connected statements of great generality that may occur as topic sentences of paragraphs or as premises of extended scientific or philosophical treatise . . . notable not only in their novelty and abstractness but also [in their] . . . mode of using language—the deduction of counterintuitive models of reality" (p. 183). When literacy is conceptualized as the production of such texts—abstract, logical, internally consistent performances aspiring to the sanctity of the syllogism—"the criterion for the success of a statement in explicit prose text is its formal structure" (p. 188). When formal features are elevated to the essence of literacy, there is little need to measure or, it appears, even to worry about a successful transaction between reader and writer: "If the text is formally adequate and the reader fails to understand, that is the reader's problem. The meaning is in the text" (p. 188).

Given this concentration on the formal features of discourse, it follows that the goal of schooling would be to transform "children's language from utterance to text" (Olson, 1988, p. 189). In textualizing knowledge, Brandt (1990) argues, Olson's view decontextualizes literacy and provides a strong rationale for the current practice of equating literate practice with certain text features. In fact, the argument with Olson's account is not with its picture of certain textual features and their usefulness, but with its theoretical and practical implications for what it means to be literate. One could even cheer this apotheosis of the essay and acknowledge it as a formidable literary and intellectual feat but still remain suspicious of the current educational practice that reduces the essence of this textual performance to a narrow set of text features. Unlike Olson's idealized essay, the textbook essay is typically defined as the presence of a thesis statement, paragraphs following standard patterns of logical development (comparison/contrast, cause/effect, etc.), transitions, and a conclusion. Reduced to teachable textual features, the textbook essay that dominates instruction is often no more than a hollow, formal shell (cf. Crowley, 1990).

But what if we aimed higher than a "limited literacy" and targeted the conventions of Olson's robust, intellectually demanding essay as basic? An even more compelling criticism of textually defined literacy lies in Brandt's

(1990) next observation: teaching textual literacy may misrepresent what expert readers and writers actually do and reinforce novice performance. In numerous cognitive studies of writers at work, she argues, the inexperienced writers are preoccupied with formal text features (as their schooling would support), while the experts subordinate such matters to a more global consideration of purposes, goals, and possible reader responses. The mental representation experienced writers appear to build is not an autonomous text but a purposeful rhetorical move. In fact, experienced readers may even work to interpret a supposedly autonomous text by transforming it into a meaningful social transaction. While inexperienced readers appear to focus on the content and textual features of a difficult text, experienced readers carry out "rhetorical" (Haas & Flower, 1988) and "point-driven" (Hunt & Vipond, 1986) reading, drawing inferences about who was saying what to whom, in what context, and why. As Brandt argues, the textbook habit of equating literacy with textuality is also challenged by ethnographic studies of literate events: here the meaning of even "explicit" texts resides not in the text alone but in its interaction with habits of problem solving, child rearing, or the storytelling a cultural group may bring to these reading and writing events. Moreover, Olson's broadbrush history of literacy as the neat march toward autonomous text seems oddly out of touch with detailed historical research that documents how literate practices and the meanings they create are constantly in flux, reflecting changing cultural, ethnic, and economic patterns. In sum, defining and teaching literacy in terms of its textual artifacts alone seems to be missing some basic features of what literate people do.

On the other hand, textual conventions are central to literacy—they embody the history of a discourse, and they shape the making of new meanings by writers and the process of interpretation by readers. The difference is that a social cognitive conception of literacy embeds texts within contexts and purposes; texts and text features are a means to an end, not an end in themselves. Moreover, they turn out to be mutable, adaptive features that reflect rhetorical and intellectual responses to social exigencies. For example, when Bazerman's richly researched history of the rise of the scientific article tracks it through the *Transactions* of the Royal Society, we see key features of the genre emerge over time as a rhetorical response to the context of that rapidly developing, individualistic, and often contentious community. The early volumes starting in 1665 are taken up with reports of natural phenomena or cookbook recipes for producing fascinating effects with vacuums and chemicals. But as writers begin reporting actual experiments and readers of this epistolary journal begin to respond with conflicting opinions and reports, the conventions for reporting methods begin to emerge as a response to misunderstanding and as a defense against attack. "As disputes arise over reported results, writers become more careful about reporting what they see and measurement takes a greater role" (1988, p. 72). Although new ways of reporting eventually become conventionalized, they begin as a direct response to the social situation of writing: "Debate and conflict push results to greater detail and precision in exactly the same articles with more detailed accounts of methods" (p. 72). The convention of an introduction that sets up a general problem also begins to emerge under the same conditions: "As experiments begin to respond to conflicts, their reports focus on the issue in contention . . . with a statement of the phenomenon in dispute and then a discussion of the opponent's work or position" (p. 76). Over this period, the genre that emerges "is a social construct that regularizes communication, interaction, and relations. Thus, the formal features . . . by which we usually recognize a text's inclusion in a genre, are the linguistic/symbolic solution to a problem in social interaction" (p. 62).

Although Bazerman and Olson are both talking about the Royal Society *Transactions*, in Bazerman's richly specified account, the features of precision, abstraction, general proposition, and evidence that Olson identified with an autonomous text turn out to be highly rhetorical, pragmatic moves that evolved within a complex social negotiation and that continue to serve a practical function in scientific discourse. In foregrounding the formal and logical features of the essay, an exclusively textual literacy ends up obliterating the human logic that produces conventions—and continues to change them.

What's in Focus: A Text, a Literate Practice, or a Literate Act?

The last few pages have illustrated how competing images of literacy can shape the ways we measure, teach, and theorize about literacy. But let us return for a moment to the question that launched this chapter: Can any of these images alone do justice to the individual literate performances of an Oren, Ron, Heidi, and Dawnise? Textual literacy and the public discourse about literacy rates, skills, knowledge deficits, and proficiency would zero in on Heidi as the model student but probably would find Ron's attempt to construct a theory of task mildly irrelevant and ask to see his freshman paper. Oren didn't even write anything. Dawnise, however, would have a well-defined spot in this literacy picture—as the problem. Her SAT scores and nonstandard expressions would quickly identify her as a remedial, developmental, or underprepared student. Her text shows deficiencies in grammar, usage, and development. She does not control the conventions of literate commentary at the level of a John McPhee or even of a mainstream student from a good suburban school. And yet, should we just ignore her personal history of using journal writing to think her way through life crises and to share her life with us (acts that have little place in the public story)? Is there any evidence of literacy in the interpretive insight and the problem solving Dawnise demonstrated in the face of new and conflicting conventions? Should her own silencing assumptions about public text be a part of the picture?

An image of literacy as a social cognitive event, on the other hand, would draw attention to the literate practices behind these performances and to the converging purposes and social interactions that created them. It would focus on the shared, conventional patterns that achieve canonical force because they are understood by other players as meaningful moves within the game (whether the game is a scientific essay or the five-paragraph theme). Some would argue that the clearly defined discourse communities to which Gee alludes are at best a convenient fiction. However, the concepts of community and practice would draw our attention to the generic, socially constructed, and discourse-specific features of literate performance. Our focus would shift from text per se to social practices ranging from the broad conventions of life history to the local conventions of thematization apparent in Oren. On the other hand, merely to catalog Oren's array of literate practices—to categorize his performance as an oral life history or depression fable—would somehow miss the point of this personally meaningful, individually constructed literate act. A social cognitive image, then, allows another part of literacy to come into focus: it shifts our attention not only from text features to discourse practices, but from social practices to personal literate acts.

A *literate act,* as I am using the term, is an individual constructive act that does not merely invoke or participate in a literate practice but embeds such practices and conventions within a personally meaningful, goal-directed use of literacy.[1] In trying to account for a literate act like Dawnise's, we begin to ask not only what the writer did but why he or she did it. Literate acts can call for the orchestration of diverse, seemingly incompatible practices; they lead writers like Ron to cross boundaries and bring his stockboy savvy with oral negotiation to constructing not just another freshman paper but to developing a theory of writing papers in this course. Literate acts also reflect the complex, even contradictory, goals and purposes that often drive meaning making. As Heidi switches from her dutiful, well-honed strategies for constructing a reading of the author's main points to her energetic construction of a social critique, she has set out on a collision course between practices. Each prioritizes different information, each demands attention, constructive inferences, and rehearsal, and each is supported by Heidi's own divergent but coexistent personal values and assumptions about what is important to learn. So when her personal curiosity dictates one reading strategy and her desire to cooperate with a presumed request for an intelligent reading dictates another, the attempt to orchestrate these practices becomes a strategic act.

Literate acts are sites of construction, tension, divergence, and conflict. They happen at the intersection of diverse goals, values, and assumptions, where social roles interact with personal images of one's self and one's situation, where individual rhetorical agendas mix with highly conventional practices. These metaphors—"intersect," "interact," "mix"—are by design inconclusive, refusing to privilege one force over the other. That is because literate acts are often sites of negotiation where the meaning that emerges may reflect resolution, abiding contradiction, or perhaps just a temporary stay against uncertainty.

III. Literacy as Action: Some Emerging Claims

I have used these comparative sketches to argue that a social cognitive alternative to the public story of literacy is emerging among educators in rhetoric and composition, educational psychology, sociology, and cultural theory. It is not that these theorists, teachers, and researchers see eye to eye or necessarily all read each other, but a new discourse about literacy is being formed nonetheless. In this discussion, for instance, literacy rates are rarely discussed because the performance they measure has little credibility. Correctness and control of privileged conventions have lost some of their status as definers of literacy or as ends in themselves. They are instead recognized as valuable tools and skills that let writers function in certain contexts (like school), even as they serve to bar the door of entry to students who are less prepared. Such skills are important, sometimes dramatically, critically important, but not because of their inherent value as a necessary building block or tool for thinking. They are important in part because certain groups of people, like teachers, administrators, employers, and readers make them so. In this discussion, students are no longer defined in terms of intellectual, cultural, or informational deficits. Expert/novice differences are useful, task specific measures of what people can do/could learn. However, novices are not blank slates, but learners who bring a great deal of cultural capital and literate experience with them (that may both help and hinder learning in school).

Perhaps the most fundamental shift in this social cognitive conversation is that it is not about literacy as a monolithic, magical entity that some acquire and others lack. It is, instead, about action, about the literate acts people perform every day, and about the different literacies people use to present a theory of optics, get a job, read the Bible, file reports, learn a discipline, make political statements, and write requests and proposals. It is also about failure and barriers, about people who cannot carry out the literate practice a specific situation demands, who cannot fill out IRS forms, write a five-paragraph theme in school, write effective technical explanations or instructions, or argue on paper with an institution or employer.

Let me articulate some strong claims that I see emerging within this conversation, at least from where I stand in it. However, please be forewarned. To call this emerging conversation a social cognitive "view" of literacy serves to sharpen its conceptual contrast to other views, but does so at the risk of masking its own internal complexity. In fact, this new perspective is itself a site of substantial conflict and it is to the rowdy, competing voices within this discussion I want to turn at the end of the chapter. But first the claims.

1. *Literacy is an action.* The starting point for literacy is a *literate act* or *practice* that is performed as part of a rhetorical, social, and cultural situation. Literacy is not a generalized ability a person possesses (or does not possess) nor a set of technical skills for decoding language. Literacy is a set of actions and transactions in which people use reading and writing for personal and social purposes.

2. *Literacy is a move within a discourse practice.* When people engage in literate action, they are doing more than decoding or producing text. They are engaging in a *discourse practice,* that is, in a transaction with text that is guided (more or less) by a flexible social script for how such things are normally done (whether it is the intensely private diary of a teenager or scientific case building). Like any social practice, it has a history with a set of expectations and conventions (including ones for text features), and it is a response to peoples' purposes, needs, and desires. A discourse practice cannot be reduced to a genre nor to a kind of text; it is a social and rhetorical situation in which texts play a specialized role.

The vignettes sketched earlier employed or referred to a variety of discourse practices: personal reflections (both written and oral), problem analyses written for a college course, sales letters (a practice that spills over into job applications). Practices themselves entertain multiple goals, just as critical reading and writing about science can be used to explain a concept (a practice often expected in college) or to develop one's own argument (as both Gould and Heidi were doing). And in the example of interpretive, documentary journalism, we saw how a developing writer like Dawnise can join in the literate practice of a John McPhee and Studs Terkel despite vast differences in literary technique. Recognizing that we are teaching not literacy but selected discourse practices opens the door to diversity. It also suggests that to be literate is to control a repertoire of literate practices that matter in one's life, to be able to switch among them, and to do so with awareness.

What does a discourse practice look like if someone wanted to teach or learn one? Some accounts focus on the typical features that help differentiate one practice from another. Bazerman, for example, sketches four overlapping stages in the development of the experimental article starting with uncontested reports of events (1665), which gave way to arguments over results (c. 1700), followed by discovery accounts exploring unusual events (c. 1770), and still later by experimental articles offering claims and experimental proofs (1790) (1988, p. 78). Although each stage has some distinctive text features (one could do a taxonomy), Bazerman's discourse analysis is after bigger game. The logic that defines these literate acts (and pushed the experimental article from one stage to another) is the logic of the social practices, personal goals, and forums that shaped this discourse. To talk about the critical features of this evolving discourse, then, we cannot rest once we have noted its methods section or conventions of measurement. Our portrait of the practice must include the ways a clubby Royal Society dealt with growing competition and the ways its ethos of sharing information dealt with a sudden need to test, replicate, and dispute the evidence of the senses.

It should be said that precise accounts of discourse practices are likely to be difficult; we are dealing with social, rhetorical transactions, not a set of canonized texts. Moreover, the boundaries that separate one practice from another will frustrate textual taxonomies, as they are both imprecise and in flux. And for good reason. The web of human purposes that motivates discourse seems happy to sanction invention, transformation, and the flagrant adaptation of literate conventions. The practice of discourse is also an individual, constructive process.

Bazerman's account of social dynamics and textual features can tell us a lot about a discourse practice, but it will take a cognitive account to fill out more of the picture and turn practice into a verb, an action individual readers and writers take. Brandt's discussion of literacy as "involvement" uses the think-aloud protocols of experienced and novice students to show how the practice of argument depends on an interaction between reader and writer, what she calls an "intersubjective experience." Her account shows how a writer imagines a reader into being in order to monitor the current state of shared understanding (created by the text so far) and to plan his next move. My elliptical paraphrase of the writer (whom she quotes in full) highlights this strategic way of rereading one's own text: "So what we've done so far is to analyze xxx to determine its significance. I think I've shown xxx and now I'm trying to talk about the general characteristics of xxx. Yes, I think we've more or less condensed what we've said before except that we haven't talked about xxx yet. Are we undercutting ourselves? Now xxx depends on assumptions . . . and we've shown that those assumptions are wrong. In fact, I claim . . ." (1990, p. 45).

In scanning his text so far, Brandt argues, this writer is "really testing the intersubjective atmosphere, sizing up the extent to which the public grounds will allow the next move he wants to make and the extent to which a reader might already be sharing the key perspective that his argument hinges on" (1990, p. 45)—the claim he now wants to make. The wonderful irony that runs throughout Brandt's argument is that novice writers do appear to operate as if they were producing autonomous, decontextualized text, but experienced writers like this student are engaged in the purposeful practice of discourse as rhetorical action. Even the "logical accomplishments [which Olson would attribute to the conventions of argument] occur within the pressure of intersubjective awareness" (p. 44). In short, although literate practices are often described in terms of text features, what educators need is an account of the social and cognitive moves by which writers actively practice a discourse.

3. Becoming literate depends on knowledge of social conventions and on individual problem solving. Success in carrying out a literate act appears to depend on two things: knowing enough of the conventions and expectations built into the practice to at least enter the conversation and having a repertoire of problem-solving strategies for comprehending and composing that can deal with the task itself and with difficulties.

As I noted before, the conventions of a literate practice that one needs to learn include, but go well beyond, formal text features (such as topic sentences, transitions, or methods sections). They include conventions about what ideas matter, how to frame an argument, and what readers expect and need. This has some important implications for education. To be literate in one practice, such as writing a personal essay for a composition course, calls for special knowledge that might include using the conventions of voice and style that signal "authentic" and "genuine" personal writing. But this success does not guarantee or even predict the writer's ability to carry out other literate practices, such as writing a placement essay based on readings or a history paper. Even the writing instructor who teaches the personal essay might appear quite "illiterate" if asked to critique a Wall Street report or might feel painfully underprepared if invited to cross town and construct an extemporaneous Sunday night prayer (the kind that weaves conventional phrases, personal thoughts, and sociable "amens" into a shared public statement). Although the grammar of standard written English and the conventions of a five-paragraph theme might be desirable in some of these rhetorical contexts, they are certainly not at the heart of the practice. Skill in one practice does not insure literacy in others.

Learning to carry off a literate practice or participate in a discourse community often depends on learning distinctive ways of thinking grounded in the social purposes of the practice—one must understand how a prayer, a placement essay, or an economic analysis functions in its community. Discourse practices, according to this new perspective, exist as tools of a *discourse community*—as functional, often historically, socially constructed ways of writing and talking that serve the purposes of some community like the developing Royal Society. By their very nature, these communities also create insiders and outsiders, and to be literate in a community like school is to acquire certain insider knowledge that comes with participation—knowledge that insiders may come to see as merely natural, a sign of innate intelligence.

But if such knowledge is often translated into conventions of practice, sometimes even text features, why do literate acts involve so much active problem solving on the part of individual writers? On simple tasks, like writing a grocery list or a genteel thank you note, the conventions of the discourse seem almost to dictate text—convention can do the lion's share of the work. Even on complex tasks, like a news story, text can emerge as a swift, sure response to discourse expectations—if, that is, one's experience as a journalist has led to the automaticity that comes with expertise. But in between these extremes lies a great deal of ordinary writing for which neither students nor experienced writers can rely on the automatic pilot of imitation or familiarity.

Problem solving is a response to the uncertainty and inherent indeterminacy of most rhetorical situations. Writers participate in the social context of writing, but my response to that situation is mediated by my strategies for reading that context and the representation I build of it—which may be radically different from yours. Writers acquire problem-solving strategies from social interaction with peers, teachers, readers, and texts, but the repertoire I have built for academic writing (which may differ dramatically from yours) is still only a set of heuristic moves, not an algorithm or formula. Moreover, the conventions and strategies we both rely on to write texts like this are not action plans—they are not even internally coherent templates for text. The practice of academic writing is a bundle of alternative moves, optional features, and contradictory expectations, united by a family resemblance. Participating in such social acts is also a personal cognitive achievement.

Problem solving is not just the mark of the elite literacies like academic writing. The "community literacy" Peck describes "values written discourse from the margins of society" (1991, p. vi) looking at the way writing lets members of an inner city neighborhood literally compose themselves for action. When mainstream college students in his study are introduced to community advocacy, they encounter a literate practice that "grows out of the dilemmas in the lives of neighborhood people, depends on a conversational, collaborative process seeking action" (p. 1). Problem-solving takes precedence over canonical forms in these literate practices: "Happening in neighborhoods, on doorsteps and in alleys, on street corners and in union halls, in food banks and in shelters for the homeless, community literate practices are utilized wherever people collaborate and use literate means to construct shared purposes and to take action" (p. 8).

To tell the whole story of a literate act, then, we also need to tell the story of individual problem solving within social contexts. By problem solving, I mean the intellectual moves that allow people to construct meaning—to interpret the situation; to organize, select, and connect information; to draw inferences, set goals, get the gist, respond to prior texts, draw on past experience, imagine options, and carry out intentions. Constructive acts are not taught by skills and drills; they go beyond imitation. Moreover, as Ron illustrates, literate performances are also *strategic actions*. The moves a writer makes are not only the product of school, culture, or convention, they are guided by the writer's goals and awareness; they are an individual writer's response to a rhetorical situation (as they interpret it). And this rhetorical situation is itself a representation writers build when they "read the situation" and call into being their image of its expectations and options.

Constructive processes can, of course, be intuitive, well-learned, fluid operations that go on below the threshold of awareness. However, at times, this process can burst into the foreground of thought and demand the conscious attention we call problem solving. Creating meaning amidst a welter of expectations and constraints, writers and readers have to deal with contradictory information, conflicting goals, and other people, with assignments by teachers, advice by friends, and their own needs and desires. Literate acts push writers to construct *negotiated meanings* that juggle constraints, goals, and expectations. Such literate acts depend on strategic thinking to read the rhetorical situation, to set goals, and to construct and negotiate meaning. Meaning making in the face of conflict is not reserved for elite literacies; problem solving and awareness are critical for everyone.

4. The new "basics" should start with expressive and rhetorical practices. If literacy is reconceived as a social and cognitive action, how shall we rewrite our impassioned but impoverished definitions of what is basic? How shall we answer the question: Where should education begin? Because people learn to be literate when they are able to/asked to engage in meaningful literate acts, the foundation is formed by giving learners, adult and child alike, occasions for genuine literate action. Instruction then builds on that foundation by helping students to enter into a discourse practice, helping them to understand the logic of the practice—who is doing what with whom and why.

If going back to the basics means finding a way for students to join in the action, then skills, drills, and rules are clearly not a very broad foundation for literacy (unless the action in question is taking tests). But what kinds of literate action will provide that foundation? In particular, what sort of literate practices should students learn; what sort of discourse community should they be invited to join? In the healthy controversy that surrounds this question, one answer comes out of our strong literary tradition with its roots in romantic theories of creativity and self-expression. A second, somewhat different, answer emerges from the equally strong traditions of rhetoric with its emphasis on transactions between readers and writers. Although my own ties are to the latter, together these complementary traditions offer a strong alternative to the message of limited literacies.

In a book called *The New Literacy*, Willinsky describes a strong grass roots movement in teaching, built on the expressive tradition, which has created a workable alternative to teaching limited literacies. The essential features of this "new literacy" education are an emphasis on writing as a social activity, a way of working on something, in a collaborative workshop setting with other writers, and in classrooms that "attempt to shift the control of literacy from the teacher to the student" (1990, p. 8). Like the rhetorical approach, it "stands against a literacy which is defined as the ability to perform at a certain level on a standardized test" and "declares that purpose and intent are foremost concerns with literacy" by setting up the classroom as a "workshop for furthering the students' intentions and meanings with a world that extends beyond the reaches of the textbook" (pp. 8–9). What distinguishes the rhetorical and the romantic approaches is what one does to achieve this. In the cluster of teaching practices and ideals Willinsky describes, "the dream is of students working as young artists" crafting artful and literate texts (p. 147). The ideology of the movement is dominated by Britton's contention that expressive writing is not only the place to start, but is at the heart of making meaning. The typical texts are personal narratives, expressive essays, and other poetic forms published in chapbooks that make everyone an "author." Associated most strongly with elementary and middle school teaching where classrooms become a small community of student writers supported by a trusted adult, this expressive tradition reflects the influence of James Britton and the London School, Donald Graves and the Whole Language movement, Peter Elbow and the practice of freewriting, and the process orientation of the National Writing Project. With this grass roots movement comes a veneration of the "craft of practice and experience, rather than direct instruction" (p. 56), coupled at times with a suspicion of theory, of research, and of explicit or strategic teaching.

As Willinsky goes on to note, however, the individualistic emphasis of the expressive tradition and its faith in simply "letting them write" seems to produce little impetus to critical thinking and critique (in spite of the emphasis Elbow, for instance, has long given to the dialectic of doubt and belief). The early assumptions that personal journal writing would increase content learning in writing across the curriculum have not been well supported. And the indirectness of the natural process approach appears to limit its effectiveness in teaching composition (Hillocks, 1986). Moreover, as Elbow (1991) has argued, descriptive, expressive writing need not be an end in itself but can serve the goals of academic inquiry when it is taught as a distinctive rhetorical practice among other practices. However, some of the apparent limitations of this tradition as it is widely practiced may also have contributed to its clear success in promoting a coherent community for literate action.

The rhetorical tradition shapes a different community that is at once a complement and a challenge to the expressive route. The rhetorical stance to literacy tends to take public discourse, rather than private expression and its artful texts, as examples of literate action. The learner is more often imagined as a young adult who is looking outside the writing classroom to the discourse practices of academic inquiry, a discipline, profession, or worldly community where the success of a literate action is not based on the satisfying artfulness of the text but on building convincing arguments, effective explanations, and insightful analyses. Such practices are difficult to master by practice alone. Direct instruction and straight talk about not only the conventions of a discourse but about ways of thinking one's way through writing all work to demystify the action and make a difference in learning.

This rhetorical tradition, then, contributes a second answer to the puzzle of, what is basic? Here the act of writing is not only an act of discovery but of communication and persuasion. Literate action is an action between writers and their readers, motivated by a sense of exigency, a shared problem, a mutual need (cf. Bruffee, 1984; Nystrand, 1986; Young, Becker, & Pike,

1970). The foundation for literacy, in this view, is having a stake, taking a stance, and having a voice in a rhetorical situation. On this foundation, readers and writers develop a repertoire of literate, problem-solving strategies. Some of these are relatively general and transferable, such as strategies for planning, organizing, reviewing, collaborating, and imagining readers and for exploring, adapting, and transforming one's own knowledge (cf. Bereiter and Scardamalia, 1987; Elbow, 1981; Flower, 1993b). Other strategies are closely tied to particular contexts and tasks, to the ways of thinking and patterns of argument in a given discourse (cf. Bazerman, 1981; Hillocks, 1986; Kiniry & Rose, 1990). This how-to knowledge goes by various names—heuristics, process plans, rhetorical or problem-solving strategies, critical thinking skills—but in essence, they are action plans for carrying out a literate act. In this rhetorical tradition, the basic, foundational skills in learning to be literate are the skills one needs to read a situation; to plan, organize, and revise; to build and negotiate meaning; to use and adapt conventions; and to figure out what new discourses expect and how to enter them.

This rhetorical version of the basics, like the expressive one, has its own built-in problems. One is the difficulty with which people transfer strategies learned in one context to another. The more abstract the strategy, the more likely it is to be generalized across tasks; however, people learn strategies best when they are grounded in a specific discourse. Transfer is, perhaps, most likely when it becomes a problem-solving task itself, when students become sufficiently aware of their own thinking to monitor and adapt old strategies to new problems.

5. *Literate action opens the door to metacognitive and social awareness.* In other words, literacy as a social cognitive act creates some opportunities for strategic thinking and reflective learning that are absent in the pedagogy of textual conventions and correctness.

First, seeing literacy as action lets us focus instruction on the points of conflict that make writing problematic—on those moments when a student's personal goals, available strategies, or history as a writer come in conflict with the expectations of a reader or teacher, the practices of a discourse, or social and cultural conventions. Some conflicts are public and social; others go on within the mind and goals of the meaning maker in the inevitable play of competing possibilities. By making such points of tension a subject of inquiry, we might better help students understand and negotiate the circle of possibilities, constraints, and expectations they face.

Secondly, this view of literacy asks students to step back from their own decisions as writers and develop greater *metacognitive awareness* of the discourse practices they are entering, of how those practices differ, of how they as writers switch among them, and the strategies they use. Texts and their conventions are no longer rules and formulas, but tools writers use and options they can take. Metacognition allows writers to reflect on the choices they made.

Third, we can encourage writers to step back even further and see how their rhetorical actions are themselves situated in the larger circle of social and cultural assumptions, some of which can empower a writer and some of which, as unexamined language and unquestioned premises, exercise tyranny. Reflecting on one's own thinking and actions within this broader context is, in part, an ethical act. It is a way to recognize the structures of authority that shape our meaning making and to resist the patterns of racism, sexism, and prejudice that are shot through those structures. Such reflection is also a means to empower writers who feel excluded; it opens a search for alternative ways of constructing one's world and for seeing the authority of one's own voice.

Since this opportunity is probably the most controversial, let us briefly consider some of the issues at stake. The social cognitive view of literacy sketched here (that is, my stance within that view) has a complex relation to current radical pedagogy. On the one hand, it parts company with many social critiques of education in that it seeks ways to help students control some of the literate practices associated with the dominant culture and its ways of invention and argument. On the other hand, it shares a position with Giroux, one of the most vocal leftist thinkers, when he charges that "radical educators have abandoned the language of possibility for the language of critique. . . . Instead of viewing schools as sites of contestation, negotiation, and conflict, radical educators tend to articulate an oversimplified version of domination [in which schools are] primarily reproductive sites . . . ideologically and politically overburdened by the dominant society" (Giroux & McLaren, 1989, p. 130).

The norm for a critical pedagogy, Giroux suggests, has been limited to "creating classroom knowledge . . . through individual oppositional readings of a text" (Giroux & McLaren, 1989, p. 148). This reduction of literate action to critique tends, I would argue, to produce yet another limited literacy that is in opposition to, yet ironically, parallel to the the current literacy of recitation in which students "spit back" summary writing in research papers, book reviews, and essay exams. Summary plus opinion is always in danger of becoming summary plus canonical critique.

Giroux's alternative takes a double stance to the problem of how teachers should deal with what students know or bring.

> It suggests taking seriously . . . the knowledge and experiences . . . by which students identify and give meaning to themselves and others. It is crucial to reemphasize that such a pedagogy is not meant to imply that student experience should be romantically celebrated; on the contrary, . . . it means developing a critically affirmative language that works both with and on the experiences that students bring to the classroom. Although this approach valorizes the language forms, modes of reasoning, dispositions, and histories that students use, . . . it also subjects such experiences and ideologies to the discourse of suspicion and skepticism, to forms of analysis that attempt to understand how they are structured by cultural and symbolic codes inscribed within particular configurations of history and power.

And at this point, Giroux's agenda takes its step beyond critique:

> Similarly, this means teaching students how to identify, unravel, *and critically appropriate the codes, vocabularies, and deep grammar* [italics added] of different cultural, social, historical, and collective traditions. The pedagogical goal here is not to have students exercise rigorous analytical skills in order to arrive at the right answer, but to better exercise reasoned choice through a critical understanding of what the codes are that organize different meanings and interests into particular configurations of knowledge and power. (Giroux & McLaren, 1989, pp. 149–150)

Giroux's argument envisions a constructive, socially situated literacy. Where his agenda diverges from the present one is in its relative emphasis on the receptive literacy of reading (including the critique of texts) in place of the production/action-oriented literacy of writing. In the constructive, social cognitive pedagogy sketched here, students engage in a range of discourse practices (including finding and defining problems, arguing and proposing, explaining, and applying reading in an attempt to solve problems or take action. Composing a critique is merely one practice, generally limited to the academy). From this range of experiences students develop awareness of not just the rhetorical, but the social, political, and cultural contexts of their own literate acts. The issue on which this difference turns, then, is partly what to foreground—the *critique* of practices or the *use* of multiple practices—not on whether each has a place. In choosing to emphasize practice, I would also argue that it is impossible to *critically appropriate* the codes of a discourse (as Giroux suggests) without learning how to carry out the practice itself—one has to understand how to write a genuine proposal, personal essay, or a project report to understand how they function in the world. Students do indeed need to learn how to uncover the assumptions of racism, sexism, and authority that are shot through our language and that structure much of our discourse. But the art of critique is itself always in danger of becoming yet another form of literary criticism, like the "Freudian" and genre readings English majors learned to do to literary texts a generation ago.

The argument of a constructive literacy is that people will best understand Giroux's "deep grammar" of literate practices when, in addition to making critiques, they themselves learn to construct and negotiate meaning within a variety of discourses and in so doing have the opportunity to reflect on their own assumptions, their own cognition, and their own texts. A second contention of this perspective is that to achieve the ideals of a democratic society that radical pedagogy calls for, it seems critical for students—especially marginalized students—to begin to control, not just critique, the kinds of discourse that affect all our lives. The issue we face is how to shape a literacy pedagogy that fosters some strategic control of meaning making *within* powerful discourse practices, as well as awareness of the context those practices invoke and the options for change.

IV. Forces in Tension Within a Social Cognitive View

The virtue of this new social cognitive view of literacy is its ability to explain more of the diversity and complexity of literate action and its willingness to tolerate, even embrace, internal tension. But that virtue comes at a price. The very terms, cognitive and social (though other terms would do) stand as poles around which different aspects of literacy cluster and conflicting fields of force seem to form. It is that tension—within literate acts and within social cognitive theory—that I want to explore.

In using this social cognitive polarity to uncover revealing tensions, I want, first, to acknowledge that there is a problem with even making the distinction. Some compositionists have built foundational arguments that would dismiss cognition (e.g., "Writing is not fundamentally a cognitive process. . . . Writing is located in the social world and, thus, is fundamentally structured by the shape of the environment" [Cooper & Holzman, 1989]). Another, more sophisticated argument (to my mind) comes from research on conversational analysis. It tries to avoid a distinction on the grounds that the very term *interaction* presupposes two essentially independent entities when the reality is an interdependent system (cf. Brandt, 1992; Rogoff, 1990). Philosophically, this move to avoid a simplistic categorization seems reasonable when we notice how hard it is to define either cognitive or social processes without recognition of the other. It avoids a sticky problem of definition by simply identifying cognition with a more observable phenomenon of social response (i.e., by simply collapsing the distinction between thinking and speaking as conversational analysis often does). But avoiding this problematic distinction gives up the opportunity for a more fine-grained (essentially cognitive) understanding of how meaning is represented and cuts off a more open-ended inquiry into the multiple (internal) forces that enter into meaning making.

A third stance, which I will take here, is to acknowledge the logical fallibility of these familiar polarities and other abstract categories that are part of this discussion. Although it is useful to talk about a cultural, social, or a rhetorical context, for instance, they interpenetrate one another in the same way the self is inseparable from society. The relationship between social forces and cognition or between different versions of context is a situated relationship—it depends on the event or activity one wants to describe. And yet these terms still have great heuristic power. If we look at the problem semiotically, they function as complex signs, ultimately interesting for the more situated clusters of experience and attitude they can help us track (Witte, 1992). This third approach to literate action, then, uses these categories as tools of inquiry but seeks knowledge in specificity rather than abstraction and looks for the points of tension and conflict that reveal more about the playing field of literacy and about who is in the game.

Consider some of the elements that cluster around the poles of this cognitive social continuum. In talking about cognition I refer to acts of thinking (e.g., interpreting, problem solving, reflecting) that go on, in real time, in the minds of individual readers and writers. I refer to what people are thinking as they read and write (insofar as we can infer it from our inevitably limited methods). Such thinking is typically far more elaborated, contradictory, and surprising than the texts they read or produce. Inquiry into cognition leads us into the irreducible complexity of individual minds and meanings caught "in the act." Although some aspects of cognition (e.g., memory search, pattern matching) are studied as basic cognitive processes, "hardwired" into the architecture of the brain, the cognitive processes and strategies we discuss here are acts of taking thought, acts of conscious attention. Such cognition, however, does not exist in a vacuum: the strategies we observe a Ron or Heidi using were learned from and are now elicited by social interactions with parents, teachers, and peers. The interpretations and the knowledge they construct is their own, but it is built out of and in response to other voices, prior texts, social expectations, and ideological alternatives. However, there is no way to isolate a social process from the minds that carry it out. Although we can treat public statements, social conventions, or interpersonal events as independent objects, if we look closer, they are the collaborative creation of individual minds over time. They only exist as meaning in the interpretations individual readers and writers give to them.

A social cognitive view of literacy is a site of controversy because the truth of the matter is so complicated. Moreover, our methods of studying and describing these events have difficulty doing justice to the interaction we know to be there. The simplifying distinctions we make are, in part, an artifact of our own methods of observation: I choose to study Heidi interpreting text by Stephen Gould as a strategic act, and someone else chooses to study Gould's claims as a piece of the intertextual puzzle of Western thought. I talk about cognitive construction, they about social; we both contribute to understanding the reality that will always elude our grasp. On theoretical grounds, then, this social cognitive distinction is a qualified one that still points to powerful distinctions in our experience.

The tensions foregrounded by this social cognitive view can be credited to competing fields of force we call by other names. Consider, for instance, the personal and cognitive elements of literacy associated with notions of expressiveness, self-discovery, personal knowledge, or with critical thinking, self-awareness, rhetorical intentions, and craft. These elements not only jostle with one another but often exist in uneasy tension with social and cultural forces identified with the givens imposed by language, by discourse, by race or gender, or with the influence of collaborators and readers, or with the shaping role of literate conventions and cultural expectations. Witte argues for how the deep "self/other" distinction and the need to continually negotiate that relationship infuses the nature of meaning making (1992). Through an unpredictable dialectic, these forces somehow converge and cooperate in the making of meaning. In socially situated acts of cognition, public and personal meanings, convention and originality are always pushing, shaping, tugging at one another.

The social cognitive view of literacy that is emerging in current discussions is a stimulating, expansive vision, trying to embrace complexity and accept the serendipitous work of dialectic. This is not to say that the educational establishment will be quick to embrace this multidimensional image of literacy and its willingness to tolerate a fruitful, disturbing dialectic. Under the pressures of outside evaluation and the exigencies of instruction, many administrators and teachers may opt for limited literacies, designating some feature (whether it be correctness, self-expression, or a disciplinary practice like literary analysis) as basic and turning it into the signifier and test of literacy. Complexity and dialectic are hard to sell.[2]

Conflict in Theory

The problem of building social cognitive theory goes deeper than embracing complexity; it is also a problem of intellectual politics. Born in a storm, this perspective attempts to reconcile strongly independent research traditions and methods that bring with them histories of attending to different phenomena, of creating different kinds of knowledge, and the habit, still with us, of gaining steam for an argument from the heat of a social cognitive, social/individual opposition. Nevertheless, this move to integration is made on the assumption that neither social nor cognitive theory makes genuine sense without the other. I would go a step further. As educators, we need to develop more responsible social cognitive accounts of how individual students—as thinking personal agents operating within and shaped by a social and cultural fabric—learn. And why they do not learn. What makes literate action possible for some, unlikely for others? Educators—and this includes not just teachers but researchers, textbook writers, curriculum developers, and the assessment industry—need to work out of an image of literacy and learning that tries to integrate, rather than deny or dichotomize, these perspectives. This is not to devalue basic cognitive research and broad social, macrostructural theory, each of which give little thought to integration, but I would argue that for educators of this generation, there is even more to be learned at the sites of interaction.

And when we stand at our chosen site of interaction, how shall we do justice to it? Let me state the strong case. A vision of literacy as a social and cognitive act starts with literate actions and events as its unit of analysis (cf. Heath, 1983; Scribner & Cole, 1981). This vision must be anchored in observation-based, grounded theories of literate action that help explain how social structures and cognitive processes do indeed interact at critical moments in reading, writing, or learning (Flower, 1989a). We cannot, for instance, build a new vision of literacy education on the notion of a vaguely specified dialectic. An observation-based theory of literate acts needs to track the twisting paths of this dialectic in diverse situations and settings; it needs to subject our intuitions and rational speculations to the tests of observation, to see what forces, what social influences, what ideological beliefs (including those implied by absence), what processes, strategies, and assumptions come onto the stage as active players, not just potential ones. We need more richly grounded but rigorously skeptical accounts of those players that are actively shaping diverse literate acts—especially the players that literacy education can influence.

Conflict in the Act of Construction

In this book, I hope to show that one revealing site for inquiry is the very process of constructing meaning. The forces that are in tension in the construction of educational theory are at work in the constructive processes of students as well, with both creative and devastating consequences. Meaning making does not always take place in a peaceful valley of the mind. The very forces that challenge theorists' efforts at reconciliation and the unpredictable, inexplicable dialectic we see in theory get acted out in real time as writers try to shape meaning. The forces clustered around the poles of self and society, public and private, convention and invention, social and cognitive, are all forces that can give structure to a writer's meaning, guide composing, or set criteria, but they often do so in alternative, even opposing ways. Constructive acts are a stage for conflict.

These tensions seem to be at the heart of education; they do not get resolved or go away but coexist like molecules in an energized field. However, the productive conflict we hope for can sometimes go awry, especially for novice writers, by which I mean any of us attempting to perform a new practice or enter a new community. Demands such as the expectations of a reader, a fear of exposing one's tentative thoughts, or a concern for correctness over content—any one force that should be held in a delicate balance by others may gain the upper hand and rewrite the script in its image. A student learning to carry out a new literate act may be standing in the eye of the hurricane.

Looking closely at an individual's thinking within a rhetorical, social, and cultural context can reveal an underlying logic to students' performance—a logic that is often in direct response to tensions writers are trying to negotiate. Moreover, some of the most problematic conflicts appear to face students who are most at risk. Consider some dramatic examples. As Erickson reports, for Alaskan native teenagers "to become literate in school terms would be to disaffiliate symbolically from their parents and other members of the Alaskan native village. . . . Caught in ambivalence between multiple cultural worlds, [they] resist adopting the complete system of school-defined literacy, and then suffer the consequences of marginal acquisition. They do not belong fully to the old ways or to the new" (1988, p. 221). Fordham's (1988) study of African-American high achievers in Washington, D.C., spells out the logic of negotiation in even clearer terms: the cultural imperative to affirm an African heritage gives these teenagers a sense of symbolic identity (kinship) and strong peer ties. "Acting white," which can generate enormous peer pressure and rejection, is, unfortunately, associated with school achievement, including specifics like using Standard English, speaking in class, doing work on time. Students who enter high school as high achievers sometimes negotiate this dilemma by keeping a low profile and what Fordham calls a strategy of "racelessness"—a behavior that entails genuine costs and that becomes increasingly difficult for males to maintain. For low-achieving students, their very failure and active resistance to instruction is a strategy for dealing with conflict. The limited meanings they construct as writers, for instance, reflect an alternative path in this negotiation. Resistance, whether it is conscious or not, is indeed a choice to fail, but it is a move that also asserts values other than the school's and repudiates the categories, such as remedial or unintelligent, that the dominant culture is imposing on them (Erickson, 1988).

For basic writers in the City University of New York's open admissions programs, drill and practice on grammar was having little effect on errors, because the attitudes and anxieties that dictated the students' composing processes favored strategies of rapid oral composing and no revision. The grammatical knowledge they did learn had no place to operate within this process. Shaughnessy's insight was to help students to renegotiate the way they dealt with grammar, errors, and anxiety, to develop a writing and revising process that let them deal with the threat of error in a different way.

This sort of conflict faced in meaning making is not reserved for at-risk students in Alaska, Washington, or New York. After talking with Ron, the student quoted at the beginning of this chapter, we learned that the critical, analytical, and reflective meaning making heard on the tape was a literate act reserved for talks with interviewers—not academic writing. His own thinking appeared in papers only after receiving repeated encouragement from his frustrated instructor and after such drafts were brought for approval in the hall. In the logic that guided Ron's learning and writing, assigned papers were high risk occasions; the goal of his negotiations was to construct expected meanings.

Looking at literacy as a social and cognitive act brings with it a newly explicit, unsettling awareness of meaning making as a site of alternatives, options, and conflict among powerful shaping forces. This book is motivated by the desire to trace that constructive process in students across different academic contexts and by the belief that doing so could give us a powerful new insight into the logic of their literate negotiations.

2

Constructing Negotiated Meaning

How do writers create literate acts—how are these individual, socially situated meanings constructed? In this chapter, I would like to propose a theory of *negotiated* construction that offers an alternative to theories based on reproduction or conversation alone. Later chapters will use this theory to tell the tale of meaning making in specific contexts. However, because our images of meaning, makers, and making are themselves surrounded by controversy, that is where we will start.

I. How Shall We Imagine Meaning?

Both readers and writers construct meaning, but how shall we describe the meaning these parties represent to themselves?[1] Describing meaning as a *literate practice*, for instance, helps us envision broadbrush, conventional categories of meaning; it foregrounds the scripts, schemas, commonplaces, the widely shared gestures and the prepackaged patterns of understanding that meaning makers share. To understand a scientific article, a freshman placement exam, or an academic essay as a practice (Bartholomae, 1985; Bazerman, 1988; Olson, 1988), we could describe its meaning as a transaction within a well-structured sociocultural landscape of like transactions (Kaufer & Carley, 1993), as an expected, "unmarked" move within a discourse (Gee, 1989), or as a thread in the fabric of an ongoing intertextual event (Bloome & Bailey, 1992). We would look at the text, but our central unit of analysis—the body in question—would be the landscape, the discourse, the intertext.

To account for the meaning of a writer's *literate act*, on the other hand, calls for a less Olympian perspective and a finer-grained analysis that can ground the meaning of that act in human purposes and in its rhetorical context. Literate acts create a unique meaning within the available patterns of discourse. These patterns, we must remember, provide at best only rough approximations of meaning; they do not provide writers with richly detailed templates for turning out introductions (Swales, 1984) or research papers (Berkenkotter, Huckin, & Ackerman, 1988) because they only exist as abstract perceptions of pattern constructed by the perceiver. They are an individual's rendering of the commonalities that she or he perceives to unite prior texts. It is easy to forget that our large-grained analyses of discourse are by necessity crude abstractions compared to the richly faceted meaning being transacted between readers and writers; discourse patterns are a form of academic currency we mint to talk about meaning, but not the coin of the writer's realm.

Literate acts transcend the patterns of a practice in other ways. For one, writers often cross the boundaries of convention, discourse, and community, adapting (or trying to adapt) multiple practices to their own ends. The result may be a deft invention or a bizarrely functional Rube Goldberg text; however, its coherence as a literate act does not come from the conventions and patterns it incorporates, but from the purposes it entertains in using them. More generally, the meaning of a literate act will not lie solely in the resources on which it draws, the conventions in which it participates, or the context to which it responds, but in the ways writers use and even transform their knowledge and resources to take action.

And yet, this picture of purposefulness is not a unified one. The purposes writers entertain are often at cross-purposes with one another. Such tensions may lurk as unexamined assumptions apparent only to readers of the text or erupt into the writer's composing process as an unavoidable conflict of goals. Whatever the writer's intentions, the patterns of discourse and language she or he uses also come with their own history of agendas, assumptions, implications, and affordances. As a result, the meaning a literate act may have for a writer is not necessarily a coherent or unified meaning. Nor is it stable. Because meaning making—even the construction of a short text—takes place over time, different parts of a given text may reflect significant changes that took place during the writer's evolving representation of the task (Flower et al., 1990).

At this point, it would seem appropriate to offer a coherent theoretical definition of meaning that could embrace these contraries and let us get on with the announced goal of exploring how such a thing is constructed. However, in the spirit of observation-based theory building, I think we have more to gain by avoiding that closure and opening up the territory with some instances that can stand as test cases for our accounts of meaning. In particular, these instances challenge such accounts to embrace both the high-status meaning making of professional, creative writers as well as the meaning making of a student writer locked in a not entirely successful struggle with text.

The Web of Meaning

To consider the meaning of the song "Homeless" as a literate act, you will probably have to hear in your mind's ear not only Simon and Shabalala's (1986) words but the bittersweet lyrical wail of those words flowing over unanticipated African rhythms. Perhaps reading the words (excerpted below) will also bring back for some of us the presence this song had in the social and political context of South African apartheid when Paul Simon's album *Graceland* was first released. "Homeless" starts with the call and response of Zulu voices that leads into the haunting image of "homeless."

Emaweni webaba
Silale maweni

....

Homeless, homeless
Moonlight sleeping on a midnight lake
Homeless, homeless
Moonlight sleeping on a midnight lake
We are homeless, we are homeless
The moonlight sleeping on a midnight lake

....

Zio yami, zio yami, nhliziyo yami
Nhliziyo yami amakhaza asengi bulele

....

Strong wind destroy our home
Many dead, tonight it could be you.
Strong wind, strong wind
Many dead, tonight it could be you
And we are homeless, homeless
Moonlight sleeping on a midnight lake

....

Somebody say ih hih ih hih ih
Somebody sing hello, hello hello
Somebody say ih hih ih hih ih
Somebody cry why, why, why?

Even if we could understand Zulu, we could not reduce the meaning we as readers construct from this text to a set of propositions nor to a list of the schemas, metaphors, themes, and conventions it evokes. In fact, for

Western listeners, its meaning involves the juxtaposition of words we can understand (and a situation we strain to comprehend) with words we cannot understand. Equally important in my representation is how the high, foreign sound of those African voices is coupled with the immediacy of the English words ("Many dead, tonight it could be you") and the inescapable, visceral pulses of rhythms that surprise my Western expectations. In my experience of this literate act, these sounds are linked to visual images of animate moonlight and midnight lakes, to the verbal resonance and the literal meaning of Simon's language, and to the emotional resonance from my own perception of the song as a political and cultural statement.

Now I am sure it is as clear to you as it is to me that the above few sentences of literary explication hardly begin to account for the complex web of meaning this literate act evokes or, more accurately, lets each of us construct. Even an extended close reading would only be another representation created in response to this text, not a replication of the elaborated cognitive representations you and I hold in our own minds. (And, of course, there is also the additional meaning "Homeless" has here as an example and a social transaction between you, the reader, and me, the writer of this text). To understand the complex (and differing) representations we have both constructed around "Homeless," it helps, I believe, to envision how a dynamic cognitive representation (full of visual and affective elements) operates.

A multidimensional meaning of the sort we are talking about is often envisioned as a network. It does not exist as statements or as a list of linguistic propositions, but as a great number of more elementary attitudes, ideas, or perceptions that are intricately linked to one another in a network that permits us to entertain multiple ways of knowing. The local elements of knowledge that stand as "nodes" of this network may be words, or they may be images, sounds, emotions, or ideas. They may be linked by verbal, spatial, affective, or visceral relations. In such a cognitive network, a concept, such as "homeless," does not exist as a coherent symbolic unit, defined by a list of necessary attributes (as it would be described in traditional views of concept formation). Instead of a logical definition, we should envision the concept of "homeless" and the meaning of "Homeless" as a web of activated ideas, images, experiences in the mind of the meaning maker, a web that is in turn part of the individual's larger, socially shaped network of knowledge. Then we envision these activated nodes linked to one another by intricate, multiple, and often shifting relations. It is to this web of meaning—of activated knowledge and its dynamic patterns of interconnection going well beyond the propositional structure of a text—that we want our theory of how writers construct meaning to be accountable. For example, my personal network for the meaning of "Homeless" includes links to notions of political action in South Africa; however, it contains a far stronger set of links to attitudes and values about African Americans at home that the song never fails to evoke. My idiosyncratic network also includes a vivid visual, auditory, and emotional memory of playing a tape of this song in a large auditorium at Penn State University as part of a talk that led to this book. However, at any given time, my "current" meaning will only be that part of this large network that is psychologically active.

This network metaphor, which we will explore in chapter 3, offers a powerful and precise way to talk about meaning as a fluid and interactional construction not limited to the propositional or even verbal representations of text. In an earlier discussion focused on "images, plans and prose," Hayes and I (1984) had proposed a multiple-representation hypothesis to explain some of the difficulty writers have transforming this sort of multifeatured cognitive network and its distinctive ways of knowing into the special representation demanded by formal prose. More recently, Witte's (1992) semiotic account of writing argues in a similar vein for the role of linguistic and nonlinguistic sign systems. As his analysis of an ordinary grocery list shows, writers use a variety of visual and spatial sign systems, including drawings and the physical layout of the store as a planning aid. My point here is not to inventory the sign systems or the forms of mental representation that make up the meaning of "Homeless" but to use this text as a provocative image of the kinds of knowing that go into the representation of "meaning." This is what a process of meaning construction is busy constructing.

How Shall We Talk about Makers and Making (or Shall We?)?

When "Homeless" was written/enacted in 1986, it was a distinctive American/South African creation that crossed racial, national, political, and musical barriers and struck many as a shared statement of injustice and a shared affirmation of spirit. Part of its meaning, then, is the history of individual and social response it generated. But "Homeless" also invites us to plumb the mystery of meaning making and inquire into how literate acts of this sort are constructed. How do individual writers (artists and students), situated within an array of social, cultural, political, and economic forces, go about the social cognitive process of creating these literate acts?

The answer I want to pursue grows out of cognitive rhetoric, but let me frame it by first recognizing that from some viewpoints the question itself might seem unanswerable or irrelevant. A romantic, expressivist, or psychoanalytic perspective, for instance, might grant a fascination with the drafts and revisions of a famous text or even with the historical circumstances of its writing but would gently scoff at the enterprise of this book—at the thought of understanding anything significant about the creation of meaning. Writers' reports are unreliable, epiphenomenal; to understand the truth of the matter, this perspective would say, we would have to plumb the deep well of the unconscious. The writer writing is "not at home," that is, as one critic would state the case,

> during the actual process of symbol making [the writer] is not in that most familiar of all places, his or her conscious mind. . . . A new thought or verbal configuration as it emerges from the moving pen is actually an insight or illumination or creation. . . . When the writer is not at home, the truth comes knocking. . . . Consciousness does not create or generate; it merely keeps the record. . . . Writing—and this includes reasoning, concept formation, reflexive and extensive composing, and the rest—comes from a place behind the screen upon which is projected what we label "reality," a place which cannot be thought or thought about, but which can be nurtured and respected nonetheless. . . . Rote copying [for example, would allow] the student's whole organism to have the experience of producing mature prose *without conceptualizing* consciously at all. (Mandel, 1980, pp. 372–376)

For radically different reasons, a postmodernist stance on the meaning making of individual writers might simply refuse the question as irrelevant. In "What is an 'author'?," Foucault celebrates the disappearance of the author, to be replaced by a notion of writing (*ecriture*) that would "allow us . . . to circumvent references to the author" and would be "concerned with neither the act of writing nor the indication—be it symptom or sign—of a meaning which someone might have wanted to express" (1977, p. 144). In the place of intention and meaning, Foucault would have us try "to imagine the general condition of each text," the space in which it is created and the time in which it unfolds (p. 144). This position points a way out of romantic theories of inspiration, expressionism, and the discovery of Meaning toward a social process in which meaning is "made" through the interplay of signs, like an unfolding game (*jeu*) that is dominated less by its "signified content" than by "the very nature of the signifier" (p. 144).

However, I will argue that it is possible to take an anti-essentialist stance to meaning making—to recognize fragmentation and contradiction within our own positions as individuals—but to still envision a constructive act that is more than the brush of discourses passing in the night. Hall, for instance, an early leader of the "Birmingham school" Centre for Contemporary Cultural Studies, takes issue with Foucault and other theorists who would abandon the issues of meaning and representation:

> Of course in so-called postmodern society, we feel overwhelmed by the diversity, the plurality, of surfaces which it is possible to reproduce, and we have to recognize the rich technological bases of modern cultural production which enable us endlessly to simulate, reproduce, reiterate, and recapitulate. But there is all the difference in the world between the assertion that there is no one, final, absolute meaning—no ultimate signified, only the endlessly sliding chain of signification, and on the other hand, the assertion that meaning does not exist. (1986, p. 49).

Hall suggests a postmodern metaphor for construction when he describes the *articulation* of ideology as both speaking forth and linking (in the way the cab of an articulated lorry ["semi"] is linked to a trailer). "It is a linkage which is not necessary, determined, absolute, and essential for all time. You have to ask, Under what circumstances *can* a connection be forged or made? Interested in ideology as a particular form of meaning, Hall goes on to see the "so-called 'unity' of a discourse" not in necessary "belongingness" but in the social forces to which it can be connected (1986, p. 53).

Cognitive rhetoric takes us down a different, but interestingly related, path in which meaning making is a rhetorical act. Here the unity and coherence Hall talks about will not be found in texts nor in the determining power of social forces that made them, but in the interaction between individual purposes and social uses surrounding literate acts. Cognitive rhetoric (as a rhetoric using the tools of cognitive inquiry) will focus our attention on thinking processes and hence on individual minds. But as rhetoric it is the study of a social cognitive process, based on the premise that the individual only exists as a rhetor by virtue of standing both within a circle of listeners/readers and within the circle of a socially structured, purposeful discourse. Historically, rhetoric has described meaning making as invention—as the discovery of possible arguments (Aristotle, 1932) and probabilistic meanings in areas where knowledge and truth are always judgment calls based on self-persuasion and consensus (Perelman & Olbrechts-Tyteca, 1969). In contemporary rhetoric, this epistemic, meaning-shaping function of the rhetor has moved even more into the foreground. So in cognitive rhetoric, the rhetor/writer is not merely a presenter of claims but the creator of a representation or a signification that is at once a personal meaning and a social act (Flower, 1993a).

The great question for cognitive rhetoric is, How does such construction happen? How do individual writers (or readers)—as thinkers, as problem-finding problem solvers, as the members of that whirling plurality of communities and discourses Hall describes, as well as seekers struggling to forge personal truths—how do they carry out these diverse literate acts?

For cognitive rhetoric, this question rises as an irresistible, necessarily empirical question. By *empirical,* I do not mean as a matter that can be resolved by the simple accumulation of facts, but, as I have argued elsewhere, as a question that calls for observation-based theory building grounded in the investigation of actual writers in specific contexts and for a willingness to be surprised and challenged by the unpredicted, by the data of experience (Flower, 1989a). It presumes, for instance, the constant interaction of cognition and social context; however, the nature of that interaction, the ways each force shapes the other, remains the compelling and inescapably open question. As a result, this stance will challenge broadbrush social or psychological theories that foreground a single deterministic force. It matters little whether that force is imagined to be a Marxist, an ideological, or a Skinnerian behaviorial *environment,* on the one hand, or a *psychology* of unconscious Freudian drives, of personality traits, or of simple existential determinism. Cognitive rhetoric would ask how they might interact with one another in the situated process of composing (cf. Bandura's 1986 argument for a social cognitive theory of reciprocity).

Once you ask *how* different writers and readers are constructing meaning, then the interaction of personal intentions, social imperatives, prior knowledge, ability, motivation, discourse conventions—this interplay of shaping forces—becomes the subject of inquiry. The motivation for this skeptical and situationally grounded inquiry is strong because the stakes are high. Cognitive rhetoric is rooted in a tradition of basic research and theory at a time when such research is attempting to combine the virtues of rigor and interpretation in building situated yet broadly useful claims. It also stands in a tradition of teaching developed in classical rhetoric and modern composition. And if diversity and uncertainty is a matter of theoretical concern for postmodernists, it is a matter of intense practical importance for us as educators. The current-traditional paradigm in English sidestepped the question of making meaning in favor of making texts (Crowley, 1990; Young, 1974). If that move once appeared to work for the traditional elite we educated or evaluated out of the system (and that is open to question), it no longer works today. And if its impoverished story of how students write was all teachers needed to socialize generations of high school students into producing research papers or to initiate countless college freshmen into the mysteries of the literary essay, that theory is not enough to understand or teach the diverse literate practices our students will encounter today or to prepare them for the significant literate acts they may need to perform.

II. Portraits of a Constructive Process

The apparent dialogue between different literate traditions in "Homeless" makes it a good example of a complex meaning. But how, we must ask, is such a process carried out? The three portraits that follow foreground some important features of this process and at the same time challenge theory to live up to their resistant complexity.

In the Public Eye

One inescapable feature of "Homeless" is that its meaning(s) seems literally *con-structed* out of *multiple voices and disparate conventions*. Because this text comes from the hands of artists/experts like Paul Simon and Joseph Shabalala, we are no doubt primed to see an integrity in its disjunctures. Nevertheless, its voices seem woven together in the same way the lyrics move easily between English and Zulu: "Somebody say ih hih ih hih ih/ Somebody cry why, why why?" The song integrates African rhythms and Western lyricism, punctuated by the piercing Zulu falsettos. However, even that trademark style of Shabalala and the Ladysmith Black Mambazo is itself a hybrid—a Zulu adaptation of the four-part harmony brought by American missionaries of the last century (Erlmann, 1987).

The piece reflects a *collaborative* process in various ways: Simon did a tape with the melody and the lines "We are homeless, homeless/ Moonlight sleeping on a midnight lake," which he sent to Shabalala "to continue the story in Zulu" (Simon & Shabalala, 1986). The "Somebody say" bridge between Zulu and English was written by Simon. He, however, lifted the melody from a favorite track of an earlier Ladysmith album. Another Zulu section of the song, which the Ladysmith musicians worked late into the night to complete, turns a traditional wedding song into a modern myth of cold and hungry people living in caves, their fists used as pillows.

These multiple "voices" point up a second significant feature of this constructive process: it appears to *transform* its elements into a coherent literate action. Its disparate voices, discourse patterns, and cultural conventions do not merely coexist; they form a unique construction. Yet within this tapestry we still hear the distinctive voice and style of both Shabalala—his poetic story/myths—and Simon—with his strings of words and metaphors crowding into a line. The unresolved contradictions of strong winds and sleeping moonlight, of singing hellos and crying whys are part of its emotional message. In a constructive process, then, the overwhelming diversity Hall talked about is balanced by the writers' powers of transformation that can—at times—turn disparate voices into resources.

A third feature of this artistic/expert constructive process is the rich *network of purposes* that appear to underlie the text. It seems to be a protest, perhaps a warning, certainly an evocation of the plight of black South

Africans, maybe of us all. Yet we would never talk about the purpose of this rhetorical act in the reductive way often seen in composition texts, as if that purpose could be equated with a singular intention, with a claim or theme to be stated, or with a mode (e.g., with the writers' intention to narrate, argue, or analyze). Writers like these are playing with a full deck, acting out of a dense interactive network of purposes that may include long-term personal, artistic, or political desires, broad rhetorical intentions looking for a way to realize themselves, specific rhetorical (and musical) goals for this text, alternative plans (including local or text-specific ones), and a set of conventional, artistic, or personal criteria invoked by both the project at hand and the emerging text. This network of purpose(s) can realize itself in bold political gestures (such as recording in South Africa despite the ban) and in subtle nuances of wording and rhythm. However, we should realize that this web of intention that shapes writing is itself a unique construction, created by the goals, plans, criteria, desires, and possibilities evoked by a specific rhetorical situation—a construction that itself develops in response to a developing text and responding readers.

To draw attention to this often unseen network of purposes is not to say that images, rhythms, melodies, and language itself are not also guiding this constructive process—even to the point of dictating the construction of meanings that may violate the writers' overt intentions (or give voice to suppressed ones). The force of commonplaces and available language may at times appropriate the meaning-making process. Moreover, much of the intentional network that writers create is fabricated from givens, from purposes supplied by culture, context, discourse, or task. Writers' purposes are always *bounded purposes* hemmed in by innumerable constraints, unrecognized givens, and shared desires. Nevertheless, and here is my point, this bounded but unique, multifaceted web of intentions that informs the making of meaning is itself a critical, creative, and individual construction. The purposes of a Simon, a Shabalala, and a group like the Ladysmith Black Mambazo are made, not born. They are both a source and a site of conflict as writers attempt to build meaning in text.

A final, but less apparent feature of this constructive process is the *negotiation* that had to occur given, on the one hand, these imagined multiple webs of intention and, on the other, the constraints of the historical and social situation of Johannesburg in 1986. Nelson Mandela was still in prison, South Africa still in a state of official apartheid. How, for instance, could one capture the meaning of displacement in South Africa in words that would not put black South Africans who sang them in political jeopardy? The ability of the Ladysmith Black Mambazo to negotiate meaning under such circumstances had let them become one of the most widely heard groups in South Africa even under the censorship of the South African Broadcasting Company. This ability had made them a sustaining voice of the Zulu and working-class tradition for 20 years (Erlmann, 1987).[2] And to this already complex web of purposes, one might speculate that Simon also brought his own history of artistic negotiation, such as an intention to once again combine his personal, enigmatic, reflective metaphors with popular, commercial success.

In the Classroom

Simon and Shabalala play out a constructive act that is at once individually purposeful and socially shaped. But their example has some limitations. Limited to the evidence of a text and anecdotes, we are forced to speculate about parts of the thinking process. Secondly, some may question if our insights into the process of "famous authors" is relevant to understanding the performance of students. The literary tradition in English studies has been reluctant to afford students the constructive potential we admire in artists. And research has indeed pointed out meaningful differences among younger and older, more and less experienced writers. But the data we will look at suggests that the differences that distinguish the struggles of expert and novice, of artist and ordinary writer are differences of degree and content rather than kind and that negotiation is an important act for both groups.[3]

Consider Darlene, a first-semester freshman, with a reading-to-write assignment on time management that asks her to draw on multiple sources and her own ideas in a short (2-page) paper (Flower et al., 1990). Here is the final text she turns in in its entirety: "I have tried to incorporate these ideas into my statement but I have been wandering in circles long enough. To continue to struggle for words would not be an efficient use of time and wasting excessive time does not seem appropriate, especially on a paper about time management."

Ask a class how this paper was written and softly cynical smiles will emerge as students talk of copping out, being out of time, and avoiding the assignment. But the response changes when the story told by Darlene's lengthy think-aloud transcript begins to unfold. As part of the Reading-to-Write project, Darlene is thinking aloud with a tape recorder as she works on the paper alone in her dorm.

> So I'm just gonna—I don't care, I'm just going to interpret them the only way I can interpret them. . . . Let's just put what the authors agreed on. *Authors agree* [she writes]—We'll just—If at least two of them concur,

> we'll say they agree. *Authors in general agree that* . . . But then they don't agree. There's nothing you can say about this. . . . Can I leave it at that? . . . Oh give me a break, I don't know what I'm doing. I'm only a freshman. I have no idea what to do.

This brief excerpt from Darlene's extended struggle on a "standard" assignment suggests some additional features of a constructive process. In her transcript, we see how multiple voices (like those heard in Simon and Shabalala) make construction a site of *conflict*. Darlene is caught between the discourse features she knows how to handle and the ones she is expected to use. Her techniques for reading and synthesizing are failing her when the authorities do not agree and she knows it. One of the problems Darlene must negotiate is the mismatch between what this new rhetorical situation appears to be asking for and what her limited topic knowledge—and tried-and-true strategies for generating knowledge—seem to supply. The rhetorical context of school is sending strong cues that tell Darlene, "Summarize by finding consensus as you have always done in school assignments." At the same time, her source texts make it abundantly clear that the authorities do not agree. There is no consensus to find, and Darlene is trying to figure out what to do.

A second feature that stands out in this glimpse of a constructive act is that it is a highly *affective* process. Darlene's performance is a response to a dilemma. She is in her first five weeks of college and her problem-solving process is loaded with feelings of uncertainty and perhaps helplessness. This is not to say she is simply awash in an emotional response: she sees changes in the rules of the game and has found a path out—to "leave it at that" and hope the teacher will give a freshman a break. On the one hand, Darlene has an unquestioned meta-awareness of the conflict; she is taking action within a dilemma she has articulated with remarkable clarity. On the other hand, her attitude toward the problem—or perhaps toward her own powers as a mere "freshman"—leads her to give up when others students, whose consensus strategy also failed, tried another tactic. Motivation, attitudes, and feelings play a part in her representation of both the problem and the text and in her decision process as a writer.

A third striking feature that the think-aloud data reveals is the importance of Darlene's personal *task representation*, the task Darlene has given herself to do. Darlene was 1 of 72 students studied in the Reading-to-Write project, working on an assignment for her freshman class (Flower et al., 1990). Their assignment was a typically open-ended one that contained the god words of college writing: "interpret," "synthesize," use the "relevant sources" and "your own ideas." Looking across the students as a whole, we saw a process with many shared features, which included students' assumptions about school writing, the culture of recitation brought from high school, and what students called their standard strategies, invoked in happy disregard of assignment specifics. But beneath this level of homogeneity, we saw that individual students were giving themselves very different tasks to do, that they held images of the task that differed not only from one another but from teachers' expectations about what it could mean to "interpret" or "synthesize." While Darlene saw a summary of consensus as an unquestioned goal, Fred was telling himself, "Don't just restate a lot of this stuff. . . . They want me to assimilate this, to come up with some conclusions, they [should] be related to something."

Perhaps more important than these differences was the evidence that students were not fully aware of such radical differences in task representation or of the options they had within a typical reading-to-write task. To test this possibility and discover what would happen if students were given the chance to operate with greater awareness, we took our preliminary observations about different representations back to the class, asked the students to recognize the version of the task they had given themselves, and then to revise, but this time to take on the demanding task we called interpreting. We found that a significant number of the students could in fact carry out the difficult "interpret" version of the task, when it was distinguished from other representations like "summarize" and they were allowed to revise. (Simply allowing students to revise and make the text "better" did not have this effect.)

The first performance of these students was not a simple reflection of ability or what they could do but what they were telling themselves they should do. Their attempts to revise revealed another level of strategic choice. Some students became interpreters; others started down that path, saw the amount of work it would entail for a mere revision, and decided to cut their losses. Another group, whom we called the Intenders, thought they were indeed building arguments and interpretations, but as the judges' ratings showed, these students were not able to carry out their intentions in text.

For various reasons then, the texts students showed us were often an unreliable indicator of their strategic process of meaning making, including their efforts, intentions, assumptions, and dilemmas. The constructive process of Darlene and her peers, which the judges never saw, went beyond comprehending the source texts, following conventions, and shaping words on a page, to include reading the context, interpreting this rhetorical situation, and charting their own sometimes surprising path for what do to in a problematic situation.

In a Community of Writers

De Shawnna offers another portrait of what can happen when the process of negotiation becomes both more public and collaborative. De Shawnna's text, titled "Let's Talk Contracting," appears with her photo and byline in a newsletter called *Going to Work*, which teenagers at the Community Literacy Center wrote to explore real-life careers. De Shawnna's text starts out with confident self-assertion: "Attention future contractors . . . . . . Do you wonder how you would get started or what a contractors days are like? I, De Shawnna Morris, a senior from Oliver High and a writer from the Community Literacy Center, had a puzzling conversation with contracting supervisor Thomas Darr, a man of contradiction."

A different perspective, however, comes from an account written by her mentor about the making of this text to describe "how collaboration can work in a crisis." Written for new mentors, it documents an impasse in writing and cross-cultural conversation. Most mentors at the Community Literacy Center are college students who take Carnegie Mellon University's Community Literacy Internship where they learn to work as collaborative planning partners, supporting the writing of inner city teenagers. De Shawnna's mentor, Tim Flower, was one of the professional people who also volunteer at the CLC, but neither his past experience as a teacher or a mentor prevented

> The Thursday From Hell—one of those days when everything seems to go wrong. For starters, neither of us felt like writing. I was tired, distracted, and worried because Shawnna and I had made so little progress; and she was obviously feeling even worse. As for the start we'd made the previous session, Shawnna announced that the computer had erased it completely. And, erased or not, Shawnna now wanted to abandon it completely. "I don't like it. . . . It's not original at all. . . . It's just gonna be like everyone else's. . . . It's boring. . . . It's no good. . . . I don't know what I want to do. . . . I don't like it." (Imagine long pauses—like eternities—between these phrases.)

As they sat together at the computer as writer and supporter with the noise of other projects around them,

> she said very little ("I just can't think today"), though her facial expressions and body language were eloquent. Mostly she stared at the blank screen of the computer, played with the color and format features, and mumbled. The few things she reiterated were significant:
>
> "I *never* have this problem! . . . I don't know what I'm doing! . . . This isn't like school writing at all!" These statements suggest that her pres-

> ent task was an attempt at something new and more complex in its demands than her previous writing experiences. At school she writes fluently, gets good grades, and writes regularly for the school paper. She'd written three articles for the paper the week before. . . .
>
> And she kept saying that she had to "do something different . . . not like everyone else," which I took to be more than a declaration of independence; I know she takes pride in her identity as a writer.

Facing terminal frustration, they abandoned the computer for the kitchen on the principle of "always change a losing game . . . we gathered up our stuff, redeposited it on the kitchen counter, and tried again."

At this point as "some interesting problems began to emerge," we start to hear some inner voices that had been speaking behind De Shawnna's silence. Like Darlene, De Shawnna has a knowledge of writing conventions that takes the form of an *inner voice* suggesting a "proper" format for objective reporting and dictating features to avoid. Unfortunately, this voice and its demands are in sharp conflict with the voice noted above that calls for originality. And both tell her that her familiar persona as a sports writer (and the strategies that give her such fluency there) are just not appropriate.

> As our brainstorming started to get interesting, we could both see that she had things she wanted to say in response to Darr, but felt she couldn't say. Why not? Because then she would have to use *I*. She used the first person mode when she wrote a newspaper column, it turned out, but felt it would be wrong for other writing. I think she identified our project with reporting; hence news, hence facts; whereas "the *I* word" may have suggested biased opinions or simply a "too personal" style. "It's O.K. when I write for the school paper, 'cause everyone knows it's me, knows about the basketball team, wants some news and opinions—how the team is doing at this point in the season" [As I posed counterarguments] Shawnna kept coming back to "can't use *I*," but we wouldn't have talked about it so much if it hadn't been for her growing acknowledgment that she wanted to have a personal voice in whatever she was about to write.

Another feature of this constructive process is its series of small *decision points*. Some are sure to be an artifact of Tim's narrative, and a mentor's hunger for turning points—this is, after all, a crisis with a happy ending: "I asked Shawnna if she'd noticed Darr contradicting himself sometimes. Eureka! Shawnna had all kinds of responses to that, and so did I. That was the breakthrough we needed." Nevertheless, De Shawnna's process, like Darlene's, is marked by a series of revealing rhetorical moves, from resistance, to simply deciding that her voice mattered, to rejecting her mentor's question/answer format (too tedious), to experimenting with variations on a dialogue format.

Although this constructive process is marked by points of conflict, discovery, and decision, it is not a tale of progress in which moves take a person either forward or backward, but of embracing and abandoning options, making connections, and making choices. It is in these decision points (as when Darlene authorizes herself to "interpret any way she can" and minutes later revokes her license to do so) that we see acts of negotiation taking place. We hear the advice of conflicting inner voices, and we can perhaps infer how outer public forces have become transformed into these inner, private voices.

The mentor's account ends by listing some decision points that had structured this collaboration (in his memory) and the rather imposing list of criteria with which the pair had been wrestling:

> We may have reinvented the wheel, but I prefer to think we devised a way to make her writing accomplish her goals. Without knowing her constraints, which emerged only in the tortuous course of our negotiation, I would not have suggested the combined genre we eventually agreed to use. We walked out of that CLC kitchen with a workable plan that would enable us to (a) use the interview directly, thereby satisfying the objectivity criterion and giving Tom Darr his own voice, (b) edit it for brevity and better focus, (c) give Shawnna a voice and a special way of addressing her audience, (d) give a theme and purpose to the piece (making the editing easy), (e) write something worthwhile that would be uniquely hers, "not like everyone else's," and (f) best of all, work through a complex problem cooperatively.

This mentor's account of De Shawnna's inner voices, of his voice, and the decision points in their collaborative process is undeniably partial, biased by his perspective and rhetorical purposes in writing this text for other mentors. And yes, for all the intensity of the experience, the wheel they invented is not exactly new. Nevertheless, like Darlene's more intimate think-aloud, this account lets us see the writer's text as a set of moves, choices, and conflicted decisions. Some of these moves we may label inspired, others unwise, incoherent, or incorrect. The center may not hold, and moves that structure the beginning may war with the logic that structures the end. Nevertheless, listening in at decision points to the inner voices and negotiations of these writers can sometimes reveal a *hidden logic* in such texts, a logic that may be only partially apparent to a teacher or reader.

De Shawnna's text is an experiment in text making, with some small unconventional gestures that a conventional editor might have deleted (but a CLC mentor would probably support or, as time allowed, question). For example, having asked Tom Darr a tough question, she tags his innocuous answer with a skeptical, but undeveloped parenthetical comment: "Have you ever had a female that worked better than a male? Yes. Everybody's an individual. You know, you don't get into female-male or color or age. . . . You treat everybody the same. (Let's find out.)"

De Shawnna's skeptical comment is a gesture not fully realized in text. Beneath that gesture is a complex negotiation among her desires to maintain objectivity, to express personal insight, and to develop a subtext about contradiction. That odd little parenthesis is the tip of an iceberg, built on her awareness and struggle with multiple conventions and strong personal goals. It operates according to the hidden logic that is also dictating her "you-are-there" introduction, her selection of questions, her unconventional formatting, her stance as a writer.

De Shawnna's negotiations led to experiments in text. In the case of Darlene, the hidden logic of her text, and the fact that it remained hidden, was far more problematic. Her protocol reveals a student's committed but unsuccessful negotiation with old assumptions and new expectations that is transformed in the eleventh hour into a plea for help. However, to readers the personal logic of this act is all but obscured by what appears to be the old logic of a student con game and cop-out.

An Unfinished Model of Construction

The portraits of Simon and Shabalala, Darlene, De Shawnna and Tim let us name some key features of a constructive process as they emerged within complex literate acts: the presence of disparate discourse conventions and their transformation into an integrated literate act, guided by a network of purposes. We see the presence of conflict in an intellectual process suffused with affect and shaped by the task representation writers constructed for themselves. And we can recognize multiple forms of collaboration ranging from coauthorship to mentoring to the more metaphorical collaboration/negotiation with one's own inner voices that help shape the often hidden logic of texts.

In a model of discourse construction that grew out of the Reading-to-Write study with Darlene and her classmates, we conceptualized the relationship among key features of this process in figure 1.

- In this model both readers and writers construct meaning within the broader context of a social and cultural context, of language, of discourse conventions (a trio that was meant to be suggestive, rather than exclusive). These form an outer circle of influence in conjunction with (and often mediated through) a more immediate circle of general

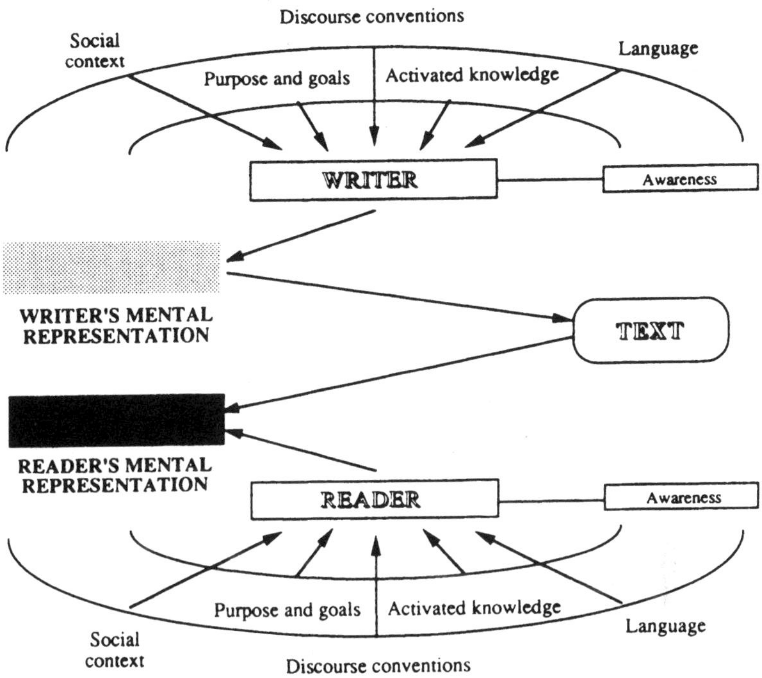

Figure 1. A model of discourse construction (figure from *Reading-to-Write: Exploring a Cognitive and Social Process* by Linda Flower, Victoria Stein, John Ackerman, Margaret Kantz, Kathleen McCormick, and Wayne Peck, copyright © 1990 by Oxford University Press, reproduced by permission of the publisher).

purposes, specific goals, and activated knowledge linked to the task at hand. In the model, both readers and writers build socially shaped, individually formed meanings.

- However, we cannot understand the link between these personal/public contexts for construction and text until we also understand the internal representations people build (represented by the inadequate convention of a box). These personal cognitive constructs mediate the context and conventions that could—in theory—shape a given act of meaning making. They account for crucial differences in the ways individual writers interpret shared social expectations or the ways students interpret a task, the conventions of a new discourse, or a teacher's response. The mental representations—the webs of meaning writers construct—tell a much more complicated story than the representation found in text, since they also include the presence of forces in conflict and roads not taken.
- Awareness, represented here with a small box on the edge of things, is a relative feature. Meaning makers may be highly conscious or

only vaguely aware of their own constructive process and the forces operating on it and within it.

Like any conceptual map, this one foregrounds certain features (such as the presence of a complex internal representation of meaning that stands as the mediator between context and text). It does so, of course, at the expense of other features (such as a more elaborated specification of those forces that range the outer circle). However, its important limitation for us is that, as a conceptual scheme, it is merely a map of the territory, not the story of how people navigate it.

The goal of this book is to animate some parts of this general model, to use its gaps as a heuristic for tracking the process of construction and, in particular, the process of constructing negotiated meanings. Although reading and writing are by definition constructive acts, under certain conditions, they generate moments of collision and moments of unlikely harmony among multiple voices and diverse discourse practices. We see writers, for instance, creating webs of intention, carrying out complex, individual, and socially bounded purposes, shaped by attitudes and feelings and other people. And within the shaping constraints of assigned writing, political oppression, strong literary conventions, source texts, cultural texts, and collaboration, we still hear the individual voices forging personal, contingent meanings.

In such circumstances, the process of construction grows into an active negotiation among some of the multiple forces that shape meaning, and writers choose (or are forced) to turn conscious attention to dealing with the options, constraints, and conflicts that would shape meaning. At these points of conflict and decision, meaning can emerge as the result of trade-offs, impulse, default decisions, faking it, compromise, or hard choices. Under these twin circumstances—conflict and awareness—meaning can be said to be actively negotiated.

How then, shall we animate the model in figure 1? One way is to think of its arrows as vectors or lines of action and to ask what happens when such a process moves into gear in situations we care about. The first column of figure 2 raises such questions about meaning making in general by asking how contextual forces enter the process and interact in building a representation and how that representation shapes text. The second column points us to this book's special concern with the construction of negotiated meanings. In a nutshell: When outer forces translate themselves into inner voices, how do writers negotiate those and other forces that shape both the meaning and the hidden logics of text?

Why pursue this process of negotiation? Within the panorama of meaning construction, with its ordinary acts of reading the paper or writing a note

The Construction of Meaning in General	The Construction of Negotiated Meaning
In what ways do the forces arrayed on the model's outer circle actually affect the individual process of construction?	How do the *outer forces* in this model transform themselves into *inner voices* that guide meaning making? What are such voices actually saying to a writer in question? Do different groups of writers hear different messages?
When this array of potentially contradictory forces (on inner and outer circles) do impinge on writing, how do they interact with one another? How, for instance, does reciprocity between reader and writer occur; how does it affect the representations each is building?	What is happening at points of conflict and points of decision? When these inner voices—and the voices of teachers, collaborators, peers—begin to talk, how do writers *negotiate* these multiple, often *conflicting guides* to meaning making?
How do these complex internal representations of meaning shape text?	How does the negotiation of inner voices shape the *hidden logic* of text?

Figure 2. Questions that would animate a model of construction

to pass in class, these moments of negotiated meaning making may not account for a large part of the action. However, the burden of this book is to argue that these moments have both practical and theoretical significance. They can have an enormous impact on a writer's performance of difficult tasks, especially if that writer is a student. Like bubbles floating on the broader stream of consciousness, acts of negotiation are moments of potential awareness and agency. In our efforts to build grounded theories of writing as a social cognitive event, these moments of negotiation offer new insight into the interplay of cognition and context. And they ask us to examine some other metaphors for how such interplay works.

III. Three Metaphors for How Meaning Is Made: Reproduction, Conversation, and Negotiation

If the process I am calling the *construction of negotiated meaning* is to be more than a truism, we need to be clear about its boundaries. Because we are individual minds operating on social experience, at some level of analysis and in some sense of the word, all meaning is negotiated or shaped in a dialogue with our world. But that vague metaphoric sense, which makes negotiation everything and nothing, gives us a blunt tool for inquiry and theory building. That is not what I have in mind. To foreground the active, dilemma-driven process we see in Darlene—to account for the "dorm room" performance that educational research rarely sees—we need to distinguish these moments of *negotiated* construction and the meanings that emerge from it from the broader category of what we might call socially *shaped* meaning and the many ways it is produced. Although thinking seriously about thinking has a long history (cf. the analytic tradition of Plato's dialogues, the mystical traditions of Taoism), I want to put this inquiry in the context of three modern metaphors for the process by which meaning is constructed: reproduction, conversation, and negotiation.

Construction as Reproduction

Writers produce meaning by reproducing existing or available meanings. The claim seems unquestionable, but when we consider some of the following strong accounts of the process, their implications fire controversy. In constructivist research on reading and on writing from sources, reproduction is a benign and honorable act. Readers actively create meaning by three means: selecting, organizing, and connecting information from texts, a process that is strongly influenced by culturally based expectations and prior knowledge (Spivey, 1987). Successful performance is typically defined by the accuracy, coherence, and extensiveness of the reproduction (Spivey, 1984). Student attempts to enter the new community of academic discourse, according to Bartholomae, are also acts of reproduction: "The student has to appropriate (or be appropriated by) a specialized discourse; . . . he has to invent the university by assembling and mimicking its language," even if doing so is little more than daring "to carry off the bluff" (1985, p. 135). In the developmental picture Bartholomae sketches, reproducing the discourse and its commonplaces will begin as approximation: "What our beginning students need to learn is to extend themselves, by successive approximations, into the commonplaces, set phrases, rituals and gestures, habits of mind, tricks of persuasion, obligatory conclusions and necessary connections that determine the 'what might be said' and constitute knowledge within the various branches of our academic community" (p. 146).

From this perspective, in which knowledge is equated with conventional connections and meaning with intertextual echos, new texts can be defined as a reconfiguration of prior texts. However, in reaction to this narrowed view of writing, some researchers are pointing out how even student writers not only elaborate but transform prior knowledge to achieve their own authority in writing (Ackerman, 1991; Greene, in press; Stein, 1992). In general, the text-based tradition of constructivism in reading has difficulty accounting for the more goal-directed processes of writers; however, it has created a richly documented account of how reproduction works as a highly valued, intertextual process in reading and learning.

Crowley expands our picture with a somewhat different image of reproduction valorized in composition's current-traditional paradigm. There the implicit process theory goes something like this. Language is cast as a perfect stand-in for thinking (i.e., what you say reveals what you are able to think). The goal of thinking is to create an accurate representation of the external world. Crowley calls this process "methodical memory" in which the tutored art of good thinking (drawing on the methods of analysis and synthesis) allows the writer (identified with reason) to refer directly to the objects, perceptions, and experience. Deep thinking with good methods can lead to a just reproduction of reality. Crowley, however, questions whether this dream of just reproduction is really accurate:

> Since language is assumed to be a docile reflection of thought, muddled discourse must be attributed to muddled thinking. No account can be taken of the fact that language sometimes fails—or refuses—to represent an author's intention with accuracy or clarity. Nor can account be taken of exigencies that enhance or interfere with the quality of a discursive production—factors such as ethical, social, or political constraints on what can be said to certain audiences in certain situations. (1990, p. 54)

In this paradigm in which good writing is faithful reproduction, the lesser writing of students would be diagnosed as evidence of the lower quality of their thought, a failure to follow "natural methods" of inquiry. When Crowley looks at composition instruction, she sees reproduction as a flawed theory of invention that obscures the more problematic and social nature of meaning making.

When Hall, on the other hand, looks at the reception of mass media, he sees reproduction as an accurate description of a flawed and intensely problematic process by which public realities are constructed. In a 1973 paper that spearheaded the development of *Screen* theory in British cultural studies, Hall examined "Encoding and Decoding in Television Discourse." He argued that meanings imposed by speaker and hearer are themselves dominated by social codes. The line between domination and determinism is a faint one. Such codes are so well learned they appear natural; they "constitute a *dominant cultural order*" (1980, p. 134). Listeners, as Hall describes them, occupy one of three positions. The first is merely to reproduce the "dominant-hegemonic position." A second is to oppose it (e.g., to read all references to national interest as class interest). And a third, of special interest to us, is a "negotiated position." However, in Hall's view, the scope of negotiation is limited, since a negotiated interpretation buys into the dominant code and its reading, but allows for local or personal exceptions (e.g., the national interest demands wage freezes, but just not in my case). Even when elaboration is recognized as a part of reproduction, it plays a minimal role.

Reproduction theory, as we discussed in chapter 1, has made a persuasive case for seeing knowledge construction as a process of unconsciously recreating the prior texts of our culture. Its implicit textual determinism has, however, been subject to the critiques of Giroux, Ericskon, and others. Turner, for instance, describes how the movement in British cultural studies (identified with the journal *Screen*) was initially dominated by "Lacan's view of subjectivity as an empty space to be filled by language. . . . In *Screen* theory, texts always and irresistibly tell us how to understand them" (1990, pp. 106–107). Turner then traces the movement away from these strong theories of cultural reproduction and reception in which a reader, dominated by text, had only a limited range of constructive options. Studies of subcultures and discourse communities pushed cultural theory toward an increasing sense of polysemy, multiple meanings, ambiguity, and contradiction. "Where once the endeavor was to alert us to the construction of a consensual reading, a considerable number of studies have now begun to describe strategies of resistance within the text; networks of ambiguity and contradiction that invite and accommodate the reader's adoption of different, even ideologically contradictory, subject positions" (p. 117). However, Turner goes on to say, that although theorists are reaching for a more balanced "recognition that texts, readers, and readings [are formed by] a complex set of negotiations and interrelations," this program of analysis has been more difficult to carry out in practice than the practice of locating dominant readings (p. 128).

In sum, meaning making that is a reproduction (to one degree or another) of others' meanings seems to be at work in many settings. It supports learning, manifests itself in intertextuality, and contributes to the cultural continuity of both dominant and resistant subcultures. But our accounts of reproduction have also come under question: Are traditional notions of reproducing reality possible? Are texts (school texts and television messages alike) actually exerting an uncontested reproductive influence on peoples' minds? And do the texts and the intertexts we study give an adequate picture of the meaning(s) readers and writers actually construct? In short, theories of reproduction may not be telling the whole story.

Construction as Conversation

The metaphor of conversation provides an alternative model. In contrast to the one-way communication of reproduction, conversation and negotiation are both dialogic processes but differ in the role they assign to personal agency and to conflict (cf. LeFevre, 1987).[4] Since *conversation* has become a fuzzy term of approbation in composition studies, I want to consider three specific accounts of it in social theory, writing research, and classical rhetoric. Although many of us use the term *conversation* to imply a general sense of dialogue, the theoretically explicit versions we consider below spell out assumptions that stand in a meaningful contrast to negotiation.

Let us start with Clark's attempt to synthesize the social constructionist position in *Dialogue, Dialectic and Conversation.* Citing Rorty, Geertz, Kuhn, Bruffee, and Bakhtin (as well as Plato, Aristotle, Bitzer, and Burke all as theorists of dialectical interaction), Clark outlines the distinctive features of a process we might call the agentless, social conversation. In this vision of conversation, there is no exigence that motivates meaning making, no logic that shapes it; rather, meaning emerges out of an "undirected interaction of equals." This disinterested constructive process is set in motion because the "responsibility for conducting their collective life" requires people to "coordinate their beliefs, values and action with others." Meaning is the output of this coordination, the ongoing record of the exchange. Unlike a rhetorical process hustling into action, this conversational process resists closure. Meaning is democratic; it "reminds readers [and writers] that they must reject the claim to authority inherent in every text" (1990, pp. xvii–xviii). In this "undirected" process, personal goals, individual agency, and power relations play an insignificant role.

The context in which meaning making occurs is an ideal one in Clark's account: "The meaning-making function of every text is situated in the free and collaborative social context described by conversation [i.e., as an undirected interaction]" (p. xvii). Although reproduction theorists might question whether this coercion-free context is indeed the norm, Clark sees conversation as the "natural experience of cooperative, collaborative interaction through which people enact the essence of compromise" (p. xvi).

Most importantly, the end of the conversational process is consensus—and more conversation. In place of persuasion that changes minds, conversation creates and maintains a consensus based on what people agree about: it produces "statements that articulate the agreements that bind us together as cooperating members of a community" (Clark, 1990, p. xvii). Conversation, then, constructs a very particular kind of social meaning (that might, for instance, differ from logical, personal, or manipulative meanings). In oral conversation, "the goal of each participant at any point in this process is to bring her individual interpretation into correspondence with the interpretations of others" (p. 37). Much the same thing is said to happen in writing, which is similarly devoted to constructing the "shared knowledge upon which the people whom a community comprises construct their collective life" (p. 48). As this passively constructive process moves toward the inevitable residue of consensus, conflict and views that are not widely shared within the community appear to drop out of the conversation or be filtered away.

In contrast to Clark's sweeping account of conversation as the social machine of consensus, Nystrand and Brandt analyze the conversational process at work in actual classroom discourse and texts, using it as a model for literacy more generally. Nystrand's (1986) reciprocity theory, which mirrors the dialogic patterns found in classroom talk, envisions both writers and readers engaged in the dedicated pursuit of shared meaning, attempting to infer the needs, intentions, and interpretations of one another. Acting like partners in a substantive, dialogic classroom conversation, both reader and writer contribute to a process in which shared understandings evolve. Texts offer their readers various inducements to join this conversation, which Brandt (1990) describes as "involvement." As an unfolding literate event in which reader and writer are actively reading each other, texts use various tricks of metadiscourse to both monitor and maintain an intersubjective context between conversational partners. They may, for example, frequently refer to "where things stand now" in the discussion and use authorial comment to simulate the response of imagined readers, or to locate what is in shared focus at the moment, or to size up agreement as a way of allowing the writer to make the next move in an argument. This view of meaning making as conversation, then, envisions a dialogue between two partners working hard to create shared understanding. The meaning in question belongs to neither—it is the product of the interaction.

Finally, let us round out this picture of conversation with a more combative model from classical rhetoric. Arguing for a revival of Cicero's *inventio*, Sloane sees the dialogic contest of forensic argumentation as the "paradigmatic" model of rhetorical invention itself. The process is to "argue it pro and con, and then find the *stasis*—that is, as Antonius says, 'the issue in doubt,' the precise point on which the dispute seems to turn" (1989, p. 466). According to Cicero, "when I have thoroughly mastered the circumstances of a case the issue in doubt comes instantly to my mind (*De Oratore* 2.24.103, quoted in Sloane, p. 466). Ciceronian dialogic invention, Sloane asserts, is the mark of a "good humanist," "a way to challenge dogmatism" (pp. 471–472). However, the available roles in this dialogic process are limited to prosecution, defense, and judge—there is no place for internal negotiation or resolution in the mind of the writer. Sloane anticipates the problem this artificial stance might pose, predicting that asking students to play both sides of the fence will run afoul of "our outworn insistence that all utterances must somehow be 'sincere'" (p. 466). Sloane's model, with its delight in adversarial dialogue, seems quite unlike Clark's genial, faceless conversation. Yet, in both, the conflict and resolution that construct meaning are external events, not located in the minds of individual writers but in the decision of a judge or the slow-congealing judgment of social consensus. Not only is conversation the agent of construction, but meaning itself exists only in conversation's unfolding interchange, not in representations any individual participant might construct. Readers and writers are merely participants in the dialogue, which it seems only the theorist/observer can perceive.

Some Problems in the Conversation

Conversation has been a productive metaphor for theorizing about the emergence of culture, communities, and disciplines. It has helped focus the research conducted in classrooms, in writing groups, and in homes (cf. Cazden, 1988; Dyson, 1986; Freedman, 1987; Heath, 1983; Herrington, 1988; Walvoord & McCarthy, 1990). It also seems to imply radically different things to different people.

Let us return for a moment to Clark's account in which agentless conversational construction is imagined as a "natural" event identified with the values of democracy. Despite this claim for natural goodness, the endless dialogue Clark outlines is, we should realize, a rather specialized process that raises at least two kinds of questions. One question concerns the psychological reality of this vision. Clark's disembodied social conversation is an idealized model of communication—communication as it should be, according to the theory. It is driven by an unflagging spirit of mutuality and supported by a faith that consensus and even shared knowledge is actually possible. Clark positions his model as *natural.* Yet, Bialostosky, whom he quotes, argues that if such a dialogical exchange happened, it would dramatically alter how people normally read and write—it would lead to Rorty's more generative, "abnormal" discourse. If this process seems so rare, is it, we might ask, a fully adequate account of how people think?

Some might also be skeptical of the social dynamics conversational theory imagines. Is cooperative dialogue and undirected conversation really the normal, natural force that leads to new meaning for individuals or society? Do the meanings a discourse community appears to share necessarily reflect democratic consensus and not the suppression of less powerful ideologies, as the reproduction model might argue? Worse yet, the dream of shared knowledge may reflect writers' misguided desire to construct their readers in their own image. As Crowley and others argue, it may be presuming too much to think we as writers can easily cross boundaries such as race, gender, and class, to assume we are holding a genuine dialogue with an audience we have in fact constructed. And what about those who write the texts that announce consensus? Are they always justified in claiming they understand and can speak for the experience of others, including the disenfranchised they would represent (Crowley, 1992)? In short, the ideals of conversational construction fail to capture some important social and psychological realities.

Finally, in their focus on broad social processes, conversational models have considerable difficulty dealing with the role of individual cognition and personal agency. The product of construction exists in the air, in the middle of the table, in the moment of interchange rather than in the minds of real people and the unique representations they construct, take home with them, or commit to paper. Kaufer and Carley's (1993) constructuralist theory challenges this view by describing meaning as a transaction that occurs in a sociocultural landscape. In what they call their ecological perspective, individuals are situated actors, components of a dynamic environment. Their actions are a function of their position in that landscape, but in interaction with other situated individuals, they are constantly influencing and changing that landscape. Their model contradicts the undirected but consensual dynamic outlined by Clark.

Although social construction theory has embraced this vision of a disembodied, agentless social conversation, many of us who use the metaphor of conversation more casually, actually envision an interpersonal, even impassioned exchange. We think of meaning created by imitation or appropriation or forged out of challenges, in heated conversations with teachers and peers, with friends and readers, and even with other writers long dead. Nystrand's reciprocity theory and Brandt's analysis of literacy as an act of interpersonal involvement articulate this position in which the reciprocity between reader and writer is a first principle of communication. In describing readers' and writers' efforts after reciprocity, they use the delicate, interpersonal tango of face-to-face conversation as a model for the complex internal tango of the writer's cognition. Reciprocity offers us a persuasive account of a key move in rhetorical cognition, but I will argue that it is still an incomplete picture of that cognition. The threats to reciprocity that lead writers to the textual elaborations that restore mutual understanding are just some of the pressures writers manage. Although in theory, reciprocity would indeed be a first principle of communication, in practice it is not the only contender attempting to guide the writer's meaning-making process.

It is not surprising that conversational analysis has stopped short of a fully articulated theory of situated cognition. When the ethnography of communication began to emerge some twenty years ago, writers like Hymes and Gumperz were arguing against a backdrop of linguistic anthropology, which they countered with "a concept of meaning as socially negotiated rather than individual, and as located or situated in the human communication process of face-to-face interaction rather than in the head of the individual speaker or in language (Philips, 1990, p. 345). Others used their conversational data to attack the limitations of the speech act theory of Austin and Searle who, Rosaldo argued, "think of 'doing things with words' as the achievement of autonomous selves, whose deeds are not significantly constrained by the relationships and expectations that define their local world (Rosaldo, 1990, p. 375). Philips's and Rosaldo's arguments for the "sociality of individuals" and "socially negotiated meaning" (first printed in 1976 and 1982) no longer seem controversial. And the narrow theory of autonomous mind they found in linguistics and needed to counter seems outmoded. (In fact, while this issue was being argued within anthropology, schema theorists in cognitive psychology were developing theories of how socially shaped and shared knowledge was constructed by individual minds and held in memory.) In attempting to establish its legitimacy, this new vision of meaning making positioned itself against a limited theory of cognition and argued for the importance of an interpersonal process by denying the existence of individual cognition. It is not surprising that conversational construction offers a revealing but partial model for the constructive process of individual writers and thinkers.

The goal of cognitive rhetoric is to understand meaning making as a process that happens *not only* in face-to-face conversation, but *also* in the minds of conversational partners—and in the socially situated but often solitary acts of writers. The metaphors of agentless conversation (that seamless, endless flow of talk at Burke's eternal cocktail party) obscure the fact that meaning and the work of construction are still located in the minds of individual agents, not in the reified construct of "conversation" itself. And the analysis of face-to-face conversation does not reveal (for the reasons noted above) how the unfolding meaning of a conversational act (as seen by the ethnographer) also leads to (differing) personal representations each party also walks away with, such as the "meaning" a student writer constructs out of a conference conversation. The need to understand these internal representations of meaning should be inescapable to teachers. Even when we create the carefully structured conversations of school (from classroom discussions to peer groups), the new understandings (in the minds of individual writers) that we so earnestly desire may not be taking place (Freedman, 1987). The real work occupying the attention of conversant learners may, for instance, be the politeness moves that will get them successfully through the conversation (Florio-Ruane, 1991).

In sum, we cannot make the easy equation of conversation with knowledge construction until we can go beyond the mere appearance of a "lively discussion" and can say what effect that conversation is having in the minds of live participants—how the representations, attitudes, associations they brought to the exchange are being restructured, expanded, challenged, reaffirmed, or left untouched by this conversation as they interpret, ignore, fail to understand, or reject it. And at this point, at which we try to specify how conversation becomes a collaborative constructive act, we may begin to invoke the more focused metaphor of negotiation, to which I will turn shortly.

Slipping Between Can, Must, *and* Ought

Do these challenges to the conversational model reveal feet of clay or deny the reality of this process? I think not. The difficulty with the conversational metaphor lies in the uses we make of it. Clark, Nystrand, Brandt, LeFevre—like the researchers and theorists who look at reproduction—have offered us some powerful and in many cases highly persuasive accounts of what can occur. They have added another piece to the puzzle of how writers and readers construct meaning by documenting ways we, under certain situations, respond to textbooks, television messages, disciplinary arguments, and classroom discourse. However, as people move from observation to theory, these situated discussions of what *can* happen (under given conditions) have a way of transforming themselves into a theoretical statement of what *must*, of necessity, be happening in the construction of meaning more generally for everyone. Clark's account of conversational construction, for instance, is a highly normative description of a particular, valued literate process. I share many of his values. But it is *a* process, not *the* process. Likewise, Nystrand's reciprocity theory enunciates an ideal, asserting a process that, he convincingly argues, must obtain if discourse is to meet our aspirations for open, collaborative classrooms and societies. This slip from a descriptive, situated, conditional *is* to the theoretical, general *must* is also apparent in accounts of reproduction, although for less optimistic reasons. Once oppressive forces or strong intertextual patterns are exposed to view in a cultural critique, it is inviting to construct a more generalized theory of discourse centered around the necessity and irresistible force of the evil empire.

This normative slippage also occurs in unquestioned shifts to the *ought* of instruction. If, for instance, our ideal model of meaning making does not always obtain in a fallen world, pedagogy ought to make it happen, creating a space and a scaffold for our valued, presumably more natural process. Yet we might take pause. As Crowley documents, when we consult our reigning images of what the writer should do, those images (such as the claims of current-traditional rhetoric) may distort the greater wonder and complexity of what people do do. Although a conversational model is a welcome assault on the authoritarian tendency of reproduction, is it itself an adequate pedagogical model? The actual conversations of peer groups, for instance, seem to fall short of the collaborative thinking instructors envisioned (Freedman, 1987). Trimbur and other left-wing critics locate a more fundamental problem, however, in Rorty's notion of conversation envisioned as "a discourse that has no beginning or end, but no crisis or contradiction, either. . . . Rolling of its own accord, reproducing itself effortlessly, responsible only to itself, . . . conversation turns into an act of assimilation (1989, pp. 606–607). Conversation, these critics claim, "downplays its own social force and the conflict it generates; . . . they suspect there are other voices to take into account" (p. 608). Trimbur's educational *ought* would shift the agenda from consensus making to consensus deferral, to recognizing the voices that are marginalized by consensus, and to learning to work together with differences that are not reconciled through an ideal conversation.

Let me be perfectly clear. The point of this discussion is not to undercut the legitimacy of these potentially conflicting accounts of meaning making. Instead, I think we have more to gain by recognizing the diverse, situated ways meaning is constructed and by being cautious about slipping from observation-based theories to the more generalizing *musts* and *oughts* that polarize thinking into oversimplified, conflicting camps. It is with this sense of the conditional reality of these accounts that I want to turn to the metaphor of negotiation: How does this process operate and what role does it play in conjunction with the other "normal" processes of reproduction and conversation?

Construction as Negotiation: A Theoretical Sketch

The agentless conversational models we have just reviewed draw attention to a relatively undirected process, in which meaning is nourished, shaped, and expanded by existing within a stream of possibilities. The meaning that emerges from such dialogue over time is the sediment of shared understandings, the gradual accumulation of a community consensus. The metaphor of conversation allows us to imagine a passive force and an agentless process in which meaning emerges through immaculate conception.

Negotiation, on the other hand, draws our gaze to a dilemma-driven and goal-directed effort to construct meaning in the face of forces that—unlike the enveloping flow of conversation—are hard to ignore. Negotiation is often associated with forging agreements in the midst of disputes at a bargaining table or summit talk (Fisher & Ury, 1983). In the rhetoric of science, the footprints of negotiation are visible not only in the citation patterns and case building in texts but in the textual history of an issue, where the pressure of competing interests and the rapid exchange of findings lead to a sequence of changes in the knowledge claims researchers make (Bazerman, 1991; Latour, 1987; Myers, 1985). Educators talk about the face-to-face dialogue between teacher and student or between ethnographer and subject as a space where meaning is negotiated. In these interpersonal negotiations, the patterns of power that structure the dialogue also give authority to some meanings at the expense of others (Clifford, 1983; Florio-Ruane, 1991; Freedman, 1992).

In these images of negotiation, individuals (and groups) come to the table as independent knowers, ready to talk. I wish to add to this picture by arguing that negotiation is also an internal process by which writers construct (rather than merely defend) personal, but socially situated meanings. Because much of this book is an attempt to explore the nature of this social cognitive process, I want to ground this inquiry in a preliminary theoretical sketch of negotiation as a constructive process. The following account is necessarily tentative, but it is also the interpretive lens through which I see the writers I study—it guides what I attend to. This lens will inevitably cast its own shadow, but trying to articulate a more explicit model of how negotiation is working creates a hypothesis that is open to testing, refinement, and revision. It also invites observation-based theory building, which asks, How does the process of negotiation described here operate or change when it appears in other significant contexts? Let me start with an operational definition of the playing field.

The process of constructing negotiated meaning comes into play for a writer when two necessary conditions hold:

- when the process of meaning making is subject to pressure, to converging constraints and options, or to conflict among goals; *and*
- when writers turn their attention at some level of awareness to managing or negotiating this problematic cognitive and rhetorical situation.

In the process we are tracking, outer forces (of social and cultural expectation, of discourse convention, of language, of teachers, of collaborators, and more) appear as inner voices, speaking in conjunction with the writer's own goals and available knowledge. As these forces open doors, promote options, and suggest action, they may come in conflict. Writers who choose, if only momentarily, to entertain and attend to this conflict (at some level of awareness) enter into the construction of negotiated meaning. In the negotiation of these forces, which we can sometimes glimpse at points of conflict and decision, the writer constructs not only a web of meaning, but the hidden logic or, more often, the hidden logics that shape the writer's text.

To say that various forces shape writing is a convenient abstraction, in that it includes goals, strategies, and constraints, as well as substantive ideas. However, the metaphor of voices may better capture the way such forces cluster and crowd into a writer's attention. The notion of a voiced idea brings with it three possibilities, any one of which might be present in a given negotiation. First, a voiced idea, unlike a linguistic proposition, comes with a body attached to it, spoken in the mind's inner ear by a thinking, feeling person who stands in a role and a relationship to the writer. Secondly, a voiced idea speaks in language that imports its own history—the resonance of its vocabulary and its link to prior texts and contexts. Finally, a voiced idea may enter negotiation as knowledge taking the name of action, as an operational idea that proffers advice, injunctions, plans, and procedures. Let me then extend this theory of meaning making with two more key claims.

Negotiation is a response to multiple voices or kinds of knowledge that would shape action:

- voices that set goals, pose constraints, propose language, promote commonplaces, reveal opportunity, demand compliance, and offer alternatives;
- voices of past experience and present opportunity—the voice of wisdom (It usually works to . . .), the voice of demand and doom (That sounds stupid and never use *I*), the voice of possibility (Isn't there a parallel between that idea and . . . ?), the voice of the discourse (How about starting, "Although many people think that . . ." or "Webster defines . . ."?), the voice of one's broad intentions and specific goals (Stick with the part that is really interesting to me, but this paragraph can show that I have done the reading), the voice of the current text (Given what I've just said, I could/I can't . . .), and the voices of readers

past, present, and imagined (Where's your topic sentence?, Yes, but why so you think that?, Can you give me an example?);

- voices that complement, conditionalize, overlap, or baldly conflict with one another or that merely present a buzzing plurality of possibilities linked by ambiguous and shifting ties.

The meaning that is constructed out of such negotiation is a provisional resolution and a response to these voices.

- As a response to multiple voices, this meaning is more than a heteroglossic pastiche of voiced language and ideas. It is a construction attempting to deal with multiple goals, constraints, and strategies as well as language. Its network of ideas, intentions, and language is forged as a selective response to, not merely as a reflection of, its shaping forces.
- As a provisional *resolution*, this meaning responds to the voices in its circle of negotiation by acknowledging and acting on certain voices, resisting, ignoring, forgetting some and transforming, synthesizing, reinterpreting others. It is a commitment to a particular representation, to a network of ideas and relations that could have been different. Imagine, for instance, the fate of a writer's intuitively "right" but contested idea. In the meaning she or he eventually constructs, it is stated as a claim (not a mere possibility, as some "voices" in her or his internal negotiation would have had it). However, it is not only qualified by an opposing perspective but subordinated to an even larger issue that emerged out of the negotiation. The structure of ideas has changed. Likewise, the writer's initial persona for the text depended on the rather formal, academic voice of the distanced report writer. This was her standard strategy from school that seemed appropriate for this forum, but it had been forced into negotiation by a need to express some personal commitments and to experiment with textual conventions. The resolution responding to these multiple, but seemingly alternative "goods" led the writer to maintain a transactional, informative voice but to punctuate it with reflective asides, short paragraphs provisionally (at least in this draft) signaled by italics.
- As a *provisional* resolution, this constructed meaning is not necessarily stable or even coherent with other resolutions that may occur across the span of a text. Resolutions may harbor unresolved conflict and ambiguity. Voices suppressed at one point may emerge at another.
- As the resolution of conflict and options, this meaning possesses a logic born out of negotiation. However, when readers of the text are not privy to this decision process and its conflicts or teachers expect

> to see their own goals met, that logic may be shrouded. The writer's resolution (e.g., her or his structure of ideas, persona, or use of conventions) will seem inexplicable, unmotivated, even illogical. Moreover, some resolutions are not stable. As certain conflicts continue to arise over the course of composing and the writer engages in a series of negotiations, the emerging text may reflect a series of local, but inconsistent logics.

Looking more closely at the key features that shape negotiation, we need to examine the role of conflict and multiple voices, the dynamics of navigation and arbitration, the question of unresolved conflict, and the role of live options and tacit knowledge.

Conflict

Negotiation emerges in the presence of conflict, constraints, and alternatives. It arises in the face of competing demands that may align the writer's initial thoughts and desires against the dragons of convention, against teachers' requirements, editors' demands, or readers' expectation. But negotiation is equally necessary when writers hold multiple personal goals (each pulling in its own direction), when they desire potentially competing goods (such as the sweep of coverage and the tight line of coherence), or when they hold a vision of more than one valued option. Conflict is the price of seeing possibility.

Multiple Voices

Unlike the dialogue of writer and imagined reader or the reciprocal shaping of Cicero's point and counterpoint, negotiation is often a site of multiple forces—of goals, constraints, alternatives, options. It is often useful to think of this melange of forces as voices each proposing its own agenda, setting its own goals, offering alternative languages, themes, points, and patterns of organization. Bakhtin, whom we will look at in chapter 3, locates these voices in the resonance of language and the heteroglossia of texts. However, Simon, Shabalala, Darlene, and De Shawnna draw attention to the way competing conventions, multiple purposes, and alternative task representations, as well as attitudes and self-images, become voices that shape meaning. Phelps introduces another set of voices when she proposes a feminist approach to analyzing controversies in composition theory. In contrast to what she calls "the excessively rationalized taxonomies proposed by some theorists" (that would play down the plethora of operative "voices"), she describes a heuristic for placing a controversy within the realm of practical reason—for uncovering not only disciplinary structures, but the categories that are "psychologically real for individuals in organizing the field for themselves" (1990, p. 23). Consider these influences on meaning:

> We began by placing an article or theorist with the question, who are her enemies and heroes? and went on to examine key words, writing style, favored genre, characteristic topics, pedagogical strategies, . . . intertextual and interdisciplinary references, modes of inquiry . . . declared identities (e.g., gender, race, social class, region, generation, institution, research program, teaching or research) and a long list of other tests for situating someone or a body of work historically and rhetorically in the field. (p. 23)

The multiple voices and the diverse goals and allegiances that feed the flames of controversy are also present within individual writers and in normal discourse. They generate conflict in meaning making not through direct disagreement over claims, but because the diverse goals a writer holds can lead to profoundly different ways to approach a topic, frame an issue, or interpret an experience.

Navigate or Arbitrate

Although the term *negotiation*, like *conflict*, may conjure up an adversarial scene, the negotiation we will see operates in two complementary ways, reflected in the common senses of the word.

- In one sense, writers do indeed *negotiate/arbitrate* the power relations inherent in the social forces and inner voices that would shape writing, deciding whose demands to acknowledge, which goals to honor, where to compromise, and how to strike the balance.
- In another sense, writers *negotiate/navigate* their way through the space of the problem, charting the best possible path across a hillside strewn with obstacles and invitations, or envisioning the swift channel down the river that reaches as many goals, satisfies as many constraints, and avoids as many difficulties as possible.

In either case, there are choices, trade-offs, and balancing acts, whether the outcome is forging a new synthesis, falling back on a default path, or simply abandoning or forgetting some problematic constraints.

The Question of Unresolved Conflict

Negotiation attempts to find a path that honors multiple goals and voices or arbitrates opposing demands. But how many voices should speak; just how far should the drive to resolution go? In student essays like Darlene's (and in academic arguments like the present one), we expect the writer to integrate her or his goals, ideas, and sources into a seamless web of meaning, into a coherent literate act and an autonomous, or at least unified, text (cf. Olson, 1988).

On the other hand, the drive to resolution comes at a price when the conventions of academic discourse filter out the individual in favor of the general. Florio-Ruane describes the problem in her research with teachers: "Because our initial formal accounts were biased toward the typical, they were unable to capture conflict, compromise, and change. In stories and conversation we had access to a great many more of the tensions and contradictions in teachers' work" (1991, p. 252).

The history of ethnographic writing, according to Clifford, is an argument over just this question: How do we negotiate the role of "other" voices and their divergent goals in text? In the 1920s, academic anthropologists began to displace the missionaries, travelers, and philologists whose accounts of exotic peoples had been disjointed compendiums of folklore and custom mixed with transcriptions of native speech and accounts. The new discourse of anthropology, on the other hand, argued for strongly thematic, theory-driven accounts: "powerful theoretical abstractions [that] promised to help academic ethnographers 'get to the heart' of a culture" (1983, p. 125). The experience of the ethnographer (not to mention the perspectives of his or her informants) were interpreted and pruned to create a "common meaningful world" (p. 129). But lately, partly in reaction to Westerners' "colonial" representations of other cultures, ethnographers are questioning the way they as writers negotiate the complex, multivocal world they, like Florio-Ruane, actually encounter. Should their texts resolve these differences in the service of theory, or should they record events that "don't make sense" (to the anthropologist) and the native accounts that "don't add up," and should they record the voice and even the interpretation of the shaman, the translator, or the informant as well as the view of the anthropologist? As a result, ethnographic writers are now negotiating a new, even more problematic set of goals: How do we represent a dialogic encounter with a multivoiced culture, while (still) achieving the authority and making the contribution to knowledge expected in academic discourse? The problem of the ethnographer is the problem of writers and negotiation in general: What is lost when conflict is resolved in the name of coherence?

Live Options and the Circle of Negotiation

But, we may ask, do all these options actually enter into the negotiation? The reproductive metaphor tends to assume that in describing the available, culturally dominant, disciplinary, or intertextual voices, we have described the thinking of individual readers and writers who participate in that culture. Conversational metaphors often treat the voices that emerge in dialogue (e.g., the resonances of a Bakhtin Word or the identities of Phelp's theorists) as eternally copresent in the mind and memory of the writer, as all and equally influential in the meaning that writer creates. However, to understand the creation of negotiated meaning, we will have to distinguish available options from live options. Out of the culturally available commonplaces, out of the ideas voiced in a class discussion offered by a teacher or peer or even recited by the student, we will have to uncover the live options that enter into real acts of meaning making over the course of composing. In other words, we must reach (1) a more discriminate understanding of the voices, goals, constraints, and possibilities that writers actually attend to, understand, or retain out of a dialogic experience (including the way writers themselves interpret those possibilities) and (2) a recognition of which voices are psychologically present in a constructive act (or present at different times).

As any teacher knows, exposure does not guarantee learning or predict the learner's interpretation of an experience, and learning does not guarantee access to knowledge or its use (Prawat, 1989). Negotiated meanings are constructed not out of the situation an observer might perceive, but out of live options and in the midst of the active voices a writer entertains. In the sketches that follow, of university freshmen, women returning to college, graduate students, and community center volunteers, we will be asking, What are the voices that most vigorously enter the circle of negotiation? What could a situated theory of construction tell us about these writers?

Goal-Directed Construction

In the conversational metaphor, meanings emerge of their own volition in the atmosphere of talk; in the metaphor of negotiation they are constructed by people with purposes. However, the negotiation I will describe complicates any notion we may have had of straightforward goal-directed thinking. The presence of multiple goals and competing voices make it impossible for us to predict what a writer will do or be able to do. For the writer, problem-solving strategies can offer only heuristic, probabilistic moves in the face of ill-defined problems. However, in contrast to the self-perpetuating drive of a Burkian conversation, negotiation is a response to a perceived exigency, to the crisis or contradiction that leads to a rhetorical act (Bitzer, 1968; Trimbur, 1989). It is this urgency, this movement toward closure and resolution that makes negotiation necessary and gives such force to those voices that become live options in this process.

Tacit Versus Negotiated Knowing

If reproduction and conversation are powerful social forces shaping the meanings individual writers create, just how much of our knowing is negotiable? This is both a question about epistemology and a question about where to place our efforts to teach writing. There is no easy answer here, but I think we can make some useful distinctions.

Some of the meanings we hold and the voices that shape the construction of new meanings appear to be relatively *non-negotiable.* Such meanings reflect some of our most basic assumptions, values, culturally dictated schemas, fears and desires—ways of perceiving that are so deeply rooted in the structure of our knowledge that we are unlikely to recognize their tacit operation and might alter that influence only with great difficulty if we did. This is the level of processing on which psychoanalytic and some broadly theoretical anthropological and ideological inquiry focuses. Likewise, research in cognitive science describes some basic mental/physical processes such as memory search, perception, and pattern matching that evade introspection and resist conscious control. Although these processes are an inevitable part of meaning making, they are not where education, wisely enough, chooses to make its mark.

Another class of meanings are also constructed with the swift, conveniently tacit and unacknowledged processes of inference. However—and this is a crucial difference—such meaning making could, if prompted, rise to the threshold of awareness. Consider the ways we "read" verbal and nonverbal sign systems, living with different representations each constructs until evidence of miscommunication makes difference an issue (Witte, 1992). Or consider how our knowledge of gender roles, power relations, or social protocol allows us to generate inferences and read between the lines of a situation almost without thinking—until for some reason we stop to think. Likewise, when readers link two ideas as cause and effect, this important "constructive" processes may be shaped by contextual/social/cultural givens without being actively negotiated—without being considered, questioned, tested, or qualified. We depend on schema-driven perceptions and these swift, unquestioned inferential acts to make sense on the fly and get us through the day. Tacit construction may also occur when readers and writers invoke knowledge that did at one time occupy conscious attention (e.g., when a relationship was first learned or questioned) but has now sunk to the level of tacit knowledge, assumptions, or automated processes. However, in contrast to the non-negotiable knowing sketched above, these meanings and the process of constructing them are *open to negotiation;* they can be dredged up, appreciated and explored, subjected to interrogation, reconsidered and revised. It is at this point that meaning making becomes the subject of the inquiry of this book.

Negotiability, then, is relative. Knowledge exists on a sliding scale of awareness where each level has its own advantages. Educators who emphasize immersion, practice, and models in the teaching of writing are placing their bets on these powerful tacit processes with good reason: they support fluency, automaticity, and intuition. Other educators who emphasize rhetorical awareness, problem solving, and strategic teaching are trying to move more of the process into conscious awareness where negotiation is more likely to take place.

Our third, and obviously much smaller, category of meanings, then, concerns those under *active negotiation* at various points in the process of construction. These meanings may hover at the back of our minds, the object of a faint but nagging awareness, or they may usurp attention, plaguing our waking thoughts, erupting unbidden into conversations. Meanings under negotiation may transform themselves before our very eyes during periods of intense reflection or may rearrange themselves without warning the next morning over a cup of tea. Negotiated construction is more than conscious awareness or metacognition; it is a response to perceived dilemmas, conflicts, and alternatives in meaning making. Writers may invite dilemmas into their thinking through problem posing or rhetorical analysis, but dilemmas like Darlene's are the unbidden guests that seem to visit us all. Negotiation occurs when the writer continues, if even briefly, to entertain rather than ignore the dilemma. Such negotiation may fill the narrow stage of conscious attention, a part of which we can tap with think-aloud protocols or selectively reconstruct through retrospection. However, even the portion our data captures reveals a rowdy, elliptical, inferential process. There is no reason to assume that such thinking will be constrained by the rules of logic or reason. Negotiated construction, as we will see in the studies that follow, can also be a highly affective event, shaped by motivation, attitudes, doubts, and desires. It can be a reflective, analytical, and private effort or the result of a fast-paced, collaborative, social exchange.

It is important to recognize that negotiated construction is a special case of meaning making within the much larger category of knowledge production. As a process it is merely an option on the far end of a continuum marked by an increasing amount of attention, focus, verbalization, critical awareness, and sustained engagement; it incorporates and builds on nonnegotiable and tacit meanings. Although we tend to value an increase in critical reflection, this heightened awareness is also selective. There is no guarantee that it will "work on" the issues an educator (or social activist or therapist) might think the most significant. Like the flame that occasionally plays on top of a burning log, negotiation must be understood as an extension of the basic processes that support comprehension and composition, including pattern recognition, schema-filling, rehearsal, analogy, inference, and recall, all of which involve information that must vie for attention and control.[5] We are dealing, then, with a limited class of actions in which complex meanings are being actively forged, usurping the attention of a mind at work (in both logical and alogical modes), negotiated in the presence of pressures and alternatives.

At the same time, these moments offer insight into the situated process of complex thought. Moreover, for many educators, these moments—when received or tacit knowledge is brought into the light of critical examination and is transformed by the purposes of the learner—are some of the defining events of education. So even as I specify the limits of this special case, I want to suggest that these dilemma-driven, rhetorically loaded efforts to construct meaning may play a more significant role in writing, especially in learning to write, than we have acknowledged. These private negotiations reveal a new dimension of students' performance and moments of high potential for growth that teachers may not see or address. More broadly, developing a theory of negotiated construction could lead us to understand better the interplay of cognition and context in which individual meaning emerges from purposeful, socially situated cognition.

IV. A Framework for Inquiry into the Construction of Negotiated Meanings

If a theory is a fully specified, integrated, and tested statement of a complex process, this book is merely a framework for inquiry. As a first step in observation-based theory building, this book will sketch a process that seems to burst unbidden into students' composing. Attempts to track the fluid movement of any process are, of course, always limited to partial, interpretive glimpses caught at the best spot we can find. The framework that I have used to structure my observation locates those "best spots" in three key events: acts of interpretation, negotiation, and reflection.

Interpretation. Negotiation begins with inevitable, often unrecognized, acts of interpretation, with the ways a writer reads the context of writing, interprets the expectations of others, defines the meaning of key words in an assignment, or envisions his or her role as a writer. Interpretation may wield its greatest influence when writers entering a new discourse must create new task representations from indirect cues. Although teachers frequently comment on text features, the writer's success also depends on understanding the goals and strategies that underlie a given literate practice.

Negotiation. Faced with options, invitations, constraints, and pressures on how they select, organize and connect ideas, writers give in, resist, integrate, synthesize, and innovate. As I argued above, some of the constraints writers must negotiate are obvious social and interpersonal ones (the teacher, peer response, the assignment), but others are less apparent—ranging from one's knowledge of the context, the voices, language or rhetorical stances remembered from prior texts, to assumptions about task, to the text written so far.

Reflection. If interpretation and negotiation are at the root of meaning construction, reflection is its coming into flower as writers move to evaluate, justify, and image alternatives. We will see writers reflect, not just on meanings they create, but on their own goals, assumptions, strategies, and habits of making meaning. Reflection is a key process in the framework proposed here not because it is an inevitable occurrence. It is important in this research framework because when it does occur, it is a unique opportunity for research to see how writers are interpreting their own experience. Secondly, it holds a privileged place in the educationally motivated theory I wish to develop here, since reflection and self-awareness can be the basis for critical understanding of one's own goals, assumptions, and strategies, and the motivation for growth and change.

Looking at Circles of Negotiation

If negotiation goes on, what is it that typically gets negotiated? In peer review, we usually assume it is the text. A confrontation over wording, a claim, or implications can lead to dialogic thinking out of which new text is born (although we know that writers may also engage in social moves and text changes designed to eliminate interpersonal conflict or loss of face and avoid any significant negotiation of meaning). However, when we gain insight into the writer as thinker, it becomes apparent that writers bring more than text into the circle of negotiation as they confront their own goals, their image of the task, their rhetorical stance or their writerly self-image. In response to constraints, conflicts, and dilemmas, writers examine their own knowledge (or what to do about a lack of it), their schemas, expectations, assumptions. They puzzle over what a given textual convention or an assigned discourse pattern (such as a synthesis, critique, or freewrite) requires of them. Another vocal constituent of this circle is, of course, other people, writers' images of other people, and the ideas and voices of others embedded in the language of different discourse communities. Institutions, too, enter into these internal conversations, often in their local instantiations as rules, authorities, and expectations. And finally we see the cumulative history of past encounters and past understandings enter into the current constructive moment. Looking closely at acts of interpretation, negotiation and reflection gives us a point of entry into these circles and allows us to ask two questions. First, what concerns (including what voices or forces) are brought into the circle of negotiation for a given student or group of writers—and what are excluded? Second, how do writers, especially learning writers, resolve these options and interactions for themselves?

To explain the three-part framework of interpretation, negotiation, and reflection that will guide our inquiry and to place my own necessarily limited observations against a backdrop of writers at work, I want to end this chapter with vignettes of interpretation, negotiation, and reflection taken from some different educational contexts. The chapters that follow will develop a theory of negotiated construction based on close examination of a few contexts. However, our best educational insights will come from the next step in this inquiry when we begin to uncover the diverse ways in which these processes are carried out—whether those differences are due to experience, motivation, discourse, or social setting.

Interpretation

The way writers interpret a rhetorical situation can tell us a lot about the circles of negotiation they construct and the problems they are trying (or think they should try) to solve. Darlene's attempt to deal with multiple authorities was part of a reading-to-write assignment: 72 students in her freshman course were asked to write their own statement on the topic of time management, interpreting and synthesizing the ideas of others presented on a brief fact sheet (Flower et al., 1990). One purpose of this open-ended assignment (with all the sacred words of academic assignments: *interpret, analyze, synthesize*) was to reveal the distinctive task representations students were giving themselves. (Students, however, tended to assume that their representation was the obvious, normal, natural, or assigned way to proceed.) The study's second goal was to help students reflect on the costs and benefits of these alternative representations and their strategic choices. In her attempt to summarize the authorities, Darlene's image of the task was shared by 43% of the freshmen, a decision in tune with the legacy of school writing and its culture of recitation, but, we should note, at odds with the expectations of many college composition teachers. Problematic patterns of interpretation appeared in another area: when some students saw themselves going beyond summary to other organizing plans (such as synthesis), the judges, looking at the plan as achieved in text, often disagreed.[6] But the more striking differences here were between classmates, first, as we have seen, in terms of organizing plans and information included in the text. While Darlene is struggling to summarize, Fred is trying to write an interpretation: "Unless I just restate a lot of this stuff, talk about the fact that, you know, it is important, . . . but that's not what they want. They want me to assimilate this, come up with some conclusions, they [should] be related to something."

The different text plans Fred and Darlene see as appropriate lead to important differences in the composing strategies they use (and perhaps in the strategies they control). After rereading the assignment, Fred sets up a new rhetorical goal for himself and starts to generate possibilities:

> I guess I'm gonna have to deal with how, how to attack the problem of time management. It sounds good, write this down, and attack problem. Yeah! Great! Things I can think of off hand, you got to put in there about. . . . [At this point he begins to review his notes, search the text, and rethink his response to one of the sources.] I guess I can do a little bit more than restate what they have in the text. I can relate to my situation as a college student. It would be easier to relate to a college student! Well, wonderful.

Because this study was designed to share its observations with students, ask them to consider their initial image, and revise their text into an interpretation, it was able to show that task representation was exerting a significant effect on what students did. Some students, without further instruction, but with an increased awareness of their options could perform academic tasks they had not attempted or realized were expected. But it raised a perplexing question, How aware were students of their initial decisions, choices, and strategies? How much control did they have of their options?

Darlene is in a dilemma, facing the breakdown of what students described as their standard strategy for doing school writing—she seems ripe for considering alternatives. Fred has read not just the familiar words of the assignment, but has read the context to infer some of those larger expectations and has translated those goals into actions in the form of writing strategies for "relating this stuff to something." Interpreting a rhetorical situation and setting goals is a key first step, but when these goals, images, available knowledge, standard strategies, and so forth come in conflict, the stage is set for more active negotiations.

Negotiation

Negotiations with Prior Knowledge

Molly is a graduate student in psychology writing an application for a graduate fellowship that asks her to synthesize and comment on three short articles dealing with supply-side economics—a topic outside her area of expertise. In Ackerman's (1991) study of how high- versus low-domain knowledge affects reading and writing, the high-knowledge writers clearly had a home court advantage. It appeared in the wealth of elaborations they generated during both reading and writing (especially in specific associations made to concepts in the source text and evaluative elaborations) and in their active, inferential awareness of the rhetorical context behind the articles they read. While the low-knowledge writers represented the task as a text-based assignment, the high-knowledge writers either privileged or gave equal billing to their own ideas and placed more new information at the top levels of the text. On such a task, it is abundantly clear that prior knowledge helps.

However, many of the low-knowledge writers, including Molly, negotiated this situation in a way that compensated for their limited domain knowledge. They plunged into the text as active rhetorical readers, not at the level of context, but at the level of discourse structures and conventions—locating main ideas and using their knowledge of text conventions to infer patterns of consensus and conflict in the corpus. Although their final texts clung more tightly to the source texts, their process of locating issues was inferential and constructive, finding a middle ground between merely summarizing and taking an independent critical or evaluative stance.

However, even within this group of rhetorical readers, Molly stood out. Instead of subordinating her personal knowledge and expertise in psychology to the patterns perceived in the text or appending her own ideas as a comment, she engaged in what appeared to be a happy struggle to read the economics texts in terms of the concept of a paradigm shift—a concept borrowed from her own area of expertise. Ackerman's (1989) study tracks this negotiated construction in a setting where domain knowledge (its presence or absence) was exerting a strong influence on the process, on rhetorical awareness, and on the shape of the text. However, as a group these low-knowledge but high-rhetorical writers chose a course that compensated for their lack of topic information. And Molly as an individual juggled her limits and strengths in a more daring way, producing an essay that showed her powers of critical synthesis and gambling that her limited knowledge of economics would not lead her into misinterpretation.

Negotiations with Teachers' Expectations

A junior history major is asked to write a report on the Marshall Plan that dictated the path of post–World War II Europe. Although she is not aware of it at the time, the other half of her class, reading the same six essays, has been asked to write a problem-solution analysis, locating problems the ensuing 30 years of the Marshall Plan revealed and suggesting an alternative. One question for both the history professor and Greene, who conducted the study, was, Would these different assignments lead to qualitatively different kinds of thinking with the material? Would they engender different analytical moves and different kinds of learning? And on average, the two groups did show two distinctive sets of what Greene (1993) called "opening moves" as the problem solvers used more content, relied more heavily on information repeated across texts, and depended on a response rather than a cluster structure for their texts.

In both the Ackerman and Greene studies, one expects the variables they controlled—prior knowledge or the assignment—to predict differences in what people did. (And that happened.) But because these studies also tracked the thinking processes that lead to texts in these different conditions, another surprising pattern emerged. An even better predictor of what writers did was the task they gave themselves, a representation that often violated or ignored the situation the researchers and teacher had designed. Although the history student sketched above received the report assignment, the task she gave herself foregrounded her own ideas rather than the sources, and her text followed the pattern of the problem solvers, with nearly 35% of her information coming from prior knowledge (compared to 38% for the problem solvers and 29% for the report writers). As the student commented in her think-aloud protocol, she "couldn't go straight from the assignment. . . . I didn't think it would be as helpful to my reader to simply recite. . . . It was more important to express what I felt was important" (Greene, 1990b, p. 33). In fact, this stance reflected the philosophical position taken in the course, which treated the writing of history "as an interpretive, constructive act" (p. 36). The plans and the interview with this student suggest that the negotiation behind her meaning was driven by a strong logic in which her image of the instructor's expectations was more significant that the assignment to "report" (Greene, in press).

Negotiations with Texts

The Community Literacy Center and Community House are in the middle of the multicultural, inner city neighborhood of Pittsburgh's North Side. When middle-class, white college students join the summer program to work with and become public advocates for children, they bring with them school-based strategies for argument—strategies that over the past 13 years of this program have sometimes failed them in the rough and tumble world of advocacy before the City Council. In 1984 when President Reagan's report questioned the reality of hunger in America and the equally prestigious Physician's Report called it an epidemic, Peck (1991), as director of this program asked, How are these college students turned child advocates reading and representing such texts to themselves as they try to build their own arguments for the needs of hungry children? The program had always immersed its interns in the life and problems of the neighborhood and in the politics of advocacy. To this Peck added direct instruction in a "data/warrant/claim" strategy for mining such texts for their implicit and explicit arguments and for developing one's own argument. For half the group, this was the major focus of their instruction. For the other half, a streamlined introduction to data/warrant/claim analysis was embedded within a larger "rhetorical/social" instruction. This focused on "reading the rhetorical situation" as well as the text (e.g., seeing the motives behind the claims) and developing advocacy arguments targeted to a specific audience. Before and after this instruction, students read the two reports on hunger, stopping at key points, thinking aloud about how they were representing the texts they were reading and writing. Would such training make a difference; would either group read and write about hunger differently from the other or from a control group who simply had practice reading and writing policy arguments?

One of the most striking features of this study was the different ways readers represented these texts to themselves as they confronted conflict between the President's and Physicians' reports and as they recognized, responded to, and, in some cases, appropriated the opposition to their own position. Before this instruction, the interns looked much like the control group—disturbed and aware of difficulty and disagreement but without clearly articulating the issues they detected. However, training in data/warrant/claim strategies turned these readers into formal critics, transformed their reading into a determined effort to locate all of the writers' claims and evidence, and turned their writing into a detailed response. By the academic standards of an argument class, their systematic analysis and representation of the text was an impressive performance.

The writers with the rhetorical/social instruction also read differently. They, too, were no longer limited to vague comments detecting difficulty, but they found far fewer claims and did a less exhaustive analysis of evidence. Instead, they read like advocates, looking only for key claims and locating the pivotal issues, while devoting far more of their attention to the City

Council audience that both groups hoped to influence. Instead of carefully analyzing the opposition, they often resorted to appropriating it, even using the president's argument against itself to advocate for children's needs. As Peck points out, these ways of negotiating conflict and opposition in texts and of plotting one's own path through an argument are likely to be valued differently in different settings. Data/warrant/claim strategies support the academically prized, careful, open-ended analysis of arguments, but such reading also turns texts into templates rather than a ground for action. The rhetorical/social strategies go for the jugular, locating the issues on which advocacy turns, ignoring secondary claims and evidence irrelevant to their purpose. They also produce what members of that community judged as qualitatively more effective arguments.

Negotiation with Multiple Readers

To pass the writing requirement at their community college, students must submit a portfolio of writing from their classes to an independent board of teacher/examiners. The history of decisions by this board have made it clear that correctness, clear, canonical forms of organization, and accurate use of source texts have great weight in these decisions. But in the composition class Higgins (1992) studied, where most of the students are returning women, the instructor places a high value on students' personal engagement with the social, racial, and gender issues that surround these women's lives and that make up the readings for the course. She encourages arguments in which writers explore their own formative thinking. But as class discussions and Higgins' discourse interviews make clear, students must eventually confront a dilemma many of them cannot resolve. Should they, with the instructor's support, venture into the territory of their own ideas—where they are certain to have more difficulty controlling both the language and structure of the text—or should they play to the critical audience they know awaits them beyond the course and write a more careful text-based commentary that is more nearly within their powers?

In her interviews, Elizabeth, a 31-year-old single mother, was in radical, private disagreement with one of four assigned theories of racism, as a result of her own experience in the South. However, it was equally clear that to turn her own experience into a source of evidence would exceed her powers of organizing the paper and producing a well-supported argument. The position she took in her final paper was based on the elegantly structured (therefore easy to use), four-point theory of the writer she most opposed. What Higgins also saw, but the teacher did not, was the subsequent second draft Elizabeth wrote for herself—a terse list of claims and warrants documenting her own position and disagreement with the "usable" authority.

As these three examples suggest, dilemmas posed by limited topic knowledge, assignments, the desire for authority, personal goals, and multiple and conflicting audience expectations force writers to negotiate intelligent, difficult, daring, and problematic paths through their rhetorical situations. The circle of negotiation—the set of concerns that call up this constructive effort—is a wide one. And as these studies suggest, the outcome of such negotiations is often uncertain and the opportunity to reflect on one's own decisions may be rarer still.

Reflection

As part of a "making thinking visible" classroom inquiry project, Aston (1993) had observed the collaborative planning of students in her developmental writing course and identified a revealing difference between rigid and adaptable planners. Denise's "rigid" strategies had transformed every assignment to fit familiar formulas, had reduced the rhetorical prompts of her supporter to a discussion of formal features, and had ignored the critical, inferential aspects of the assignments. Aston's description of this strategic process helped to explain the frustration and failure of students like Denise who continued trying to "write by the rules" in a reading/writing course focused on issues of sexism, racism, and education, structured as a Freirean, problem-solving environment designed to empower students to speak in the culture of power. For students like Denise, this invitation to critical, analytical reading and writing often remained an opportunity not taken.

Aston's hypothesis, however, took a new shape when she invited students to reflect on these observations and on their own resistance to the goals of both collaborative planning and the course itself. For an experienced community college teacher, whose students may work a 25-hour week, it is no news to hear that students do not want the responsibility of discussing the readings: it is the teacher's job to lecture and tell them "the meaning." "The idea that authority should rest with the writer was, indeed, a very foreign notion" (p. 184). However, those assumptions turned to anger when the class read an unvarnished analysis of high school tracking that laid out the "banking" expectations set for the low track and the "critical thinking" goals afforded to the high. As Aston reports, "The class erupted [with] surprise that tracking was an *intentional* action on the part of educators. *Although every student in the class had been tracked into a low track in high school, none knew of the term tracking*" (p. 184). If critical thinking was missing from their image of the options for school writing, the expectations for the low road were clear: "When I was in high school, I was a low track student. I was never taught to compose an essay (like this one), never taught to think for myself, or do scientific work. I was taught how to do my taxes, fill out job applications, and sit quietly without asking questions" (p. 181). In this class, anger and awareness created the ground for change, but they did not make the difficulty of change or learning go away. Aston's study of her class does not stop with the emotional empowerment of those "successful" class discussions. It takes us instead into the ways five students then negotiated this conflict over the rest of the term. Two of these students clung fatalistically to practiced behaviors in the face of conflict, but three of them risked change, daring to comment on controversial topics like racism or ask questions of the readings, even though they ran the risk of "sounding stupid." For these three, the experiment with critical and rhetorical planning strategies appears linked to a reflective understanding of their old repertoire of strategies (of what they could and could not do). Over the course of the semester, their reflections also reveal a startlingly clear sense of the shifts taking place in their own thinking, of the increased cost in time and effort such writing takes, and of the personal justification for learning when old strategies are still rewarded elsewhere and this is the only class "that was not, as they put it, 'a banking course.' "

Studies like these suggest that not just the construction but the negotiation of meaning goes on behind the texts of student writers. The studies that follow will use the theoretical framework proposed here to track the process of meaning making and to uncover the strategic knowledge guiding writers in a set of varied university contexts.

3

Construction as a Metaphor for Meaning Making

How is meaning made? Sidney, that most artful of Renaissance poets, made a famous case for artlessness in the making of written meaning:

> Loving in truth, and fain in verse my love to show,
> That the dear she might take some pleasure of my pain,
> Pleasure might cause her read, reading might make her know,
> Knowledge might pity win, and pity grace obtain,
>
> I sought fit words to paint the blackest face of woe:
> Studying inventions fine, her wits to entertain,
> Oft turning others' leaves, to see if thence would flow
> Some fresh and fruitful showers upon my sunburned brain.
>
> But words came halting forth, wanting Invention's stay;
> Invention, Nature's child, fled stepdame Study's blows;
> And others' feet seemed but strangers in my way.
> Thus, great with child to speak, and helpless in my throes,
>
> Biting my truant pen, beating myself for spite:
> "Fool," said my Muse to me, "look in thy heart, and write."
>
> (*Astrophel and Stella,* 1591)

Sidney had an ear for the resonance of prior texts, a genius for re-creating those voices from "others' leaves" noted in stanza two. In fact, the polished allusions to both rhetorical and Petrarchan conventions in the first three stanzas make those stanzas themselves an eloquent argument for writing as the reproduction of "borrowed" meanings, for how our ways of knowing reside in the socially constructed language and tropes of a tradition. But the muse in the final couplet urges young Astrophel to a rather different image of writing, one in which meaning is born of an expressive process in which truth, originality (and maybe even a persuasive fourteen-line argument as well) exist to be discovered in the heart. The muse's metaphors of search and discovery have worn well since 1591; they seem to capture the artless, tacit, intensely personal, and serendipitous dimensions of this process that metaphors of reasoned invention, convention, and imitative craft in the earlier stanzas deny. And yet the success of the poem as a whole depends on its power to represent both of these perspectives; it enacts a process of meaning making marked by tension, conflict, and uneasy resolution of multiple ways of knowing, in which emotion, intention, social convention, and craft all assert their presence.[1] It constructs a negotiated meaning.

Although the poet appears to pit the stepdame of tradition and convention against the muse of personal inspiration as a source of meanings, the poem itself constructs a meaning in which they interact. For instance, while Sidney challenges the constraints of the sonnet, he nevertheless chooses to write a technically demanding sonnet that resonates with the Italian and English history of the form. Two hundred years later, Wordsworth echoes this sense of bounded independence:

Nuns fret not at their convent's narrow room;
And hermits are contented with their cells;
. . . .
In truth the prison, into which we doom
Ourselves, no prison is: and hence for me,
In sundry moods, 'twas pastime to be bound
Within the Sonnet's scanty plot of ground.

Wordsworth presents his sonnet as a desire for constraint, a brief solace from "too much liberty:" freedom and constraint are set up as opposites and options. Likewise, in the surface text of Sidney's poem, Invention (Nature's child) is in conflict with Study, until the Muse speaks up for the unstudied wisdom of the heart. That, however, is the surface text. The subtext of Sidney's sonnet echoes, I believe, a more modern stance on this conflict. In place of opposition and choice, the poem itself (as artifact) demonstrates the interaction and the interdependence of tradition, convention, and personal creation. The case for a more unstudied art of invention is made through artfully crafted play with those very conventions. Sidney's sonnet constructs a negotiated meaning by weaving a sophisticated network of relations among all of these "truths." Its meaning does not reside in the claims it makes, but in the resonance, ties, and tensions it creates.

We are used to honoring literary texts (and literary readers) for their ability to construct complex even ambiguous meanings (even though the ties and tensions that Sidney, Wordsworth, and we perceive may only partly overlap). However, this same interactive sense of meaning also exists in the minds of writers—literary and normal writers, experienced and student. It is this individually created network of relations and tensions that a social cognitive theory of meaning making needs to explain.

I. Exploring the Metaphor of Construction

Using the metaphor of construction to describe how writers create a complicated web of significance for themselves (and others) is a loaded choice. Unlike the metaphor of discovery, construction does not suggest a pre-formed truth waiting to be found. And unlike the metaphors of social construction and transmission, it asserts the importance of personal agency in the creation of bounded but individual purposes. Construction, as a cognitive metaphor, locates meaning making in the actions of individual writers creating a sonnet, a scientific paper, or a student essay. And this in turn poses open, empirical questions about how these writers do in fact negotiate the voices of tradition, the whispers of the muse, and the rhetorical demands of their own unpersuaded Stellas.

In this chapter, we will review some of the key concepts that inform this idea of a constructive process—notions of representation, knowledge networks, dialogue, and schema theory. And we will be asking:

- How might we envision the interdependence/interaction of cognition and context, individual and society and at the same time account for individual constructive acts?
- Can we build a more finely-grained working theory of how this process of construction actually operates?

The constructivist tradition in cognitive theory is often traced from Bartlett's 1932 studies of how British readers "reconstructed" a Native American myth in their attempt to understand it. In the enigmatic mythic account, a wounded young man who feels no pain returns from his encounter with the spirit warriors and tells his story.

> He told it all, and then he became quiet. When the sun rose he fell down. Something black came out of his mouth. His face became contorted. The people jumped up and cried.
>
> He was dead (p. 65)

British readers, however, remembered shouting on the battlefield and "a voice said, 'The black man is dead.' And he was brought to the place where they were, and laid on the ground. And he foamed at the mouth (p. 72)." Or they supplied a more plausible medical scenario in which villagers bear home their sick comrade, who "as the day drew to a close, . . . became rapidly worse (p. 75)." Unfamiliar with the cultural and discourse schemas of this text, their "reading" and recall of the story was marked by omissions, transformations, and rethematization—they created a new, coherent, and culturally meaningful text for themselves. Reading research has described the processes of organization, selection, inference, and connection that support such construction (Spivey, 1990). Cognitive rhetoric takes the question a step further and asks, How do writers carry out their socially embedded but even more explicitly goal-directed and rhetorically motivated process of knowledge transformation?

As Bartlett's readers demonstrated with their bizarre reconstructions, meaning making starts with acts of theory-laden perception. We can no longer accept the early positivists' hope that perception can give us an objective and independent touchstone—a set of facts on which all could agree and against which we could test our claims. Like Sidney, we perceive our own experience within interpretive frameworks. Philosophers such as Kuhn (1970) argue that we must in fact learn to see by serving an apprenticeship within a theoretical paradigm; we learn to practice science, for instance, by learning to perceive with the lens it provides. And, as psychologists like Bransford show, new information only becomes comprehensible when the reader can construct a meaningful context for it. Consider the simple two-paragraph passage which begins: "The procedure is actually quite simple. First you arrange things into different groups. Of course one pile may be sufficient depending on how much there is to do. If you have to go somewhere else due to the lack of facilities that is the next step, otherwise you are pretty well set. It is important not to overdo things. That is, it is better to do too few things at once than too many." The procedure may indeed be simple, but readers exhibited little ability to recall it—until they were told *at the beginning* that this was a passage on washing clothes. With that small change, comprehension and recall more than doubled (1990, pp. 134–135). As Bransford and others show, in reading for understanding, we draw heavily on our prior knowledge and construct a context that makes the words meaningful.

Having said that we operate with theory-laden perception out of interpretive paradigms does not mean that we should leap from the dreams of positivism, simple objectivity, and romantic individuality to equally naive determinism. It is still the case that our interpretations are held accountable by the data of perception that can challenge theories and rewrite paradigms. And in the same way, individual writers move among many interpretive frames whose features and conventions they can appropriate for individual purposes. The real problem is understanding the different forms this interaction takes in meaning-making situations we care about, whether that situation is resisting ideological oppression, learning a new discourse, or writing for self-understanding.

As we set out to explore the metaphor of construction, let me note some presuppositions that may distinguish our starting point and our focus from that of other literary, social, and/or cognitive accounts. To begin with, our investigation locates the process of making meaning as, first of all, an event that occurs in *the minds of individual thinkers whose cognition is embedded within and shaped by the social contexts and emotional realities.* Focusing on individual cognition acknowledges but cannot spotlight or do full justice to the social or emotional dimensions of meaning. We need, for instance, to acknowledge that the relatively artful, self-conscious, or reasoned moves of cognition we choose to teach will always be operating in conjunction with tacit, alogical, and emotional knowing. Likewise, it is critically important to learn how meaning emerges out of historical processes, in which claims can metamorphose into "scientific" fact (Latour, 1987), to understand how culture-specific assumptions become reified as "natural" facts or to discover how concepts like literacy undergo unacknowledged (intertextual) redefinition to reflect changing social and political functions of reading (Resnick & Resnick, 1988). Meaning itself is both a social and an individual construct. So how can we justify a deep and inevitably partial focus on cognition, beyond the obvious virtue of promoting complementary perspectives in the field?

The strong case for cognition lies, I believe, in the fact that the agent in even a socially extended process of making meaning is not society, community, or a discourse; that is, meanings are not made by an abstract, theoretical construct but by individual writers, readers, speakers, and listeners who are interpreting inferred meanings around them, constructing their own, and attempting to share those meanings with or impose them on other members of their social or cultural collective. Individual meaning is not *sui generis*, but it is nonetheless a cognitive construction, created out of prior knowledge in response to the multiple layers of a writer's social, rhetorical, and cultural context.

Given this vision of a socially embedded, constructive process, the problem is how to understand it better. A cognitive perspective draws our eye not to certain discernible patterns of public knowledge and ideology or to the patterns of social interaction that help create and certify meaning but to the *interpretive acts—to the transformations of knowledge and the internalized social negotiations by which individual writers construct personal meaning.* With this set of cognitive/social/affective presuppositions as a backdrop, let us look at some of the concepts from cognitive theory that give specificity to the metaphor of construction, trying to recognize both the theoretical power they offer us and their limitations.

Representations and Networks

According to Gardner, a "core assumption" that underlies the cognitive revolution in psychology is the central role of *representation.* Although it is often useful to account for human thought in terms of behavior, neurology, cultural influences, or the phenomenological experience, "for scientific purposes, human cognitive activity must be described in terms of symbols, schemas, images, ideas, and other forms of mental representation" (1985, p. 39). Although the debate still rages about "the best ways of conceptualizing mental representations" (p. 39), for the purposes of cognitive rhetoric, I would argue that a multiple-representation hypothesis helps account for some central problems in writing (Flower & Hayes, 1984). This thesis makes three key claims.

1. Writers at work represent their current meaning to themselves in a variety of symbolic ways. These different modes of representation can range from nonverbal imagery to abstract knowledge networks and schemas (often waiting to be instantiated with specific information) to abstract linguistic propositions (that, like deep structures, can also be instantiated at the point of utterance in a variety of lexical and grammatical forms). And, of course, mental representations can take the form of rich semantic networks, as well as the increasingly constrained semantic and syntactic patterns of speech and prose (cf. deBeaugrande, 1984; Fiske & Linville, 1980).
2. From the writer's point of view, where the end of the line is prose, these representations differ in the amount of linguistic information each representation provides. Different kinds of symbolic representation are adapted for different sorts of cognition and understanding. Just as poetry gains certain advantages by dropping the unambiguous reference and explicit relations expected in prose, and "pre-text" allows fluid revision (Witte, 1987), so nonverbal imagery and partly verbal abstract schemas may let a thinker perceive patterns within large and complex bodies of information or experience. However, expository prose and the discourse of many fields call for meaning to be represented as a fully articulated, densely interconnected semantic and syntactic network of language and ideas.
3. One source of difficulty and evidence of craft in writing is the writer's ability to move among these representations and ultimately to translate the current meaning (one's current internal representation) into prose. Writing produces a kaleidoscopic series of current meanings

> (some of which are written notes and drafts) represented in the multiple symbolic languages of the mind. In this process of re-representation, instantiation, and translation, the final text is simply the version done last. Moreover, as a written representation abandoned to the world, it is not to be confused with the complex, multimodal, growing, changing, and decaying internal representation in the writer's mind or with the equally dynamic, internal representations soon to be constructed by readers in their own minds.

Within this world of independent, yeasty, and hard-to-control representations, the text is still the lingua franca, the version that both aids personal reflection and allows communal knowledge to be built (LeFevre, 1987). However, if we are to understand the construction of meaning (in readers and writers) and to see texts as a member in this family of symbolic representations, we need to go beyond analyzing texts alone. We need a way to talk analytically about representations beyond the border of the text. And because these representations are rhetorical, social, and cultural constructions (not just information or a string of logical propositions), we must find a way to talk about purpose (the goals, plans, and criteria that shape writing and reading) and about the ways knowledge and purposes participate in their social contexts.

One attempt to create a more precise tool for tracing mental representations is the idea of a memory network. Unlike a text in which lexical and structural choices have been made, a memory network is made up of multiple nodes, any two of which may be connected to each other by a variety of complementary, conflicting, or just plain serendipitous links. The nodes that make up such a network may include ideas, images, goals, criteria, emotions, concepts, phrases, as well as textlike language. Some nodes, such as key concepts, have a wealth of highly activated links to other parts of the network; some nodes have few. Some links are merely associative, others may reflect a logical connection between nodes (such as an unspecified sense of causality), while other links will be more fully articulated or defined. The act of committing ideas to text is (like the teacher who asks for "transitions") notorious for forcing us to discover and name these links.

In linguistics, cognitive psychology, and artificial intelligence, the idea of the network has been used to develop theories of the structure of human memory. Networks can account for the mind's flexible, multiple ways of organizing information and are precise enough to predict not only the speed of comprehension (and how it changes for different kinds of information), but patterns of recall and reconstruction, which can serve as tests of a theory (Lindsay & Norman, 1972). In these discussions, the basic unit of analysis is the proposition—a subject about which some predication is made. Nodes may stand for propositional subjects, for concepts or events; links between nodes are predications that specify meaningful relations among the nodes.

Imagining our own knowledge (and constructed representations) as a network has some real advantages for rhetoric. For one, it foregrounds the multiple, and contradictory, links that often exist between key nodes. For example, figure 3 is a network reconstruction based on interviews with a schizophrenic patient, Leon-Gabor. Although this fragment of Leon-Gabor's memory is not particularly troubled by logic, it shows how the node called *I* (on the left of the figure) can unite multiple nodes and associations. And it can at least hint at the ideational and emotional complication of human memory. The network shows how some elements, such as *my father*, can stand apart, as isolated pieces of the fabric of memory, weakly connected to or constrained by the rest. In trying to read a semantic network, we need to know a few formalisms: a link labeled *is* denotes an identity relationship; *isa* denotes a class inclusion relationship. Links are also created by actions named on the network (such as *abuse*) and by logical relations (such as *because*), but in this associative network they need not be named. Nodes with only a number, such as <C5> are nodes defined by a cluster of features that may or may not have the attached feature of a name.

Despite its bizarre content, this sketch helps us envision the networked structure of a fragment of knowledge and lets us imagine some of the transformations writers must work in order to turn such networks of knowledge into a purposefully organized, articulate representation in text. But as a conceptual tool, there are also problems with this image of knowing. The formalism of propositional analysis that Lindsay and Norman use to represent a memory network treats the proposition (composed of a node, arguments or predications about it, and links between a node and its arguments) as the basic unit of meaning. Although this formalism has proven to be a powerful tool for predicting and measuring recall for texts, the attempt to treat it as the "*lingua franca* of cognitive systems" has come under attack. "The fact that computers can—and usually do—transmit information in only one symbolic form is no reason to assume that human beings do the same" (Gardner, 1985, p. 129). For our purposes it is important to distinguish between a generative concept, like knowledge networks, and the simplifying assumptions and formalisms that make research possible—a distinction that psychologists like Kintsch are fully aware of: "However, the decision to use a propositional representation does not imply that all other forms of knowledge are considered to be unimportant or nonexistent. [He has just referred to spatial imagery, mental models and affective systems.] It would be desirable to expand the [present] model to include non-propositional representations, but one would first have to learn how to operate with such forms of representation" (1988, p. 166).

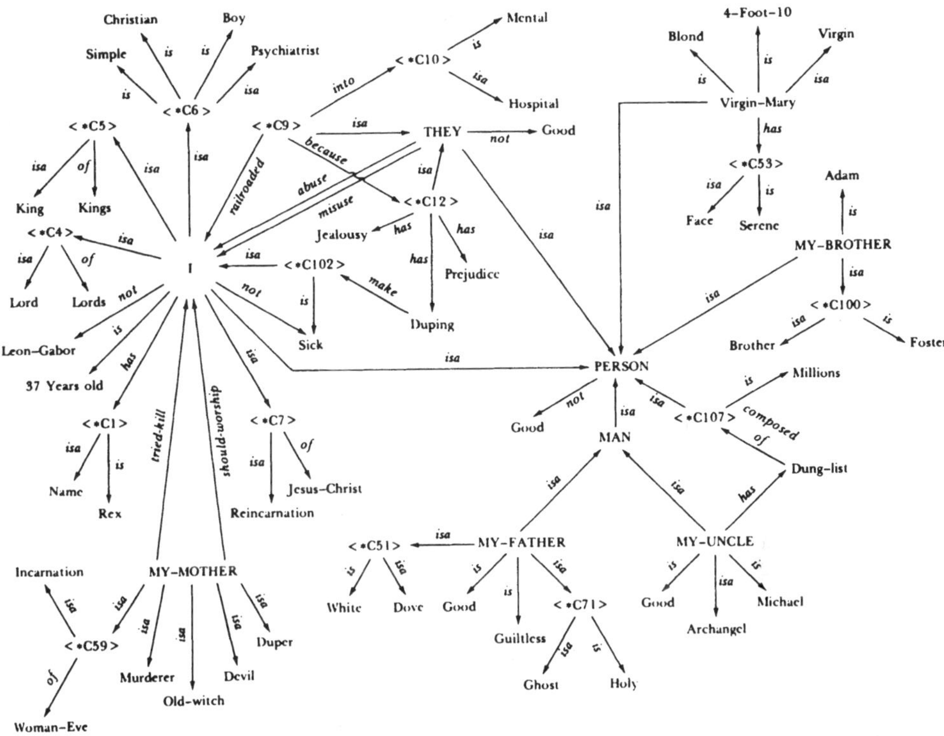

Figure 3. A segment of a memory network (figure from *Human Information Processing: An Introduction to Psychology* by Peter H. Lindsay and Donald A. Norman, copyright © 1972 by Harcourt Brace & Company, reproduced by permission of the publisher).

As Kintsch acknowledges, formal representations like propositions, which can indeed support inquiry, are at best a partial approximation of the multiple symbolic resources of the mind. But what if the mind is not limited to our traditional notions of symbolic representation either?

The most compelling challenge to the idea that we think in exclusively symbolic representations has come from connectionist theories of memory (Bechtel & Abrahamsen, 1991; McClelland, Rumelhart, & P. D. P. Research Group, 1986).[2] In a symbolic architecture, knowledge resides in symbols (ideas, linguistic propositions, the physical expressions of a computer). And thinking depends on rules. The mind operates on these symbolic entities with logical and transformational rules: the rules of logic (if P, then Q), the linguistic rules of grammatical transformations, or strings of condition/action rules that make up a production system in a computer (if condition P is present, then initiate action Q). Connectionism, on the other hand, deconstructs these symbols into smaller elements of information that make up a dynamic network. Knowledge is not in the elements but in the connections. In place of rule-governed logic, thinking is a process of making connections that activate parts of this network (Bereiter, 1991).

To illustrate, let us think of Leon-Gabor as a writer, orally constructing a representation of his mother as Woman-Eve in a session with his therapist. In a symbolic architecture, the concept *Woman-Eve* would exist and be defined by a set of key attributes. It would be evoked (or remain absent) as the result of a logical operation (e.g., the concept *A* obtains if *x*, *y*, *z* are present but not *m*) or as the result of a set of serial, "if/then" production rules. By contrast, in a connectionist network, knowledge is structured as an intricate network of simpler units that for Leon-Gabor might include a detail of the biblical Eve, images from a Renaissance painting, sexual fantasies, associations with woman (maternal, sexual, nurturing, sinful), to Eva Gabor or Aunt Eve, and specific thoughts of his mother, including (and this is central) a multitude of elementary units too small to be meaningful by themselves until they become part of a pattern on this activated network.

A connectionist network operates by parallel processing—instead of the step-by-step logic of rules, its elementary units of relevant memory are activated in what are called cycles of *spreading activation*. This means that like a spreading chain reaction, certain combinations of activated elements can spread the activation to others across the network. As Leon-Gabor discusses his mother, we would also notice that the links between activated elements appear to have different "weights"; that is, some links will be much stronger than others. The process of spreading activation is highly sensitive to these weights, so that the heightened weighting or strength of one part of the network has the power both to *increase* the activation of other elements and links (e.g., the link between Eve and original sin) and to *depress* the activation or presence of others (e.g., in this context, the link to maternal love is probably depressed well below the threshold of awareness. Although it is part of Leon-Gabor's memory network, we would not say it is an active part of his representation of mom). The weights or strength of certain connections affect, of course, how likely they are to be activated. These may have been developed over time through experience, or they may be generated on the spot by inferences Leon-Gabor draws as he speaks. This pattern of spreading activation ultimately settles into a steady state, its active connections giving shape and definition to an idea while other elements (potential knowledge) are suppressed. This process allows the network to respond dynamically to its environment—to associated ideas, to the suggestion of a conversant, to emotionally loaded memories, or to purposes. This is not to say that symbolic units of meaning have no place. A network architecture can also be envisioned as a hybrid model in which symbolic representations are also a part of this dynamic net.

This expanded image of the potential information that makes up a writer's representation takes us well beyond the picture available from a linguistic or propositional analysis of Leon-Gabor's utterances or a rational portrait of a concept plus its defining attributes. But even this is not enough. A complete social cognitive description would want to include other possible dimensions of Leon-Gabor's representation such as his awareness of the therapeutic situation; his rhetorical goals of pleasing, manipulating, and shocking his listener, and his current emotional/mental state that might affect the way different connections are made and weighted. And we would want to acknowledge, even where we could not document it, how part of the network associated with *Woman-Eve* had already been created by the ideologies with which Leon-Gabor grew up; by his own past history with church, mother, father, and doctors; and by his own schizophrenic interpretation of both ideology and experience. Leon-Gabor's meaning making, then, is not a logical recognition that his mother possesses the required attributes and fits a preestablished symbolic representation. Rather, his knowing is a complex constellation of weighted, activated knowledge, which includes the symbolic element he shares with us, the name *Woman-Eve*.

This theory of memory, Bechtel and Abrahamsen argue, has a number of advantages for thinking about constructive acts. First, it has neural plausibility; the architecture of parallel, distributed processing is more likely to replicate the way the brain itself works. But more important for us, this way of dealing with information is able to work within what are called soft constraints. To illustrate: if we were to use a symbolic system (e.g., logic or linguistics) rather than a network system to model how Leon-Gabor's memory search works, it would impose hard and fast constraints on the operation of ideas—that is, in order to say that Leon-Gabor is thinking about *Woman-Eve*, we would have to assume that entire concept, as an intact symbolic unit, was present (or absent), according to a logical, rule-governed decision (e.g., are all the defining features present?). Having been recognized as present, the symbolic unit presumably arrives pulling its set of defining attributes in tow. By contrast, in a connectionist theory of mind, we could assume that at the mention of *mother*, Leon-Gabor is in fact activating a large set of independent features. When weights or connections exist between a certain set of those features and the activation of those elements reaches a certain threshold, the equivalent of the concept of *Woman-Eve* can be said to be present even if some (possibly relevant) features are absent or not activated at this moment. The network's less rigid conditions for making the recognition, *Woman-Eve*, are satisfied.

This means that the mind can respond well to multiple simultaneous cues and constraints. It can accommodate the complex desiderata that rich or ambiguous meanings impose on understanding. It can recognize patterns when only some of their features are present. This also means that the concept *Woman-Eve* does not "exist" as a prefabricated symbolic unit of knowledge, but it is in essence constructed anew each time our writer thinks it. As a result, the mind also works well in a pinch: it can operate with scrambled or missing information, and it can search memory in a myriad of ways, since "ideas" as units do not have to be filed within categories.

From our point of view, connectionism is a theory not of memory and how knowledge is *remembered* but of how it is *constructed* out of memory. Because connectionist theory places inference at the center stage of this process, it gives us a more operational way to explain the creativity and unpredictability of constructive acts: "Within symbolic systems remembering is a process of retrieving a symbol that has been stored away. But in connectionist networks, remembering is carried out by the same means as making inferences; the system fills in missing pieces of information. As far as the system's processing is concerned, there is no difference between reconstructing a previous state, and constructing a totally new state (confabulating)" (Bechtel & Abrahamsen, 1991, p. 64).

For many people, models of thought based on formal logic, Chompskian linguistics, and the production rules of computer operating systems have seemed limiting conceptions of mind, even though they have given us powerful tools to test theory and extend understanding. Connectionist theory is unlikely to be a final answer either. In fact, within cognitive science where this debate is going on, it is unclear whether the future will see the success of one architecture over the other, or pluralism (each doing what it does best), or hybrid models like the current semantic networks that include symbolic expressions within dynamic forms of parallel processing (Bechtel & Abrahamsen, 1991, pp. 19–20).

What does this mean to cognitive rhetoric? Given our concern with performance, the cognitive science debates about the underlying architecture of the mind's operating system may ultimately be irrelevant. We must remember that what these theories say is that *people behave as if* knowledge were indeed distributed across a dynamic network whose units are not only symbols (i.e., unified conceptual entities) but also perceptual, physical, affective, imaginistic, procedural, or spatial information. And because these are data-based theories, they offer a robust, richly specified account of human performance—of how people perceive, what they ignore, what they remember, and how they interpret it. What these theories offer rhetoric, then, is a data-based metaphor of the mind. And unlike some traditional metaphors, they bring with them a fine-grained analysis of how this process might actually operate. They let us think more precisely about how writers construct meaning not as a logical manipulation of static symbols but out of a dynamic network of knowledge that can be reconfigured in small or radical ways in response to the internal or external context of thinking. What is at stake in this connectionist/symbolic debate and in the schema theory we shall turn to shortly is not locating the "truth" about the mind's architecture, but achieving a better approximation—a more generative theory—of the complex performances we see. By generative theory, I mean a more richly specified account that can be tested and changed against the data of performance as well as a theoretical framework that lets us anticipate, understand, and intervene in students' performance.

The Multiple-Representation Hypothesis—Revisited

The multiple-representation hypothesis noted earlier (Flower & Hayes, 1984) was motivated by an appreciation of writers in action. To explore the play of mind that constructs meaning in writing, we argued, we need a conceptual tool that allows the networks of the mind to come alive. In a multirepresentational network, the nodes are not limited to propositions or even to symbols alone, nor are its links limited to specified linguistic relations. The "knowing" that constitutes this system of relations may be represented as images or as abstract, affect-laden, partly verbal schemas for going to a restaurant (Schank & Abelson, 1977) or being "duped" or "railroaded" into a hospital. Nodes may exist as clusters (*My Mother*, *Devil*, and *Woman-Eve*) where borrowed, or richly intertextual meanings are knit together by experience, fear, imagination and desire (links that the fig. 3 network does not reveal). Knowing may also have the character of an episodic memory that resists verbalization (Tulving, 1972)—whether it is a hour spent in dappled sunlight or an incident of being "misused" for Leon-Gabor. Or it may take the form of procedural knowledge for making hill starts with the Alfa in a Pittsburgh winter, a knowing that eludes a declarative representation.

Reading theory has concentrated, understandably, on the content knowledge constructed during reading and at the point of recall. However, research in composing shows that writers also construct a representation of their rhetorical purpose, generating goals, plans, and criteria based on their interpretation of the task and in response to their own evolving text. This representation also evolves over the course of composing (Flower, 1988). A full picture of a writer's representation, then, will have to include not just topic and discourse knowledge, pre-text, and textual choices, but the network of plans, goals, criteria, the associations and emotions, the evaluations and suggestions of collaborators, and so on—the activated network that makes up what a writer means.

Reviewing these complex networks of significance, we glimpse the mind's multiple ways of coding its experience and knowledge (and recognize traces of other ways *not* articulated in these psychological theories). Unlike mimetic, rational, or unconscious theories of mind, the multiple-representation hypothesis conception foregrounds the diversity of representations and the multiple and flexible connections with which writers are working. It allows us to account for the generative serendipity of discovery, the considerable difficulty meaning making can pose, and the important role problem solving plays in literate action.

One striking limitation of this conception, and of the multiple-representation hypothesis Hayes and I posed in 1984, however, is its inability to account for social dimensions of knowing within an individual mind. As the data we will turn to in later chapters makes clear, the ideas and language writers are working with do not come into composing as discrete or anonymous bits of information, shorn of all connections to a social past. Even in the data of think-aloud protocols and of collaborative talk (which may only offer traces of richer mental representations), we see instances of language, plans, and ideas that bring with them a vivid sense of who said or thought them, in what context, and why.

Hearing Voices, Responding to Contexts

Symbolic representations with which writers think and work not only have a social history, they often bring a social and affective reality with them onto the stage of the writer's attention.[3] The most provocative theoretical account of this phenomenon is Bakhtin's (1981) notion of heteroglossia, a multivoiced meaning that reflects the primacy of context over text. It gives a vivid image of how a cognitive network—the construct of an individual mind—is at the same time an intensely social representation and how the construction of meaning for a text can be an ongoing negotiation with the "presence" of other voices. Bakhtin uses heteroglossia to describe a dialogic literary style in which meaning arises from the juxtaposition of heterogeneous voices, each still calling up the associations and acting out the intentions supplied by its own history. For some readers of this text, the political agendas, philosophical claims, and the evocative, literary resonances Bakhtin's words call up will enter into just such a dialogue with the decidedly cognitive, research-oriented talk of this chapter. When writers/readers begin to construct their internal representations, the same sort of sometimes desirable, sometimes just unavoidable, dialogue can arise across the landscape of their own knowledge.

Looking at mental representations through the lens of heteroglossia might let us expand the cognitive concept of networks in some provocative ways. In a heteroglossic network, certain locations on this network would become interanimated. It is a rather outré image, but we should visualize these elements of the network not as mere lexical nodes, concepts, or even images but as, in effect, talking heads. As writers talk about *Woman-Eve* or contemplate the "pity" that might "grace obtain," they represent meaning in the form of voices plucked from prior conversations and prior texts. Moreover, as these voiced ideas enter into the current context of composing, they (the ideas) continue their conversation with their prior context in the writer's own mind. Unlike some other kinds of representations, such as spare propositions, these voiced nodes reflect what Bakhtin describes as social speech types and individual voices. More generally, he sees this "internal stratification of language" as a critical feature of discourse:

> The internal stratification of any single national language into social dialects, characteristic of group behavior, professional jargons, generic languages, languages of generations and age groups, tendentious languages, languages of the authorities, of various circles and of passing fashions, languages that serve the specific sociopolitical purposes of the day, even of the hour (each day has its own slogan, its own vocabulary, its own emphases)—this internal stratification [is] present in every language at any given moment of its historical existence. (1981, p. 262)

We need to imagine for a moment how knowledge might function as a voiced, intentional speech act (what Bakhtin refers to metaphorically as the Word). When these acts enter into the network of meaning a writer is creating, such nodes and links are not inert additions of information but continue a conversation with the world from which they came; that is, these nodes maintain a rich network of connections to the writer's prior experience with the language (the concept, image, episodic memory) he or she is using and, beyond the writer's experience, to the socioideological belief system in which that language emerged in the first place. But now, as part of a new network of significance created during writing, as a node linked to other nodes in the writer's personal construction of meaning for this text, these talking heads may begin a new conversation generating links with new purposes and ideas. It is a process of cumulative juxtaposition. Bakhtin suggests how such a process works in the novel. It starts with the fact that any topic a writer might choose and the language, jargon, or style with which it is addressed brings a history of talk and tension with it:

> Any concrete discourse (utterance) finds the object at which it was directed already as it were overlain with qualifications, open to dispute, charged with value. . . . It is entangled, shot through with shared thoughts, points of view, alien value judgments and accents. The word, directed toward its object, enters a dialogically agitated and tension-filled environment of alien words, value judgments and accents, weaves in and out of complex interrelationships, merges with some, recoils from others, intersects with a third group: and all this may crucially shape discourse. (1981, p. 276)

The novelist, trying to express purposes that are too complex to reduce to flat statement, exploits this possibility of language with the technique of the neutral narrator who simply allows these different voices to coexist: "This interaction, this dialogic tension between two languages and two belief systems, permits authorial intentions to be realized. . . . The author utilizes now one language, now another, in order to avoid giving himself up wholly to either of them" (p. 314).

The multiple-representation hypothesis would suggest an even more animated network by envisioning not just *talking* nodes (where knowledge is encoded only in the language people use) but *performing* nodes in which images of people performing in particular ways, for particular purposes, in particular settings link with one another to form multiple small networks of knowing. In other words, the social, emotional, interpersonal experience that attends speaking and writing is also a part of our representation.

What does this mean when we begin to compose a text of our own? When Bakhtin asserts rather categorically that the "living utterance, having taken meaning and shape at a particular historical moment in a socially specific environment, cannot fail to brush up against thousands of living dialogic threads, woven by the socio-ideological consciousness around the given object of utterance" (1981, p. 276), he is speaking as a literary critic and philosopher of language, drawing a broadbrush picture of possibilities. At some abstract level of analysis, his assertion that an utterance "cannot fail" to brush up against thousands of other threads seems meaningful and true. But in trying to understand the cognition of individual writers, we must also remember that language in dialogue is not the *only* representation in town; it must share the stage with other ways meaning is represented and constructed in the mind.

It is important to place Bakhtin's (rather unqualified) philosophical claim in the context of individual cognition. It is, for instance, quite possible that these internal dialogues he projects *as possible* do indeed occur, but only as insignificant dissonances, or slight encounters where the "brush of threads" is located on the dim margins of awareness. Under these circumstances, their role in meaning making would be more potential than actual (and we might ask Bakhtin to situate his sweeping claim a little more carefully). On the other hand, does this dialogue sometimes go on at the center of attention, where it is taking up working memory, pushing itself to the center of a writer's constructive process, where it wields a significant influence on meaning making? The data in chapter 6 seem to suggest both possibilities. We might also suspect that this sensitivity to the social dialogue around one's own language is not limited to novelists (and denied to poets as Bakhtin suggests). And if these voiced representations form part of the networks of us all, are they, for instance, present with equal force in the constructive process of experienced and developing writers? To know just what possibilities and problems a "talking network" creates, we obviously need a fine-grained analysis of real writers in real contexts at work. My own supposition is that the dialogue of these talking nodes can exert at times a potent force on writers. Moreover, as expository writers create a personal network of meaning, they (unlike the neutral narrators in a Dickens novel) may have to actively resist certain prior connections and appropriate others. Such construction may call for negotiation.

Schemas and Expectations

The way writers construct meaning is also strongly influenced by the ways their knowledge is already organized (Langer, 1984). Schemas are highly structured patterns of knowledge that guide how we make sense of new information (Schank & Abelson, 1977) For instance, word schemas for concepts such as *break* and *murder* lead readers to scan and rescan texts if the agent for the action is not immediately specified, attempting to fill a critical slot in the schema. Our schemas for restaurants and birthday parties help us comprehend and even predict bizarre events (such as a young woman who announces her name to tell us she is our "bread girl"). And schemas are the social scripts of prejudice that replace reality with stereotypes.

Schemas operate like a structured body of knowledge that contains slots for expected information (there should be a menu at the restaurant and it is inappropriate to ask for seconds). They also provide default values that can fill those slots in the absence of complete information (we assume that candles on the birthday cake are to be blown out, not burned for incense). These handy default assumptions are so strong they can actually replace or distort perceptions (people will remember a chocolate layer cake with candles, whether it existed or not, and schemas for street gangs will supply teenagers waiting for the bus in a poor neighborhood with a menacing slouch and an air of loitering).

Although it is convenient to talk about schemas as though they were objects in memory, with their slots and with defaults ready to fill the slot, it is more accurate to think of them as blueprints or recipes for how to construct meaning out of experience. Schemas are the necessary meaning makers that guide perception and separate the wheat of significance from the chaff of information that drifts through our minds. Fiske and Linville describe schemas as "a set of category-based expectations" that guide social perception as well as learning (1980, p. 550). The use of schemas and the building of schemas alike depend on four key principles (this specificity helps to distinguish them from looser concepts such as ideology or a linked network of ideas). They argue that

- schema-based understanding is an active, constructive process, rather than a veridical copy of the perceived world;
- the schema itself is an abstraction that has been created in the mind of the perceiver out of multiple instances, not merely a collection of raw data or instances;
- the structure of the schema is based on experience rather than being determined wholly by genetic factors or the current environment—we each create our personal versions of publicly shared schemas; and
- the organization of a schema, which guides perception and construction, works (for good and for ill) in the service of adaptive efficiency rather than accuracy. Default values make us fast on the uptake but slow to question what the schema makes "obvious."

Not all organized meanings—especially the special purpose ones of writers—have the stability, organizational complexity, and therefore the generative power of schemas, to shape what we see by their patterns of expectation. Nevertheless, a writer's current meaning can influence perception. An event of no apparent significance (e.g., a glance from the unreachable Stella) may gain meaning because the writer perceives it as linked to those reverberating "others' words," that is, because that glance fits a familiar schema or echoes a commonplace. A stray thought or phrase may rocket to significance on this network when the writer sees a possible link to a prior goal (such as moving Stella to pity). For a writer to build such a network, information from the densely interlinked storehouse of memory, from experience, or from a text at hand must be *selected* according to some principle, *connected* by inference, and *organized* into a pattern shaped by both convention and the writer's purpose (Spivey, 1990). As Spivey notes, the available organization may dictate/predate selection.

To say that meaning is constructed in the mind's multiple ways of coding its knowledge and held as an internal representation, only partly captured in a text, gives us an expanded picture of the writer's meaning. But even if this representation includes notions like talking heads, it cannot describe how the writer as thinker interacts with the stepdame of tradition, the Muse, the reader, and other influences, in the process of making itself. Even if we no longer assume that meaning can be transmitted intact from books, discovered as an essence through self-examination, or simply supplied to us by a context or the dominant culture, just how radical is this constructive, transforming process? The constructive perspective leads us, on the one hand, to recognize the role others' texts, others' thoughts, and available language play in creating a network of significant information and a web of purpose. On the other hand, it also leads us to ask, How do individual writers go about constructing meaning out of prior knowledge, and why do they shape these personal representations the way they do? In particular, how do students, attempting to learn a new discourse and its distinctive ways of making meaning, shape their representations? These are some questions we will attempt to answer in terms of some specific student writers in the coming chapters. But first, it might be helpful to consider how the social cognitive perspective we will take differs from ideas of social construction and social interaction.

II. Social Construction or Social Interaction?

In a comparison of what he calls social constructionism and social interactionism, Nystrand (1990) suggests that these perspectives would give us very different stories about how meaning is made. Using Nystrand's matrix of differences, we can compare these positions in terms of the object to which they devote their attention, the assumptions they make about the constructive process, and the response they are likely to take to what they see. From a social constructionist point of view, the major object of attention is the norms and canons of literate practice—the productions of a social group rather than those of an individual. Because these socially constructed patterns are broad and highly variable, the level of analysis is necessarily coarse grained, the patterns only broadly specified. The concepts used to describe constructive process(es) suggest the power of external forces: interpolation, reification, initiation, and in some cases, oppression and determinism. It follows that perhaps the most appropriate response to these processes is to engage in critique as theorists and resistance as students and writers.

Social interactionism, as Nystrand sketches it, differs in its object of attention. Instead of social norms and forces, it investigates texts and patterns of talk ranging from classroom discussion to readers interacting with text. The process of interest here is a dialogic, reciprocal one. One response this perspective engenders is visible in Nystrand's (1986) own work—to use a closely situated examination of the dialogue that occurs in school and in developing writers to describe ways to improve the conditions that support reciprocity in education.

This sketch of differences does not do justice to the germinal thinkers associated with either perspective, who tend to complicate the central tendencies of a position. But it suggests both meaningful differences and a problem. The strength of a social construction perspective lies in its power to create vivid descriptions of how attitudes and assumptions can be knit into the larger fabric of an ideology and to see how social and economic conditions and unexamined "natural practices" can govern the construction of meaning. In the hands of its philosophers, social construction theory is a powerful statement about epistemology—or about a critical aspect of meaning making.

However, alongside this rich description of social patterns, we are beginning to see problems arise when broad philosophical claims about these patterns are used uncritically or didactically to justify educational policy or chart practice. The problem of social construction theory is a problem shared with other metaphysics of process, whether that ideology envisions writing as a romantic, expressionistic process—"the writer is not at home" (Mandel, 1980)—or uses a Marxist metaphor of the factory system to see writing as a process of production. These approaches often combine strong claims about how meaning is made with an unobservable, underspecified, and untestable theory of process. Physicists faced the same problem when they tried to deal with chaos: the theoretical mathematical descriptions of air and water currents were satisfactory as long as one continued to plot the fate of abstractions. However, once someone made the fatal error of looking at the data of experience—watching a water current hit a rock, air masses move across open fields, or faucet drips careen into the patterns of chaos, then complexity and internal contradictions began to challenge the elegant simplicity of theoretical claims.

Standing above the data of experience is a useful stance in a metaphysic, but it becomes unsettling in a theory of action and education. A good example of this problem appears in a review of Rafoth and Rubin's book on social cognition, in which the imperatives of social construction theory were used to criticize the authors for their failure to define *social* as *ideology* (ignoring the agenda or perspective the book itself was taking). The reviewer, Bizzell, supports her belief that an ideological (social) analysis would be more revealing than the observational research the authors did with an anecdotal claim:

> For example, I have a large number of women students whose difficulties in mounting academic arguments stem, in large part, *I suspect* [italics added], from the effect on them of cultural assumptions concerning feminine compliance and modesty. But if I were to turn my suspicions into a research hypothesis along the lines of those explored in this volume, I anticipate that my students would say that sexism is a thing of the past and that their fathers have told them they can be whatever they want to be. (1989, p. 485)

I, too, *suspect* that few readers would disagree about the existence of ideology as a powerful force in our lives. But they might hesitate at the ease with which an unsupported (and apparently unsupportable?) suspicion—that compliance and modesty are significant causal forces in writing problems—is elevated to an assertion. In fact, in the analysis Bizzell claims should have been done, there is little chance a rival hypothesis would emerge, since for the social critic it is already "expected [that one will] find social inequities reproduced in schooling" (Bizzell, 1989, p. 486). But what if those particular inequities, which as Bizzell suggests one can always find if one expects them, what if they are not a particularly significant causal force in her students' writing? What if other goals, pressures, assumptions, or strategies are more effectively guiding their thinking? If so, a critique of the social forces that lead to such attitudes might not empower students to structure forceful arguments. If we could imagine other possible reasons for the difficulties of Bizzell's students and our own, what we would need is a way to evaluate our own suspicions and reasonable rival hypotheses.

The problem for social construction theory—when it tries to assign causes and shape a teacher's practice—is that there is little interest in this discourse in generating rival hypotheses about the process and the problems of meaning making actual writers might face. And in the rejection of research (because social constructionists fear their "expected" answers may indeed be difficult to support), there is no means by which to consider the "unexpected," and maybe unwelcome, alternatives that do emerge. Its philosophical strengths, which rest on the abstract analysis of broad social patterns, can sometimes make it invulnerable to internal contradictions, leaving educators divorced from grounded inquiry, from the data of experience, and from the situated process of individual thinkers.

A Social Cognitive Perspective

Drawing distinctions between entities as amorphous as these theoretical perspectives is a heuristic not a definitional act: it foregrounds what each is good at giving us. We can see discourse as a social interaction and still affirm the value of exploring the patterns of ideology and socially shared discourses. Each perspective has its own object of inquiry—if we are cautious about how it is applied. In the same spirit, I want to extend this comparison to foreground what the social cognitive view of discourse taken here adds to the conversation. Although this perspective shares Nystrand's strong commitment to observation-based theory building, the focus of attention in social cognitive theory is not on texts or talk for themselves, but on the play of mind of individual writers. It uses text, talk, thinking, drawing, and even the silence of pauses to understand how the mind of a writer works in context to make sense of its world and to take action in it. And unlike Nystrand's reciprocity theory, which takes an ideal case as its model of discourse (the collaborative give and take of a supportive conversation), the theory of negotiated construction developed here envisions a more problematic process of building representations of one's situation, one's meaning, and one's readers.

Finally, the social cognitive view developed here also hopes to go beyond merely asserting that writers do interpret their rhetorical context and negotiate situations and meaning. In attempting to build observation-based theory, it asks us to discover how individuals and groups of writers actually conduct this negotiation. Should the negotiation in a given context be described as appropriation, co-option, cooperation, or resistance? How do constraints such as gender, race and class, ideology, prior knowledge, strategic repertoire, goals, and awareness affect this process? And how does education make a difference? A social cognitive stance tends to valorize unanswered questions and research into the nature of construction over broad political or philosophical claims and to see education as a way to expand writers' awareness, repertoire, and control.

Seeing meaning making as a social cognitive process also has some important limitations, one of which is knowing what it is missing. As a data-based perspective, cognitive rhetoric tries to push the boundaries of understanding by focusing on what we can observe (or infer with evidence) while maintaining a responsibility to evidence and reliability. So the difficult question becomes, Just what sort of processes are left out, underacknowledged, or even misconstrued by a focus on those that can more forcefully draw our attention? Because some parts of the writer's process (such as emotions, personal history, diffuse social influences) will be inevitably underacknowledged, it will be important to make good inferences about how they affect the more clearly visible processes that students can understand and manage and that we can teach.

Another critical problem for social cognitive theory is to develop new methods of observation and analysis that do justice to this vision of coexistence, interaction, and negotiation. Many traditional methods rooted in either social or cognitive paradigms are blunt tools for such discovery. As we will see in chapter 5, expert/novice comparisons, so widely used in cognitive research, tell an interesting story about collaborative planners, but they also cover up a perhaps more telling process of strategic choice. Studies like those that follow are not only forays into understanding meaning construction, they are also experiments in observation and interpretation.

In the context of such questions and goals, the second half of this book will explore some specific episodes of meaning making in which the voices of social convention and Sidney's "others," as well as the voices of "Invention" and "Study" are heard with unusual clarity. Tracking the constructive process of students engaged in collaborative planning, composing, and reflection will give us some insights into meaning making as a social cognitive act, but it will also raise questions about the way this process is shaped by school.

4

Construction Sites
Observations of Meaning Making in Learning, Development, and Literacy

A constructive act does not always end up in text. Some of the most revealing sites of construction are not acts of reading and writing but the activities of children trying to make sense of the world and the everyday cognition of adults trying to solve problems in it. In trying to develop more fully specified theories of learning, development, and everyday cognition, researchers in sociology, psychology, anthropology, and education are attempting to trace how these social cognitive processes work. And they have raised some perplexing questions about how formal education should enter into the picture, especially if it purports to teach people to construct genuine, relevant meanings.

In this chapter, we will begin by touring some of the "construction sites" described in educational research. From these conflicting images of knowledge construction, we will turn to the knotty problem of teaching a social cognitive process and ask, Where does the negotiated construction discussed in chapter 2 fit? And how could education support a process like that? My answer to those two questions is at best a provisional one, but it will suggest some reasons why the direct attention to strategic thinking found in cognitive rhetoric, with its focus on writer's goals, strategies, and metacognitive awareness, could be an important addition to other kinds of situated learning.

I. Constructive Processes in Learning, Development, and Literacy

Knowledge Construction in Learning and Development

In developmental psychology, the constructivist tradition associated with Piaget and Vygotsky has shown how the learning and development of a child is not a process of merely imitating or absorbing knowledge, but one of appropriating available information and using conventions and cultural forms to make sense of the world, to carry out social purposes, and to solve problems. Children construct meaning (Piaget, 1932). Piaget's work, focused on how children develop the forms of scientific reasoning, would note that Darlene's difficulty (chap. 2) occurs precisely because she is engaging in the difficult process of logical analytical reasoning, attempting to construct an explanation that recognizes and resolves conflicts and inconsistencies. Not satisfied with thinking in what Piagetians would called associatively linked "chunks" of information, she is trying to impose a particularly adult form of reasoning on her world. Rather than "discovering" a preexistent meaning in the text before her that simply includes contradictions, she is attempting to construct a coherent, consistent account in response to a perceived conflict. Such construction in the face of conflict is, in Piaget's terms, the basis of learning.

Vygotsky's (1986) work shares many constructivist assumptions with Piaget's but his focus on language development in social contexts suggests another critical dimension of this process. The very notion of consensus building with a series of "authors" or authorities is a cultural form, a convention, a literate practice, like the comparison/contrast pattern the writer might also have used. In the midst of this literate, social event, Darlene is trying to appropriate that convention to carry out the pressing goal of "interpreting"—another literate practice she is struggling to learn. As a learner, Darlene is engaged in a constructive, problem-solving process, which is shaped, Vygotsky's work would argue, not only by the cultural forms and literate conventions available to her, but by the social context of her learning and writing. Children depend on parents and peers not just to model new patterns of talk and thinking but to provide a scaffold for performance—a supportive structure that extends a child's blurted word into meaningful request, question, or observation. Darlene's request, "Can I leave it at that?" (made to herself?, to her tape recorder?, to the teacher who might some day hear this?) recognizes the social situation of a student making an effort, realizing her limitations, and hoping that in the great scheme of freshman writing, she would not really be expected to resolve a problem of these dimensions. After all, "I'm only a freshman," and this is where a teacher is supposed to step in. The irony and problem for formal writing instruction is that the supportive social scaffolding that nurtures early language development is rarely available when older students try to develop more sophisticated rhetorical skills—teachers rarely hear these dorm room cries and the scanty text they do see ("There's nothing you can say about this") masks the attempt and the specific problem that stopped the writer in her tracks.

Developmental research makes it clear that socially available knowledge and conventions of cognition both create options and put constraints on knowledge construction. But we cannot stop with that truism. The individualized networks of meaning and the webs of intention learners (and writers) create within these constraints are complex, unique constructions of enormous practical and social importance. These individual differences in making meaning are the reason we read one another. For good and ill, they are one reason some succeed and others fail at school, at work, or at achieving social and economic mobility. They are the basis of personal agency and action and the source of meanings that resist, contribute to, and perhaps revise the social conventions that seem to be indelible givens. This dialectic relationship between the individual and cultural practice is the focus of the sociocultural theory we shall consider next.

Meaning Construction in Sociocultural Practice

The publication of "Situated Cognition and the Culture of Learning" by Brown, Collins, and Duguid in *Educational Researcher* led to a revealing debate about the role of culture in schooling. In the exchange that followed, there was general agreement that situated cognition offers a radical alternative to "the Cartesian thinker cogitating in the solitude of his study" (1989, p. 5) and poses a challenge to the traditions of "didactic, decontextualized instruction" (Palincsar & Wineburg, 1989, pp. 5–8). These educators agreed that knowing is tied to doing; that in authentic activity, concepts and knowledge are always under construction forming new relations; and that knowing involves a sense of personal agency that treats knowledge as a flexible tool for achieving one's own goals and confronting new, ill-defined problems. But they did not agree on the place of culture in this portrait of the ideal conditions for learning. Just what is the culture that schools need to reproduce if they want to support situated cognition?

In this debate, the culture that enables learning (not unlike the notion of "discourse community into which writers are initiated") is defined by one group as the practitioners' art (e.g., the art of working historians, mathematicians, football players, tailors). It is the storehouse of usable knowledge and tools that requires years to acquire, which includes technical jargon as well as insider knowledge on the field's rivalries and trendy concerns. Is this the worldly, practicing culture that schools need to reproduce to make meaning making possible? Or can situated cognition and learning in reading, writing, math, and history flourish within the culture of an academic environment, one that preserves a zest for learning and respects the diverse cultural traditions of a multiethnic society (what its advocates call "a tall enough order for our schools" [Palincsar & Wineburg, 1989, p. 7])? If this were the case, the relevant belief system of the culture (say mathematics) would not be the professional's, but might depend on beliefs such as having a sense of personal agency in one's own learning and a sense-making attitude to new information that seeks to apply it to genuine problems (such as learning how to make change). It would depend on a set of general principles, rather than a set of expert algorithms. As we will turn to later, the hard decisions about what to teach and how to teach it present a real challenge to theories of sociocultural construction because they ask for a new specificity about just how this process can and should operate for individual learners. This articulation of how culturally embedded meaning making might operate in school is clearly a notion under construction.

Learning and meaning making are not limited to children and school, and, in fact, they appear to take a somewhat different shape when embedded in everyday practice. Standing at the junction of anthropology and psychology, practice theory is a family of theories that attempts to explain how the sociocultural order is maintained. Although this macrostructural system is seen as the fundamental unit to be accounted for, practice theory argues that the sociocultural system *is realized* in the experience of individuals in everyday action in the world (Lave, 1988, p. 192). In seeing *everyday practice* as "the central mechanism for the reproduction of the social system" (p. 14), practice theory stands in contrast to earlier views in sociology that saw first socialization and then rituals as the most powerful formative factors in the maintenance of the social order. In this more dynamic view of cultural practice, society is not characterized "as a set of macrostructures in place, a *fait accompli* to be internalized by individuals born into it," in which consensus is achieved by "cultural transmission or socialization" (p. 7). Instead, individual and system, cognition and context, stand in a dialectic, each shaped by and continually shaping the other. Lave's own influential research on everyday cognition works toward what she calls "a theory of active social actors, located in time and space, reflexively and recursively acting upon the world in which they live and which they fashion at the same time" (p. 8).

Lave's work focuses on "math literacy" in the everyday practices of calculating best buys at the market, managing family finances, and following the rules of Weight Watchers, but two features of the constructive process she illuminates, are, I think, central to writing—and they are ones that traditional research in psychology and anthropology does not see. The everyday cognition Lave and others study is like writing, typically dilemma-driven. But in contrast to the isolated problem-solving exercises students are given in school, cognition is deeply embedded in an activity or a social setting that not only structures cognition but provides resources that in essence do much of the work. A few examples will suggest how the "structuring resources," material realities, and/or the technologies of a situation actively shape a constructive act. We should, however, emphasize that Lave's notion of how resources might shape activity is critical of social epistemics that act as though social structures operate through a simple deterministic process. Her dialectic stance not only assumes but foregrounds "the partially determined, partially determining character of human agency, thus emphasizing the impact of practice on structure as well as the reverse. . . . Internalization is a less-important mode of contact with the world than action in the world" (p. 16).

As social theorists, Lave, Scribner and Cole, Saxe, and others they cite are distinguished by the way their data-based, finely-grained analyses of constructive acts in situ strive to develop theory through a careful description of the relations among these social and cognitive dimensions. As Lave suggests, since the "structuring resources" that contribute to an action rarely do so in equal proportions, that relationship "must be empirically determined" (1988, p. 147).

The definition of context in everyday practice is a critical concept, since context involves first, the higher-order institutional frameworks, the macrosocial, political/economic structures that constitute, for example, a supermarket. "At the same time, for individual shoppers, the supermarket is a repeatedly experienced, personally ordered and edited version of the [larger sociopolitical context]. . . . Some aisles in the supermarket do not exist for a given shopper as part of her setting, while other aisles are rich in detailed possibilities" (Lave, 1988, p. 151). The *context* of constructive acts, then, is defined by Lave as *the dialectic, problem-driven relation among these elements*. The notion of task representation developed in the Reading-to-Write project is a relationship in this sense, which reveals one way writers negotiate these multiple dimensions of context. It was that created context—as a relationship among the students, the class, the assignment, school and their history with it, and so on—that guided the text students constructed. Although the Reading-to-Write project accounts for less of the socioeconomic and political structuring resources than Lave describes in supermarket shopping, task representations, as a site of construction, are one place for rhetorical research to see writers' invented representations of shared situations, created as Lave would describe out of a dilemma-driven dialectic "among people acting, the contexts of their activity, and the activity itself" (p. 48).

In everyday cognition, knowledge construction does not just happen during an activity, the activity itself does part of the work. For the new initiates to Weight Watchers, mathematical thinking and invention were often inseparable from everyday objects and conventional social practices. On day one of their program, Weight Watchers went through an elaborate, school-like measurement routine for a glass of milk: "Look up allowed serving size of a glass of milk. Get out measuring cup, milk carton, and drinking glass. Pour milk in measuring cup. Pour milk from measuring cup into glass. Wash measuring cup and later the glass." The mathematical transformation they soon invented became: "Get out glass and milk carton. Pour milk into glass up to just below the circle of blue flowers. (Wash the glass.)" (Lave, 1988, p. 128).

In this study, the nine new dieters invented their own units (four swallows = four ounces) and 134 measuring devices, replacing formal mathematical procedures with efficient processes structured or supplied by objects at hand, by other people, or by store packaging and conventional practices (e.g., a "slice" of bread).

The informal, mundane quality of these mathematical techniques highlights Lave's second point: the constructed processes that make up the practice of math in everyday cognition are not rational, highly generalizable procedures (cf. "just below the circle of blue flowers"). They do not fit the venerated model of mathematics as objective, scientific thought or the formal, algorithmic procedures taught in school. In fact, many everyday practices, like home money-management practices with "mad money" stashes and delicate "his/her" negotiations, actively violate the ideology of rational mathematical/monetary practice to achieve other social and interpersonal goals. And the more such techniques are embedded in people's ongoing activities (like grocery shopping), the more situationally specific the math "invention" is going to be and the less communicable it will be to others (1988, p. 14).

Lave's observations of everyday cognition in math suggest some important parallels for how writers operate within cultural, social, and rhetorical situations and her methods illuminate the nature of situated cognition in a vividly realized way. At the same time, this work does not fully realize its desire to show how conflicting aspects of context or conflicting available structures produce genuine, significant dilemmas for people (or for learning). Nor does it model a way to track how very broad sociocultural forces actually impinge on meaning-making activity—other than to assert the nonsurprising fact that they do. One reason, I believe, is that Lave chooses to argue for the importance of looking at activity by vigorously attacking the failure of traditional cognitive science and sociology to do so. However, her cognitive science is a remarkably reductive straw figure; it operates with a research agenda that looks only at rationality and algorithmic, means/ends procedures and with a body of theory unacquainted with the richer conceptions of schema theory, ill-defined problem solving, or the work in education we shall look at next. I raise this limitation because Lave's work does, indeed, draw our attention to a very important goal for education: we need more sensitive ways to see where and how the macrostructures of culture and society impinge on the critical activities of education—on teachers trying to teach, students trying to learn, and writers trying to compose—not just in general, but at points where that dialectic is susceptible to change. That Lave's particular approach fails to make these links simply highlights the difficulty and the need to do so.

For Lave, the fact that school practices do not parallel everyday cognition constitutes a prima facie indictment both of education and of educational research that deals with the more abstract and more or less socially decontextualized procedures school necessarily teaches. However, other important studies of everyday cognition see the problem more in terms of uncovering the practices and capabilities students may bring to school and building bridges between the two. For example, in Saxe's (1991) intensive study of Brazilian candy sellers in the streets of Recife, the idiosyncratic math six 15-year-old children used to make deals and change was part of a complex cultural practice adapted to eking out a subsistence in a fluctuating monetary system. The cultural practice of candy selling supplies a set of general goals (such as adjusting to the constant inflation). Other people (such as the wholesale store clerks) are key parts of the calculation process for the young candy sellers. At the same time, Saxe's constructivist account shows how candy sellers construct new math procedures as part of a goal-directed activity (e.g., new ways to price candy combinations or to calculate a break-even point while bargaining with customers). These novel understandings, in turn, influence the emergence of subsequent goals (e.g., packaging and selling strategies). We would best understand constructive cognition, he argues, by looking at the relationship between peoples' goals, their social life (and cultural practices), and the individual cognitive forms (such as counting techniques) they invent as part of a goal-directed activity. Moreover, the interplay between the different cultural practices (math on the street versus math in school) can be central to learning. For example, the candy sellers who had been to school used standard notation systems, but it did not improve performance. However, second graders could use their selling knowledge to do better in school—a relation teachers needed to realize.

I chose to look at the research on math first because this is where the arguments for the special features of everyday cognition have been made most forcefully. Here some principles of socially embedded cognition stand out with special clarity. Cognition is not a purely mental procedure in the mind of a solitary thinker but interacts with an ongoing social (or physical) activity that provides structure and resources such as people, tools, techniques, and conventions. Nor is cognition always (or even often?) a rational, objective, process—even in math—but is an affective, inventive, and goal-directed effort to do something in the world. To make these assertions the research on math must attack its particular bête noire, a vision of cognition as algorithmic rationation. Literacy research must confront some similar misconceptions that hold that the strategies we label as critical, creative, or literate thinking are universal patterns of thought. Consider, for example, the comfortable assumption heard in English departments that a particular literature, cultural critique, or argumentative writing course we require is developing general, transferable capacities "to think," quite independent of the local discourse practice of the course.

Scribner and Cole's (1981) landmark study of literate practices among the Vai people of West Africa set out to challenge the notion of literacy as a generalized capacity or form of thought. They examined the multiple, quite distinct forms of literacy held among the Vai in a single community who used Vai script, Arabic, and English. They found that each language was associated with different literate practices, such as the record keeping and ritual writing done in Vai, the ritual reading of the Koran in Arabic, and the essays of Western schooling in English. More importantly, these distinctive literate practices called for and developed distinctive cognitive capacities. To be literate was to be in control of the literate practices valued in the community one—at the moment—was in. Western, "schooled" literacy was just one of these practices.

When cross-cultural studies of literacy like these look closely at cognition, they can throw into relief the way our educational system fosters certain ways of making meaning not just in the abstract, but at the level of specific cognitive strategies we teach or (more often) simply expect. And as these analyses become increasingly fine-grained portraits of thinking, the implications for teaching diverse communities of students become more direct.

Reviewing some of the claims for literacy as the generator of logical, self-consistent meanings and general statements, Rogoff notes that most of these descriptions apply to practices valued in and associated with Western school-based performance and assigned prose. For instance, people with Western schooling develop the ability to remember long, unrelated lists of information and to classify and organize ideas into a taxonomic system, exhibiting deliberate strategies such as rehearsing, categorizing, or elaborating connections between items (1990, p. 47). Nonschooled people are more likely to develop functional arrangements and do not spontaneously engage in strategies to organize. As Goody (1977) has argued, list making, comparison, classification, and hierarchical arrangement are closely associated with literacy. He goes on to argue that the technology of writing makes these practices possible. However, the fact that Western children exhibit these skills may be seen more accurately as an interaction between cognitive capacities (shared across cultures), the enabling technology of writing, and social practices that value such skills. Mayan nine-year-olds, for instance, were slightly better than Western children at remembering information when it was embedded in a meaningful context (such as a story setting with toy figures). Why? One possibility Rogoff suggests is that American children's rehearsal strategies—adapted to the school task of memorizing unrelated lists one often does not understand—may actually interfere with these everyday, out-of-school tasks. As Rogoff argues, literacy is an excellent example of the ways technology, cognition, and society interact.

Heath's (1983) description of reading, writing, and speaking practices in different sociocultural communities brings these issues closer to home and to the question of how teaching can/should and currently does fit in the picture of how students develop a cognitive social practice. To cite but one example: the children on front porches in Heath's African-American community practice a performance-oriented way with words—a literate practice in which the goals are to capture and keep attention with a story, language play, and imagination. Meanwhile, other children in a neighboring blue-collar, white community are learning to point to familiar objects in picture books and recite names—a literate practice tied to social values and activities like Bible reading—and, it turns out, one that clearly supports success in first grade. From the teacher's point of view, verbal performances can be disruptive in a class of 25; from the child's perspective, when the workbook exercise of naming the obvious has no history or connection to activities such as reading with mother, the whole enterprise can seem confusing, if not pointless. There is a sad irony when discourse practices that would fit one rhetorical situation are misfits in another—although an African-American child's performance literacy may be better adapted to the creative and argumentative writing expected in later grades than recitation, that child is likely to be turned off or out of school long before.

II. Teaching a Constructive Process

How can or should education respond to this emerging portrait of situated cognition, in which knowledge is distributed across a social group used as part of ongoing, goal-driven sociocultural activities and in which new knowledge is constructed and structured in the context of practice? Consider some of the hard questions this research raises: What is the place of school with its formal math, its rules of standard written English, or its conventions for the essay, if it presumes to prepare people for life after school in which the blue flowers on the glass and other women in the neighborhood will be an operative part of one's math and writing process, and if, as the research suggests, formal procedures and general principles seem to have a dismal record of transferring to new situations (i.e., being seen by the student as relevant and used to solve an isomorphic or closely related problem)? What is the place of school knowledge in which patterns of ethnic, racial, and sexual discrimination are built into the practices and the cognition it values? To be more specific, if literacy is seen as a set of distinctive literate practices that are valued and effective in some communities (but often not in others), what should we teach? Indeed, can we even expect that school can help learners cross communities? Is education, even when it pretends to teach principles and transferable knowledge, ever able to do more than teach the situated cognition and practices called for in school? In short, how do social cognitive processes, especially constructive, meaning-making transformations, get taught? Could we do it better?

Traditional and Cognitive Apprenticeship

One persuasive image of what teaching might be goes under the names of guided participation and apprenticeship. It is persuasive in part because it rests on a rich body of descriptive research about how learning is, in fact, organized in many normal settings. Rogoff's (1990) impressive *Apprenticeship in Thinking* moves from a richly developed theoretical statement of cognitive development in a sociocultural context (discussed above) to a review of how guided participation structures learning. Learners may be infants strapped to the back of a working relative; 2-year-olds making small "toddler tortillas" alongside sisters; apprentice weavers in Guatemala who observe, asking no questions and receiving no explanations; or preschoolers in American working-class, African-American communities where young children are not seen as appropriate conversational partners and so must gradually find ways to enter the adult discourse. Such learners are swept into the ongoing activity of the working, adult world. They learn by participating, not in textbook exercises, but in complex events that have social and economic value. Through participation, they encounter the executive routines that organize the game. Adults typically structure the "apprentice's" participation in light of the learner's current skill: apprentice tailors, like preschool "cooks," are given jobs they can handle without the risk of serious or costly failure and only gradually take over the total operation. However, the amount of direct instruction may be minimal. "Nash reports that the method of learning to use the footloom in a weaving factory in Guatemala is for the learner (an adult) to sit beside a skilled weaver for some weeks, simply observing, asking no questions, and receiving no explanations. The learner may fetch a spool of thread from time to time for the weaver, but does not begin to weave until, after weeks of observation, the learner feels competent to begin" (Rogoff, 1990, p. 129).

In apprenticeship, the assistance of adults—prompting a narrative with "what next?" or testing the job by giving the screw the last turn—is often not intended as a lesson. It grows out of what Rogoff describes as intersubjectivity—an understanding between people based on a common focus of attention or awareness, cooperative intentions, and a shared set of presuppositions that make communication possible (p. 71). There are large cultural differences in how explicit adult guidance is and whether intervention comes in the form of silent scaffolding, correction, diagnosis and repair, or tutor's hints, but Rogoff's notion of intersubjectivity makes communication in one form or another central to guided apprenticeship. Intersubjectivity has many parallels to Nystrand's (1986) argument that effective communication depends on a reciprocity between writer and reader. In the meaning making Rogoff reviews, intersubjectivity reflects two people's joint participation in a shared decision-making process, which the individual learner later internalizes and then appropriates for his or her own uses.

The events of *guided participation* Rogoff describes are primarily accounts of how infants and young children develop fundamental social and cognitive skills outside of classrooms. The theory of *cognitive apprenticeship*, developed by Collins, Brown, and Newman (1989) would reshape how reading, writing, and mathematics are taught in school. (This is not to say it should replace other kinds of learning, but it would give a very different place to lecturing, for instance.) If we ask how such teaching might support the construction of meaning, the parallels and points of contention between traditional apprenticeship, cognitive apprenticeship, and various process approaches to teaching writing are revealing.

Apprenticeship has been passing along the world's knowledge far longer than schools. The strength of traditional apprenticeship lies in observation and participation. Extended observation lets learners develop a conceptual model of the task or process in its entirety. Although the apprentice tailor may graduate by slow steps from ironing finished garments, to cutting, to sewing easy straight lines (i.e., practicing subskills) he or she sees how they fit into the full garment. The apprentice is also immersed in a social organization in which successful work counts and a culture of experts in which he or she has access to multiple ways of doing a task. Classes in which both the students and the teacher see themselves as writers try to create such a context in the classroom, as do courses, in the tradition of Dewey, that embed instruction in larger, collaborative projects. Apprenticeship creates an occasion for situated, purposeful learning.

Cognitive apprenticeship, however, differs from traditional apprenticeship in two key ways. First, it "is aimed primarily at teaching the processes that experts use to handle complex tasks" and at using conceptual and factual knowledge to solve problems in a variety of contexts (not just in the tailor shop or on a specific assignment) (Rogoff, 1990, p. 457). In this sense, the goal of learning supersedes the task in which it is embedded. The teacher chooses tasks in order to illustrate the power of certain techniques or methods and to give the student practice in diverse settings. In fact, although apprenticeship derives its instructional power from knowledge in use, the goal of cognitive apprenticeship is to then decontextualize that knowledge to make it transferable by practicing these problem-solving techniques in a variety of contexts.

Secondly, in cognitive apprenticeship "the focus of the learning-through-guided-experience [is] on cognitive and metacognitive, rather than on physical skills and processes" (Rogoff, 1990, p. 457). This places a special demand on the teacher, especially in writing. While in traditional apprenticeship settings learners can observe the actions that lead to the creation, evaluation, and refinement of products (e.g., teachers can share outlines, drafts, and revisions of text), in cognitive apprenticeship, the teacher needs also to externalize the thinking processes associated with planning, invention, self-monitoring, diagnosis, self-correction, and other key moves.

In both kinds of apprenticeship, the teacher/mentor is a performer rather than a lecturer; the student's performance, rather than a body of knowledge, is the focus of instruction. Cognitive apprenticeship depends on three chief methods of instruction. The first is to *model* expert performance, demonstrating/expressing the thinking process, which learners may never see in traditional expository instruction. The second is to *coach*, working directly with the learner's own performance to diagnose problems and shape it in action. The third is to *offer a scaffold* for the learner's performance (providing the prompts and support at key points that allow the learner to succeed in the task) and then to *fade* out of the performance, relinquishing control, withdrawing structure and intervention as the learner takes over the process him or herself.

One of the striking success stories of cognitive apprenticeship in reading instruction has been Palincsar and Brown's use of what they call reciprocal teaching in reading. In various studies with children at high risk in the school system, students' reading ability rose from between 15% to 40% accuracy on comprehension tests (scores that put children in remedial classes and low tracks) to 80% accuracy (i.e., reading at grade level) that continued well after the studies had ended (Brown & Palincsar, 1989). As Collins et al. note with understatement, "these are very dramatic effects for any instructional intervention" (1989, p. 461). The success of their approach appears to depend on its powerful mix of socially situated, cooperative learning and direct strategy instruction. As students work through a text in small groups, the role of the leader, who models interpreting the text and asking questions, is passed around. In initial sessions, the teacher demonstrates the use of four reading strategies and metacognitive skills that are strongly associated with expert reading—formulating questions, summarizing what one has read, clarifying and exploring problems that arise, and predicting or forming hypotheses about what might come next. Eventually, the modeling, coaching and scaffolding comes entirely from students helping each other read, in groups where both the cognition of interpretation and the metacognitive strategies that support it are unusually explicit.

Cognitive apprenticeship, as Collins et al. (1989) are quick to point out, is not a replacement for all other kinds of learning. Likewise, I would argue that it is not the only way writers learn to construct meaning within a discourse or for themselves. But in one form or another, it may play a large part in both formal and informal education. And because the theory of traditional and cognitive apprenticeship offers a well articulated statement of how cognition and context interact in teaching, we will look in the next section at how it applies to writing.

Apprenticeship, Cognitive Apprenticeship, and Cognitive Rhetoric

In the last few pages, we have looked at some of the diverse ways meaning is constructed in learning and development, in everyday cognition, and in literate acts. Research into these events makes it clear that social and cultural structures, activities, and other people play a large role in people's constructive processes. The hypothesis of this book is that the acts of dilemma-driven, intentional cognition (negotiated construction) also play a critical role in situated cognition. As we saw in the Reading-to-Write project, students' attempts to build a representation, read expectations, and choose a strategic path through the task were highly problematic—each move was a gamble one had to take. Moreover, it was the subject of extended rumination in students' "dorm room" problem solving. In other research on planning, a similar portrait emerges—we see a process marked by frequent decision points, options, and conflict, in which one mark of experienced writers is the frequency and willingness with which they entertain conflict and the ways they choose to resolve it (Flower, Schriver, Carey, Haas, & Hayes, 1992). Making sense of the task and making sense in the text appears to call for active, problematized engagement.

In helping students deal with such problems, how does cognitive apprenticeship compare to traditional apprenticeship? And what does the strategic instruction of cognitive rhetoric add to the cognitive apprenticeship?

Cognitive Rhetoric

Cognitive apprenticeship, like guided participation, is often associated with the development over time of basic skills. Instruction associated with rhetoric has often combined a strong apprenticeship and practice model with explicit talk about heuristics—starting with Aristotle's advice for finding the available means of persuasion and the sophists' sensitive adaptation to audience and context. Cognitive rhetoric extends the purview of rhetoric to include the thinking strategies of writers, and the comprehension strategies of readers. It uses expert/novice distinctions to articulate these strategies more clearly, and it emphasizes metacognitive awareness and the conscious control of one's options. Like cognitive apprenticeship, it builds on the foundation of strategies such as modeling, coaching, scaffolding, and fading. However, cognitive rhetoric gives an even greater role to the learner's own processes of observation and reflection. Cognitive rhetoric shifts a significant part of literacy instruction from the arena of cognition and practice to metacognition, from apprenticeship and imitation to rhetorical awareness, negotiation, and engagement. This change is perhaps a matter of degree, but it can change what teachers do and students learn.

Some Limits of Apprenticeship in Current Practice

In current approaches to teaching writing, apprenticeship is strongly associated with traditions of immersion, coaching, and practice. It also reflects the elements of traditional apprenticeship in the deliberate absence of direct instruction, especially in thinking strategies. There is no denying the power of immersion in writing instruction. But there is a downside to the metaphor of apprenticeship and some problems with immersion *alone* that we should consider.

One strength of traditional apprenticeship and techniques like workshopping and coaching is that ideas and techniques are situated in a real activity. But another way to put that is to say that the goal of the activity is a crafted product or an effective social transaction. It is designed to fit the novice/initiate into a production process, not to empower the learner or to equip an individual with transferable strategies or flexible knowledge.

Consider a craft where technical and artistic innovation and individual handwork are prized: apprenticeship has been a central part of education in watchmaking since Chaucer's time. Until the 20th century, it was common for an apprentice to sweep floors and make tea for some years—to look on. Most never graduated beyond doing piecework—contributing their bit to the successful production.[1] And apprentices were notorious for running away. Traditional apprenticeship and the guild system that sustained it was good for business; it is a good way to sustain a social system. And it is still a good way to learn if we deal with its limitations, too.

In writing instruction, the apprentice idea often takes the form of workshops and projects in which the teacher is a coach and students are working on a meaningful literate production. The apprentice model also lies behind the notions of immersion and initiation in which direct instruction is replaced by practice or is limited to talking about texts. In immersion, learning how to think like the teacher or a writer is a tacit process (Greene, 1992). The following excerpt, published by a writing student looking back on her graduate training, is clearly intended to valorize what she saw as traumatic immersion, in which students learn to sink or swim. The writing instructor is the kind of dad who, to teach you to swim, would "take you to a lake in the middle of nowhere. Where the water is murky, where you can't see the bottom, where the cold wetness is a shock under the hot sun. And here's how he'd teach you to swim: He'd toss you in. He'd let you figure out what swimming is" (Flecker, 1990, p. 16). But from an educator's view, the cost in students who do not make it may be one of the undesirable side effects of tacit teaching.

My own premise, it should be clear, is that the best way to teach writing as a meaningful rhetorical act and to create opportunities for socially situated cognition is to enlist the enormous power of apprenticeship. However, in current writing instruction, the idea of apprenticeship is typically associated with traditional apprenticeship. In the absence of any clear cognitive goals, it depends on *tacit* instruction and on *immersion*, in which the teacher's chief goal is to create a *supportive* environment—one that can support students' interests and the expression of natural abilities. Traditional apprenticeship works; it can even produce brilliant results. While supporting many of the goals, I want to draw attention to three problems it has in practice.

Fictions of Cognition

When instructors have little access to students' thinking processes, when what students are actually doing is unexplored and unknown, there is a tendency to fill that gap with fictions of cognition. Teachers imagine students' cognition as a mirror image of the teacher's own instructions—an assumption the Reading-to-Write project called into question with its picture of students' diverse readings of a simple assignment. Or teachers construct theory-driven images of what *should* be happening, given the premises of their instruction. (Compare, for instance, Crowley's (1992) discussion of 19th-century rhetorics and their influence still seen in modern assessment procedures based on the modes.) Collaboration and peer critique offer a good example. In theory, collaboration is described as a consensus-building effort, in which critical skills are modeled by the group and elicited from the democratic circle of partners (Bruffee, 1984; Gere, 1987). However, a growing number of studies that look closely at what students actually do and the clues to the thinking individual students may actually be engaged in (such as actively avoiding evaluation of one another or negotiating the demands of the exercise, rather than the text's meaning) suggests that we need to fill that gap with more observation and less imagination.

Some theory-driven fictions of cognition may even be impervious to contradiction. Assumptions about the cognitive deficits of students we label as remedial seem to persist with little evidence and to resist the contradictions of fact. As Hull, Rose, Fraser, and Castellano argue, the construct of remediation allows teachers to construct fictions of cognition with alarming ease. Maria had been a successful, bilingual student in high school. But her energetic engagement in her remedial college class takes the form of inappropriate interruptions, poorly timed questions, and comments that violate the standard IRE participation structure of classroom talk in which a teacher *initiates*, a student *replies*, and the teacher *evaluates* or comments on the reply. She talks up like a student in an honors section might. For the teacher, these conversational missteps are evidence of cognitive deficits: she labels Maria "Queen of the Non Sequiturs," and in the face of successful writing (from which she evaluates Maria's "thinking . . . [as] clear and logical"), the teacher surmises that Maria had gotten help from her parents (who, in fact, speak little English). In the final interview, the teacher concludes that "Maria has thinking continuity problems" and predicts she will not pass the next class "because it requires coherent thinking. Maria's interactional patterns in class become not just an annoying conversational style, but the barometer by which to measure her cognitive abilities. Her bothersome conversational habits become evidence of a thinking problem—evidence that is so salient that it goes unqualified even in the face of counter-evidence that Maria, in fact, wrote rather well" (p. 311). True or not, fictions of cognition can affect real cognition: Maria, the high school student who had written a novel and earned a speech team scholarship to college, left the class thinking that she now "had some problems with . . . English," that she was "not a very good speaker" (p. 317).

Slow Instruction in the Face of Diverse Demands

Apprenticeship, initiation, and acculturation are all slow processes. They are well adapted to the extended processes of growing up, language development, or developing expertise. Unlike direct instruction, tacit training makes less demand on the mentors, who are, after all, engaged in the world's work. Moreover, there is probably no alternative way to achieve full membership in any complex discourse community. If even graduate students (and their professors) struggle with academic writing, what can we expect of students? On the other hand, this slow and indirect process, with its goal of full and flexible initiation is a poor fit to the realities of school and the goals of a liberal education. Unlike professional or vocational programs, liberal education gives students relatively brief exposure to diverse literate practices: a historical report and a response statement to a poem due today, an economic analysis based on a Keynsian model and personal essay next week. Students (unlike apprentices who are not allowed to ruin the watch) are expected to try on different discourse practices, to explore, to fail and try again with successive approximations—and most of all, to read the situation and learn quickly what matters here. Being a "quick read" is a useful ability; learning "how to learn" and how to enter new discourses has a high survival value. But the strategies of immersion and learning by doing are not well adapted to these situations or to a timetable of exploring new options.

Supporting Insiders/Mystifying Outsiders

The conflict between the fast clock of education and the slow processes of tacit teaching matters most for students not already primed to succeed. Instruction based on creating supportive situations sets up environments in the classroom that invite students to write. It assigns activities that create opportunities to experiment and assumes that natural capabilities can often make up for inexperience or instruction. These assumptions are often right: supportive environments (that avoid direct instruction and ignore cognition) can achieve remarkable results, especially with a portion of the class. But *opportunities* to perform or to learn always offer the greatest benefit to the most prepared. Situations that *support* performance (only) depend on students' prior knowledge and their ability to read the situation accurately, to seize the opportunity, and to perceive the indirect cues to the thinking this situation allows (and tacitly calls for). The critical problem is that supportive situations support insiders most.

Delpit, who wrote "Skills and Other Dilemmas of a Progressive Black Educator," notes that "writing-process advocates often give the impression that they view the direct teaching of skills to be restrictive to the writing process at best, and at worst, politically repressive to students already oppressed by a racist educational system. Black teachers, on the other hand, see the teaching of skills to be essential to their students' survival" (1986, p. 383). At stake, Delpit argues, is the culture of power and the rules for participation in that culture, which institutions like school help transmit. However, "if you are not already a participant in the culture of power, being told explicitly the rules of that culture makes acquiring power easier" (Delpit, 1988, p. 283). In Delpit's own fieldwork as an African-American, Louisiana-born Ph.D. working with villagers in New Guinea and Alaskan Native communities, she says: "I have found it unquestionably easier—psychologically and pragmatically—when some kind soul has directly informed me about such matters as appropriate dress, interactional styles, embedded meanings, and taboo words or actions. I contend that it is much the same for anyone seeking to learn the rules of the culture of power. *Unless one has the leisure of a lifetime of 'immersion' to learn them, explicit presentations make learning immeasurably easier*" (italics added, p. 283). But here is the catch: people with power, those who move easily in the culture speaking its language, catching its innuendos, and practicing its strategies are the least aware of it, and in the case of liberal and radical educators, most uncomfortable with acknowledging their "insider" status and information. "Liberals . . . seem to act under the assumption that to make any rules or expectations explicit is to act against liberal principles, to limit the freedom and autonomy of those subjected to explicitness" (p. 284).

In a variation on this assumption, some argue that sharing insider knowledge of rhetorical strategies for problem solving, goal-directed action, or audience awareness signals teachers' complicity with unjust systems and indoctrinates students willy-nilly into their beliefs (Berlin, 1988). From Delpit's view, on the other hand, the desire to raise consciousness of powerlessness without teaching students the tools that give one power—the theory without praxis—is a form of liberal/radical racism.

Immersion may create the greatest barriers for students when learning also means recognizing powerful but conflicting schemas and previously learned strategies one brings to the task. Although such strategies may have brought writers success in other contexts, they can throw up solid, but invisible, barriers when students encounter new literate practices. As we saw in Aston's description of her community college students in chapter 1, the invitation to empowerment always remained for some an opportunity not taken (Aston, 1993). Her students needed the explicit expectations of collaborative planning to recognize how their history of tracking in high school history had translated itself into sources of "genuine oppression" in their own actions and to begin to construct alternative and obviously difficult strategies for critical reading and writing.

To sum up, in attempting to create situated instruction, we must recognize the strengths of apprenticeship and its critical limitations. Much of meaning making does go on by tacit and socially structured means, but in the face of conflicts and alternatives, meaning making becomes problematic and writers rise to the construction of negotiated meanings. By the same token, these may be critical points where learning is also problematic and where instruction should no longer be tacit. When students come to writing with limited prior knowledge, with conflicting schemas, and with the history of an outsider who needs to read the cues and learn quickly, then immersion apprenticeship needs to become cognitive apprenticeship in which thinking is not just a by-product but a part of the process that teachers model, coach, scaffold, and fade out of.

From Apprenticeship to Collaboration

The leisure of traditional apprenticeship and the forms of guided participation Rogoff describes are well suited to the slow clock of a child's intellectual and social development. When the fast clock of education often looks for other ways to structure the social dialogue, collaboration among peers offers some interesting trade-offs, especially for older learners. Unlike guided participation that involves an adult or Vygotsky's older, more expert peers who could be expected to demonstrate the optimal ways of doing a task, collaboration offers the learner diminished guidance and a more problematic model. On the other hand, as a form of joint problem solving, it gives learners a new degree of authority over their own actions. When partners are involved in the co-construction of an idea or solution, the social interactions that promote learning become much more salient (or, more accurately, *can* become so). For instance, collaboration on a problem brings multiple perspectives into the picture; it puts conflict on top of the table; it leads partners to model alternative solutions and strategies to one another; and it can lead them to make their criteria for evaluation more explicit. Collaboration brings the learner's process and ideas under negotiation. Just as cognitive apprenticeship alters the focus of traditional apprenticeship to extend its power, collaboration alters the ways the social context supports learning.

In the chapters that follow, I would like to take this process of cognitive apprenticeship one step further for writers by exploring how cognitive rhetoric might structure the process of collaboration. The instructional experiment we will examine draws its key strategies from the long tradition of rhetoric with its emphasis on problem-solving heuristics that support invention and persuasion. In addition, cognitive rhetoric will add explicit attention to cognition of writer and reader and make metacognitive awareness a part of its educational strategy and goal. Just as writers need to turn at times to the active negotiation of meaning, it is important for instruction to go at times beyond supporting cognition to engaging metacognition, to go beyond the modeling and coaching of apprenticeship to a focus on the learner's strategic knowledge, where instruction deals not only with students' strategies but with their goals and their awareness of their own options.

5

Collaborative Planning

An Educator's Account of a Constructive Process

Carter is a freshman in the second semester of college. In high school, he was used to getting A's and B's with what sounds like an efficient knowledge-driven approach to paper writing. As he tells his planning partner below, his recipe for success starts with procrastination—put off planning until the deadline demands prose and shrinks your goals down to producing a given number of pages that "sound intelligent." He expected that what had worked in high school would work in college. "So, we had to write a 5-page paper on African nationalism, which I had no idea, and I waited like the night before I was due to start [. . . .] I thought, why this is just like high school."

Carter describes himself as "not a very good writer," but he appears to fit the profile of an able average student who has learned to use the efficient strategies of knowledge-driven planning to advantage. In his first semester of college, he had discovered to his shock that this "BS" technique for fast text production no longer worked: "In college they don't go for that stuff. You gotta really, you know, go write, and you can't BS your paper, because they'll know right away that you're doing that." Nevertheless, the solution he describes is still a better recitation of knowledge. In talking about both high school and college writing, Carter concentrates on content—on the presence or absence of ideas and on the quality or correctness of his coverage of an assigned topic. The road to successful writing appears to lie in better knowledge telling.

When Carter walked into his freshman writing class in the second semester, he entered a rhetorical situation he probably did not expect. In this new context, some of Carter's past strategies for success were seen (by the instructor) as part of the problem, and the instruction and assignments he received were designed to come in direct conflict with his first-draft-final, knowledge-driven approach to writing. As a student, Carter had entered an intentionally orchestrated conflict in which the route to success was *not* to pile up information, but instead to change some of his goals for writing, to alter his process and habits. He was being asked to use new strategies for a task that only a year ago his old strategies were handling with relative ease. To succeed in this new rhetorical situation, Carter would have to "read" this message from the context of the class and to do so with enough critical awareness to resolve the conflict.

Carter's situation is not unusual. As Bartholomae has described, many classes in college introduce students to a new discourse community in which the parallel of initiation to the rites of a secret society is not farfetched. Students often feel (and perform) like outsiders to these communities in which the language, the conventions of speech and ways of arguing, and the commonplaces, concepts, and genres are new (Herrington, 1988). Moreover, the expectations of this new discourse are often unclear, its features uncertain, and the cues to change hard to read (Flower et al., 1990).

What may be unusual about Carter is that his comments come from a "collaborative planning" session in which he, as the Planner, is developing and explaining his plan for a paper with the help of a partner or Supporter, who questions, encourages, and prompts him to develop a more reflective rhetorical plan. These sessions allow us to glimpse part of this constructive process in action. Chapter 5 will give an account of the process as an educator might expect it to work by exploring the theoretical framework that supports collaborative planning. Chapters 6 and 7 will then examine the acts of negotiation and the strategic knowledge that gave a logic to what students actually did.

When students like Carter use a collaborative planning session to construct meaning, we can see them trying to bring their past experience and tried and true strategies into synch with the new rhetorical situation. However, the metaphor of initiation, with its emphasis on the expectations of the group, may gloss over the different ways individual students interpret and negotiate this context. At times, one sees negotiation in the hard-nosed sense of the term—writers considering what values, interests, ideas, or strategies they must give up, what to hang on to, what instruction and advice to accept, and what to ignore. But this adversarial image that pits student against the system may at times blind us to the equally important interpretive enterprise students embark on and the good faith effort they make in doing so. In these other sessions, students negotiate the context of learning as one might negotiate rapids in a white water canoe, trying to read the stream for cues, looking for the waves that harbor rocks, and for the deep channel to shoot through. To negotiate the terrain is to find the best path. The study of Carter and his class will try to model some of the distinctive ways both kinds of negotiation helped shape the construction of meaning in the collaborative planning of these freshmen.

Tracking a Constructive Process

Meaning making is difficult to study. Texts, writers' reflections, and readers' responses can tell us a lot about meanings but less about the making. The creation of a writer's meaning (that mental network of multiple symbolic representations) goes on while students are daydreaming in class discussion, recalling feedback from previous papers, or talking with a roommate. It is formed during planning, in the shaping of pre-text, the crafting of sentences, and the process of evaluation and revision (Britton, Burgess, Martin, McLeod, & Rosen, 1975; Hayes, Flower, Schriver, Stratman, & Carey, 1987; Witte, 1987). Most of this process is private and internal; it is hard to track from behavior or infer from texts. And like other mental representations, it may also be hard for the writer to recall or report after the fact.

Given the elusive nature of this internal representation growing over time, research on planning is a little like Muybridge's classic photographic study of a running tiger, which is shot with a series of rapid stop action frames. There are significant dimensions of this process the photographic data does not record, such as the soft footfalls and the tiger's reason for running. But from the sequence of images we can capture, we may be able to infer a repertoire of moves the tiger possesses, to distinguish a slow lope from the preparation for a leap. Although each pass before the camera will be unique, just as each act of making meaning will adapt to an endless variety of local conditions, process tracing helps us infer larger patterns in the process that help explain local events. Here are some of the trade-offs we considered in choosing to focus on planning.

Planning data (the combination of the notes, drafts, interviews, and concurrent records of writers planning aloud) are especially good for doing certain things. One is to track representations that are in flux. Whereas discourse interviews are especially suited to eliciting writers' tacit knowledge about conventions (Odell & Goswami, 1985), planning data tend to foreground goals, conflicts, and real-time decisions. Compared to written text, the fragmentary, elliptical language of planning talk may also give us some indication of schematic, episodic, or "I know what I mean, but can't say it" representations that are part of the writers' thinking but resist being turned into text. It may also reveal some mismatches between the current structure of a writer's knowledge and the structure the task calls for. Planning, then, is a good place to look for transformations of meaning.

Planning is also a place to observe how writers negotiate a social and rhetorical situation. In planning, writers choose to work with a representation of meaning that is at points more abstract and simplified than either their own network of meaning or a fully elaborated text. By suppressing detail, plans throw the priorities writers are setting into sharper relief and reveal the issues that capture their attention. In this data, issues in the spotlight include teachers' expectations, students' attitudes, the meaning of an assignment, and the problematic or expected features of a genre. Planning talk provides a window on the strategic way writers interpret, are cued by, and negotiate their rhetorical context.

Collaborative planning sessions, which will be an important source of data in the study to follow, offer a different perspective on constructive acts and another set of trade-offs. As a source of data, collaborative talk clearly changes the local features of planning; it alters the path of the tiger in ways we may not realize. It also shapes the process in some useful ways we can predict. Although the sessions record naturalistic, student-controlled events, they telescope a number of planning problems into a short period of time. Unlike extended think-aloud protocols of individual writers, collaboration condenses the attempt to create, rehearse, and elaborate a plan into shorter periods of focused effort (10 to 20 minutes in these sessions). Unlike after-the-fact interviews, the sessions are themselves occasions to plan. The presence of a partner forces writers to explain, elaborate, or, in some cases, simply try to articulate thoughts, doubts, fragments, assumptions, and ambiguities that are often left unsaid in thinking to oneself. And of special interest to us, collaborative data gives us some insight into how writers handle the social and interpersonal negotiation of meaning. At the same time, these sessions impose important constraints on how we interpret this data. The path of the planning process we observe here is the path of a collaborative act—there is no way to separate the contributions of the Planner from his or her Supporter since their process is the product of an interaction. Although some students say that their normal "solo" process in fact includes collaborative sessions not unlike this, this data is not about individual writers but about the repertoire of strategies the collaborative process calls out and the sorts of meaning these collaborators construct. Although this and other studies (Burnett, 1991; Higgins, 1992; Wallace, 1991) suggest the usefulness of collaborative planning data, the more important point is one Ericsson and Simon made in describing the kinds of information different methods yield. No research method, whether it is textual analysis, protocol analysis, thick description, or test scores, is good or bad in and of itself. Data of such observations is still and only data (1985). What matters is how that data is interpreted and the standards of evidence that it is asked to meet.

I. A Theoretical Framework for Looking at Planning

This study of Carter and his colleagues is a chapter in our field's larger systematic exploration into writers' planning and into the knowledge and strategies they bring to different rhetorical situations.[1] Likewise, the collaborative planning we observed was part of an educational effort to support students' rhetorical planning, which had in turn grown out of a body of research on planning and a theoretical account of constructive planning. Since the course Carter took, the collaboration he did, and the interpretations we make of the data were shaped by this research and theory—by the prior texts and by the assumptions, hypotheses, and questions we brought to it—I want to start the story of Carter and his meaning making with its theoretical background.

Planners are opportunists. An intriguing idea or a bon mot floats into view and the writer goes running after it, happily revamping her or his plan to embrace this unexpected possibility. The presence of opportunism and serendipity reminds us that planning rarely seems to follow the tidy, top-down procedure promised by some textbooks (e.g., choose a subject, limit your topic, select relevant ideas). However, this does not mean that the planning process is unstructured—even if the writer does not consciously control that structure. One important source of structure comes from three planning strategies that appear to operate as executive-level strategies; that is, they give a distinctive overall character or structure to the process of setting goals, generating ideas, and testing the plan (Flower et al., 1992). Executive-level strategies describe a global plan or approach that can call an array of more local moves and strategies into play. In comparing these three executive strategies—knowledge-driven, schema-driven, and constructive planning—the question to ask is, Who (or what) is providing the goals and the structure for the plan?

Schema-Driven Planning

Imagine the scene: a distinguished colleague is coming to lecture. Composing on the run, a writer is drafting an announcement that says *who, what, where*, and *when*. His schema for lecture announcements has not only prompted him to fill in the 4W's, it told him to add an academic title and affiliation to the speaker's name and to fill in the *what* slot with the title of his paper. As he approaches the desk of the departmental typist, his announcement schema conjours up an image of the finished text—the familiar, bare, dittoed announcement—and he feels the mismatch between that text and the scholarly context he had projected for this lecture. In searching for a better fit to his "distinguished lecture" schema, he now envisions an eye-catching poster done up on the Macintosh in 24-point type, but he eventually decides to go with the more personal touch of another schema: a memo addressed to faculty and graduate students.

In this example of schema-driven planning, once the writer's social knowledge about the care of visiting dignitaries suggested the need to write an announcement, his knowledge of discourse conventions could step in as an efficient guide to the construction of meaning (in the form of this announcement). I am using the term *schema* here in the restricted sense to refer to a well-structured body of information that can be shown to be shared in some meaningful way within a community, as in our schemas for eating in restaurants or going to birthday parties (Schank & Abelson, 1977), for reading a physics paper (Bazerman, 1985), or for writing an English placement essay (Bartholomae, 1985). Of course, these special purpose schemas will embed within themselves a host of more generic schemas. Some of the most important for writers are the discourse frames of the sort proposed by Meyer (1982) and Bracewell et al. (1982), which include narrative, descriptive, conversational, and problem frames. Although schemas like these represent socially shared knowledge, we must remember that they are constructed by individuals who abstract them piece by piece from experience. These networks of information contain many specific instances (such as the memory of a particular memo or a store of appropriate words and phrases), but they operate primarily as abstract or prototypical representations (Fiske & Linville, 1980). When it comes to writing, this is both the strength and limitation of a schema.

To use a schema, as an executive-level plan, a writer may have to instantiate or flesh out an abstract structure with new specifics. However, at some point such re-creation can become so effortful, and can require so much generative work that it is hard to distinguish it from "creation." To say that the writer, in such a case, is drawing on something as underspecified as a schema for academic papers has little explanatory power—the claim seems true at some level, but useless. Used in this broad, hand-waving sense, all knowledge fits into some schema (some structure) and the notion becomes "mush" (Fiske & Linville, 1980). To pin down the significance a given schema may have for a writer, the question to ask is, How well does it function as a set of instructions, first, for interpreting a new situation (i.e., by identifying it as an instance of the schema) and, second, for generating schema-supplied information to fill the gaps in what is given? How much of the constructive work can it do?

The distinguishing feature of schema-driven planning is that a schema, such as the discourse conventions for announcements, is doing the lion's share of the planning work. It is setting the appropriate goals and suggesting plans or subgoals and even appropriate language. During composing, it prompts the writer for what to generate next, and it suggests a structure for the text itself. If a problem crops up that is a recognized part of the schema, it can provide a prepackaged solution. When schema-driven plans operate at the executive level to guide composing, the planning process can be fast, efficient, and assured. The writer is reaping the rewards of learning—all those years of reading and writing department memos have not gone to waste. On the other hand, schema-driven planning leads to trouble when the task is more complex than a writer's available schemas. Even a well-developed schema for academic papers or well-structured arguments would quickly run out of advice if we tried to turn it into a computer program for producing our next journal article. Schema-driven planning works when the writer has a schema that fits the rhetorical occasion and when the schema in the writer's mind is specified in adequate detail to guide the drafting of text—when instantiating a schema can be distinguished from creating a plan.

Knowledge-Driven Planning

Imagine a later scene: writing up notes for today's seminar, our exemplary writer realizes that more students might show up at the lecture if in class he briefly discussed his distinguished colleague and her work with the new genre of "interactive" computer fiction. Although his schemas for writing lecture notes, reviewing a research design, and so on, come into play, this planning process is guided at the executive level by his knowledge of the topic. If we could enter the labyrinth of his memory, we might see that a part of this network is organized around the general topic of computers and writing (he will need to start his comments there); another part is organized around the narrative theory behind these texts and the continuing controversy over story grammars (that should be mentioned); and finally a smaller and more recent cluster concerns interactive fiction and the speaker's latest computer "text"—a murder mystery. In planning comments to make in class, this richly specified, well-organized body (bodies) of knowledge essentially drives the planning process, setting goals for what to cover, prompting the planner's "what next" moves, and supplying both content and organization.

Knowledge-driven planning can produce sophisticated and complex texts if the writer's knowledge is adequately developed and already structured to meet the needs of the rhetorical situation. It lets writers breeze through essay exams, reel off how-to explanations, and spin out letters to the folks back home. At the same time, it accounts for "writer-based" prose with its narrative or descriptive structure and focus on the writer thinking out loud to herself. For difficult tasks, knowledge-driven planning and a writer-based first draft may be a first step toward a reader-based text revised in the afterlight of a more rhetorical plan.

However, Bereiter and Scardamalia (1987) have argued that a special form of knowledge-driven planning they call knowledge telling may be a dead-end strategy that, in fact, precludes "knowledge-transformation." Based on their extensive research with young writers, they have proposed a model of knowledge telling that operates with a very simple "what next" process of selecting the topic (usually from a prompt given by the teacher), locating relevant topic knowledge, filtering it through genre constraints (e.g., opinion paper, description, etc.), and writing it down, pretty much in the order generated. This limited, yet highly productive process lets youngsters write school essays without resorting to goal setting, goal-directed knowledge search, or reorganization. They argue that the strict efficiency of knowledge telling makes it an alternative rather than a stepping stone to more complex planning, and its record of success for so much school writing makes students reluctant to give it up—even when the occasion does demand more. The knowledge-driven planning strategy we have described in adults is more sophisticated in that it allows serious encounters with one's knowledge as writers try to come to terms with what they think or try to synthesize their reading with an intelligent organizing idea (Flower et al., 1990). Nevertheless, it can pose the same problems as schema-driven planning—it works if the writer possesses the appropriate topic knowledge and if the structure of that knowledge already fits the demands of the task or the needs of the reader.

Constructive Planning

Sometimes a rhetorical situation asks for more. Instead of presenting knowledge, the writer must transform it, and instead of instantiating a prepackaged schema, the writer must actually construct a plan tailored to this unique rhetorical situation and devise a way to carry it out in text. When, as it turns out, our announcement writer is also asked to write a letter of recommendation for his colleague who is being considered for a position at a nearby university, he comes to the task with well-organized topic knowledge and a fairly well-developed schema for student recommendations. But for this letter, he will be forced to go beyond those schema- and topic-based plans and rise to constructive planning in response to problems and facts like these: What is his task in this context anyway—to reassure a conservative department that interactive fiction is still fiction or to confirm his colleague's place on the cutting edge of forming a new canon? If he decides the task is "to reassure," how does he turn that daunting intention into more specific rhetorical goals, into how-to plans that help select and organize information, that help set tone and language? And what about the conflict he suddenly sees between using reassuringly familiar language and concepts while wanting to praise some unique but unintelligible concepts in interactive software design—concepts with such patently frivolous names as "random punts"—for which his colleague's work is known?

Constructive planning is a response to tasks that knowledge- and schema-driven planning cannot handle. It operates at the executive level to construct, elaborate, and monitor progress on a rhetorical plan of the writer's own making and to transform knowledge and adapt schemas to meet the writer's goals. To say that a writer is using a constructive strategy is simply to say that the writer is approaching the task by constructing not just a plan of what to say, but a rhetorical plan, by setting goals, imagining readers, considering alternative moves, and so on. Note, however, that one of those moves might be to create an introduction that lets the writer turn quickly to a familiar topic—and switch into knowledge-driven planning. Constructive planning is like a jazz musician who *uses* a musical scale (as opposed to simply practicing scales); as an executive strategy, it frequently embeds both knowledge-driven and schema-driven planning within itself, fitting them within the rhetorical plan it is creating. In making a useful distinction among these three strategies, the question to ask is still: Who or what is doing the lion's share of the executive-level planning; where are the goals, process prompts, how-to plans, and tests coming from—a text schema, a topic knowledge network, or an adaptive, problem-solving process? It should be apparent that all of these planning strategies draw on what we might call knowledge that is at some level "socially constructed" or shared and that in all three instances our writer was participating in a social process of making meaning. However, because the first two strategies are designed for efficiency more than for flexibility, only constructive planning is likely to prompt our writer to a critical examination or reflection on this social process and shared knowledge.

Like the other two strategies, constructive planning poses its own problems, and they are significant ones. Its greater flexibility and rhetorical power means the writer must juggle even more constraints and decisions. To make a constructive planning strategy work, the writer must often leap five intellectual hurdles associated with the processes of representation, development, integration, instantiation, and conflict resolution (cf. Flower et al., 1992). Although it is reasonable to think of these five hurdles as identifying abilities writers need to develop, their theoretical implications point out an ambiguous virtue. The very processes that give constructive planning its rhetorical power and that support independent, expansive thinking also bring uncertainty, conflict, and disorganization. Like many good things, constructive planning comes at a price.

1. The writer must read the context and build an *initial representation* attuned to multiple features of the rhetorical and social situation. The writer's task cannot be taken as a given.
2. Based on this initial representation, the writer must generate a body of *supporting goals*, subgoals, and plans to deal with the situation and the problem as he or she has defined it. The appropriate response is not a given.
3. In elaborating goals and ideas and in taking advantage of opportunistic planning, writers are giving themselves a more fully realized rhetorical problem. But this expanding universe of information comes at a price when writers must then *connect, integrate, and even reconfigure* the disparate pieces of a developing plan.
4. Elaborating, integrating, and testing meaning at the whole-text level are possible because abstract plans and goals offer a more manageable representation for thinking than a text does. However, such goals must still be *instantiated* with a workable plan at more concrete levels, for example, in the choice among alternative discourse conventions or in the generation of specific language. And the more abstract the plan, the less likely it is to suggest or supply these concrete instantiations of itself.
5. Finally, the processes of construction, elaboration, integration, and instantiation all create added occasions for *conflict*, which can occur at all levels of the plan. To manage this process, the writer must be able to resolve the conflicts it produces.

Knowledge-Driven Planning: The Default Strategy for School

Constructive planning appears to be a high-effort strategy that is worth the effort when a situation demands adaptive planning and when a knowledge- or schema-driven strategy cannot do the job. It often makes use of sophisticated kinds of thinking, such as simulating a reader's response, and of the discourse knowledge that lets writers play out alternative moves. It is not surprising that constructive planning often appears to be an expert strategy, an option the expert writer is more likely to take. But the picture is not that simple. Observations of writers styled as younger, inexperienced, student, or novice convince us that these individuals can rise to sophisticated, inventive, rhetorical planning. And yet, the bulk of research clearly suggests that what is possible is not the norm.

Consider some cases where investigators hoped to see more constructive effort. Bereiter and Scardamalia (1987) have documented the way knowledge telling dominates the writing of young children. When they compared 10-, 12-, and 14-year-olds, the amount of planning activity per se more than doubled for the older students, but the preoccupation with content planning remained at nearly 90% in contrast to the 10% devoted to conceptual planning. Emig, who hoped to see a reflexive engagement with writing, saw in her case study of Lynn a polished and efficient student whose fluency with the five-paragraph theme and whose smooth knowledge-driven production could turn out effective student papers with little reflective effort. Langer found that 10th-grade students differed in how their knowledge of a given topic was organized. If that prior organization fit an assignment, they did well. For instance, a diffusely organized knowledge network can lead to success on thesis and support assignments that encouraged free elaboration, but not on an assignment that posed a question or problem.

A mismatch between the task and a student's knowledge structure (as Langer measured it) was a good predictor of lower paper scores (Langer, 1984). Langer used these findings to emphasize the role of prior knowledge. But they also suggest that the students were not using writing as an occasion to restructure what they knew. Although the rhetorical situation (the assignment) asked for a comparison or a response to a problem, the texts reflected the writer's current structure, not the sort of new, adaptive construction we expect of writers. Likewise, Durst's (1987) high school juniors, who were asked to do analytical writing, did engage in more generalizing and global planning than students with a summary assignment, but the texts were hard to tell apart. When Beach asked high school revisers to describe their strategies, they summarized content, but perhaps they did not understand the question. On a new form that asked for comments about the content, the function, and the audience for each paragraph, "the students gave content summaries in response to all three questions" (Beach & Eaton, 1984, p. 163). In all these studies, requests for adaptive, interpretive, reflective thinking seem to be met (by a statistically significant group of students) with some form of knowledge-driven response.

In college, 68% of the freshmen in our Reading-to-Write study responded to an open-ended assignment with either a summary or a form of review and comment (Flower et al., 1990). The freshmen later predicted that Master's students (to whom they attributed greater freedom and sense of personal authority) would have represented the assignment differently as an invitation to interpretation. Although the writing protocols showed students making their own elaborations and applying the readings in personal ways, little of this information made its way into the text. In interviews, the culture of recitation figured strongly in the way these freshmen represented writing to themselves, echoing Applebee's (1981) description of secondary schools in which only 3% of class time was devoted to writing that involved at least a paragraph, and most of that for purposes of examination. College juniors and seniors got a more challenging reading-to-write task in Kantz's (1987) study, which asked them to apply articles on creativity to the problems of a particular group of freshmen students. While some students took a synthesizing stance, approaching the sources and task as an "explicator" or a "builder," others still saw their role to be a "paraphrase-and-commenter" or a "summarizer."

This mixture of strategies is apparent in graduate students as well. When Ackerman asked Ph.D. students in business and psychology to read and write about an issue within their discipline, they engaged in a highly context-sensitive rhetorical reading and use of the sources. But faced with a task outside their expertise, these moves disappeared. They continued to exhibit rhetorical awareness, but it was focused on discourse features and conventions rather than context, and writers shifted to more "text-based" images of the task, using the structure of information in the source texts to guide their interpretation in reading and their summary and synthesis strategies in writing (Ackerman, 1991). In the descriptive study of expert and novice planners noted above, it was the experienced writers who as a group created more elaborated complex plans, who integrated those goals at both the high and low levels of their goal networks, and who dealt with conflicts not just by switching goals but by reexamining their plans. The student writers—particularly the problem students—focused by and large on their knowledge, even when it proved difficult to make it fit the audience and assignment (Flower et al., 1992).

These studies and others point to the way knowledge-driven planning surfaces when writers lack experience or face difficult tasks and to the primary role knowledge-driven planning plays in school, where it is combined with well-learned schemas for theme writing. Teachers, it seems, read school writing as a display of knowledge, whether the topic is textbook learning or personal experience. Students become adept at planning that is devoted to searching, organizing, and reciting what they know or have learned, so adept, in fact, that when tasks call for students to speak the language of a new discourse, they still offer a knowledge-telling, five-paragraph theme, and so adept that when the situation calls for rhetorical planning, for a unique plan that adapts information to the needs of a reader or the purpose of a writer, students still rely on knowledge-driven planning.

And yet each of these studies and our own experience offers exceptions. Looking for the rationale behind students' performance, it is often hard to separate the way students *represent* a task to themselves, or what they *choose* to do, from what they might or might not be *able* to do. Students' performance may reflect the simple fact that knowledge-driven planning is admirably adapted to most school writing, that it fits the expectations of that social and educational context—it is the smart choice. Or it may arise because constructive planning can be difficult to do and may rely heavily on things a learner would typically lack, such as deep topic knowledge, fluency with a discourse, or experience with a particular rhetorical situation. And yet, when experienced writers face an unfamiliar task, we see them still acting in constructive ways, generating and evaluating their own goals, accepting conflicts, consolidating plans, and rising to a meta-awareness of their own process and the way it is working.

We think one reasonable conclusion that can be drawn from this contradictory picture is that students, especially the young adults one sees in high school and college, are capable of doing adaptive, constructive planning in many areas of their life, including writing, and that on certain occasions they do. However, in most school-sponsored writing, knowledge-driven planning is the default strategy. It is the strategy that normally works, the strategy students control most fully, and the strategy of choice we might expect writers to use unless instruction or the context of a class leads to an alternative. In contrast to the efficiency and simplicity of this default move, constructive planning asks students not only to set rhetorical goals, but to examine them and to critically consider the fit between their knowledge, their intentions, and the new discourse they are often trying to learn. Because it is also difficult, we should not expect students to be adept at a process they may have had little occasion to practice.

There is evidence that simply prompting students to consider the things knowledge-driven planning ignores can make a difference—if the prompt occurs in the planning process itself (that is, not simply in a textbook, lecture, or classroom activity that encourages but cannot intervene). Carey (in preparation) created a set of prompts designed to address the very processes we saw missing in the Flower et al. (1992) planning study and to answer the question, Are these missing processes the result of writers who *cannot* or simply *do not* construct and consider a plan? The context was slightly improbable: a computer called the Collaborative Writer would compose a paper, if the writer would develop the plan, thinking and talking out loud in response to the computer's questions and prompts. The paper assignment, which asked the writer to adapt and transform knowledge, drew on material from a course all the undergraduates had just completed.

With surprising willingness, students participated in this fiction, even though it involved an hour to an hour and a half dealing with frustrating questions from this computer, such as "I really appreciated all your plans so far. However, I still need your help because I was programmed not to accept the first plan given me without considering alternative plans. So could you give me some alternative plans to consider for this text?" And later, "I just had a thought. Maybe we can use more than one of your plans after all. Can you think of ways of combining your alternative plans to form a new plan?"

This study had some surprising results. Even with these prompts, it was always possible for writers to resort to talking solely about content, and some did. However, many freshman students exhibited a remarkable degree of constructive thinking about their purpose, their audience, and the features of presentation and organization. In fact, half of the freshmen (those who had had a composition course that emphasized problem solving and planning) resembled the experienced master's students in the study on certain measures, such as the amount of initial rhetorical planning. It seemed clear that prompting could make a meaningful difference in at least the kind of thinking students did. The greater surprise was that our subjects, the students, appeared to value doing what we saw as a demanding sequence of tasks designed to answer a research question, not to engage a student. Subjects asked if their roommates could participate in the study and wished they had been able to use the program (which of course did not really write anything, only asked questions) for a final paper just written for their psychology course. In essence, the students were telling us this was a useful learning process. And the data were telling us that collaboration in the form of on-line supports and prompts could help students abandon the default strategy of knowledge-driven planning, that constructive planning was a strategic choice students were willing, with help, to make.

II. Collaborative Planning: A Scaffold for Constructing Meaning

Research of this sort is food for thought. It offers a conceptual structure for understanding differences in planning, interpreting performance, diagnosing problems, and recognizing patterns of growth. But turning insights into instruction is a different matter. Collaborative planning started as an attempt to translate the implications of process research into a workable plan for teaching. As an experiment in instantiating theory in practice, collaborative planning has since taken different shapes in different contexts (Flower, Wallace, Norris, & Burnett, 1993). The study that follows set out to explore how that "translation" was working in a freshman course and to develop a more grounded, observation-based theory of how constructive planning operates in the context of school.[2]

Collaborative planning is a loosely structured planning process under the control of the student. In it the writer (as planner) explains and elaborates his or her plan (or partial text) to a partner (as supporter). The supporter listens, asks questions, and encourages the writer to develop his or her plan. These informal sessions are structured in part by the collaborative roles of planner and supporter and in part by a set of rhetorical prompts called the Planner's Blackboard. The immediate goal of a collaborative session is to develop a more elaborated and rhetorically sophisticated plan. Writers are shown how to encourage each other to go beyond information-driven plans "to say" something in order to create rhetorical plans "to do" something in writing (1) by focusing on purposes, key points, audience, and textual conventions, (2) by trying to consolidate those goals, and (3) by reflecting on their thinking. These three moves reflect the long-term goal of collaborative planning: to help both students develop strategies for constructive planning and to gain more awareness of their own choices.

The collaborative, supportive, and social nature of this experience is at the heart of the process, but it also differs from some other social arrangements for learning. Although complex thinking strategies like this can develop through extended social interaction and feedback, as we see in traditional apprenticeship (Rogoff, 1990), we wanted students to take more self-conscious control of this process. While writing this discussion, I came across the pottery and words of Maria Martinez in the small Millicent Rogers Museum outside Taos. Maria Martinez' reinterpretation of a traditional art and her mentoring of young potters had shaped the pottery revival in the New Mexico pueblos in the 1920s and 1930s. And above those striking pots and sepia photos was a very different description of learning: "Me and my sister just started. . . . I myself started on little pots, and my mother used to say, 'Don't go over and bother your aunt. . . . If you want to learn that, go ahead and learn slowly . . . without bothering anybody. Just go ahead and watch her . . . then you can make it yourself.' "

Although we do not know how Martinez herself mentored others, she describes a form of socially embedded, but indirect, inexplicit instruction. And in fact, some educators in the constructivist tradition feel that learning that comes through unprompted personal discovery is better learning, and they equate more direct instruction with mechanical teaching and a reductive sets of steps and procedures (Pressley, Harris, & Marks, 1992). But other constructivists argue for a process that is both dialectical and direct: students start with what they already know and can do, but their effort is extended into what Vygotsky called the the "zone of proximal development" through strategic instruction. Students are supported by a scaffold of prompts and explanations, by extensive modeling, by in-process support, and by reflection that connects strategic effort to outcomes (Harris & Pressley, 1991). Strategic instruction of this sort tries to integrate social and cognitive processes. It has taught us that people learn strategies best when they are anchored in a specific context, but learners construct a repertoire of flexible strategies only by working across different contexts and learning to make conditional judgments about which strategies to use when (Bransford, Sherwood, Vye, & Reiser, 1986; Bransford, 1990). And they take ownership of those strategies when they are able to interrogate, reflect on, evaluate, and transform those strategies (Meichenbaum, 1977).

The problem as we saw it was not how to guide planning (in the way a teacher, tutor, checklist, process activity, or computer program might). The problem was how to help students themselves construct a robust strategy for being a constructive planner. The ultimate goal of collaborative planning then is not a particular sort of process, plan, or text; it is the personal invention of an intellectual repertoire. The logic behind its design was to create a purposeful social event that engages two people in the use of powerful rhetorical strategies. In teaching, the synergistic combination of social and rhetorical moves may achieve what neither can accomplish alone. Social support alone—unstructured or uninstructed collaboration—often fails to grapple with important goals and writing problems (Freedman, 1987). Likewise, instruction in heuristics and text features can settle into inert knowledge unless a social situation engages that knowledge, calls a process out, and makes rhetorical moves happen. In our hope for a social cognitive synergy, this technique is closely related to other approaches Collins et al. (1989) have described as cognitive apprenticeship. Collins et al. emphasize six features of learning in this paradigm. Cognitive *modeling*, in-process *coaching*, and *scaffolding* or support based on the learner's current knowledge are the key instructional processes. These are tied to techniques that support students' efforts to *articulate* and to *reflect* on their knowledge, reasoning, and problem-solving processes using this understanding as a springboard to *exploration* on their own.

In the social dynamics of collaborative planning, not only the teacher but each partner models constructive planning in the form of rhetorical, reflective thinking, for the other. The supporter and prompts provide a scaffold (Applebee, 1984) that helps writers not only attend to parts of the problem, but to persist and elaborate their insights and to consolidate what emerges. Although the planner and supporter have distinctive social roles to play, the interpersonal atmosphere of talking out one's ideas makes students partners in shared problem solving (Freedman, 1987). This exploratory "talking out" not only creates a climate for reflection, but what may be more unusual, it also allows students to observe and talk about their own ways of approaching a writing problem and/or collaborating. The session itself can become a springboard to observation-based insights and a shared understanding of normally private experiences.

The second source of structure in collaborative planning comes from prompts embodied in the Planner's Blackboard, which is essentially a visual metaphor for the theory of constructive planning. It asks writers to imagine a planning space within their own minds on which ideas are posted as on a mental blackboard whenever they occur (cf. Hayes-Roth & Hayes-Roth, 1978). As figure 4 illustrates, writers may focus on topic information and build a knowledge-driven plan "to say something" in writing. Or they may work with the fuller blackboard (fig. 5) and construct a rhetorical plan "to do something" through writing.

The categories or spaces reflect familiar elements in rhetoric, but the blackboard conceit calls attention to how well a writer is actually developing each of these areas in his or her plan. The large background field on the blackboard is, of course, topic information, which includes things to say in the text. But the complete Planner's Blackboard places three other concerns in the foreground—Purpose and Key Point, Audience (which includes both readers' characteristics and their imagined responses) and Text Conventions

Figure 4. Planner's Blackboard for developing information-based plans *To Say* (figure from *Problem-Solving Strategies for Writing,* fourth edition by Linda Flower, copyright © 1993 by Harcourt Brace & Company, reproduced by permission of the publisher).

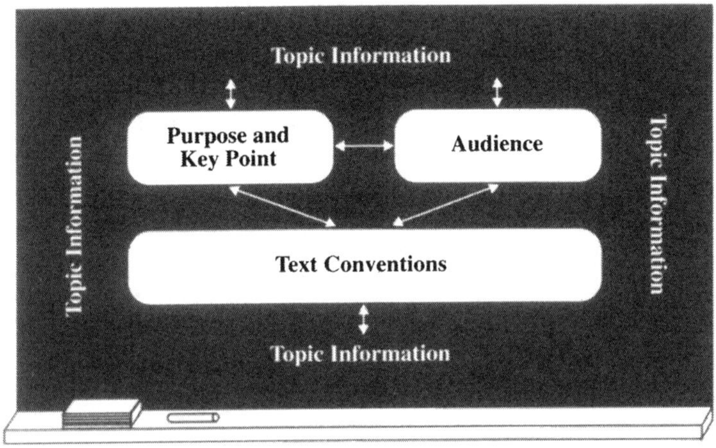

Figure 5. Planner's Blackboard for developing rhetorical plans *To Do* (figure from *Problem-Solving Strategies for Writing,* fourth edition by Linda Flower, copyright © 1993 by Harcourt Brace & Company, reproduced by permission of the publisher).

(which include matters of organization, format, style, and the gamut of discourse-specific conventions). As the research we reviewed earlier suggests, while experienced writers devote time and attention to these three areas, less experienced writers often ignore them (Carey & Flower, 1989). Taken together, the four empty blackboards encourage writers to construct a fuller, multidimensional plan.

The blackboard's second visual message is a prompt to metacognition. We presented it as a reminder that many inexperienced writers do indeed do extensive planning, only to find they have been devoting all of their attention to generating things to say—posting information on the metaphoric Topic Blackboard alone. The blackboard encourages writers to consider the current state of their own plan. More experienced writers not only consider the other elements of the blackboard, they periodically review the state of their plans and look for ways to create links across these different concerns or to consolidate their ideas by looking at the big picture. This consolidation is symbolized by the arrows linking all the boards to one another. For instance, experienced writers think about ways they might adapt their Key Point to some special interests of their Audience, or they ask themselves how different ways of organizing the paper (Text Conventions) would help carry out one of their Purposes.

The message of the blackboard metaphor as we taught it was relatively simple: "Remember those parts of a writer's plan that, in the heat of struggling with content, you might forget to think about. And remember to consolidate these ideas and reflect on the state of your own thinking." The rationale for turning this prompt for planning and metacognition into a visual metaphor is that it might be used by both planner and supporter as a flexible aide-mémoire and prompt in the midst of collaboration when such advice has the power to actively intervene in the process. The reality of how the blackboard was used turned out to be even more interesting.

The nature of the planning sessions we have observed in classes and on audio tape range from some rather formal question and answer sessions (by students who have yet to take full control of the process for themselves), to freewheeling sociable explorations, to sustained discussions about a particular planning problem both writers were facing. Like the tiger in the Muybridge photos, collaborative planning can take different paths, some obviously more productive than others. We encouraged flexibility combined with an insistence on three principles we saw as fundamental.

- Authority (and the floor) belongs to the planner who is encouraged to think, talk, elaborate, and explore options and ideas. Unlike peer editing, the spotlight is on the writer's intentions rather than on the reader's response to a text.
- The goal of this collaboration is to create a more elaborated representation of meaning for the writer—an expanded, interconnected network of goals, plans, ideas, alternatives, and possibilities alive to all the areas represented by the blackboard.
- The social dynamic of this collaboration (and the job of the supporter) is to create a setting that actively supports and engages the writer in both inventive and critical thinking about purpose, audience, and text. But equally important, by making this normally private process more explicit, collaboration gives both writers a new way to observe and reflect on their own thinking and writing process.

To sum up, collaborative planning is an attempt to engage students in the kind of constructive and reflective processes observed in the research on planning. To help stage this experience, rather than describe it, collaborative planning hands the process, the prompts, and the responsibility to make it useful over to students. Since the project began in 1987–88 (when data for this study were collected), we have learned a lot about how to teach and support this sort of collaborative planning. Although there are other good ways to translate planning research into practice, this route has shown some advantages. One is that the social nature of collaboration can create a supportive and structured invitation to plan and reflect that can intervene in the ongoing process.

Second, the concept of collaborative planning has proven adaptable to very different kinds of classrooms and kinds of writing. It became the basis for an extended classroom inquiry project at the Center for the Study of Writing and Literacy, Carnegie Mellon University, where it has been used by teacher researchers and students from fifth grade through college in western Pennsylvania. The publications from this Making Thinking Visible project document ways these teachers shaped collaborative planning to some very different intellectual goals, such as helping high school students incorporate literary conventions from reading short stories into their own writing in an English class. But in World Cultures, in which the instructor focused on purposes and key points, the goal was to let students use their experience as writers (with purposes) to see how the sacred primary source texts of history were also writing shaped, like theirs, by the purposes, audiences, and conventions in their own time. In a college course, collaborative planning became the means to another end when students used their taped sessions to reflect on their own strategies for switching among the different discourses of college writing. The history of these instructional experiments suggests that what is interesting about collaborative planning is not any one version of it as a classroom activity, but the theory it tries to represent and the ways teachers reinvent the practice to meet those larger goals in their own setting (Flower, 1993b; Flower & Ackerman, 1994; Flower et al., 1993; Making Thinking Visible Project Series, 1991, 1992, 1993).

Finally, one of the outcomes of collaborative planning most relevant to this study is that these sessions offer a platform for research by making elements of both the cognition and the social negotiation of writing more observable. The sections that follow give us a close look at the social and cognitive process of 22 freshman writers.

6

"Welcome to College"
Construction and Negotiation in a Freshman Class

Chapter 5 left us with a problem (how to encourage more constructive thinking), a question (would collaboration support such moves?) and a hypothesis (that collaborative planning might not only help students but offer us an unusually good opportunity to study construction and negotiation in their writing). This chapter will take us into the midst of these processes with an in-depth study of collaborative planners from two freshman composition classes.[1]

The Rhetorical Problem

Students were asked to read two chapters from Peter Farb's *Word Play* (chapters on how language and conceptual labels affect what we see and know) and to write a short (1–2 page) paper "that analyzes a 'discourse' problem of your own choosing." Finding and defining real problems was a theme of the course that had appeared in earlier assignments, as had the idea of discourse communities and awareness of one's own writing process. In their preparation for this assignment, students were urged to consider

> a realistic "discourse" problem you or other students encounter. As you plan the paper, give some thought to your own purpose in writing the paper. Sometimes people analyze a problem in order to think a question through for themselves. Or in order to explain a problem or issue to someone else. Or maybe to discuss a possible solution to a problem or even persuade readers to act on one solution. Decide on our own purpose, let your reader know what it is, and use it to organize your paper. What do you want to accomplish in this paper?

Students received the four criteria on which the papers were to be evaluated in advance.

1. Did you apply your reading to a real discourse problem or an issue that you define in the paper?
2. Did you use the material from Farb's book for a purpose of your own, and did you make your own purpose as a writer apparent to readers?
3. Did you use your purpose and/or your sense of a problem to organize the rest of the paper? Is each paragraph relevant to your purpose and to the logical development of your analysis?
4. Did your paper meet college-level standards for correctness and style?

Although it is likely that freshmen might perceive such writing as a "pseudotransactional" rather than a fully rhetorical act (Petraglia, 1991), a genuine effort was made to engage students in the purposeful formulation of a problem they and others would find relevant. The task, by its nature, seemed to call for constructive planning.

As they had done on previous papers, students were to meet outside of class with a partner of their choice for a collaborative session once they had developed a preliminary plan. Because collaborative planning was being used in this course for the first time on an experimental basis, instruction in how to conduct a collaboration was spare. A class was devoted to introducing the idea of the Planner's Blackboard and students were given a handout on how to track their own process that told them to (1) conduct a short self-interview about their plan on tape before the collaboration, (2) tape the collaboration, and (3) conduct a final wrap-up interview with themselves on what they had observed or found interesting. These collaborations were discussed but not graded.

The Issues That Emerged

These transcripts document a crossroad where literate actions collide, where learning and performing make competing demands, and where strategic cognition, social contexts, and prior knowledge are in visible and vigorous interaction. In trying to describe how these collisions and collaborations affect meaning making, four issues, which will organize the rest of this chapter, stand out.

The social negotiation of meaning. Entering a new discourse, trying to build a satisfactory representation of meaning leads these writers into active negotiation of the interpersonal and social context of writing. Negotiation here is a two-way street: students are not only reading this context and interpreting its cues but are in turn translating their understanding into action in the goals they set and the strategies they invoke.

The collaborative construction of plans, task representations, and texts. Collaborative planning sessions appear in many cases to support constructive planning and to challenge or change students' representations of both the task and the text they are writing. Writers are negotiating some sophisticated demands on meaning. Moreover, the parts of their plan that come under the most direct scrutiny (from both the blackboard prompts and their partner) show up in significant parts of the final text, such as the introduction, conclusion, or major examples. Out of these observations, I will propose a model of the writer as learner that highlights the strategic choices learners must make.

The strategic nature of individual differences. Students use collaborative planning in significantly different ways, measured in terms of the perceived quality of the session (a holistic judgment), the extent of constructive planning, and the amount of reflectiveness. These differences, however, are not adequately explained by ability, paper grade, or strategies alone, but appear to reflect the strategic knowledge—the goals, strategies, and awareness—students bring to the collaboration. The final section of the chapter will compare three ways to interpret this data: with an expert/novice comparison, with strategic analysis, and with statistical pattern finding.

The strategic nature of our research. As researchers (making meanings about students' meaning making), we can gain a great deal from the pattern-seeking techniques of expert/novice and statistical analyses with their emphases on those "variables" with broadest accountability. But to build a theory of construction and negotiation and to understand the interaction of social and cognitive forces, we need to extend the picture with a strategic analysis that recognizes the goals and awarenesses that help drive the behavior we observe.

I. Negotiating the Social Context of Learning: "Welcome to College"

When two writers work together, some of the social negotiations that help forge meaning move into the spotlight, and some of the normally silent cognition behind these negotiations can be heard. To take the large view, the episode of planning transcribed below—two students and a tape recorder behind the door of Jennie's dorm room—could be read as a tiny event bobbing in the open seas of its wider social context. This event has been quietly shaped by Western culture and the tradition of a liberal education, the ideology of success and competition in school, and the middle-class context of university life. Together, Carter and Jennie are tacitly responding to the obligations and opportunities created by this particular freshman class, to the signs that reveal their teacher's expectations, and to the social protocol of a course-sponsored collaborative "date." Within these layers of context, some forces, like the desire to succeed in school, are likely to operate simply as givens, as distant and indirect forces like faraway thunder that create a disposition and attitude. Other, more directly observable forces, like the assignment to find a "meaningful problem," appear not only to shape specific decisions the writer makes but to be negotiable social influences, mediated by the writer's awareness of them. Not surprisingly, these transcripts offer, at best, weak evidence of how larger social and cultural forces (such as capitalism, orality, literacy, and educational institutions per se) figure in this event, allowing us to do little more than speculate on which of these forces might be shaping some specifiable feature of Carter's writing or how they operate to do so. However, these collaborations do reveal some critical points at which these writers are interpreting the more well-specified situation of school, of this class, and of this collaboration. In reading this level of the context for cues to action, students are not passively responding to the social meaning of their situation but actively negotiating it. That is where our analysis will focus.

Grades are an emphatic social sign about one's place in the structure of school. But there are many ways to interpret a C- on one's first college paper in World History. When Jennie, at turn 31, asks for an example of how different writing styles can actually cause a problem, Carter reads last semester's C− as a meaning-laden sign. In the story Carter tells, he transforms the response of his high school and college teachers into a direct comment on his own writing strategies and his (Carter's) assessment of the effort required. With his partner, Carter *constructs* the significance of this school experience. (The conventions of transcription used for these sessions are covered in detail in the Appendix which contains a longer version of this session. In particular, note that standard ellipsis dots within brackets indicates editorial omissions, whereas three dots indicate pauses by the speaker. The abbreviations in square brackets at the end of each turn are a coding scheme based on the Planner's Blackboard, which will be explained in detail in the next section. Here *S* stands for supporter.)

31 S: So, what kind of examples are you gonna use? Can you give me an example? An example... [*tx con*]

32 Carter: Um... Okay... I'll give you a real big example. Switching from high school writing to college writing. [*info*]

33 S: Uh-huh. [*off*]

34 Carter: In high school, you could—most of the times for any class you could get away with, you know, BS in a lot of papers. And you'd get good grades, just 'cause it sounded intelligent, even though it really didn't say much. In college they don't go for that stuff. You gotta really, you know, go write, and you can't BS your paper, because they'll know right away that you're doing that [. . . .]

37 S: [. . . .] So some of your main points are gonna be that from high school to college—in high school, you can get away with saying things that aren't really relevant. In college you can't. But how are you gonna explain that? Are you gonna give a specific example in your life? With like... In high school I did this in college I can't do that. Like I think it would become more real. [*key pt/tx con, R*]

38 Carter: Yeah. Okay. I can do this. In high school, in my senior year, we had to write a thesis paper. And we had an entire semester to do it. And, just like me—I waited until like the last three weeks of the semester to start doing it. And I didn't have all the research done that I should have, but I started working on it real hard. And I had a lot of pages. It ended up being 15 pages long... /wow/ with bibliography and... Well, that's what she expected—she said 10 to 15 pages. And it was really long and drawn out, and it didn't really say much of anything, but it sounded like it did. You know what I mean? [*info*]

39 S: Yeah. That's a good example. I really like that. [*tx con*]

40 Carter: I got an—I got an A on it... [*info*]

41 S: Oh! Congratulations! [*off*]

42 Carter: It really didn't say anything, so I was so happy and I got an A in English, and that made my day, and then I graduated, and I was even happier. But, for college... [*off*]

43 S: Yeah. That's a good example. [*tx con*]

44 Carter: I'm not done yet. [*off*]

45 S: (Laughs) Sorry, Carter. [*off*]

46 Carter: (Laughs) Okay. And comparing that to the—the first semester of college... I took a class [on culture and history], which is probably the most boring class I've ever taken in my life. But, we had to write... [*info*]

47 S: I hope [name] doesn't listen to this tape (giggle). [*off*]

48 Carter: Well, I'm done with it, and I got a B in it, or whatever. But anyway... [*off*]

49 S: Whatever. [*off*]

50 Carter: So, we had to write a 5-page paper on African nationalism, which I had no idea, and I waited like the night before I was due to start that... [*info*]

51 S: You have a bad habit of doing that. [*off*]

52 Carter: I know. Well, I put all that into my writing-style analysis paper, so that's all there. So, anyway... So I wrote five or six pages on nothing, but I included the words *African nationalism* in there once in a while. I thought, why this is just like high school, I can get away with doing this. I got the paper back, and it was a C−, or a C, or something like that. It said "no content." And I was introduced to the world of college writing. [*info*]

In the explanatory account Carter appears to have constructed last semester in history, he cast himself as a writer who had options but made the wrong, low-effort choice (cf. Nelson, 1990). His instructor's comment was read as a direct reply to that choice. Now, in response to Jennie and the assignment to explore problems, he re-creates this story for a new purpose. Making a new link in his personal network of meaning, Carter now sees the history class experience as an *example* of a writer who needs to learn the ropes of college writing. The process of interpreting, reinterpreting, linking, and reorganizing this network of ideas, attitudes, and personal experiences serves two purposes: it is a way to construct meaning for the paper at hand and to interpret, hence negotiate, the social context of writing.

Carter has been constructing a socially negotiated meaning of school for some time. As this vignette suggests, his approach to schoolwork grows out of a string of encounters in which he has been interpreting the context of writing as a guide to action and, with each encounter, changing his script and redrawing his image of what is expected. With each of the small social negotiations recorded here, Carter elaborates his theory of the task of college writing starting with the "welcome to college" story Carter told himself last term in the wake of his shocking C-. He supports this reading with another construction—an interpretive flashback to his prior habits of negotiating high school expectations. The meaning-building process continues in turn 38 as he tries to embed his first-semester understanding within a new, second-semester situation that is asking him to extend the "transition" and figure out the "writing styles" different courses demand.[2]

Another artifact of a previous social negotiation turns up in Carter's description of what is expected in two of his current courses, Strategies for Writing and Science and Technology.

56 Carter: Yeah. Well, I can give a specific example for that. For a problem analysis paper in Strategies for Writing, my first draft... It wasn't very well organized, and... [. . .] [*tx con*]

62 Carter: But... And she told me how I could structure it better, you know, make it more smoothly flowing, and whatever. And... And so I wrote it like that, as, you know, real paragraph form, everything was ordered, and everything like that. Good spelling. Good grammar. Good punctuation. [*info*]

63 S: Yeah. So that's necessary in an English paper. [*info*]

64 Carter: Yeah. But in Technology and People, we have papers due almost every Friday, and most of them are... They'll give us a problem, and they'll ask us to give a possible solution of the problem. You know... in a report form sort of. And my papers for Tech. and People... Usually, they'll have maybe a paragraph. And then maybe a problem, like an equation worked out or something like that. They won't really be structured. I mean, I'll just have like one, problem one, and then all that, you know, so it's really different. [*info*]

No doubt, the instructors would not be entirely satisfied with Carter's interpretation of the key features they look for in writing. Nevertheless, this vignette shows a student looking closely for the cues that will guide action—trying to forge an operational definition of what matters in each class and how to write differently. In their demands for "content" and for "organization," each course is asking Carter to transform his knowledge and to structure that knowing in a particular way. The point here is that Carter's reading of the situation attempts to turn contextual cues into specific literate practices.

The sections of Carter's transcript just described let us indulge in social archaeology, digging up evidence of how past interpretations and negotiations guided the construction of meaning. However, we should recognize that these paired retrospective stories of reading a situation are probably being constructed in part for this occasion. In fact, it is likely that the need to plan and write the current paper is itself leading Carter to this more articulated representation of his experience. Thus, another form of social negotiation happens in real time in these sessions when the planner must deal face-to-face with the prompts, criticisms, and requests of the supporter.

Face-to-Face Negotiation

In her study of classroom discourse, Cazden (1988) sketches a number of ways the talk between teachers, students, and peers can support learning. One way is by serving as a catalyst that stimulates, even demands, change.

Another is by adding the missing bit the learner needs to perform, through scaffolding a conversation, completing and extending thought, or playing a complementary role (such as prompter or critic) that the learner might eventually internalize. One of the points of contention in this research is whether discourse supplies the catalyst and support for change by engendering conflict and cognitive dissonance (a position attributed to Piaget) or whether it dictates the path of growth by providing new models and forms of thought that the learner immersed in the experience then internalizes (a position attributed to Vygotsky). This polarization is unfortunate, since neither Vygotsky nor Piaget intended to exclude a cognitive or social influence and since discourse seems able to do both—to contribute models of performance and to engage students in a process for constructing their own knowledge. Moreover, as Cazden points out (quoting Leont'ev, another Soviet psychologist), internalization is not covert imitation: "The process of internalization is not *transferral* of all external activity to a preexisting internal 'plane of consciousness'; it is the process in which this internal plane is *formed*" (p. 109). Internalizing a new process is itself a constructive act in the sense presented here.

Vygotsky's and Piaget's theories were trying to account for the rapid cognitive and social development of young children. When we turn to the collaborative talk of the young adults in this study, we see that this friendly discourse continues to provide models for thought (coming in the form of Planner's Blackboard prompts, students dropping into teacher talk with a self-conscious laugh, or partners' suggestions for "how I would do it"). The discourse is also full of contradictions, conflicts, requests—offering a catalyst and a process for change. However, it would be naive to envision these writers as mere passive recipients, absorbing or even responding to all influences of the discourse. The reality of this social situation, and the meaning of all this talk, rests in how the writers interpret and choose to use it.

Within collaborative planning, one of the most important social negotiations to track occurs when the supporter confronts the planner with a face-to-face request for a constructive act. These are critical occasions in collaborative planning in which the partner goes beyond merely prompting the planner to tell more (about a topic or to talk about the audience, for example) and actually raises a problem or pinpoints a place where knowledge-driven thinking will not work. How do writers interpret this request for constructive planning when the request is no longer an indirect cue, such as the "no content" comment written on a finished paper? Here is an invitation to thinking happening in real time directly tied to the task at hand, in which the student's response is likely to reflect on the self-image he or she is trying to project.

We attempted to answer this question for Carter and the other 21 students in the study by locating points at which the supporter's comment or request called for constructive planning.[3] For each such prompt, we asked: (1) was the request to construct knowledge itself rejected or deferred; (2) if the planner did engage the request, what knowledge or possibilities were constructed (or rehearsed from memory) in response to it; and finally, (3) do traces of this response appear in the text or not? This analysis has some important limitations because there is no appropriate control group for comparison. We cannot claim that the partner's prompt caused the constructive thinking we see (as we will discuss in a moment). And since students do do constructive planning without such prompts, we cannot assume the writer would have never generated these ideas alone. What it does answer then is, What effect did these partners have?

The four occasions on which Carter received a direct request to rise to constructive planning involved some of his central ideas. For example, at turn 20, Jennie questions whether Carter's broad claim about everyone needing or even wanting to switch styles is really true (see table 1). Carter responds first by becoming more tentative and then by narrowing the focus to his audience of college students, for whom this would be relevant. The final text begins with a statement that anticipates a reader like Jennie, asserting that people are asked to switch styles "throughout [their] educational careers."

Just what effect does such a prompt have on Carter's thinking? It could

Table 1. Carter's Response to Prompts for Constructive Planning

Prompt at turn	Reject or defer	Knowledge/possibilities constructed	Trace in text
20. Is claim true?	no	Decides some people may not care but switching is important to students.	¶1. Different styles are a problem for students.
27. Adapt focus to audience.	no	Gives example of switching from high school to college.	¶3. Hardest transition is high school to college style.
37. Make it more real.	no	Tells story about high school versus college paper.	¶4. Learning the hard way is an example.
75. Give solution or just talk about it?	no	Proposes to help reader catch on to differences sooner.	Final ¶. Problems caused by confusion, so think before writing.

be any one of the following: In the case of greatest influence, (1) it could lead to the generation of a new idea or set of connections, or (2) it could lead to the elaboration and extension of an idea he already had in mind, or (3) it could simply have the effect of making a previous idea more salient, tagging it as interesting, problematic, or important. In Carter's case, a taped self-interview just before the session suggests that he had planned to address "mostly freshmen" (turn 20), that he already planned to talk about confusion over styles and switching from high school to college (see turn 32, "Okay... I'll give you a real big example"). So Jennie's first two prompts are probably leading to elaboration and qualification. However, it appears that the idea of using his senior thesis and his World History papers as specific examples was freshly created in response to Jennie's prompts (see turn 38, "Yeah. Okay. I can do this. In high school...").

Although some students initially assume that collaboration is supposed to give them new ideas, the more interesting and common kind of knowledge construction may take the form of expanding, connecting, and qualifying the network of information already in the writer's mind (cf. chap. 3). Moreover, changes of this sort can have a significant effect on texts. When we track the ideas that emerge from Jennie's prompts to do constructive planning (i.e., to target his text to a special reader and to adapt his experience to respond to a problem or to readers' needs), we find they achieve a prominent place in the final text, including the introductory and concluding paragraphs. As we saw with turn 20, the challenge to an idea Carter already held led him to qualify that idea and to counter a possible misreading by asserting its importance in a prominent place in the final text.

For Carter and some of the other 21 students, this face-to-face prompt to make a constructive planning move left an imprint on planning that can be tracked directly into the text. In table 2, students are listed in an order based on a holistic quality score (column 2) given to each session (this scoring will be discussed later). The table shows the number of direct prompts to constructive planning given by the partner followed by the number of occasions on which the planner ignored, deferred, or refused to engage with this request for constructive effort. The column entitled "Writer constructs" shows how often the writer then responded to the prompt by constructing a plan (or rehearsing one already in mind) there in the transcript. (Note that a writer could recognize a need or accept a prompt or criticism but not actually generate ideas in response.) The next column then tracks those ideas into the final text: Did the information generated in response to the prompt turn up in the student's written text? A fraction indicates that only some (e.g., two out of three) of the idea clusters mentioned in the transcript made it into text. The codes show where that information turned up. The

Table 2. Constructive Prompts from Talk to Text

Writer	Quality score	Partner prompts	Prompts refused	Writer constructs	Location in final text	Abbreviated version of prompts
Jennie	4	2	0	2	Intro, Con	Try to do in conclusion? Work on conclusion.
Carter	4	4	0	3	Intro, Con, MEx	Adapt to audience. Make real. Solution?
Liz	4	5	0	4	MEx, Con	Do not reiterate Farb. Why problem exists. Solution?
Patrick	4	2	0	2	Intro, Con	Is that a problem? Turn to a problem.
Fran	4	7	0	7	Intro, MEx, Con	Problem? Relate to context. Be specific. Important to audience?
Kate	4	3	0	2	Claim 1/2	A discourse problem? Show to audience in different light.
Han	3	0	0	0		
Ben	3	2	0	2	MEx. Con	Relate to audience?
Tomas	2	3	1	2	Paper missing	How relate to anything? Will audience know that?
Paul	2	3	0	3	Intro, Claim 2/3	Use Farb? Audience already knows.
Vince	2	4	4	1	Intro, Con	What is point? Conclusion? Just examples?
Bob	2	3	0	3	New topic	How does that relate?
Ron	1	4	3	1	Con	Purpose? Explain cause?
Linda	1	1	1	0		Your insight?
Tracy	1	1	0	1	Intro	Relate to Farb.
Sara	1	0	0	0		
Gary	0	3	0	3	Intro 2/3	What is interesting? Do for audience?
Laura	0	3	0	3	Intro, con 2/3	Purpose? Conclude?
Chanda	0	2	0	2	New topic	Purpose? Audience response?
Janine	0	2	0	1	New topic	Purpose?
Yun Ho	0	0	0	0		
Lisa	0	0	0	0		
Average for group		2.45	0.41	1.91		
for 4/3 scorers		3.13	0.00	2.75		
for 1/0 scorers		1.60	0.40	1.10		

Note. Intro = introduction; MEx = major example; Con = conclusion.
Fractions show the number of ideas used over the total constructed, when only some are used.

final column is a shorthand version of the prompts themselves, some of which came as suggestions (e.g., to "make it more real"), while others are marked as questions (e.g., "what are you going to try to do in the conclusion?").

Perhaps the most interesting observation here is that these supporters, who had little or no instruction in being collaborators, much less peer tutors, are asking questions in 82% of the sessions that call for more than knowledge-driven planning and that the answers planners make to those questions almost always show up in the text. Moreover, these responses show up in some of the most important parts of those texts—in the introduction where the problem is framed, in the conclusion where the writer's own position often appears, and in the major examples used to develop the paper. This trail from prompt to text is most visible in the top eight sessions, which received quality scores of 3 and 4. These sessions also averaged 3.13 prompts, which yielded 2.75 instances of information constructed in response. By contrast, the 10 lowest-scoring sessions averaged only 1.60 prompts with a yield of 1.10 constructive responses. (The average was 2.45 prompts yielding 1.22 constructions.) Although there is a difference in the total activity (prompts and responses) of the students with high and low quality scores, perhaps the more important figure is the impressive 89% (response/prompt) rate of yield for these prompts across groups.

It seems fair to say that collaboration is not only providing an occasion for some of the cognitive, conceptual work the instructors hoped for but that some key parts of the writer's representation and text are being brought into this social negotiation. If we read this conservatively and assume the weakest case in which the supporter's prompt simply foregrounds selected parts of a representation that already exists, that influence alone could help the writer structure this paper around salient issues or anticipate readers' responses in the subtle way Carter does from prompt 20. This data also raises an interesting question: Would prompts from a tutor or teacher yield a higher rate of response but produce a different kind of negotiation?

At any given prompt, it may be hard to assert which process is happening—new generation, network reorganization, or simply selection and foregrounding. Nevertheless, the trail from collaboration to text at these points shows that meaning is being developed as both a socially negotiated and a personally constructed representation. Looking at the entire transcript, of course, reveals other dimensions of the writer's representation built from the active interplay of cognition and context. For instance, it is not enough to assume that Carter is simply "responding" to the social context of school, to his grades, or to his collaborator's prompts in predictable ways: the "meaning" of these contextual cues is not dictated by the context itself. In constructing his own, rather complex, but coherent web of meaning, Carter turns a past success on his senior paper into a causal explanation in his "welcome to college" story. That story is itself transformed into an example of a discourse problem. And in response to Jennie's gentle prompts, Carter restructures the stories he told himself into a new text for two new readers—other freshmen and a composition instructor. Since social negotiation is likely to be a tacit interpretive process, these transcripts may reveal only the tip of the iceberg, but enough to show us that a highly constructive process is going on, the imprint of which can be seen in both plans and text. Let us now look more closely at the process itself.

II. Constructing a Representation—in Collaboration

A collaborative planning session is a sort of compression chamber for planning: some of the decisions, confusions, challenges, and epiphanies seen in an extended solo process can be telescoped into a 10–30 minute session. External influences, such as the instructor's criteria and the reader's expectations, turn up as direct prompts the writer must negotiate on the spot, while the need to explain can call the writer's own private agendas to the surface. In this section, we will look both at the process of such meaning making and at the representations these writers construct.

It is important to recognize that this study is by necessity and design a descriptive analysis, not an experiment to validate an instructional technique. In fact, we learned a good deal about how to teach collaborative planning from this close look at a relatively untutored process. Unlike an experimental curriculum study, there is no control group of solo planners and texts for comparison—indeed, we saw no good way to capture a comparable individual performance and were skeptical that the blunt instrument of holistic evaluation would tell us much about the effects assigned collaboration might be having. The most relevant comparison to make with this data is against our own expectations based on the research described in chapter 5: Do these planners fit a novice profile in which knowledge-driven planning is the default option for managing a school task? Or does collaboration take these freshmen into the rhetorical thinking the instructors hoped it would? However, the most interesting questions here cannot be answered with a yes or no, since the real focus of this study is on what these writers did with this instructional prompt—how they interpreted it within the context of this course and their own goals and strategies for writing. In fact, I will argue, one of the most important but least understood features of an instructional process like this is not the procedural package the teacher proffers, but the strategic knowledge with which individual students use it.

The Focus of Attention in Planning Talk: Coding the Transcripts

The categories of the Planner's Blackboard and the predictions from previous research on planning offer a starting point for analysis: Where are students focusing their attention? How much of that attention is devoted to generating topic information, in relation to effort spent on purpose, audience, and discourse options? The quantitative analysis will include the comments made by either the planner or supporter, telling us about the collective representation—the image of possibilities—that emerges over the course of the collaborative session. Clearly, some of these ideas will remain options that the writer may or may not use, but this collective analysis lets us see the kinds of ideas and goals that are brought under consideration as these writers plan. Since the intent of collaborative planning is not just to improve a given paper but to engage students in a supported constructive process and to help them reflect on their own thinking and collaboration, the nature of this jointly constructed representation is of special interest.

The coding scheme used to analyze these transcripts is of interest because it reflects not only the theoretical predictions embodied in the Planner's Blackboard, it shows how this metaphor was in fact interpreted by the students. As one test of reliability, the rules for identifying planning comments were elaborated and refined using student transcripts (ones not included in the analysis), and they offer revealing operational definitions of what a category like "purpose" means in this context. The unit of analysis is a conversational turn. If a turn includes more than one kind of planning statement, it is double-coded to capture each category and its abbreviated code indicated in brackets at the end of the turn.

Topic Information [info]

Statements are coded as topic information (*info*) when the student talks over ideas that he or she finds interesting and might want to include or recites a more developed discussion he or she already has in mind (see Carter, turn 32). At times students even drift away from the paper itself into sharing their own knowledge or experience with the topic. When topic information dominates the discussion to the exclusion of other concerns, we see evidence of the knowledge-driven planning strategy. (We should remember that this is on its own a valuable move supported by a number of process activities taught in composition classes, such as freewriting, journal writing, and brainstorming, which focus on the fluent generation of ideas.)[4]

Key Point and Purpose

The coding for this blackboard category distinguished between three kinds of purpose statements: key point, rhetorical purpose, and generic purpose.

Key Point [key pt]. Out of the wealth of ideas generated as topic information, these statements are ones that would serve as major claims or thesis statements (a topic plus comment) and that are in some way marked as a key point the writer wants to make (or are marked by the supporter who hears a key point and reflects it back to the writer or offers one as a suggestion). Note that this category does not include ideas that *could* function as a key point or that become marked as one *later on* in the process. As a result, this coding highlights the way key points are often constructed in the process of planning as a student moves from a network of "interesting" ideas (coded Topic Information) early in the session to a rhetorical focus on the key point he or she wants to make. For example, Patrick opens his session at turn 1 talking out a still tentative, exploratory review of the territory that will eventually yield his point:

> After reading chapters 8 and 9 of *Word Play*, the ideas that I've come up with are these. Something that struck me as most important, they've got me confused maybe, was in chapter 8 Farb quotes this guy, Ludwig Wittgenstein of Cambridge University and Wittgenstein says uh, the limits of my language mean the limits of my world and says, uh, I'll read one paragraph. [100 words of talk and reading later] I think Farb... kind of, I mean he said this and it seems to me as though he agreed with it. But he sort of contradicted himself later on. I mean with the examples of color [terms]... [*info*]

Eventually, in turn 23, Patrick hammers out the first statement of his point, which revolves around Farb's contradictory and misplaced emphasis:

> All right, my main point I suppose would have to be that Farb is very concerned with discourse between different communities and that's good an' all when you need to go to that other community. But basically, I mean the main thing that we need to understand [. . .] is communication within our own community. [*key pt*]

However, by the end of a session trying to untangle Wittgenstein (turn 40, "All right, let's start over here. What did you think this dude was saying here?"), Patrick has in fact decided to argue against Wittgenstein's later position that one must learn to accept the limitations of language. In his final text, Patrick, a first-year design student, describes how the invention of new color terms can improve communication within the design community. This new key point, which emerged near the end of the session in turn 60, is reflected in the introductory paragraph of his eventual text:

> If there was one thing I never wanted to do in a paper it would be to dispute one of the most "influential philosophers" of this century, but I disagree with Ludwig Wittgenstein's thinking concerning language and I feel obligated to show why. [from final text]

In our analysis, Patrick's first comment, tentatively exploring ideas that "stuck out," would be coded as a discussion of topic information in contrast to later comments where certain ideas are more clearly marked with the status of a key point. Patrick's pattern of exploration, followed by a marked (though still tentative and revisible) key point assertion, is common in these sessions.

Rhetorical Purpose [rh pur]. These statements set an explicit intellectual, personal, or audience-based purpose that indicates the planner's desire to produce some kind of effect. The Planner's Blackboard presents key point and purpose as separate but linked concepts (on the same blackboard), because at times writers think of their purpose in terms of asserting or presenting a given idea (a key point). That is clearly a form of purpose. But at other times, writers create what we are calling a rhetorical purpose by constructing a set of specific intellectual or rhetorical goals for this particular text. The reader may figure strongly in these rhetorical purpose statements, as in Carter's intention to "prove it to them that different writing styles exist, and I want my audience to be able to relate their own experiences to this, and maybe see how it affects them" (turn 30). Rhetorical purpose statements can also focus on a writer's personal desire to think through or answer a question or explore an issue. As Patrick puts it, "I'm writing to question what he [this 'philosopher guy'] said later on [in his career]."

Rhetorical purpose statements, then, had to meet the criterion of setting specific, substantive goals particular to this paper. The threshold for statements to enter this category was set high: comments that depended on highly general verbs such as "I want to say," "show," "describe, or "explain XYZ" were not admitted and were coded as Key Points or, if in the context discussing purpose, as Generic Purpose Statements.

Generic Purpose [gen pur]. This third purpose category (not named on the blackboards) emerged from the freshman transcripts as an important form of purpose statement. With it, writers refer to generic discourse plans used to describe the purpose or direction for the paper. Although these plans do not explicitly involve an audience or the unique intellectual goals we typically associate with rhetorical planning, these statements occur in the context of shaping the overall goals of the piece (and may be described by the writer as "my purpose" or "plan"). They define purpose in terms of whole-text text conventions and reflect the students' concern with managing the demands of a minigenre or a kind of discourse. Some plans coded as Generic Purpose plans reflect simple formulas or textbook genres such as a thesis and support paper, but other episodes show students in a sophisticated struggle with the demands of a relatively new kind of discourse, such as a problem analysis.

This category provides an important alternative to key point and rhetorical purpose as ways of representing and thinking about purpose, since it may tend to absorb the attention of students learning a new genre, perhaps to the exclusion of other versions of purpose. It also helps us examine the difference between a formulaic and a heuristic use of these generic plans. For instance, we see Patrick and his partner considering ways to carry out the generic purpose of writing his assigned problem analysis, trying to define the problem the paper will address. Talking about the barriers language creates (an example of a problem), Patrick notes that an artist and a basketball player would indeed have trouble talking about the composition of a painting; however, he concludes that this problem is "kind of obvious [. . . .] I think disagreeing with this philosopher is a little more important as far as his point" (turn 61). His partner, however, does not appear to see finding a *significant* problem as a major constraint in school writing and replies to the charge of obviousness with: "Yeah, but you can argue that just for being an argument."

Both writers are talking about purpose in terms of what the genre—a problem analysis or an argument paper—asks the writer to do, but the partner's image appears to focus on surface features more than rhetorical qualities. He interprets this generic purpose in a more limited and formulaic way. Because these generic purposes are, like other high-level goals, relatively abstract, they must be instantiated with more specific goals and key points. It is at this level of planning that students choose whether to argue with Wittgenstein or rehearse the athlete/artist barrier. Did Patrick's partner recognize this challenge to his goals? If teachers are to convey these qualitative differences to students, they may need information they normally do not have about the specific goals writers are setting for themselves and the way a generic injunction (e.g., "find a problem" or "support a thesis") is being interpreted.

Audience [aud]

These statements mention a particular audience, describe its characteristics, or (more rarely) project a reader's response. As we will see, some ways in which students use the notion of audience serve to test and elaborate their ideas, but some ways, which textbooks often sponsor, do little more than conjure up a fictional reader who is conveniently disposed to hear the points the writer plans to make.

Text Conventions [tx con]

With these statements, planners indicate their awareness of a wide range of conventional features of text such as examples, conclusions, lists; organizing plans such as point/counterpoint; design factors and visual cues such as bullets and italics; and the conventions of various genres. Unlike the plans coded as Generic Purpose, these deal with local decisions or specified parts of the text and frequently drift into a discussion of topic information. Some of these planning statements indicate the students' conscious awareness of textual patterns and options (see the discussion of examples and comparisons in Carter's session, turns 30, 35). But in other cases, these terms may be simply woven into our language for talking about content. At times, it seems that students possess a language for talking about text without the awareness or control to take full advantage of what they know about examples, conclusions, or format.

Consolidations [consl]

In these turns, two or more elements from the blackboards are consolidated in the sense of being talked about in an integrated manner. Each comment that counted as a Consolidation was also included in the counts for the two or more blackboard categories it contained. Only rarely did the planners give indications of attempting an overt, self-conscious consolidation. Occasionally, writers referred to two or more blackboard elements during a turn without integrating them. These turns were double-coded but not counted as Consolidations.

For example, Patrick and his partner eventually worked out a key point asserting that "communities are limited by language but that they shouldn't be." In turn 70, the supporter restates this point and then shifts his attention to the issue of audience—an example of a nonintegrated, double-coded comment. However, this prompt leads Patrick in turn 73 to try to consolidate his rhetorical goals with his image of a reader and to link his genre-based purpose (to discuss and undermine a quote) with specific features of a text (examples, conclusion)—a comment in which these concerns are consolidated. (In the text, consolidations are indicated by the slashes between categories).

70 S: Limitations need to be broken down. Okay. All right, I kind of think so. And you're writing to this philosopher guy. [*key pt, aud, R*]

71 Patrick: Well, he's dead. I mean I'm writing against his philosophy to... damn I don't know who I'm writing to 'cause he's dead. [*aud, R*]

72 S: You could just say like to anybody that agrees with his philosophy. [*aud, R*]

73 Patrick: I'm writing to the people who are going to listen to his philosophy. I'm writing to question what he said later on [in his career]. What about this? How am I to write my paper? I guess I'm going to write about... to discuss his quote, and then I'm going to use the examples that Farb has [of how communities adapt]. And that's going against what he says. And then I'll just conclude with, basically I'll just write with the examples. I don't know about my conclusion. [*rh pur/aud/gen pur/tx con, R*]

74 S: Okay. [*off*]

75 Patrick: I'll just conclude with the main point about how this isn't true what he says. [*key pt/tx con*]

75 S: All right. It sounds like we worked something out. Okay. [*off*]

Off [off]

Collaborative planning sessions include a good deal of valuable social talk as well as revealing metacomments about the planning itself. However, since these do not make a substantive contribution to the representation or plan itself, they were coded as Off for this analysis. For the same reason, prompts, such as "Who is your audience?," or fragments, such as, "My purpose, ahh..." that mentioned a blackboard category but failed to supply any propositional content were also coded as Off and not included in the counts for the blackboards, since they add little to the network of meaning. Off also includes uncodable fragments.

Interrater reliability, calculated by Cohen's Kappa among three raters on 20% of the transcripts, averaged 73% agreement across all categories plus all major combinations (to account for occasional double-coding of episodes).[5] Instances of disagreement were discussed and resolved among the three coders.

Constructive Planning Scores (0–6)

To make quantitative differences in students' use of the planning blackboards more apparent, we created an operational definition of constructive planning in which each session was given a score from 0 to 6 based on the amount of attention given to each of the three categories of purpose (rhetorical, key point, and generic) and to the audience, text convention, and consolidation blackboards—that is, to effort that took the students beyond knowledge-driven planning. Sessions received a point for each area in which their number of comments was at or above the average number for the group. To eliminate the skewing caused by a few high-scoring sessions, the modal rather than the mean average was used.

Reflection [R]

An important goal of collaborative planning is to create opportunities and support for critical reflection on one's own ideas and one's own thinking process, both during and after the session. For this analysis, reflection was operationally defined as any turn during the session that included (1) an evaluative comment or a problem identification, (2) a justification or request for justification of plans or ideas, or (3) the generation or consideration of plans or ideas marked as an alternative to those already posed. A reflective turn is marked by *R* on the coded transcripts. Interrater reliability for identifying reflection was 89% (pair-wise comparisons).

Quality Scores (0–4)

This scoring let us compare the preceding analytical descriptions of collaboration against a more holistic judgment of their intellectual quality and usefulness. Although we could have based the quality of these collaborations on the instructor's grades for the paper, we felt that the tangled skein of relations between paper grades and collaborations would be hard to interpret with confidence. For example, apparently unsuccessful sessions sometimes do their job by leading students to a complete change of topic or to later thinking we never see. On the other hand, a successful freshman session might do its job by raising a C− paper to a C+ or even by starting to expand the student's image of the task for the next paper. Paper grades are also social tools teachers use to challenge or encourage individual students or to emphasize the importance of some particular feature of an assignment. A session like Carter's may be productive, even impressive, in some areas, but ignore other criteria, such as explicit use of the source text on which the paper is graded. Paper grades are included in table 4, Quality Scores.

However, for this descriptive study, we felt the most appropriate and most sensitive quality measure would be a teacher's judgment of the session itself.

We asked four judges to read the transcripts and rate the generative quality of the sessions as if they had overheard their own students planning and were holistically evaluating the quality of the discussion. The four judges rated each transcript on a simple high/low scale for generative quality, so the maximum score (high by all judges) was a 4, the minimum (low by all judges) was a 0. Agreement among the judges averaged 75% (by pair-wise comparisons).

Going Beyond Knowledge Telling

Did this collaborative process lead to rhetorical, constructive planning? The coding and scoring schemes described above were designed to answer this predictable teacher's question. And they offer some encouraging answers. However, to anticipate the discussion, let me say that the transcripts also challenged the adequacy of these categories to describe this planning process. Students in these sessions were not going about business as usual merely planning a text. They were also learning new ways to plan and to write, and in doing so, they were interrogating, interpreting, and reflecting on a social/rhetorical situation. The remainder of this chapter, then, will propose a model of what *planning while learning* entails, and the analysis will cover not only the differences we expected to find (i.e., differences between knowledge-driven and constructive planning processes), but also differences in students' strategic negotiation of this event (i.e., differences created by limited versus challenging goals and by writers' reflective awareness).

Given the social and cognitive assumptions of collaborative planning, the analysis begins with the simple question: Where are students focusing their attention? Has the pattern of knowledge-driven planning predicted from other studies been altered in any significant way? Table 3 records the total turns for each session, divided into those coded as Off and as Substantive (i.e., the remaining comments). When the Substantive category is broken down in the columns that follow, we see that students' comments are distributed across the blackboards in a somewhat surprising way. Substantive talk appears in all the categories listed across the top, including consolidation and reflection. The bottom three rows of the table show the total and the mean number of turns devoted to each category. The final row allows a closer comparison among the categories by showing what percent of the substantive comments each category garnered.

Students appear to be going beyond the default moves of knowledge-

Table 3. Planning Categories

	Total turns	Off	Substantive turns	Information	Key point	Generic purpose	Rhetorical purpose	Audience	Text conventions	Consolidations	Reflections
Jennie	127	68	59	7	13	8	13	25	23	23	39
Carter	134	66	68	17	5	6	10	16	33	13	34
Liz	103	43	60	1	8	48	4	12	3	14	37
Patrick	75	23	52	21	17	11	1	7	3	7	28
Fran	56	10	46	24	3	0	0	9	9	2	27
Kate	57	12	45	26	4	0	0	8	7	0	19
Han	65	18	47	17	27	1	0	2	13	8	29
Ben	79	35	44	30	4	0	1	6	3	2	11
Tomas	90	33	57	32	10	1	2	7	8	1	4
Paul	89	42	47	26	9	2	0	5	13	4	28
Vince	101	62	39	13	15	7	0	3	12	6	17
Bob	40	16	24	17	2	0	5	5	0	4	11
Ron	70	35	35	7	8	5	0	5	16	3	12
Linda	38	23	15	4	6	0	0	5	1	1	7
Tracy	43	24	19	5	3	2	0	4	8	3	6
Sara	24	14	10	3	2	0	1	2	2	0	0
Gary	19	2	17	1	3	4	2	7	6	5	8
Laura	24	11	13	0	5	0	2	5	8	5	2
Chanda	34	11	23	7	4	2	0	4	8	2	1
Janine	24	9	15	6	3	1	0	1	4	0	1
Yun Ho	21	9	12	3	1	3	0	3	6	3	0
Lisa	16	6	10	1	1	0	0	4	6	2	2
Total turns	1,329	572	757	268	153	101	41	145	192	108	323
Mean	60.41	26.00	34	12.18	6.95	4.59	1.86	6.59	8.73	4.91	14.68
Percent of substantive				35%	20%	13%	5%	19%	25%	14%	43%

driven planning that we might have expected. Moreover, when we collapse the three kinds of purpose statements into one category (see fig. 6), we see that purpose, at 39% of the comments, is even gaining slightly more attention than information at 35%. Audience accounts for 19% and text conventions for 25%. Collaborative planning is clearly drawing students' attention beyond content and correctness and to matters, such as purpose, which the research reviewed above would not lead us to expect from either solo planning or peer review. (Remember that comments that simply repeated a prompt for purpose or audience, etc., without additional propositional content, were counted as off.)

From our point of view as educators, these results were clearly good news. Collaborative planning appeared to be intervening in the process itself at a generative moment, to be expanding students' rhetorical awareness, prompting concerns that had not been raised in the pre-session self-interviews, and generating knowledge that made its way into important places in the text. However, the study was not designed as a test of a polished pedagogy (it was taught by instructors using collaborative planning for the first time, without the emphasis on being a supporter or on reflecting, both

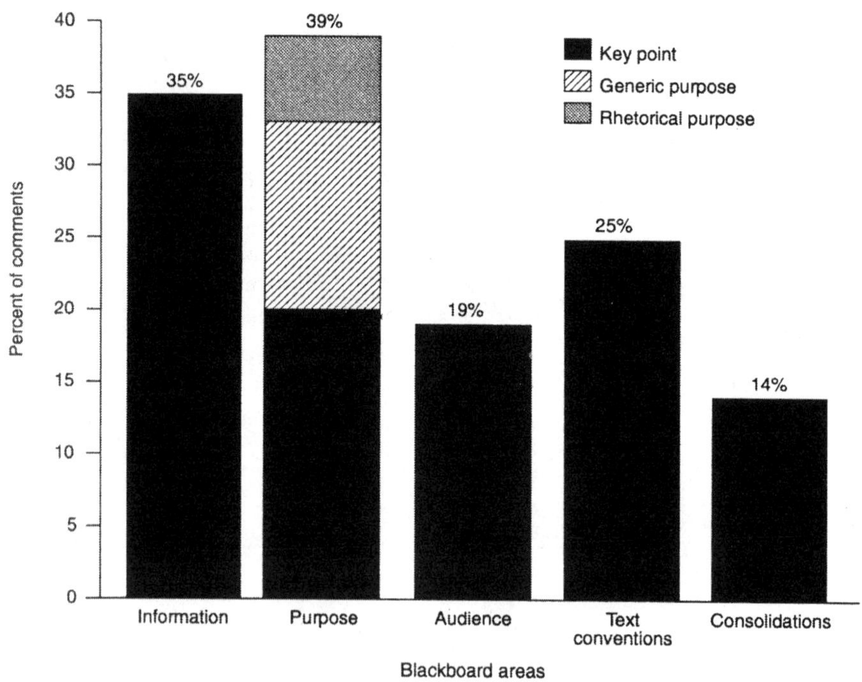

Figure 6. Focus of attention

of which became essential parts of later instruction). Because our inquiry focused on how students interpret and use this process, the important question here is, What can these patterns of planning and thinking tell us about the nature of students' constructive process?

Although students are going beyond the patterns of knowledge-driven planning one might have expected from novice writers, a look at the transcripts suggests they are not performing like experts more generally nor even in ways their instructors may have been expecting. The facts of the matter suggest a more complicated and revealing interaction between writing and learning to write in school. Consider, for example, how the collaborators went about constructing a purpose, starting with the different frequencies for the three kinds of purpose plans (fig. 6). In this composition class, one might have expected to see attention given to rhetorical purposes: the instructors encouraged and valorized the creation of unique personal, intellectual, or audience-based rhetorical goals for a text. The assignment and the criteria for evaluation invited such thinking. However, the extended attention Carter paid to such rhetorical goals at turns 18, 30 and 76–82 was not typical. These concerns did not seem to be particularly relevant to most students: only 5% of the total comments are devoted to discussing rhetorical goals. Are students unable/unwilling to do necessary rhetorical planning, or is there another logic to their use of this collaboration that frequency figures do not show? (The breakdown of comments in table 3 lets us compare Carter's activity in each category, e.g., 10 rhetorical purpose comments, to the group's mean number of comments per blackboard, e.g., 1.86 Rhetorical Purpose comments, found at the bottom of the table.)

From one perspective, the attention paid to Generic Purposes (13%), coupled with the slight glance given to broader Rhetorical Purposes (5%), seems at odds with the rhetorical emphasis of the course. However, a closer look at how students and teachers talked about purpose suggests that representing one's purpose in terms of genre may have been a pragmatic, successful move in this context, despite the announced goals of the class. Even though rhetorical planning is often necessary and probably helped Carter turn his insights into a well-supported argument, did this freshman assignment really require such planning to do a credible job? It is even possible that Carter's preoccupation with the personal, realistic aspect of the task led him to ignore another aspect—using material from Farb—that, as we will see, his instructor saw as necessary. Carter may have dropped one constraint in order to deal with another. Another reasonable hypothesis is that the "arhetorical" situation of school writing and the power relations of student speaking to teacher do not provide—some would say prevent the possibility of—any motivation for the rhetorical thinking we wish to encourage. To some extent, this is undeniable, especially for a short paper in a freshman course. And yet we do see such thinking even here. We also see it increase as students take more control over their own learning (see chap. 8) and as they discover meaningful ways to assert their authority within the intellectual community of teacher and learner (Greene, 1990b).[6] Although social and cultural critique can point out forces that shape and may at times dominate thinking, it is a great oversimplification to assume that these abstract forces predictably dictate writers' constructive acts. Reality is more resistant.

Another interpretation, which I think the data supports, gives more weight to students' reasonable attempts to negotiate the rhetorical situation. At this point in the course, most students are clearly struggling with the new "genre" of problem analysis that encourages them to find and define a meaningful problem for which there is no easy solution. Problem finding and analysis is both a rhetorical act done in relation to someone (Freire, 1989; Young, Becker, & Pike, 1970) and a complex discourse convention (Carter, 1988). Under these conditions, concentrating on the intellectually demanding purposes associated with this convention *as a convention* may represent a sensible way of negotiating the demands of the course and a sensible learning move, even though students may not be fully aware of the options they had or the decisions they made. (This also suggests that if teachers expect students to do significant rhetorical thinking about audience and purpose—when those students are also learning a new genre or a new topic—the teachers may need to do more than merely "expect" or create assignments that "invite" such thinking.)

III. A Model of the Writer as Learner

If the planning process observed here is indeed a learner's process—an overdetermined, strategic, adaptive, and variable social cognitive event—how shall we account for this complexity? Let us consider for a moment some of our options. Our standard methods of analyzing students' performance are likely to be too unidimensional or abstract to account for even the glimpse of the process these transcripts afford. Performance measures, such as quality scores, paper grades, or the frequency of constructive moves, speak to what happened but not why it happened. Broad social explanations, on the other hand, are eloquent on the possible whys—locating the logic of the process in selected cultural or social forces beyond the students' control or attributing it to the students' status within (or outside) of a presumed discourse community. The satisfying sweep of such explanations, however, is achieved at the expense of sensitivity to strong situational and individual differences. Social critiques raise awareness about important potential forces that may be acting on students (e.g., the arhetorical, asymmetrical power relations that structure much school writing), but the generalized level of analysis at which they do their work is impervious to contradictory data. More importantly, such methods of analysis are unable to account for the role of students as agents negotiating these social contexts.

Another option is a descriptive analysis guided by the model of expert/novice differences that initiated the study. It can achieve some of our goals: it will make our theory building more responsible to the data and more sensitive to the multiple forces that can influence what writers do. However, it cannot adequately explain the logic of performances that do not fit these expectations. Expert/novice comparisons (i.e., fine-grained analyses of expert and novice performances in different settings) arose as a way to avoid "deficit" or categorical theories of student performance by concentrating on what people at different levels of experience actually do. Although such comparisons are critical to theory building and to setting educational goals, such comparisons alone have an important limitation. They do not adequately model the *logic of writers in the process of learning to write differently.*

A theory of a writer as a learner would foreground the fact we are witnessing an educational process, not just a writing performance in which producing text is the only objective. It would recognize that learners are likely to take risks, make a guess, take a stab, or rely on old skills until proven ineffective. (This differs from what a merely inexperienced, novice journalist, for instance, might do. We need to make finer distinctions within the category of novice that can recognize, for instance, how a writer experienced in one domain, an "expert," can be a novice in another and may also choose to act as a learner.) Such a theory would recognize expert student performance and offer diagnostic insights into less effective learning efforts (Bereiter & Scardamalia, 1982). It would help us build an image of learner expertise, of success and difficulty that is sensitive to this process of developing a new understanding about writing and/or about a particular form of discourse. In this study, for example, students appeared actively engaged not only in understanding a new task and "reading" the class but in testing the water—would their normal strategies learned in other contexts do the job? Collaborative sessions (like papers written early in the course) can be an informative trial run to see what strategies transfer, what strategies do not, and what sort of meaning this new situation requires.

A theory of how writers as learners construct meaning must recognize that more than one kind of work is going on. A *model of a student learning to write* would assert that in such situations two kinds of meaning making matter—in addition to the final text—and that performance may be an indicator of a learner's uncertain strategic choices.

1. ***Students are building a representation of the task.*** This representation is not only a broad theory of the task (an image of what college writing, a problem analysis or a paper for English, might entail), but also a more immediate working representation of what this particular assignment entails (including the goals the writer chooses to shoot for). Students report that talking over the task is one of the most important ways they use collaborative planning. In a more indirect way, challenges, prompts, and questions from a partner can work tacitly to expand or alter a student's theory or image of the task, even though they may have no material effect on the current plan or paper.
2. ***Students are building a representation of current meaning—the basis for text.*** This evolving understanding is the foundation for what writers will do and say in a paper. However, this representation (and the process of constructing it) is likely to be a site of conflicts, possibilities, and ambiguities that shape the student's text in both visible and invisible ways.

In such events, the logic of students' performance will be more visible in this representation than in the eventual text. Moreover, the final text may be a very uncertain guide to students' ability. A student model calls for broader, more informed evaluation by making the following assertion.

3. ***Students' performance will reflect how they are interpreting the instruction they receive and how they are choosing to negotiate the multiple demands of this rhetorical situation.*** For example, to understand these collaborative planners we would want to look at which aspects of the rhetorical problem students attend to (e.g., which blackboards) . We need to examine how different students interpret and use the instruction itself (e.g., the planner/supporter roles and the blackboard metaphor). (These differences will be reflected in part in both Constructive Planning and Reflection scores.) And we would want to consider the generative quality of students' planning sessions. (These differences will be reflected in part in Quality scores.)

In the spirit of this expanded analysis, we will start with students who "fit" the model of expert/novice differences, that is, for whom this model seems to offer a useful and well-supported account. Then we will look at some performances that complicate and challenge these expectations and require a more finely-grained strategic analysis that draws attention to how students negotiate this situation. I hope to show how this additional level of analysis, focused on a student's strategic knowledge, can make a significant difference in understanding not just what these writers did, but why.

Constructive Versus Knowledge-Driven Planners: An Expert/Novice Analysis

Planners in this study differed in some ways the research had prepared us to expect. Table 4 lists students in terms of the holistic, generative quality of their planning session (in column 1), followed by scores they received for constructiveness, reflection, and the paper. In general, the planning sessions divide into those who marked by generative talk, constructive strategies, and reflectiveness and those with lower scores in all these areas. Some students look more like expert planners than others.

A Constructive, High-Scoring Session

Carter's planning session (see the Appendix) has the earmarks of an engaged and productive educational experience. Above average in all six categories expected in constructive planning, his constructive score puts him in the company of five other students who earned high scores of 5 or 6 (see previous discussion of scoring). This planning session also earned the highest quality score of 4, rated as having a high overall generative quality by all four judges. As a benchmark for what a productive planning session might look like for these freshmen, Carter and Jennie's collaboration shows writers constructing an image of both the text and the task. and it fits a reasonable expectation that a high quality score and constructive, rhetorical thinking should go hand in hand.

Carter and Jennie are as much involved in building a representation of the task as they are in constructing the current text; that is, they are collaborating on how to write in college not just what to say here. Because Carter's effort to get a grip on college writing is itself his paper topic, we see him talk about his theory of the task in unusually explicit detail, identifying what he sees as the key features of the task (a set that may differ from that of his instructors) and turning those general criteria into working goals for his paper. At the same time, this representation is clearly a sort of working hypothesis, subject to expansion by Jennie and disconfirmation from his teachers. For instance, the final discussion about "the most interesting part" of Carter's paper (turns 85–93) explores a qualitative dimension of this task, and the writers begin to use their own responses to predict what will interest readers.

Carter's content is also undergoing development. His initial self-interview shows that his major ideas were all present in some form before meeting

Table 4. Quality Scores

	Quality score	Constructive score	Percent reflections	Paper grade[a]
Jennie	4	6	31%	a
Carter	4	6	25%	c+
Liz	4	5	36%	D+
Patrick	4	4	37%	C
Fran	4	2	48%	B
Kate	4	2	33%	B+
Han	3	3	45%	a
Ben	3	2	14%	F
Tomas	2	4	4%	a−
Paul	2	5	31%	b+
Vince	2	4	17%	a−
Bob	2	2	28%	C
Ron	1	5	17%	d−
Linda	1	2	18%	C+B−
Tracy	1	3	14%	b−
Sara	1	1	0%	B−
Gary	0	4	42%	a−
Laura	0	5	8%	D
Chanda	0	2	3%	C−
Janine	0	0	4%	D+
Yun Ho	0	2	0%	b−
Lisa	0	0	13%	D

[a]Uppercase from class A; lowercase from class B.

Jennie. Collaboration did not produce the bouleversement or "ah ha" some students expect as evidence of change. As Carter puts it, the session helped him "think a little bit more about my examples [. . .] specifics [. . .] audience [. . .] and definitely my text conventions." At the same time, the examples Jennie elicited and her prompt to build a more useful conclusion produced material that turned up in key places in the paper (as we saw in the earlier analysis). Those bits that helped him frame his own experience as a shared problem may have had a more significant impact on his representation than Carter realized.

In general, the expert/novice model (in which Carter and Jennie are expert learners) gives us a useful way to understand their performance. However, their performance also raises a problem to which we will return later: the quality of the planning does not always predict the grade on the paper.

A Knowledge-Driven, Low-Scoring Process

Janine's session is a contrast in terms of both the work going on and the scores received. As tables 3 and 4 show, her planning is below the average in all categories, receiving a constructive score of 0 and a quality score of 0 (i.e., no judge rated it as a high-quality session). Her rambling knowledge-driven process repeatedly overrides the supporter's tentative prompts for constructive or transforming moves. Looking for more focus from Janine, the supporter prompts her with a tentative topic statement, then a request for a comparison, and finally a straight request for a main point or purpose. But Janine is still in the process of exploring her own knowledge and responds by plunging back into the incidents and examples she wants to draw on, responding with either topic information or a loose and baggy key point on 7 of her 10 substantive remarks.

4 S: How are you going to compare it [body language], like use different words, maybe like [. . .] [*gen pur*]

5 Janine: Well, the thing is, um, I'm gonna show from my experience with acting, like on the stage, like as far as how portraying a character and how that you're more aware of your facial expressions and your body movements on the stage than in real life. Like real life you're aware of things, but not as, you're constantly aware of them, as when you're portraying a character in a play. And, um, because when you're on the stage you're, as well as words but your facial expression and your body movements mean a lot too because once you're on the stage you're trying to look like a real character to the audience. [*info*]

6 S: Wait, I understand that, but what does that have to do with... I don't, I guess I don't understand what your... could you just give me like one sentence of your main purpose? [*key pt*]

Although Janine has found a wellspring of personally relevant ideas, her planning fails to focus or transform her stream of associations to and examples of body language into an idea she can articulate for herself or others. Her knowledge-driven process in this session could not deal with the contradictory and multiple connections in her own thinking about body language, projection on the stage, and unintentional emotional leakage that occurs off stage in conversation. The paper she eventually turns in is on a different topic (a topic that was discussed both by her partner and by Farb).

A Mixed Session

Vince offers us a third profile that is closer to the average for this group, with a constructive score of 4 and a quality score of 2. His quality score is perhaps read most accurately as a mixed performance in which half of the judges credited it with a generative process, but half did not. A closer look suggests why. The important educational work in this session is the friendly interrogation of Vince's representation of the task. In two separate episodes, Vince's laid-back but direct partner, Tomas, draws attention to Vince's limited aspirations, challenges his assumptions, and asks for more. This is the sort of advice—straight talk from a peer—that teachers hope will come out of collaboration:

16 S: Yeah. What is your key point? [*off*]

17 Vince: Well, it's just to discuss how this [the use of idioms and clichés] comes up in life, and how people just use it to avoid like say... [*key pt*]

18 S: Are you gonna be saying, "This is good, this is bad." What are you gonna be saying? [*key pt*]

19 Vince: Well, I'm just... I'm not gonna be saying... I'm not gonna be making any kind of judgment. I'm just gonna like discuss it. Really, I think the paper's gonna be a little too short to be into making judgments. There's also another reason why I think people do it. Sometimes they do it to avoid. . . [*gen pur* and *key pt*]

20 S: I don't know. It doesn't seem like much of a point to me. It doesn't sound like you're making a point. [*gen pur*]

21 Vince: Well, I'm just discussing something. Well, it's my—That's my purpose is to *discuss* this. [*gen pur*]

22 S: Okay. Okay. Sure. [*off*]

23 Vince: All right? [*off*]

24 S: Sure. [*off*]

25 Vince: Thanks Tomas. [laughs] Wish you were marking this paper. What an agreeable guy. No. Well, my purpose... to discuss this. This point—this topic... this situation. [*off*]

S: Yes. [*off*]

Unlike Carter, Vince does not appear to have subjected his image of the task to much scrutiny before this moment, choosing to rely on his "standard" strategy (turn 37). Hoping for a contribution from Tomas, he is instead steered back to the central problem: he has a topic but no point to make and no rhetorical plan for doing more than knowledge telling.

37 Vince: Now. My text conventions. Ah... I was planning just... Well, they're sort of like a standard way I write my papers. I just—I just—You know—start out with an introduction. I usually give some examples, and—and—you know—I mean, I finish it up with a conclusion. [*tx con, R*]

38 S: Hm-hm. [*off*]

39 Vince: You have any input here, Tomas? [*off*]

40 S: What would you conclude? I mean, you... I haven't really seen any conclusion you'd come to yet. [*gen pur, R*]

41 Vince: Well, I know. That's why we're talking about it. See, you're supposed to help me, Tomas. [*gen pur, R*]

42 S: Well, I'm just... [*off*]

43 Vince: Oh, no. [*off*]

44 S: I was thinking if you had a more definite key point—maybe—maybe you could have a more definite conclusion here. [*gen pur, R*]

45 Vince: Well, yeah. Ah... I mean, I—I do... In my mind, see, I have a key point. I know—I know what I want to discuss. [*off, R*]

46 S: There's a difference between having it in your mind and on the paper. [*off, R*]

47 Vince: Yeah. A whole grade difference. [Laughs] You know. Whatever's in my mind's not gonna get me an A on the course. Ah... That's beside the point. I mean, I know what I'm gonna discuss; it's how people use idiomatic speech. [*key pt, R*]

In terms of our model of the writer as learner, this collaborative session is doing important work on the first task—challenging Vince's comfortable and limited representation of the task of writing. And maybe that is enough to expect from a 10-minute session with a friend. On the other hand, Vince does not in the end take responsibility for extending his image of the task—he relies on his skills of social negotiation to get Tomas' tacit acceptance:

(80) S: So what I get from this is that—that you're just gonna go over certain examples, that's all the paper is gonna be... [*gen pur*]

(81) Vince: Yeah. [*off*]

(82) S: Go over certain examples of... [*off*]

(83) Vince: Yeah. But it's gonna... I mean... Yes. That's about it. [*off*]

As a result, this session contributes little to our second desired outcome—to building an expanded representation of the writer's meaning or a more developed text. As we will discuss, the A's Vince receives with his well-developed knowledge-driven planning may have called both such effort and the value of learning different strategies into question.

Limited Versus Challenging Goals: A Strategic Analysis

The three profiles of planning we have just seen fit an understandable pattern of expert/novice differences; that is, they differ in their use of knowledge-driven versus constructive planning and in the extent to which each pattern of planning meets the rhetorical goals of the assignment, which asked students to engage with a relatively complex rhetorical problem in a purposeful, reader-sensitive way. For a number of students, the high, low, or mixed scores for constructive activity run parallel to high, low, or mixed quality scores for the session, and the expert/novice paradigm helps us describe the difference teachers judged holistically. However, it is the cases that do not fit this pattern to which I want to turn now, because in complicating the picture, they challenge some reasonable, if convenient, assumptions we may make as educators.

In teaching, in evaluation, and in studies like this, it is normal to focus on large and obvious dimensions of practice: the papers one can grade or analyze and the activities or behaviors one can teach, observe, and measure. There are good reasons to do this. The bottom line in evaluation is finally the paper a writer can produce. And in teaching, our claims for the value of one method over another need to rest on reliable and repeatable measures of what was done (Hillocks, 1986). However, these standard approaches and their methods of analysis may be missing something important when they tell us what the writer as student *did* without an understanding of *why*.[7]

As we will see in the benchmark cases below, a description of strategies and/or knowledge alone cannot always offer an adequate explanation. The students in this study who challenge the pattern do so because of the goals they bring to this session. Because of those goals, a session devoted almost exclusively to knowledge-driven planning was the basis for a high-quality discussion, violating the expert pattern. Yet another session that appeared to be constructive (according to the scoring system) was a low-quality exercise.

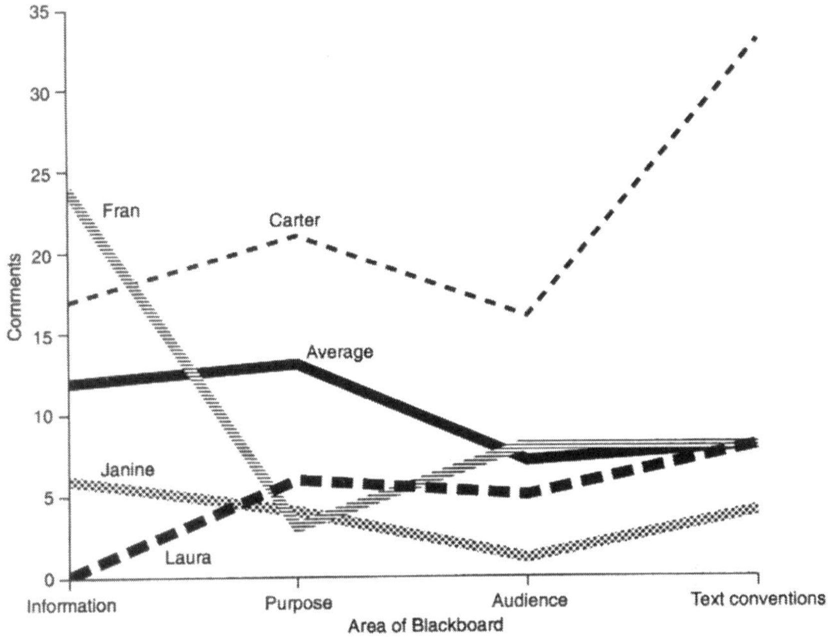

Figure 7. Benchmarks of difference

Figure 7 lets us plot these apparent contradictions graphically. Across the top of the graph, we see Carter's frequent use of all the blackboards (17 planning episodes devoted to topic information, 21 to purpose, 16 to audience, and 33 to text conventions). Janine's line runs along the bottom; and the average frequency for the group is plotted with the heavy line running near the middle. (These figures are taken from table 3.)

Limited Goals

Now consider Laura. She takes a relatively low road across this graph with 0 planning episodes devoted to topic information, 7 to purpose, 5 to audience, and 8 to text conventions (see fig. 7). Although she is somewhat below the mean average in her use of most of the blackboards (see table 3), the more lenient modal average used to calculate her constructive score gives her a favorable score of 5. This stands in apparent contrast to the low quality score of 0 she received from the judges who read her transcript (table 4). If Laura is carrying out the planning activity her instructor requested (attending to the various areas of the blackboard), why do the teacher/judges fail to value the result? And why does her graph take such a nose dive at the category of Topic Information? A closer look that takes account of the writer's goals suggests a rigorous sort of logic behind this performance.

Laura shows us a schema-driven planning strategy, as efficient as any alchemist could desire, for turning a simple idea into a five-paragraph theme. It starts (she tells us in the initial self-interview) with the discovery of an assertion. While reading Farb, she "came to the conclusion that our language is basically limited and we have a problem with that [. . .] because there are not enough words in the English language [to explain all we know]." By the time her brief, 24-turn collaboration begins, this observation has been transformed into a thesis that will be stated in the introduction, then lead to three points, each with supporting examples, to be neatly wrapped up with a conclusion. In such schema-driven planning, topic knowledge is called in to fill in the template; the five-paragraph discourse schema packages ideas in such a clearly defined way that the structure itself becomes generative—a thesis in search of examples. In turn 13, this schema-driven plan confronts and briskly co-opts the problem analysis assignment, which, ironically enough, had been designed to conflict with a pat thesis and support plan.

12 S: How are you going to write it ? [*tx con*]

13 Laura: First I'm going to make the introduction, which states the problem or the purpose of writing it. Then I'll have my supporting ideas, which are the problems. And then I'll conclude it, and I don't think I'm going to try and solve it or give a solution because I don't think there is one besides changing our entire language. [*tx con/rh pur*]

14 S: But wouldn't that be a solution?... [*tx con*]

15 Laura: Yeah, but it's sort of unrealistic to change the entire English language. [*rh pur*]

Notice how Laura deftly inserts the instructor's request for a problem into her five-paragraph theme schema—her supporting ideas will mention problems, and since the problem is too big to solve, her thesis can itself serve as the conclusion. This formulaic schema appears to assimilate the prompts of the Planner's Blackboard into its agenda as well. At turn 6, her partner's skepticism about the broad, unfocused audience of "everyone" prompts Laura to a move used by a number of freshmen. She simply redefines the audience as people who are interested in her topic.

6 Laura: Well then... I don't know. All right my audience is to... This is going to be directed towards students that don't realize that the English language has so many flaws. [*aud/key pt*]

7 S: All right. [*off*]

In essence, the audience is a shadow cast by Laura's topic and thesis. As a function of the point she intends to make, it plays little role in constructing or testing the plan or challenging her conclusions. Her partner appears to share Laura's strongly schema-driven approach to the paper, prompting her for supporting ideas, organization, conclusion, and length—wrapping up the session with approval after 24 brief turns. The paper follows this plan closely.

Although these transcripts did record a few sessions that deftly avoided planning by treating the session as a perfunctory exercise or a campy social event, Laura's tape does not suggest a desire to resist or avoid the demands of the assignment. Laura and others like her may be operating with the confidence that they are doing precisely the task the instructor had in mind. Although Laura is considering the *issues* her instructor requested, the limited *goals* she sets for herself are so easily satisfied by surface features of the text, that attention to audience and purpose loses much of its meaning. In the same vein, there is nothing wrong with a schema-driven strategy per se, but in this case, Laura has invoked a schema with rather limited aspirations and criteria in a situation that calls for more critical and constructive thinking. To understand the low quality of Laura's session and the mixed evaluation of Vince's ("I'm just discussing something"), we need to look not only at the strategies they invoke but the goals they are setting for themselves. The main difference between these two may well be the partner: Vince's partner challenged his image of the task, Laura's bought into a familiar plan. In the six cases that received low quality scores from all four judges, we see the signs of limited engagement—the total number of turns, blackboard and reflective comments are typically below average. The problem with these "problem cases" is knowing whether students' strategies stem from limited engagement or personal investment (as the cause) or whether such limited engagement is itself a result of the goals students give themselves. Because goals are so rarely made public, students like Laura may continue to assume their tried-and-true high school goals are acceptable even if a given paper was not.

Like Carter ("welcome to college writing"), Laura is receiving an introduction to certain features of academic discourse. But if our analysis were to stop with this fact—to see, for instance, all these students as the product of a culture of recitation and five-paragraph themes, determined by their own assumptions, placed in a power relationship that compresses the scope of their authority, operating as the uncertain initiates to a frequently mystifying discourse—if we were to look no deeper than the social, contextual reality these students are likely to share, we would be missing an important part of the picture. It will take a deeper, finer-grained analysis to distinguish among these students who, for all they share, are handling school in significantly different ways. This strategic analysis will let us build an explanatory account of why students differ based in part on the different ways students are reading, interpreting, and, in a sense, constructing not only textual meaning but the teacher's instructions and their theory of the task. It would show us one way personal agency operates within the powerful, shaping context of school as some freshmen writers set, reflect on, question, and revise their own goals and test and modify their strategies, while other students cling to old formulas by avoiding engagement (Vince) or perhaps by failing to see the alternatives that exist (Laura).

Challenging Goals and Reflective Processes

If a strategic analysis that recognizes students' goals can account for the logic of some low performers (based on quality scores), how can we account for the high-quality sessions that do little constructive planning? Figure 7 plots the performance of Fran who (like Kate and Ben on table 4) received a high quality score from the judges but gave scant attention to the rhetorical elements of her plan (particularly her point and purpose). Fran's session exemplifies an energetically goal-directed collaboration but one in which her goal is not to shape and develop a paper but to explore ideas, examine assumptions, and to precipitate an issue out of the clouds of her ideas. Fran's goals (for the collaborative process itself) are not the ones the instructors had in mind—hoping students would use collaboration to elaborate and test an initial plan in this new, more rhetorical context. Still at an early point in her writing, Fran treats collaboration as an occasion for discovery. At the same time, she is willing to engage with a demanding image of the task—one that expects her to find a real issue—and to accept and wrestle with goals she cannot yet meet. Like Patrick, trying to work out his answer to Wittgenstein ("My thoughts are all jumbled, but that's good"), Fran is willing to accept the tension and uncertainty generated by hanging on to high expectations. Unlike Vince ("I'm just gonna like discuss it"), Fran accepts the gambit each time her partner poses a difficult question. The apparent contradiction in Fran's high quality but low rhetorical performance is resolved when we we have access to the writer's goals—when we see this as a goal-directed strategic process in which the student put off the constructive planning the teacher expected, while accepting the challenge of finding a problem.

However, I want to argue that the logic of this performance emerges even more clearly when we look at a third aspect of Fran's strategic knowledge—at the strategic or metacognitive awareness she is bringing to this session as she monitors her own thinking process and considers her options. Look for a moment at not only the rambling path of Fran's conversation but at the way she is monitoring and reflecting on the process. Fran's session brings us in on the genesis of a plan. As she says in her self-interview before the collaborator arrives, "I really don't know what I'm doing my paper on, but that's all right, 'cause that's what I'm here for." The starting point, she tells us, is what "stuck out in my mind" when she reviewed Farb. This appears to include a sense that society is linked (somehow) to language, followed by a jumble of interesting examples (of something)—for example, Apaches and Amazons with strange classification systems, German words that do not translate, a Connecticut roommate whose abrupt "Northeastern" style made her seem cold. Out of all of this, Fran is trying to find or define a problem, supported by a persistent and faithfully optimistic partner (whose occasional interjections appear between /slashes/):

30 S: It seems that all these things are the result of some problem, but what could it be?... [*info, R*]

31 Fran: The larger problem or a smaller problem? Larger problem... people would just—people aren't aware of the way people talk and... / aren't they?/ in other communities necessarily. /well... / They don't quite realize everything... I mean, sure if they'd been there for a while, they would get to know it, but just like going somewhere else... like... people from... [*info, R*]

32 S: (Begins to speak with a Southern accent) Well, everybody's heard about how everybody talks down South, I mean I knew about that and I've never been there, well, I've been there, but I was too young to know. [*info, R*]

32 Fran: Yeah. (laughs) [*off*]

33 S: Well, the very fact that I know, I mean, doesn't necessarily help me. So I don't know if the problem is awareness of how they talk. [*info, R*]

34 Fran: What I was thinking was the people that go... like someone from... like out in the country, he doesn't really hear a lot because they're out in the country and separated from everything and then they go to the city and they try to communicate... [*info*]

35 S: Why can't you make a drawing (laughs)? [Fran is a design student.] [*tx con*]

36 Fran: It's subconscious, well it's not subconscious, I don't think about it as drawings, I just start drawing and my drawings kind of relate to what I'm saying. By the way, there's lots of arrows and boxes on my page here. When these people will go to like the city, they

wouldn't quite realize that, there are just certain things you don't do or say or act. That people in the city aren't quite as friendly and open as people out in the country might be. Umm... I feel like I'm like running around something, but never quite getting anywhere... I think I need to think about this for a while longer and just let it sit in my mind and let it grow. [*info, R*]

37 S: Yes, see, like you said, the worst part is, is that all these ideas are related, somewhere, but... [*info*]

38 Fran: Somewhere. [*off*]

The faith that "all these ideas are related, somewhere" could be the theme song for other collaborations that received these mixed scores. The Kate and Han transcripts resemble Fran's in their preoccupation with sources, problematic or conflicting ideas and examples; in their high scores for topic information; and in their limited concern with either putting that knowledge to use or constructing a text. All three are using the conventions of problem analysis as a heuristic for invention rather than the design of an argument, as they are pushed by supporters who ask, "Now why is that a... I don't really see that as a discourse problem" (turn 29, Kate). Their high quality scores may reflect this persistent engagement with their own knowledge. Their low scores for constructive planning also indicate how this dedication of attention to one part of the rhetorical problem has put other calls on hold. True, they have not lived up to all the instructional intentions of collaborative planning at this point, at least not to the level some students did. However, in adapting the planning session to their own uses and immediate needs in fruitful ways, they are exhibiting the kind of strategic cognition we expect from experts including expert students. Unfortunately, this strategic dimension of a student's performance is not always available to the instructor.

Setting challenging goals (even when they are not the instructor's) appears linked to metacognitive awareness in another way, in that the planning process does not stop when the assigned activity is over. Kate's final self-interview is a revealing glimpse of a process guided not by the automated moves an expert might have, but by the reflective awareness of a learner. During this self-interview, Kate listens to the planning tape made with her partner and evaluates both what she accomplished and what she didn't do: "Okay I really don't think that our collaboration went that well, so I'm kind of writing down ideas as I listen to it [the tape], and I think I got a really good idea here. What I think I really want to do is... " After an extended, 850-word planning session with herself, she concludes that "just thinking this through" helped more than the collaboration did. Yet, stepping back, it is also obvious that this focused, productive second session alone [with her tape] would not have occurred without the first. As Kate, herself, concludes: "It might help though, if I get together with my partner again, and I get somebody to talk with me about this. I think that's what I'm going to do next."

These two students, Fran and Kate, like the low-scoring Janine ("body language"), are lost in their own networks of knowledge, trying with mixed success to see some pattern in their own sense of unarticulated conflicts, to link their experience to Farb, and to see how these disjunctions in discourse are, to quote Fran's partner, "the result of some problem, but what could it be?" All three focus their collaboration on unraveling this tangled skein of topic knowledge, but the strategic knowledge—in particular the challenging goals and metacognitive awareness—Fran and Kate bring to this process is different from what Laura brings in some striking ways. First, both writers are highly reflective. What does this mean? Terms like *reflection, metacognition,* and *awareness* are often used in a broad sense that includes performing a cognitive action (such as planning) as well as being aware of one's action and/or able to articulate that awareness (cf. A. L. Brown, 1980; Durst, 1989; Higgins et al., 1992; Paris & Winograd, 1990). Because we are interested in how writers use reflection and self-awareness to manage their own process and negotiate rhetorical situations, this study defines reflective comments in the more limited and rigorous sense. For a comment to be coded as a reflection (see the last column of table 3), it had to exhibit either (1) an evaluative comment or a problem identification, (2) a justification or request for justification of plans or ideas, or (3) a comment that generates or considers plans or ideas marked as an alternative to those already posed. As table 4 suggests, the reflection scores turned out to be highly correlated with the quality scores for collaboration (even after length was factored out, $r=.66$, $p<.05$, Pearson Product).

How do these reflective moves translate into the generative planning the judges saw? For Fran and Kate, this reflective stance includes an awareness of their own process and options. When Fran's partner raises a constructive challenge (such as, "What is the problem?," "How is this related?," "What does this have to do with the audience?"), Fran treats these questions as a necessary and natural part of writing—even when she knows she cannot yet answer them. She accepts the gambit, goes as far as she can. Moreover, she appears to be monitoring the changes in her plan as a whole and to see the parts of her representation (the different blackboards, in effect) as connected to each other. At turn 43, when this monitoring pays off and she sees a way to consolidate her ideas, she recognizes that this new decision has reverberations across her plan:

42 Fran: Let's see, maybe like all these little things I've been talking about are kind of topics under this larger context.

43 S: Who's the audience, again?

44 Fran: Audience, okay. Now it's all changed again. I've got to think, who is this important to... to whom is this important? [. . .] Actually, maybe like... something like *Psychology Today*.

Collaborative planning appears to support reflective thinking for some students, but, we might ask, does this awareness depend on sophisticated powers of introspection? Does reflection have to be intentionally initiated or guided by explicit knowledge about options to consider? As far as we can infer from this data, Fran's strategic awareness does not arise as a deliberate choice but as a sense of options invoked by a challenge or triggered by an opportunity. She might not be able to describe precisely what she does to a floundering Janine (even though she might be a good supporter). Kate's transcript, however, shows a more explicit awareness of her own process as she reviews what she accomplished, set against a set of goals that are clearly more demanding than Janine's ("body language") or Laura's ("about three paragraphs"). In Kate's second, private session with the tape, she in fact prompts herself to face a potential criticism: "So that's a pretty broad subject. But I think that... All I really want to do is just analyze this, and in analyzing it, I want to explain to my reader that this does exist." One can imagine the internalized voice of a teacher in Kate's diagnosis, "That's a pretty broad subject." And a few minutes later, she engages her textbook's author (whom she does not know) by name in a simulated dialogue, walking herself through what the author might say: "She tells us, you know, first we're supposed to explore the subject. Well, I think just by being a student I've more or less explored the subject [e.g., understanding the language of a new discourse like physics]. And... let me see [. . . .] What did she tell us to do next?"

Kate wraps up this self-interview with the decision to have another collaborative session, not only reviewing and evaluating the status of her own thinking, but making plans that guide her own process. Kate is not an expert writer even by freshman standards (her paper received a B), but she is a good model of a student expert, using both the collaborative experience and the self-interview to experiment, observe, reflect, and learn about both her topic, the task, and her own writing process.

Strategic Choices and Quality: A Statistical Analysis

The strategic analysis we have just done adds to our understanding of student planning in two ways. It tries to incorporate data on writers' goals and awareness that a traditional analysis focused on outcomes and activities would exclude. And it looks not only for the broad patterns of difference an expert/novice model would suggest but for individual writers or small groups of writers who depart from those patterns in meaningful ways. The statistical analysis that follows offers converging evidence of and a different perspective on these patterns by asking, "What actions predict the quality of a session?" The regression model that offered the best fit to these data identified three factors (in descending order) as the best predictors of the judged quality of a session: the number of substantive turns, the percentage of reflective comments, and the constructive planning score. (The R^2 value for this model was a high 0.929; the adjusted squared multiple r = 0.840. Beta weights for the three factors in order were 0.076, 0.029, and –0.229.) At first glance, it seems counter-intuitive that the constructive score would be negative. However, the first factor, number of constructive turns, contributes heavily to making this a strong correlation, and its strength, combined with correlations among the factors, reduces the apparent role of the other two to the point of showing a negative value for constructiveness. However, all three of these elements are needed to create the best fit regression line, and in a post hoc test of individual elements in the best fit model, both reflection ($F = 6.962$, $p = 0.017$) and constructive score ($F = 5.089$, $p = 0.037$) are significant explanatory variables. Given the low N of some categories, these results must, of course, be read as converging evidence, not strong predictions.

The overall pattern suggests that, on the one hand, substantive engagement (not surprisingly) combined with reflection and, to a lesser extent, with constructive planning predicts a quality score. On the other hand, the fact that constructive planning is not a reliable predictor argues against a simple linear correlation. Looking at the logic of students' strategic process earlier suggested why the relationship is unstable. Students working with limited goals can turn complex issues (like purpose) into a routine exercise, while writers setting challenging goals may adapt knowledge-driven planning in valuable ways to their own current needs and purposes. This analysis suggests that quality depends on strategic choices about how to use an activity more than which activity one uses.

The regression points up the same need for closer analysis I argued for above: the expert/novice pattern (defined in terms of knowledge-driven versus constructive planning) identifies a meaningful difference in how students use collaboration, but it can only tell part of the story.[8] A check for possible outliers, that might call the regression model itself into question was negative. However, an analysis based on Cook's distance, identified two students whose scores, given this small sample, were highly influential in depressing the predictive value of the constructive score. One student was Tomas with his low reflectiveness; the other was Gary. The Cook's measure identifies problematic cases within the data that depart so far from predictions that they influence the larger pattern. Gary has much in common with Laura—a short session in which the Blackboard Planner topics are brought up but not followed up. What makes him so influential in the statistical analysis and worth scrutiny is a high reflective score, which is based on Gary's uncertainty and his partner's persistent, but unrequited reflective questioning:

> 10 S: What's this going to do for them, though, them reading your paper?
>
> 11 Gary: That's a good question.
>
> 12 S: I mean, what are they going to get out of it; is it just going to be examples or what?
>
> 13 Gary: It will be a lot of examples and just my point of view on... I mean, it's a discourse problem, but [. . .] I guess really there isn't too many ways you can solve it.

Like Laura, Gary's image of the appropriate goals for a college paper appear to set a ceiling on effort and a comfortably low threshold for success. As the statistical analysis suggests, the quality of the session is linked to significant strategic choices.

> 17 Gary: It will be a typical like essay, where, you know, you start with your introductory paragraph and then offer a few examples, a few paragraphs with examples, and then a concluding paragraph. I mean, it will all relate to each other, each paragraph will sort of have something to do with the one before.

To sum up, looking at these transcripts in terms of expert and novice performance helped us name some key features of rhetorical planning. Our analysis based on these expert/novice patterns had broad explanatory power for a significant number of students. And it gave us one way to measure whether collaborative planning (a dorm-room activity) was in fact leading to rhetorical thinking (the set of intellectual moves we hoped to support). The statistical analysis let us confirm that rhetorical planning was linked to what teacher/judges saw as high-quality planning, and it added two other factors that predict quality—the persistence or engagement that leads to more turns and the reflective frame of mind that considers problems, reasons, and alternatives. In their different ways, analyses like these can help us design and evaluate an educational practice in general. However, these analyses are also turning up people and performances that do not fit the general picture and do not belong in the statistically significant majority. In the next chapter, I want to argue for the value of a strategic analysis that also tries to explain pattern breakers (the Frans, Lauras, and Garys) and the perplexing performances (Carter's C+ and Vince's A−) by asking not only what did they *do* but what the *logic* of this process is from the learner's point of view.

7

Strategic Knowledge and the Logic of a Learner

I. Uncovering Hidden Logics

Teaching is often dictated by the representations we build of students. Cognitive psychology has defined itself as the study of how people build and use such representations (Gardner, 1985). Poststructuralist cultural criticism has taken up this idea as a cause, arguing that our institutional practices depend on a set of socially constructed agreements about how to represent entities—literacy, the canon, or the remedial writer. However, as writers like Derrida and Foucault argue, these representations are not stable approximations of a more objective truth. When an identity is stabilized, when we achieve a socially subscribed representation, we do so by "repressing the play of differences within and between what look to be (but are not) separate things" (Poovey, 1990). Popular representations of remediation, for example, build an equation between nonstandard English, low test scores, social background, and intellectual failure, creating an enormous but questionable gulf between those who succeed and fail on these measures (Hull et al., 1991; Rose, 1988). When we represent literacy through one set of literate practices, we repress the other practices writers may control or choose to use. Our representations have political and social consequences.

At the same time, these unstable identities, selective representations, and the very re-conceptualizations writers like Hull and Rose try to create are necessary to teaching. They let us define differences that matter to us and set priorities. It is useful, but not enough, to mount a philosophical critique based on the fact humans create such representations, remaining in the safe moment of skepticism. Nor is it enough to stop after a critique of the specific (and inevitably partial and problem-ridden) representations that we now use. The problem for educational research and teachers alike is to build better representations that accommodate more of the resistant reality of what students know and do and recognize the play of difference our current images may obscure.

In chapter 6, we saw how one way of representing students' performance, the expert/novice paradigm, gave us some useful insight into an important *part* of what a significant *part* of the students were doing. It helped answer the question teachers cannot neglect: How are students interpreting and using a strategy like collaborative planning—in practice? There were indeed a number of things that could have happened. Perhaps students' well-learned strategies for knowledge-driven planning would be impervious either to rhetorical prompts or to the social presence of the partner. Or perhaps freshmen, preoccupied with the conventions of academic discourse, would be like Laura ("about three paragraphs") immersed in a schema-driven creation of text. Or perhaps the planning session would turn into a familiar peer critique where authority would be wrested from the planner by a more vocal, able "supporter." After all, these freshmen did not receive much instruction in how to be planners or supporters, nor did they have the opportunity to reflect on their own performance in class—two things we would emphasize in later instruction. On the other hand, maybe merely creating an opportunity and framework for self-directed inquiry in a supportive, collaborative setting would unleash a wealth of rhetorical thinking. We might see students elaborating personal rhetorical goals to investigate a problematic idea or to convince another freshman, considering alternative text conventions that might work best. The expert/novice comparison let us track the fate of our hypotheses and our instructional practice.

What we found, however, was a pattern of even more provocative difference. Yes, many students were engaging in the expert, rhetorical moves the planning session was designed to support. The good news. But the students themselves could not be adequately understood by this expert/novice grouping, even though it was useful for other reasons. Working on the problem of both doing and learning a difficult task, the students were making a variety of strategic choices. Whereas an experienced writer might draw on a repertoire of strategies for formulating problems out of ambiguity and contradiction or call up well-developed text schemas for analyzing them, these students had to work through this process in a far more ad hoc and experimental way, adapting the knowledge they did have, compensating for what they did not. And, as it turned out, those choices did not add up to a predictable or even a consistently successful or unsuccessful pattern.

To understand these students is to track the logic of a more problematic, experimental, and unpredictable student process. Neither experts in such writing nor novices (new to the game), they are learners, in the act of adapting the knowledge and strategies they have to a new problem. But that adaptation takes place on a number of different fronts; a student's performance is not a unitary process. For instance, students differed in which features of the discourse and the assignment they could handle successfully (or chose to tackle). They differed in the grades they received. Students differed in their use of the reflective and rhetorical strategies encouraged by the instructor and the Planner's Blackboard and in the perceived quality of the sessions themselves. And yet, none of these measures could fully predict the others; some students appeared to succeed in one area and not in another. Likewise, it would not be enough to examine any single feature of this performance, whether it is the students' response to instruction, their social interaction, or their texts. As we saw in the statistical analysis, correlational patterns tell a useful story for a significant portion of the data, but they can also lead us to ask about the remainder. Taken alone, none of these stories could account for the diversity at the level of detail an instructor needs to diagnose problems or describe the grounds for success—that is, to understand what individual students are doing or why. This chapter is about how we might accommodate more of that difference by looking at the logic that guides individual performance and the strategic, adaptive process of a learner.

In trying to understand the problems of basic writers (and the reason good models, instruction, and feedback did not always "take"), Mina Shaughnessy demonstrated that there was a strong underlying logic to the process of the writers she studied and to decisions they made. When teachers did not address the logic that was guiding action, their instruction often missed the mark. For instance, the common practice of drills on isolated bits of grammar was futile in the face of a reasonable (though faulty) grammatical rule system students had already developed. And the error-dominated image of writing these writers held not only led to certain disaster-prone strategies (e.g., overcorrecting during composing but avoiding reviewing), it made these strategies impervious to change. Subsequent research in other areas of learning is revealing the persistent, seemingly reasonable, but "buggy" routines (flawed algorithms) children develop as they learn to do math, and the commonsense intuitions, the pre-Newtonian assumptions, and problematic schemas students bring to learning science (Larkin, 1983). Nor is the problem limited to children or basic writers. Advanced medical students (soon to be your doctor) bring an array of necessary and helpful metaphors to learning physiology and diagnosis. Unfortunately, the complexity of the subject means that each of these metaphors is also partly faulty—a source of misunderstandings and misdiagnoses (Feltovich, Spiro, & Coulson, 1989).

This search for hidden logics is not a hunt for knowledge deficits that can be repaired by the addition of information. For instance, Hull and Rose (1989) examine a basic writer's attempt to summarize a nursing report by trying to look beyond the surface of its fragmented organization and illogical pastiche of personal and paraphrased information. Using a videotape to prompt Tanya to recall some of her composing decisions, they find a set of confused "rules," consistent, disaster-bound strategies, and reasonable but flawed assumptions. They show how Tanya's techniques for using sources are decisions with a history that grow out of a fear of plagarism from high school and an intense desire to succeed in college. For Tanya, this translates into a plan to display her knowledge while at the same time to show her teacher she is not "the kind of student that would copy." Unfortunately, this set of intentions leads to unconventional text if, like Tanya, one does not control the textual conventions for mixing quotations and comment. When these goals are combined with another strategy that selects information by its personal relevance (the same "True, Important, I Agree" strategy seen in mainstream freshmen [Flower et al., 1990]), the result is a "bizarre word salad [that] is, perhaps, not so bizarre after all" (1989, p. 151).

How shall we account for the logic of a student's performance? One familiar way is to describe the knowledge and schemas learners bring to comprehending or producing texts, especially the genre features or conventions that they do not possess or the problematic ones they do (e.g., Tanya's ignorance of conventions for quotation). Another way is to describe the behaviors or thinking strategies we can observe or the context and messages it sends. But to understand the logic behind an open-ended, social, and constructive process like collaboration—to recognize the stubborn complexity of individual actions—we may need to ask about students' strategic knowledge as well. Strategic knowledge is understanding in action. *As it is used here, strategic knowledge refers to three critical elements of what writers know—their goals, strategies, and awareness.* It is this combination that turns knowledge into a strategic act and that lets writers embed the conventions, criteria, and moves they control in a coherent theory of action.

If we want to understand the hidden logic of the students who present us with contradictions or who fail to fit the pattern of our instructional expectations, we may need to look deeper at not only the *strategies* they use and the knowledge they receive but at their *goals*—the priorities they set, the criteria they think are important, and the task as they represent it to themselves. The goals these student collaborators set are a kind of interface between their store of knowledge about what could be done and what they actually choose to do or realize is possible in the immediate situation. These goals also reflect the students' reading of the context and its expectations, whether that context is the culture of schooling or the persistent prompt of a collaborator. In setting (and in forgetting, revising, or elaborating) their own goals, writers turn their theory of a task and their reading of a rhetorical situation into actions they can take and into evaluative criteria. These goals can be more difficult for observers to see or infer than composing behaviors, cognitive strategies, or discourse knowledge, but goals provide the logic that governs why and how writers use what they know.

Imagining Goals

It is difficult to imagine other people's intentions. The formalisms used in artificial intelligence gain precision and predictive power by reducing complexity to goal-fate graphs and condition/action rules (*If* the assignment says "compare," *then* . . .). Ethnography solves this problem with case histories rich in observed events and contradiction where patterns of intention are inferred from histories of behavior. Nevertheless, such observers' descriptions rarely plumb the logic of individual performances as the writers themselves were seeing it. Writers operate out of a web of intentions—of goals, values, constraints, assumptions, criteria—that no single representation will capture. As we discussed in chapter 3, imagining the intentions of a writer like Carter as a network of goals, constraints, and criteria brings some of this dynamic knowing into focus.

Constructing a strategic reading presents two challenges. The first is to recognize the heterglossia of a goal network: the diverse faces, voices, assumptions, rules, values, conventions, intertextual echoes, rhetorical goals, and tentative plans that have a place on this network. Our strategic reading of Carter, for instance, highlights his rhetorical goal to "help people catch on to these differences sooner than I did" and his specific ideas for carrying this off in text. But it also shows how the face-to-face requests from Jennie ("make it more real," "give me an example") function as generative goals calling for plans and text, while memory calls up voices asserting "no content" that challenge older plans that linked procrastination, BS, and A's in English. These social events and snippets of personal history take up residence on Carter's emerging network of goals in the form of criteria for success, constraints, and a standard operating plan that is now called into question. Looking more broadly, we can also read in Carter's web of purposes a tacit agreement to play the game of school, even when the rules change. And we can see already the hints of trouble to come when we compare his priorities—the goals he seems to privilege—to those privileged in the assignment. In sum, we can see how not only his problematic interpretation of the task but his social experience, cultural values, and personal history all translate themselves into cues to action.

If the first challenge of a strategic reading is to seek out more of the socially supplied elements of this web, the second is to discriminate possible influences and available plans from those that participate in a given constructive act. We know that everything the culture dictates and every past experience—as well as every model text, teacherly suggestion, and assigned requirement—do not necessarily make it into the logic of any given performance. The question is, What did? What does the "activated" network of purpose that guided this constructive act look like? A strategic reading complements a broader cultural, social, conventional, and textual reading by attempting to see this network, as best we can, from behind the eyes of the writer. It seeks to recognize the social values, the remembered advice, the personal goals, the assignment features, and so on that have come to voice in *this situation* and taken life as the active goals and strategic forces participating in *this constructive act*.

Acknowledging Awareness

However, looking for goals and strategies alone does not capture the dynamic nature of the writer's process or the way goals may change as an idea or text develops. *Awareness*, I will argue, is the third critical, if little understood, element of strategic knowledge. Awareness can be triggered by circumstance (like Fran's) or more consciously invoked (like Kate's); it can be active or reflective, and it can extend over many areas (like Kate's and Carter's) or seem quite painfully limited (like Janine's). This metacognitive awareness affects how writers monitor and control their writing process; it allows them to examine their own knowledge and to reflect on their own goals, their assumptions, expectations, or reading of a situation. Our understanding of the role metacognitive awareness does and could play is surprisingly limited given the value we place on self-reflection. This blind spot may come from equating such awareness with the meager, after-the-fact declarative knowledge writers appear to possess. Meanwhile the real action is occurring elsewhere: in situated, in-process cognition and in acts of negotiation.

For example, as Carter and Jennie are putting the wraps on their session at turn 85, Jennie rather unexpectedly opens it up to reflection: "Well, Carter, what do you think is the most interesting part of your paper?" As the coding for rhetorical purpose, consolidations, and reflection shows, the comments that follow are an occasion for some of the most integrated rhetorical thinking of the session (they offer an image of student expertise).

But they also allow insight into the strategic knowledge Carter and Jennie may bring to the task with its vision of possibilities and its blind spots. To Carter, the most interesting thing about his own paper on discourse communities is, in fact, the possibility of awareness for a reader (imagined as an earlier self):

90 Carter: Because, I... I don't think people think about this, you know, too often. Like when they sit down to write—"Oh, it's different from like the Strategies paper. " [*aud/gen pur, R*]

91 S: Yeah. And by reading your paper they'll sit down and see... [*aud, gen pur, R*]

92 Carter: Maybe they'll be able to realize their own differences, and everything, realize that they exist. [*rh pur, R*]

Although this freshman discussion may not be sophisticated, it is important to recognize what is happening. Carter has grasped the principle that discourse communities differ, understanding it not as a truism or an abstraction to parrot, but as operational, working knowledge that influences his writing. Moreover, he is aware of how this difference operates in his present context (e.g., his Strategies for Writing class versus Technology and People) and in his own history with school (e.g., "welcome to college").

A strategic analysis invites us to compare Carter's pragmatic awareness or difference to Jennie's representation and to note how each functions as a criterion used in evaluating writing. Jennie also finds the fact of difference the most interesting part of his paper ("Just so I can see that. Yeah, it's really different."). But like other commentators on school discourse (Bartholomae, 1985; Bizzell, 1989), she is especially concerned with what is expected.

93 S: And even though there's nothing you can do about it—even if there are boundaries set on you, and that's a given, and you can't really change that—but if you're aware of that, you can be more aware of what is expected of you, and you can work with that. That's really good. [*rh pur, R*]

We lack enough evidence to confidently interpret Jennie's understanding, but at this early date in her college career, she appears to see those boundaries as given by others and unmovable. We might speculate that in her own intellectual development she is still working out her relationship to such authority. Or we might describe her thinking as participation in a set of cultural assumptions that preserve the status quo by reifying boundaries into givens—thinking that fails to recognize her own role in interpreting/constructing those givens or her own power to transform them. We might contrast her attitude to that of Patrick who chose a riskier experiment: "If there was one thing I never wanted to do in a paper it would be to dispute one of the most 'influential philosophers' of this century, but I disagree with Ludwig Wittgenstein's thinking . . ." However, it is ultimately Jennie's strategic awareness (not our interpretive account of it) that will guide her attempt to "work with that."

A strategic analysis of the sort I am proposing acknowledges that students' awareness of their own assumptions is an important dimension of their knowledge. It also acknowledges that we as outsiders may have difficulty interpreting such awareness. In the studies that follow, we see students themselves conducting this strategic analysis by reflecting on their own planning and thinking. Moreover, our interpretation of what Jennie realizes may be far less important than the fact that she is engaged herself in the act of interpretation. Although Jennie does not see these boundaries as open to change, her assumptions about difference have become, in the sense of this book, more fully open to negotiation. Reflecting on what she found interesting in Carter's paper, these assumptions are being considered and articulated to a listening ear. Interestingly enough, her own paper explores the problem of interpretation and struggles with Farb's claim that language does not duplicate reality but comments on it and with the unavoidable way interpretation constructs our memory of past events. In her own self-interview, Jennie comments, "The most interesting part of my paper, for me at least, will be just writing it down to help me see how people really do twist things around, and how something in reality that has happened could be so different from the story that's told." In these reflective comments, we see students' awareness of their assumptions, decisions, and quandaries playing a role in their negotiation of meaning.

It is important to keep in mind the difference between an observer's reading of a student's performance and the writer's own strategic knowledge. Hull and Rose, for instance describe their search for hidden logics as an attempt to locate literacy events of underprepared students in four contexts: the present task, current schooling, the writers' literacy history, and a general social/cultural domain (Hull & Rose, 1991). This broad social cognitive conceptualization lets them demonstrate how Tanya's assumptions about summary grow out of her personal history and reasoning while their own wider theoretical perspective as observers/teachers/researchers adds a new interpretive frame not present in Tanya's reading of the situation (Hull & Rose, 1989). But, as they also demonstrate, there is another side to this coin. When observers (teachers or researchers) do not have insight into students' strategic knowledge, they may bring their own well-meaning interpretive frames and impose their own "social constructs" on a performance, just as Tanya's teacher did (Hull et al., 1991). Such constructs can distort our reading of students, misdirect our response, and disempower students by dismissing their goals under the name of improving their technique.

The strategic analysis we will pursue in the chapters to come has many parallels to the multilayered observer's analysis Hull and Rose (1991) describe, but these two complementary approaches tell a somewhat different part of the story. Although both are clearly interpretive, a strategic analysis is less concerned with the frameworks *we* (the observer) can bring to a writer's performance than with the ones the *writer* brings. It leads to research methods that engage writers in observation-based reflections on their own performance. And it turns attention to the kinds of awareness writers possess, the options and alternatives they see, and problems they are actively negotiating.[1]

Feedback That Speaks to the Learner's Logic

Understanding the logic of the learner's process by looking at the more inclusive picture of strategic knowledge helps us see how individual writers are making sense of the situation. But it is also likely to complicate the situation for both student and teacher. For instance, if Laura ("about three paragraphs") and Vince ("I'm just discussing something") used these planning sessions as a way to reflect on their own goals—to compare them to the instructor's image of this task or to Carter's, Jennie's, or Fran's—it might call into question a strategic process that had perhaps stood them in good stead for 12 years of school. It would complicate the learner's job, suggesting that the task had changed and that they must not simply use what they knew, but reevaluate it. For Laura, who received a D+ on her thin paper, this might in fact demystify what had gone wrong with a plan that had "sound[ed] pretty good" to her and her partner. But despite the limitations of Vince's collaboration, his paper on idiom was a soundly organized elaboration on the source text, using a mixture of details from Farb and his own examples "to show how this comes up in life." He received an A−. His limited goals and knowledge-driven strategy, combined with engaging personal examples from his trip abroad, were effective and efficient for this two-page paper. Although the teacher noted the vague sense of purpose, this was a well-written short paper on other counts. Should Vince try for more?

By contrast, Carter, who plunged into what the judges saw as a highly generative, reflective, and constructive process, who used this paper to interrogate his own assumptions, to revise his theory of the task of writing, to confront the problem of switching discourses, and to "make it real" for his readers, received a C+. The goals Carter set were well suited to learning, but the task he represented to himself, perhaps in his focus on a "real problem" led him to ignore other goals set by the course. These included the second criterion on the teacher's handout: "*use the material from Farb's book* for a purpose of your own" (italics added), which was a highly salient feature of the assignment in the teacher's eyes (see chap. 6). If Carter read and pondered Farb, beyond the fact that discourses come into conflict, there is no indication of it in the transcript or the paper. As Carter's average grade and Vince's A indicate, strategic knowledge, whatever its logic, operates within a social context. The goals writers set and the metacognitive awareness they develop become meaningful (good, bad, useful, original, empowering or not) within a resistant social and rhetorical context (which may be serenely indifferent to the writer's interpretation of it). Rhetorical or academic success may depend on which purposes one chooses to entertain.

Understanding the logic of the learner might alter the feedback a teacher would give. In addition to giving him an A−, we might help Vince recognize the limits of his well-developed knowledge-driven strategies, to face the challenge of Tomas' questions about purpose, and to realize that in deftly avoiding the issue, his limited goals led to a session of limited value. We might want the feedback Carter receives to balance his C+ with a positive recognition of what he did accomplish. It could affirm that his desire to help readers "sit down and see" something, as well as his energetic inquiry into the task and his own assumptions about writing, are central to good writing and to learning to write. At the same time, it could show how this rhetorical situation involved the additional constraint of using source texts, typical in college assignments, that he ignored. Such feedback might locate the problem where it lies: not in his writing ability but in his reading of the rhetorical situation.

Insight into hidden logics might also help teachers intervene at an earlier point in the process. When Wallace studied students writing a fellowship application in response to certain guidelines, he found some ran aground before they were fairly started by failing to set "*useful* intentions" that is, plans that transformed information to fit the application criteria by turning lists of personal facts into general statements and experience into evidence. For example, while Tamara saw how she could mine her experience at Sears as evidence of responsibility and self-control in the face of heated customers, Mary assumed she could do little more than list her employment: "saying that I worked at K-Mart... I mean I don't know how far that will get me" (1991, p. 93). As it turned out, creating these useful intentions was an even more consistent predictor of text quality than whether the writer went to a community college or a private university. Mary's thin text began with her fatalistic assessment of the rhetorical situation and her assumptions about what counted as valid information.

II. Strategic Knowledge: A Site of Social Cognitive Negotiation

There is no question about it: a writer's strategic knowledge—her or his goals, strategies, and levels of awareness—will be harder to see and measure than content knowledge, text quality, or behavior. The writer's strategic knowledge will be harder to describe than the textual knowledge—the conventions and commonplaces of a discourse or the structural patterns—that teachers intend to impart. And interpreting a strategic action of individual writers will be more problematic than subsuming an individual within the categories of broadbrush social or educational theory. Why then do a strategic analysis, teasing out goals, desires, reasons, attending to alternatives, conflicts, options, and asking about the choices, decisions, assumptions, and uncertainties that stand behind writing and texts? And why go to the effort of close-grained observations of not just the text but the thinking of individual writers?

Let me suggest a possible rationale for including strategic knowledge in our picture of what writers know by looking at collaborative talk and power relations as two cases in point where a strategic analysis can be revealing. But first let me note some reasons for valuing this kind of knowing.

Some Premises

As active constructors of meaning, students approach writing with powerful, often contradictory, and sometimes problematic logics that inquiry into strategic knowledge could help reveal.

Understanding acts of strategic cognition and the repertoire of strategic knowledge students bring to writing gives meaning and dignity to both success and shortcomings. Social construction theorists in composition, such as Bartholomae, Bizzell, Bruffee, and Berlin whom we discussed earlier, have drawn on current literary theory to illuminate the social patterns that constrain, even, they might claim, constitute our knowing. However, the image of the student that falls out of this line of theorizing is one largely constrained to acts of imitation, to being appropriated by rather than appropriating conventions and commonplaces, to awkwardly approximating a discourse rather than interpreting it, and to using her or his critical powers not to construct meaning but to uncover and confess her or his own derivative assumptions and intellectual complicity in an ideological system. Like many,

I value the political awareness this work brings to composition and its announced agenda of demystifying academic discourse by unveiling the conventions and commonplaces an outsider must learn. Bartholomae's (1985) criticism of cognitive modeling is also well taken: basic writers (or any outsider to a privileged discourse) need to learn conventions as well as thinking strategies. However, as a cognitive rhetorian, I am not persuaded by the polemical, dichotomizing stance of much social theorizing, with its rather overdrawn picture of students' writing as a generic, culturally dictated social process; by its inability to account for how cognition and context interact; or by its tendency to broadbrush speculative generalizations about students supported by assertions and political value statements in place of evidence that might complicate or qualify the story (Flower, 1989a). More important, I am not persuaded that reified social forces and discourses (rather than mutually influenced thinking people) exist as independent constructors of meaning in any place other than the minds of consenting theorists (who are engaged in interpreting and responding to one another).

I would argue that research with individual writers gives us a vigorous picture of students as interpretive agents whose goals and awareness make a difference. As the earlier discussion should have made clear, the *logic* of a learner is not the logic of a formal syllogism or even of explicit informal reasoning. As the rationale for action that gives meaning to what a writer does, this logic appears to exist as a fragmented body of goals, personal habits, cultural and socially derived assumptions, inferences, and serendipitous plans. Through observation (rather than speculation) we can also begin, like Schaughnessy, to uncover some of the problematic logics, shared by groups of students, that thwart learning. However, observation can be an equally powerful tool in the hands of students as well. Events like collaborative planning make the process of constructing meaning more conscious, articulate, and negotiable. They create a microcosm in which tacit social expectations become more explicit and patterns of response become visible and open to question. They can, at times, push meaning making into the arena of negotiated construction. And when these events become the basis for students' own observation-based reflection, they open the door to informed negotiation.

Our emerging social cognitive theories of writing need to be grounded in and tested by the kind of observation that can build a situated, interactive picture of cognition in context.

Acts of strategic cognition are a prime site for observing the interaction of social and cognitive forces. We can think of these acts (e.g., goal setting, reflection, strategic choice) as sites at which the social and rhetorical context is often being interpreted and mediated and as sites at which context in turn cues and shapes cognition. Strategic knowledge is not the only point of interaction, but it is one of the few that is explicit enough not only to suggest but challenge theories.

In moving toward a social cognitive theory, I am using a metaphor, "interaction," which some worry suggests a separation of society and the individual mind, where they see "identity" (Feltovich et al., 1989; Rogoff, 1990). The reality of this relationship is obviously more complex than any single metaphor, and "identity" may offer a better framework for understanding the processes of acculturation, socialization, and learning in early childhood or for explaining broad social and historical patterns. But to wash out the distinction between individual and group blinds us to the ways individual minds interpret, negotiate, reinterpret, and resist social constructs—even as they are learning them. From the vantage point of cognitive rhetoric and its focus on individuals rather than groups, it is equally important to explain the development of personal agency and individual differences in these young adult writers. Exploring the interaction of cognition and context can, I will argue, reveal some of the distinctive ways writers learn to negotiate a social process and a rhetorical situation.

This emphasis on interaction builds on the dual assumption that individuals are indeed part of a social fabric and its shared knowledge but that they are also the active constructors of personal, internal representations of meaning. From a social perspective, the individual writer is operating within a cultural, interpersonal, and rhetorical context. The intentions writers hold are always bounded intentions, circumscribed by the expectations and constraints imposed by others as well as by the tacit assumptions of what is acceptable or normal. The roles writers take, whether the social role of "student" or the persona of a text, come with culturally defined patterns of expectation and response. This context then is loudly or subtly suggesting goals, reinforcing certain strategies and not others, and "naturalizing" some responses (e.g., avoiding *I*) by pushing them below the threshhold of awareness or above objection. But context is not an unmoved mover, and bounded intentionality is still intentionality.

From the perspective of individual cognition, the social context, its patterns and expectations, do not exist as reified objects, independent of the minds that conceive them. The important question is how individual learners construe that context, as they do in reading a situation, in attending to cues selectively, and in interpreting the signs and symbols, the advice, instructions, and feedback that surround writing. In building both a theory of the task and a representation of the immediate assignment from that blurred ditto handed out on Tuesday, writers are translating the context of writing into a meaningful image and a plan for action. Unacknowledged individual differences here may spell critical differences for success in school.

Another premise of this interactional picture of writing is that it cannot be reduced to a simpler, deterministic story dictated by single causes. In trying to account for the social foundations of thought, Bandura has proposed a theory of reciprocal causation or triadic reciprocity that tries to consolidate a large body of social and cognitive research. Simply stated, Bandura's theory clusters the influences on human action into three agents—cognitive (including other personal and motivational factors), the environment, and ongoing behavior itself. It argues that in any action these "all operate interactively as determinants of each other" in different blends that are related "probabilistically rather than inevitably" (1986, pp. 23–24).[2] For example, we can see Carter's high school success supporting a similar strategy in college—until the environment speaks back with a C+, which he then interprets as a comment on his planning and the grounds for a new action—which we see him carrying out with Jennie. And in that process, the emerging text plan prompts Jennie to raise a difficult question, and that in turn leads to new knowledge and a changed plan and text. In even this slight sketch of reciprocal causation, note how often some immediate "cause" is itself based on an interpretation Carter or Jennie has made—an interpretation that they might well have made differently, leading to a different causal influence on performance. In sum, because an interactional perspective assumes a dynamic interplay of these influencing forces, it leads us to ask how that interaction is working.

Strategic knowledge is a good place to study social cognitive interactions. This trio of goals, strategies, and awareness is at once the site on which this process occurs, the result of social shaping, and the source of personal agency. Insight into a writer's strategic knowledge is a grandstand view into meaning making as a social cognitive act. For example, the goals a writer sets reveal her or his reading of and immersion in a social context—even in the moment-to-moment reader/writer interactions Brandt describes (Brandt, 1990; Nystrand, 1986). Setting goals is a mechanism for participating in a social act while building an individual sense of meaning. The strategies writers call up translate goals into action—they are the operational definition of what it means (for this writer at this moment) to live up to the expectations of a rhetorical situation. The goals and strategies a given writer exhibits reflect not only the socially available options but a personally constructed body of moves, like the difference between knowing the steps and performing the dance. Awareness is the wild card in this process: it is the force that has the potential to change the shape of the interaction, to call both social influences and personal assumptions into question, and to support or resist the state of play.

In the final section of this chapter, we will look at the collaborative talk in this study as a site of social and cognitive interaction and at the strategic knowledge of these students as a place where social and cognitive forces are negotiated. More specifically, I would like to bring this strategic perspective to the discussion of two important questions being posed by other educators. The first concerns the strong yet problematic relation between collaborative talk and individual learning. Does one necessarily lead to the other? Second, we will look at the problem of authority and resistance as a prime site for negotiation and ask, How are students in this study negotiating some of the power relations in school?

Collaborative Talk Is a Strategic Event

Talking to other students in school is a goal-directed event: the goals that shape the social interaction also shape the cognition of the talkers and the kind of learning and meaning making that goes on. Classroom talk, peer response, and teacher/tutor conferences all set up distinctive patterns of social interaction, just as the relation between the planner and the supporter gives collaborative planning its own signature. These different forms of talk appear to elicit different kinds of thinking. But even more interesting are the strategic choices students make within a given practice and the way those choices determine the link between collaborative talk and learning.

Collaboration is one of those family concepts, harboring many different realities. In their review of the research on response groups, DiPardo and Freedman concluded that it is not enough to idealize collaboration or response groups; we need to understand how "peer dynamics can support the larger goals of writing instruction" (1988, p. 143). They then make a strong and potentially controversial prediction about the influence those dynamics have. In comparing the success of different types of instruction, they say that "the instructional mode would not be the key variable; rather, the degree and type of social interaction would" (p. 142). Our observations on the cognition of collaboration in this setting may both support and qualify that claim. This study does not compare the success of collaborative planning as an instructional mode to others, such as the presentational or natural process modes Hillocks (1986) describes. And unlike most process-product research, it is not seeking to measure correlations between an instructional process and an successful outcome or product. Nevertheless, the process tracing analysis does show that neither the fact of collaboration as a mode nor the presence of an instructional prompt was enough to insure a high-quality session; what mattered was how students interpreted the prompt and how they used the situation. Garrison has mounted a philosophical critique of process-product research on the grounds that it cannot account for an intervening variable—the intentions a given instructor brings to the use of any instructional technique (Garrison & Macmillan, 1984). Our study suggests that the intentions of learners and their ways of putting instructional activities to use may be an equally important, and even less acknowledged "key variable."

Although Gere and Stevens concentrate on the virtues of and theoretical justification for writing groups, they raise the question of quality in much the same terms I would use: What sort of cognition does this interaction actually produce? "Collaboration is a necessary but not sufficient condition for collaborative learning. While the democratic give-and-take of collaboration is essential, it does not by itself guarantee that any learning will take place. Participants in collaborative groups learn when they challenge one another with questions, when they use the evidence and information available to them, when they they develop relationships among issues, when they evaluate their own thinking" (1985, p. 69). Claims for "group talk" as an instructional mode cannot be supported by generalizations about collaboration per se but must be based on observation of the actual patterns of talk in question and the way they shape cognition, learning, and text, if they do.

The patterns of interaction we see among collaborative planners often differ from the dynamics observed in the studies of response DiPardo and Freedman (1988) review. These studies show a variety of relations based on *information giving*, on *consensus*, on *conflict*, on *scaffolding*, and on *collaborative problem solving*, some of which are in clear contrast to what we observed. For instance, Gere and Steven's 46 students, scattered across elementary, middle, and high school, operated under rules of peer response designed to minimize the cycle of criticism and self-defense that peer editing can engender. Under these instructions, writers are not allowed to "comment on, or apologize for, the selection read," while readers comment in turn on their "strongest impressions of the writing" (1985, p. 86). Of the 7,928 comments Gere and Stevens analyzed, 88% were devoted to giving information (usually about an item of content) or directives, while only 12% (941) elicited information (presumably from the writer). Collaborative planning is designed, obviously, to reverse this dynamic. Supporters try to elicit ideas from writers, rather than evaluate, and to shift the focus from content per se to uses of that content (a move that these collaborative planners apparently made with 65% of their comments devoted to the rhetorical blackboards.)

For similar reasons, perhaps, this pattern also looks different from the series of 34 student-teacher conferences Sperling (1990) observed for a small group of ninth-grade students. Most discussion was stimulated by the teacher's written comments, but when discussion was devoted to planning future text, the number of "student-owned" topics ranged from 0–3 per student, and the number of student-initiated cooperative units of talk (such as question/answer, offer/acceptance) ranged from a grand total of 1–8 per student over the combined set of conferences. In the short conferences conducted by this experienced teacher, student-initiated planning appears to play a small role.

Nor did these collaborations exhibit the drive toward consensus building Bruffee describes as the goal of collaborative learning (Bruffee, 1984). In fact as the analysis of reflection showed, students were engaging in evaluation, problem finding, alternative making, and justification—creating the patterns of conflict and cognitive dissonance that, the Piagetians argue, can lead to learning (Higgins et al., 1992). However, the form conflict takes is important. Plans are fluid creations under the control of the writer. Just as there is little need to forge consensus or agreement (this is the writer's plan, after all), there is also little need to defend or cling to a text in which one has some investment. The cognitive dissonance in these sessions appears to sit easily in the air. Writers, not invested in a text they have labored over, are willing to entertain significant alternatives.

Two telling exceptions we have observed are Han's session (in which the supporter vigorously argued against the claim that man is at the mercy of language) and in tapes of a pilot session in a local high school where the instructor felt the blackboard categories and notion of being a supporter would be too complicated for his students to keep in mind and downplayed those features. His instruction led to lively, argumentative episodes of peer response, some of which he later described as bull sessions and barroom brawls. Typically focused on the writer's claims, they were high in overt conflict and pressure for agreement but showed few signs of cooperative problem solving. Comparing these videotapes with tapes of supportive collaboration seen in other inner-city schoolrooms and to the freshmen described here, it appears that the way teachers present or students perceive the "rules of the game" can make a visible difference in the social interactions and in the kinds of cognition collaborative planning elicits. Burnett's (1991) adaptation of collaborative planning for business writers led some students to engage in generative, substantive conflict—a practice that was correlated with more successful writing.

Another form of interaction described by Vygotsky (1987), Bruner (1983), and Applebee (1984) goes under the name of scaffolding, in which learners participate in a structured situation and in doing so, enter their "zone of proximal development," going beyond what they could do on their own. The term is sometimes used quite metaphorically to justify or valorize instruction based on group talk by drawing questionable analogies between the language development observed in infants and toddlers and the classroom experience of 15- to 25-year-olds . In the developmental examples, mothers build scaffolds of language that turn "Doggie!" into complete sentences, or adults and older peers create talk with empty slots that let the child participate in increasingly sophisticated linguistic structures. When scaffolding is used in writing instruction, the role of teachers, older partners, or peer groups can range from stimulating or extending the learner's efforts, to coauthorship with or even co-option of the writer. Differences in the way such social scaffolding works, then, may be informative. For instance, the scaffold in collaborative planning is not provided by the knowledge of a more capable peer but by the blackboard metaphor when it functions as a prompt both partners use, and by the role of the supporter who distributes the responsibility for metacognition and monitoring. Nor is there the "hand-over" process (Bruner, 1983), which one might see in oral language development, in cognitive apprenticeship (Collins, Brown, & Newman, 1989) or even in peer tutoring in which the "caretaker" or "master" introduces a new procedure and gradually "hands it over" to the learner. In fact, much of the "modeling" of the process, so critical in cognitive apprenticeships, is done by the writers themselves in response to a prompt and observed when students switch roles, reflect on the session, or listen to their tapes.

A more precise description of the jointly constructed scaffold for learning and writing we observed is probably the collaborative problem solving that both Freedman (1987) and Nystrand (1986) observed and that other instructional techniques such as reciprocal teaching (Palincsar & Brown, 1984) and procedural facilitation (Bereiter & Scardamalia, 1987) also strive to support. Differences in the ways all of these studies analyze their data make precise comparisons difficult, but the following excerpt will illustrate the patterns of interaction that stand out as a signature of these collaborations. It also shows how the collaborators' strategic choices provide a powerful logic for this talk that leads to certain kinds of thinking and not others.

When Vince (whose limited goals we saw in action earlier) switches from a planner to a supporter, he does not take the role of a capable peer tutor whose input is designed to diagnose, gently lead, or advise his partner, Tomas. Nor is he a critic, an editor, or a coach. His input appears to have two main goals: to play the role of a blackboard reminder (at turns 6 and 10) and to elicit enough information to make sense out of this plan for himself (at turns 8, 12, 16, and 32). Vince's skeptical comments reflect his own effort after understanding. The rather simplistic key point Tomas offers at turn 11 would only make sense if one projected a particularly "ignorant" audience, as Vince does at turn 12. Although Vince is raising a pertinent question, he is not doing so out of expertise as a tutor or teacher. His prompt is engendered by a gap or conflict in his own image of the situation and by his attempt to construct a purposeful, rhetorically sensible, commonsense meaning out of Tomas' plan. And as a result, Tomas tries to elaborate and alter his own representation. The roles of collaborative problem solving (informed by the partner's drive for meaning) appear to provide an important scaffold for this process.

6 Vince: All right. That's your topic?

7 Tomas: That [the previously mentioned idea that words have several meanings] is my topic.

8 Vince: How does that relate to anything? I mean, words with different meanings...

9 Tomas: Okay. The point... The key point...

10 Vince: The key point. Key word.

11 Tomas: Yeah. The key point that I'm gonna make in this paper is—um—that these words with several meanings—um—make people unfamiliar with the language being used—it makes them confused. Um—both in the sense that they don't know how to... They don't know the usage, so they have trouble using them in context, and they also don't understand the meaning several times when they're used in context, and so they don't understand when people are talking to them.

12 Vince: In other words, these people are just ignorant?

13 Tomas: Yeah. No. I mean, it's beyond ignorance. I mean...

14 Vince: They're beyond ignorant? They're a piece of wood?

15 Tomas: It has nothing to do with ignorance. It's just lack of knowledge about the language. It could happen to you in German.

16 Vince: [. . . .] This... I don't know... Just doesn't sound like... Can you like sum it up in like one sentence—what your key point is?

17 Tomas: The key point is that words with multiple meanings confuse people that are unfamiliar with the language. Is that good?

Tomas' request for a little social approval leads to some joking until Vince launches his next effort to imagine this audience who, he feels, will need to "know like what you mean" before they read the paper.

18 Vince: You read that very well. (Laughs)

19 Tomas: No. It's not written on my paper. It's not written like that.

20 Vince: Oh. All right. Looked like you were reading it. Um—Okay. Who's your audience?

21 Tomas: Okay...

22 Vince: Say, Tomas, who's your audience?

23 Tomas: The audience would be—um—people who have encountered these problems, either being on the receiving, or the giving end. Like they're either talking or they're listening.

24 Vince: So people before they read this paper are gonna know like what you mean? I mean... You're gonna give this paper a title? Right?

25 Tomas: Yeah. I'm gonna give it a title and introduction. So... So I'll introduce it. So they'll know about that. And... let's see. The audience will also be those interested in general problems of discourse.

At this point, Tomas seems to think he is off the hook with Vince—that a few standard moves such as a title and introduction are all that was missing. But Vince, (the Vince who was reluctant to consider the purpose of his own text) is still not ready to see Tomas' point as a self-evident or self-justifying problem and continues the discussion.

26 Vince: Maybe these people will be too stupid to know what this paper's about. (Laughs)

27 Tomas: Well, I guess it'll be for the people who know what it's about. (Laughs)

28 Vince: (Laughs) I think you just have to make it clear like when you're writing—like your introduction, especially...

29 Tomas: I don't see what you're getting at.

30 Vince: Well...

31 Tomas: Are you saying that people can't understand why this would affect people?

32 Vince: Well... Maybe what I'm saying is that *I* [emphasis on tape] don't understand what your paper's gonna be about. All right—I understand that it's gonna be about like people get confused... Why don't you give me an example?

Talking with Vince becomes an occasion for *shared metacognition*—for thinking about thinking by monitoring and reflecting on their own responses. In the face of Vince's confusion, Tomas has to articulate his own image of what the reader is expected to bring to the conversation—to be "people who know what it's about" (turn 27). Vince meanwhile uses his immediate response (his skepticism and uncertainty about the point) to imagine what it would take to create the response Tomas expects—i.e., a reader primed by a title, prior knowledge, and a clear introduction (turns 24, 28). What sort of social arrangement brought about this shared metacognitive effort that leads Tomas to build a more elaborated, rhetorical image of his own meaning? It appears to depend not only on the structure and prompts of collaborative planning but on a partner who makes an opportunistic, in-process use of them as needed and a writer who accepts the goals of the enterprise.

I do not want to overstate the philosophical significance of these moments of metacognition. We have seen writers like Fran and Kate who were more reflective and articulate. In fact, what is important to notice is that thinking about thinking can emerge as a practical and natural event when partners remind each other to think about rhetorical issues or prompt one another to try some of the difficult cognitive moves (such as simulating a reader) that students often ignore. Perhaps *ignore* is even the wrong term here. As Bereiter and Scardamalia (1982) have argued, one of the hardest things young writers must learn is to monitor their own thinking and to develop the "executive routines" that remind them to generate some more ideas or to try another angle when they feel stuck.

These writers are adults, but rising to metacognition is an effortful act. Perhaps it is no coincidence that nearly every session starts with the writer at least attempting to describe a key point but that nearly all the comments about purpose depend on a prompt from the supporter. As one writer said, "I'm not used to thinking about my purpose." Although both Vince and Tomas ask probing questions as supporters, as planners they follow the same plot with a different script, only considering their point and purpose in response to repeated prompts. In collaborative planning, the partners share the effort of metacognition—the burden of projecting the current plan against its larger rhetorical backdrop. Like Vince, they help monitor whether the current version of the plan makes sense, especially in light of issues involving purpose, audience, and discourse conventions. Even when there is no immediate problem, they remind the writer to consider rhetorical issues or to rise to a metalevel survey of his or her own thoughts. For these freshmen, thinking about purpose clearly depended on the partner's reminder or meta-awareness of a problem (as we saw in Vince's own planning session). On the other hand, the rise to metacognition seems to be shared in other ways. For instance, episodes of reflection were almost equally initiated by planners and supporters (Higgins et al., 1992).

But are all versions of shared metacognition equal? To answer this question requires a strategic analysis that goes beyond identifying general patterns of interaction and looks at how students use collaborative talk. Freedman's study of response predicted that the "achievement of cognitive gain [in a group process] depends on the substance of the social interactions" (1987, p. 8). On the basis of the present study, we would suggest that both the educational quality of the experience and the pattern of students' interactions with each other are influenced by the way they interpret the prompt and interpret or negotiate this school-sponsored meeting. Some writers treat the prompts (meaning both the questions and the issues they represent) as a relatively simple checklist to be run over. As we saw in Laura's ("about three paragraphs") session, the prompts can be read in a literal, reductive way; the planner responds by reciting a few key facts or simply naming the audience or purpose. The student may even (like Vince) reject the request, declining engagement as though this item on the checklist (e.g., purpose) were not applicable to him. Collaborative planning, like other forms of group work, not only reveals simple differences in what teacher and students find important, but it can be susceptible to partners who bring lowered thresholds of acceptance and less sophisticated evaluative criteria (Newkirk, 1984).

By contrast, other students use the prompts not as a checklist but as a heuristic. In the excerpt above, Vince jokes with a split awareness of the different ways these prompts can be taken. His question about audience at turn 20 starts as an effort after meaning. When Tomas delays, he comes back with a mock version of a checklist question, but Tomas' serious response returns the exchange to a heuristic effort. As a result, Vince replies by raising both a genuine problem and a practical, if partial, solution. When metacognitive moves (such as the move to imagine a reader's response) are treated as a heuristic, they become a road into a problem or a discovery. They often lead to an extended inquiry rather than to a short question/answer session. The meaning of even a simple prompt borrowed directly from the blackboard (such as, "What is your purpose?") can be read as a broad invitation to engagement with a problem or a possibility. As a whole, these transcripts show us sessions of shared metacognition operating in both the checklist and the heuristic modes. They contain cooperative sessions at which both partners seem to share the same representation of their task (whether checklist or heuristic). They contain frustrating sessions at which the supporter persists in expecting more and disappointing sessions at which a planner seems primed to explore and the supporter is ticking off items on his shopping list. What we were not able to do with the students in this study was to go back with this data and ask: Do you see these differences, too, and which sort of session would you prefer if you could orchestrate your collaborative planning sessions for your own purposes? But that is the direction in which strategic analysis will take us in subsequent chapters.

To sum up, the relationship between social patterns of talk and the learning or text they produce cannot be reduced to truisms about the virtues of collaborative talk. Different kinds of collaboration request and support different kinds of cognition from information giving to consensus, conflict, scaffolding, and collaborative problem solving. The social structure within which talk happens helps shape the cognition that goes on. However, the thinking individual students actually do is not at all determined—or even reliably predicted by—the social arrangements teachers construct. Collaborative talk is a strategic act; it is shaped by purposes students bring, the options they see open, and the strategies they use, whether those strategies are checklist questions, persisting after understanding, or metacognitive monitoring and heuristic search.

How Do Collaborators Negotiate the Power Structures of School?

When educational researchers describe the supportive patterns of peer talk and teacher conferences, the scaffolding that nurtures a child's development, or the patterns of cognitive apprenticeship that foster skills, they point to the natural, positive ways social structures nurture the individual, guide cognitive development, and increase options.

However, these social structures that instruct and initiate are at the same time power structures that impose their authority, assert their values, and set their own priorities. The paradox for educators lies in being committed to active instruction based on strong educational objectives and at the same time to the objectives of democratic participation that increases students' authority. Teachers talk about the problem of their own institutional power, but given the established structures of school, much of the resolution rests with how students deal with the situation. Collaborative planning is an excellent case in point of this paradox. It takes a natural social event, like talking with a friend, and imposes a structure upon it; that structure is derived from educational research, and it is intended to engage students in a particular kind of thinking they might not otherwise choose to do. (Of course, *why* knowledge telling became the default is another question.) In fact, some students who have developed finely honed strategies for midnight inspiration and writing under pressure find this purposeful, rhetorical approach to writing an actual interference. And some educators who emphasize self-expression, the privacy of writing, or a concern with language and style better handled in revision, might find collaborative planning irrelevant as well. My point is that the literate practice of collaborative planning is an educator's construct that is neither a "natural act" nor the unquestioned "right way" to write. It is assigned because the teachers who use it believe it will be a means to achieve certain goals. As such, it is a clear instance of both power relations in school and the structures, such as assigned activities, which maintain them.

The paradox is that the goals of collaborative planning are not to achieve a specified product or a valued voice or a teacher-imposed ideological perspective. They are, in fact, to encourage students to take more responsibility for their own thinking, to take their sense of purpose beyond a formulaic representation into a more fully elaborated web of intentions. The goal is not to initiate students into compliance with a discipline or genre (whether it is journal writing or five-paragraph themes) but to help writers explore options and recognize that they control a repertoire of text conventions. As an educational construct, collaborative planning was designed to foreground the real problems of writing for an audience and of entering any discourse that one may only partly control. From the instructor's point of view, collaborative planning is a forum for students to build a representation of the task, to figure out what is expected, and to imagine how readers, including teachers, respond. In short, it is intended to help students take control of their writing and to manage whatever situation they find themselves in, in a more purposeful way, just as all of us do who write for our jobs or personal ends within the social structures we inhabit.

Collaborative planning, then, embodies the paradox of power seen in many educational innovations: it does not presume to "give" independence but to use the power structures of school to help writers develop ways of achieving rhetorical power and personal authority in their writing. At least, that is the intent behind this social arrangement. But as our strategic analysis of collaborative talk emphasized, the real question is, How do students themselves negotiate their ways through these tricky waters of opportunity and constraint?

Patterns of Power

To understand the multiple ways learners achieve power, we have to bear in mind the multiple ways writers negotiate meaning. In the first sense that I argued for in chapter 2, negotiation is an act of path finding: writers must set a course through a territory of constraints and criteria clamoring for their attention, strike a path guided by their reading of the situation and the logic they (as learners or experts, insiders or outsiders) impose. Negotiation is a set of trade-offs among conflicting goals, a series of decisions among valued alternatives each competing for the writer's attention. A good path honors as many values and goals as possible. Sometimes these concerns are internally generated; sometimes they are the artifact of an interpersonal negotiation in which the talk between two people sets agendas, charts paths, and confers social value on some choices and not others. In the world of negotiation as path finding, there are no simple dichotomies or adversarial certainties but a complex web of possibilities and desires.

However, when we look at meaning making in its political sense, we see negotiation operate as a move within a set of power relations in which decisions can represent the give and take of assertion, resistance, compromise, or capitulation. The web of possibilities associated with path finding seems to shrink to a conflict between sides, and the outcome is not a uniquely created path but a question of whose path. Finding the balance of power is also a central part of negotiating meaning in school. Schools are institutions that bumble along perpetuating the unjust social patterns that created them, and students must learn to speak within such systems. Teachers' expectations often conflict with students' personal needs or cultural values. Readers (teachers, classmates, journal reviewers) want to hear the comfortable commonplaces of their present community even as writers chafe to strike out for a different discourse. Negotiation within these patterns of power (where power is not necessarily unjust, but usually problematic) is at the heart of rhetoric, both classical, modern, and cognitive. It is also part of the paradox of education—an institution committed to using its power to help students develop their own.

When meaning is forged in a conversation with power, some theorists would invoke reproduction theory to argue that the practice of written literacy, which so clearly reflects the cultural practices of the social elite, is a critical tool in reproducing its values and social patterns. Meaning making in school, the argument would go, is certain to be a hegemonic practice, in which the powerless engage in the very practices, supplied by the dominant culture, that keep the powerless in their place. Some educators, like Berlin for instance, assume rather categorically that students have so fallen "victim to reification" that this condition should be the focus of writing classrooms: "Students must be taught to identify the ways in which control over their own lives has been denied them, and denied in such a way that they have blamed themselves for their powerlessness" (1988, p. 490). However, Erickson, whose work in sociolinguistics and educational anthropology has focused on issues of racial and cultural equity, criticizes the answer of reproduction theory as "an overdetermined social theory that denies any autonomous reality to social life and choice at the level of everyday conduct of life—in this case, the level of everyday life in classrooms. . . . We have seen empirical evidence of such choice . . . and the importance of such choice making by learners and teachers in the interactional construction of learning environments that foster or inhibit student learning" (1988, p. 220).

Resistance theory, Erickson argues, "lacks some of the flaws of its parent," by showing how "non-elite students cooperate in this situation of unfair competition by disadvantaging themselves still further by refusing to learn." Resistance is a self-defeating move, but one in which "the student resists being defined by the school as a person of less worth than others" (1988, p. 219). Resistance theory can often give us a powerful explanation of why intelligent students "choose to fail" (Fordham, 1991) or how other less vulnerable mainstream students resist and critique school requirements (Chase, 1988). However, is resistance (with its assumptions of unremitting class conflict and a tendency to polarize and at times valorize conflict) the best explanation for every act of assertion or poor performance? As Erickson points out, "Giroux (1983) takes resistance theory to task for fallacies of loose thinking, especially for the fallacy of overgeneralization. Every instance of student misbehavior—scrawled writing on an assignment, failure to complete an assignment, fighting, taking drugs, absenteeism—cannot be interpreted as evidence of resistance" (p. 220). Resistance as Giroux (1983) defines it is an ideological critique of patterns of social domination leading to struggle, and as such, it is necessary in a democratic society. But is it the only desirable form of critical awareness and the only reasonable response for learners to make to the power structure of school?

We need, I believe, to conduct more supple and grounded analyses of students' negotiations with power, analyses that do not obliterate strategic choice by an overlay of more simplistic or categorical social explanations. For example, Greene's argument for a "social-cognitive epistemic" notes that while social critics "like Shor, Berlin and Knoblauch speak of reflection, critical consciousness, and action, . . . it is the teacher who identifies, abstracts, and problematizes certain themes in this method. . . . We do not find much specific discussion about how individual students can take ownership of their learning, or how they can negotiate the complex tasks of unmasking ideology, of becoming agents, or of learning the modes of inquiry that can potentially give students access to the disciplines they wish to join (1990a, p. 162). When Greene brought this social cognitive perspective to the writing in a history class, his study went beyond previous constructivist studies of writing and challenged the traditional wisdom that students achieve "authority" either by inserting their own ideas or by citing other authorities. His finer-grained, strategic analysis let him complicate this dichotomous image of literate authority, which typically reduces students to either imitators/manipulators of received ideas (Bartholomae, 1985) or to assertive, but typically naive, claimants whose limited "own ideas" about the Marshall Plan are likely to reflect their status as learners. Greene (1990b) adds compelling evidence of what he calls students' *constructive authority* at work as they interpret the task (e.g., turning a report into a problem-solving inquiry) and as they transform information in their texts, appropriating and restructuring source information, repositioning the authorities themselves to meet their own discourse goals.

The present study did not set out to discover how collaborative planners negotiate power structures. Such research, based on more contextual data than we collected, should be done. However, the transcripts, grades, and instructors' comments we do have point to a strategic response that is often more complicated than a choice between capitulation or resistance and that involves not only choices but awareness of alternatives.

In this study, collaborative planning represents one clear-cut form of imposed social power—both as a set of announced rhetorical goals and as an assigned activity. Students constructed meaning in response to such power in at least three interesting ways: by cooperating with it, by appropriating it, and by engaging in what I will call compliance.

Carter and Jennie take the road of cooperating with the goals of instruction. Their comments on tape and their teacher's evaluation reflect their attempt not only to please and impress the teacher but to maintain a good-natured, good faith effort to "play the game" to see what it yields. And they do so in a productive way, developing an enlarged image of the task and of what readers, including teachers and peers, look for in a paper. As their concluding comments indicate, they find it easy to combine useful, even inventive, collaboration, with maintaining social relations and keeping a eye on the clock.[3]

Kate ("I don't think our collaboration went that well") reveals a more critical or at least a more assertive intellect at work. Kate deals with authority by appropriating it. She uses the planning session for her own purposes, to explore her ideas. In doing so, she makes a sensible strategic choice, even though she fails to engage in the rhetorical process the course was trying to teach. Yet this is a case not of resistance, but of negotiation, charting an individual path. As we saw, she later chooses to take on the mantle and voice of a teacher in a rather experimental manner, walking through the textbook's advice to see what it would yield and evaluating the result. And she ends the session with the intention to collaborate again, to cooperate with the program. If, in that later session, she had tried to engage with the difficult issues of purpose and reader, she would have taken the cooperative stance of Carter, much as Fran ("these ideas are all related, somewhere") did, willing to participate as a learner in a process she does not fully control. If one is trying to learn something, cooperation (on at least an experimental basis) that leads to appropriation and critical awareness appears to be a useful way to deal with the structures of school. However, a note of caution: if we want to see sustained critical reflection, we have to make it a part of the school-sponsored structure of doing collaboration. As we found in later the classroom inquiry project (Flower et al., 1993), teachers who expect collaboration to support critical cognition and reflexive awareness have to make reflection a genuine activity that merits class time and attention.

These patterns of cooperation and appropriation are easy to understand, as is the more consciously oppositional stance of resistance. But what about the students who engage in passive compliance, who turn strategies (meant to be the means to some intellectual end) into exercises (where doing the procedure is itself the end). Such students choose to go through the steps without learning to dance.

Sometimes the logic is not hard to find. Donna, who is joined by two other drama students, may have a more important social agenda to manage, which includes her relationship with the teacher: "Okay... I have this idea—wait a minute. That was the waiter. Okay. (Laughs) We're in the Yard [a student hangout]." After various diversions ("I love this song"), Donna states her topic (inside jokes and expressions that different groups of friends do not understand), then checks the recorder, and puts her partner on notice: "Do you have any other questions, Isaac, or would you like to tear my idea apart?" Isaac replies, "I don't understand your idea yet" and begins to ask what her "insight" is.

13 Donna: Insight! Well, the only insight that I can think of that I have is just because like I've had these experiences that I have often. And that I've found it is totally impossible to try to bring these friends together in a room and things like that because they don't get along. They don't understand each other... I don't know. This is not insight. This is shit but I think I'm really confused about what to do. I really need a drink of water right now.

14 S: Time out beep.

15 Donna: Ask me some more questions.

16 S: What are your key points?

17 Donna: My key point, oh good God. That's not it. That's a bad question. Can we come back to that?

18 S: Okay.

19 Donna: I really have not thought about this much because I've too many other exams. It's true Steven [instructor's first name]...

20 S: This assignment comes at a bad time for all of us.

21 Donna: Really bad time. It's true. Hello, Steven, we're in stereo now which I'm sure will really be exciting for you cause it really is for us. Ask some more questions of me, Isaac.

Donna's personal style and self-image, the social situation ("dramats" are expected to be casual, witty, "onstage") and the relationships that need to be juggled among Isaac, Eric, and the instructor probably play a much stronger role in this negotiation than either the instructor's intentions or the student's own apparent interest in the topic. Even the heavy hand of academic evaluation seems to be more of a fact than a factor: "This is going to be a really bad paper unless I change what it is going to be." For this freshman, the authority of school (the forces to negotiate) may be identified primarily as a social relationship with the instructor (which appears to be itself subordinate to other relationships). Given her priorities at this point, going through the steps may seem enough.

A more perplexing version of compliance, however, comes from Vince and Tomas whom we excerpted earlier as an example of a mixed quality session. They illustrate more clearly that paradox of power: the authority of school is being used here to ask Vince to take authority by learning to take purposeful control of his own writing. The course had emphasized rhetorical thinking. The assignment and evaluative criteria had called for Vince to find a "real discourse problem" and a "purpose of . . . [his] own" that is not only "apparent to readers" but used to "organize the rest of the paper" (see chap. 6). The Planner's Blackboard prompts for purpose. But even more importantly, Vince's partner, Tomas, makes the issue unavoidable with his persistent questioning about Vince's point—whether he has one and what he will conclude. To all of this, Vince consistently replies, "Well, it's just to discuss how this comes up in life." A little interpersonal negotiation gets Vince off the hook, getting his partner to laugh and agree, "Okay. Okay. Sure."

The meaning Vince negotiates reflects the legacy of school—in response to these new requests and expectations he maintains the knowledge-driven plan he enunciated in his pre-session self-interview: "I picked the topic of like idiomatic speech [mentioned in Farb]. The way people just have certain ways of saying things, and they just fall into these ruts and they always use the same reply even though it's not really how they may feel. Uh... the key—key point and purpose of this paper is to—to discuss this and show how it comes up in everyday life [. . . .] This paper's pretty general." He concludes, "Probably the most interesting feature of my paper is that I will use another language beside English," drawing on a trip to Germany for foreign clichés. This is a paper Vince knows how to write.

What I find interesting is the way Vince negotiates the situation itself with this peculiar strategy of compliance. It is true that teachers and/or the institution of school often deny students authority and, in demanding cooperation, deny the possibility of true cooperation. Some educators might even applaud or encourage these small, indirect forms of resistance as a way for students to subvert the system and deny agendas they have not made. And yet Vince is neither assertively resisting nor consciously challenging the rules of the game. Instead, he has turned (what was intended to be) a heuristic process into a "teacher's process," an exercise that is fulfilled when one goes through the steps. Vince participates in the activity but not in its goals. Like other educational activities—freewriting, journal keeping, peer review, problem finding—such planning makes most sense when students engage with the goals that make the activity worth doing. The event the teacher had in mind was an intellectual event in which a student like Vince would not just parry questions but attempt to see his writing as a rhetorical act, to explore his own purposes or interests, to imagine a reader, or question his plan.

There is, of course, a logic to compliance just as there is a logic to the paper Vince has in mind. Both Vince and Tomas are A students described by their teacher as smart, stimulating, and a little cynical about school. And even though Vince's instructor noted the lack of a real point in the paper, his "discuss it" strategy was enough to produce a well-organized short paper with nice examples and to earn an A in this freshman course.[4] A cynic might say, "So what? Vince didn't need rhetorical planning to get his A. Why should he bother to do more?" (It is part of that paradox of school power that it can never realistically motivate the effort it requests; it must ultimately count on students to set goals that stretch them despite the artificiality of a classroom.)

And yet, is Vince's choice really a choice or an unexamined habit of negotiating school? What is the strategic knowledge, the logic behind this "teacher's process"? Bringing students' awareness of their strategic choices into this equation might complicate our analysis in a useful way. Stacked up against other options, Vince's compliance seems to buy him little: (1) he could have engaged in an active, critical resistance to this approach to writing or to collaboration, or his partner's questions; (2) he could have avoided this nongraded assignment, cutting it short to study for a calculus test, order a pizza, or whatever was higher in his priorities; or (3) he could have attempted to engage in his partner's requests, even if he did not want to change his plan for the paper. Yet Vince gives little indication that he is really aware that in doing the "teacher's process," he has given himself an exercise with low aspirations and limited value to himself. It is not clear Vince is aware that he has, in effect, chosen to spend this collaborative time on a low-investment, but low-return strategy.

Compliance—stepping through strategies and ignoring their goals and doing so with limited awareness—is a way to maintain some sense of internal authority while still staying within the bounds of school. But it is a way that offers students little in return, since it supports neither learning nor effective rhetorical action. Choosing to blow off an English paper in order to finish an architectural drawing, as some of these students did, is a reasonable move, a legitimate assertion of a student's priorities and part of learning how to negotiate as well as influence structures of authority. Compliance, on the other hand, is like the practice without theory that Freire (1989) describes—an action without awareness.

This attempt to understand the strategic knowledge that is guiding Vince is decidedly post hoc, a speculative interpretation of the logic behind his actions that may be only partly right. The critical issue is really Vince's awareness. The studies which follow, however, offer some support for this reading. In them, students begin to conduct observation-based analyses of their own thinking, using tapes from their planning sessions to reflect on features they found interesting. We will hear from a number of students who discover that their own unacknowledged assumptions about the "teacher's process" and "teacher's expectations" led them to ways of imagining authority and negotiating school that precluded taking authority over their own writing. More interesting, such reflection seems to confirm students' authority to apply more personal, more demanding goals and to design these sessions into a process that actually works for themselves.

I think Vince raises two issues for us. One concerns teachers. To understand the ways students negotiate the power structures of school will take a strategic analysis that recognizes the strategies writers control as well as the goals they set and the awareness they possess of their own actions. Bringing students' strategic knowledge into the picture is central to building a social cognitive theory of writing and to responding to individual students. However, the real potential for change comes when students themselves undertake observation-based strategic analysis of their own actions. When writers come to realize that they are engaging in strategic acts shaped by their personal goals as well as by social and cultural assumptions, then it becomes clear that strategies are open to change and that there are multiple ways to negotiate the authority and structure of school.

8

Metacognition
A Strategic Response to Thinking

Is Metacognition Really Necessary?

This book began with an image of literate action as a social cognitive process and as a theory of how writers construct negotiated meanings through acts of interpretation, negotiation, and reflection. However, the following chapters argued, the logic of these socially situated constructive acts becomes apparent only when we recognize writer's strategic knowledge—their goals, strategies, and awareness. Strategies or heuristics have long been seen as central to the art of rhetoric, just as goals are the driving force in cognition and motivation. But the place of metacognitive awareness is less clear. Is metacognition really necessary to learning or meaning making? And if so, does it follow we should teach it?

Consider this freshman in the Reading-to-Write project (chap. 1) as she describes in class what she discovered about herself from her own think-aloud protocol. "Since I was talking out loud, I was very conscious of the fact that I was making connections to what everyone [in the source material] was saying. Using my own—using things that have happened to me to connect to the people talking... And I realized that I actually do have strategies to read. I thought I didn't. I thought I was some kind of odd person who didn't have any strategies ever."

Observation-based self-reflection seems to be succeeding in convincing this young woman that she is indeed making strategic choices, where six weeks of class discussion had failed. Yet, for all the wonder of her discovery, she had done well enough without this knowledge to make it into the freshman class of a competitive college. Vince ("I'm only discussing this," chaps. 6, 7) not only succeeded in high school, he was on the road to success in his freshman class, holding on to his well-developed knowledge-driven strategies and not particularly eager to to call either his strategies or his assumptions about writing into question.

There is a strong tradition in liberal education that values, even venerates, reflection and awareness—a set of assumptions I tend to share. But as an educator, one cannot merely assume that the discourse practice of reflection is really critical to learning, much less to all students. There are reasons to take a critical look. To begin with, reflection is not a mimetic act mirroring an inner reality; it does not function as a gesture of pure awareness. It is, after all, a historically shaped discourse practice with a long tradition that includes philosophical *pensées*, the "confessions" of an Augustine and Rousseau, the "apologia pro vita sua" of a Newman and the Puritan practice of religious self-examination that helped shape autobiographies of a Pepys, Rousseau, or Boswell, as well as the emerging form of the novel (Watt, 1967). It includes the guided journeys of psychotherapy in its many forms and the implicitly rule-governed practices of an "authentic" personal essay (Macrorie, 1970), the freewheeling, freewriting style encouraged in journal writing (Elbow, 1981), or the politically directed action/reflection designed to create critical consciousness (Freire, 1989; Giroux & McLaren, 1989). Reflection, my point is, exists not as a faithful mimesis of inner experience but as a set of codified discourse practices, a kind of thinking one can learn to do. To say this does not deconstruct the practice of reflection into a mere game or deny the possibility of its enormous personal and educational value, but it does ask us to treat the educational significance of any given reflective practice as an open question.

When reflection is self-motivated and incidental—something good students do on their own time—its value would probably be unquestioned. But consider the harder case when intentional, strategic reflection forms part of the content and the writing of a course. Then reflection as a literate practice, chosen in place of other practices, needs to be accountable. And at this point, other voices that also equate literate action with liberating education enter the discussion. I hear Delpit (1986) arguing that many liberal, white "process" teachers fail to listen to the black teachers when they assert that what their students need is not a place to express their voices but straightforward instruction in how to handle the conventions of power—the patterns and conventions of Standard English. And I hear Hull and Rose (1989) writing about underprepared students for whom the five-paragraph theme is both a revelation and a generative structure. And I hear Peck (1991) standing in the midst of an interracial community center, where people on the streets of the city's North Side do not need to be "made aware" of their oppressed condition (even if the middle-class kids in nearby colleges do), but they do need to control the kinds of literacy that lets them act, the rhetorical strategies for making plans and arguments that can lead people in a neighborhood into concerted action. If we are going to listen to these voices, we have to be sure that acts of reflection are not just literate classroom performances that produce charming texts with the cadences of engagement and discovery that make teachers feel good. We have to ask, Is guided reflection a robust occasion for learning, or is it just frosting on the cake? It is in that spirit of skeptical commitment to the possibilities of reflection that this discussion is written.

Let me clarify how the sometimes interchangeable terms of *metacognition*, *awareness*, and *reflection* are being used here. Metacognition, as the most inclusive concept, signifies thinking about thinking at many levels of awareness. Metacognitive awareness, when it takes the force of a verb, signifies acts of observation, alertness, and noticing when a part of attention or working memory is devoted not just to action but to the recognition that I am performing this action. Awareness, as a noun, refers to the knowledge possessed as a result of this divided attention. However, as think-aloud protocols often demonstrate, such "knowing" can be a fleeting event, pushed out of memory by the press of business, as my colleague, Dick Hayes, once brilliantly but inadvertently illustrated. Giving a seminar on protocol analysis to a group of writers in Washington, he was demonstrating the process, composing aloud on a difficult topic and promptly running into a planning problem with which he struggled for some minutes. Later, when asked if he had had any difficulty planning, he blithely reported that it had gone quite well as he reiterated his final, triumphant plan. It was only when he was reminded in front of the group of the details of his struggle that awareness of the dilemma returned.

Reflection, as I will use the term, is an intentional act of metacognition, an attempt to solve a problem or build awareness by "taking thought" of one's own thinking (Flower, 1989b). In the collaborative planning study in chapters 6 and 7, awareness was pushed to more articulate reflection by a dialogue with a partner in which it was used to identify problems, pose alternatives, or justify decisions. It was a side effect of collaboration. In the chapters that follow, awareness is the result of an intentional and assigned act of reflection.

I. The Debate over Metacognition

Meta, as in *metaphysics*, *metaphor*, and *metacognitive*, suggests a level of awareness that floats somewhere above more concrete events. But the link between knowing and acting and the content of what people know can be highly variable. In practice, the different meanings of *metacognition* cluster around two levels of metaknowing: the in-process acts of regulating cognition and those of reflecting on it. The first level of cognition about thinking is often relatively tacit, a process of regulating or controlling other cognitive acts. Readers engage in such metacognition when they interrupt fluent reading to monitor a failure in comprehension, to reread, to try to form a gist, to clarify a momentary source of confusion. This level of metacognition, which Baker and Brown (1984), describe as control strategies, monitors cognition and redirects attention, putting on the brakes, calling up new processes, setting a new goal for the thinker. In writing, acts of planning, detecting, and diagnosing problems are all control strategies that let writers monitor and guide cognition. Experienced readers and writers tend to make a greater number and/or different versions of these metacognitive moves than less experienced writers (Bereiter & Scardamalia, 1987; Flower et al., 1992; Hayes et al., 1987). But in all these cases, metacognition as control can be a highly automated, extremely fast, and tacit process.

A second level of metacognition refers to the knowledge one has about cognition—"to the stable, statable, often fallible, and often late developing information that human thinkers have about their own cognitive processes; traditionally this has been referred to as *knowing that* " (A. Brown, 1987, pp. 67–68). Such knowing has a privileged status as Brown asserts: "Several theorists from quite disparate schools agree that the most stringent criteria for understanding involve the availability of knowledge to consciousness and reflection; thus permitting verbal reports" (p. 72). Metacognition is knowing that you know something and being able to inventory and talk about your own knowledge as content and as process, that is, being able to talk about what you know (and what you do not, how your knowledge is organized, etc.) and secondly, about how your thinking operates. The object of cognition about cognition, then, is not only the topic knowledge one possesses, but one's own thinking processes and strategies, as well.

However, are all forms of this statable metacognition equally useful to a learner? One form, which has not fared well in educational research, is that "knowledge of pertinent facts" that is often a "permanent part of one's naive theory on the topic" (A. Brown, 1987, p. 68). It is the sort of information tapped by questionnaires and clinical interviews that ask people to generalize: to estimate their memory span (Flavell & Wellman, 1977) or to describe their normal writing process (Rubin, 1983). Unfortunately, when asked to retrospect about their own thinking and decision process, people not only "tell more than they can know" but are often demonstrably wrong (Nisbett & Wilson, 1977). Or, as Rubin found, such knowing may simply reproduce the reigning conventional wisdom rather than describe real performance. Or, like sentence diagraming or truisms about thinking about the reader, it may tap the "inert" knowledge students can produce on request but have never learned to access when needed or to use for real purposes (Bereiter & Scardamalia, 1985).

In contrast to these generalized "naive theories" and retrospections, a much more limited form of statable metacognition is clearly tied to successful performance. It is often referred to as the ability to mention as well as use, to recognize, or to access one's strategies. Such knowledge may be statable as no more than the unelaborated comment we see in think-aloud protocols (e.g., an in-process recognition that "I think I need an example here to make the point"). However, such recognition marks a great watershed in learning, as evidence that a student has achieved both access to and control of his or her own knowledge. As A. Brown says, "children who know perfectly well how to use a strategy or have the relevant prior knowledge, often fail to access it on appropriate occasions" (1987, p. 72). Many see this as the classic problem of learning—getting access to what you know (Prawat, 1989). It is only, A. Brown argues, when learners have conscious access to and control of their own knowing, when knowledge is no longer welded to the situation in which it was learned, that we achieve the flexibility that is the hallmark of higher intelligence (p. 71).

There are also some strong educational implications from metacognitive research. On the down side, many metastatements are merely inert theory. However, as Vygotsky argued, it is clear that one form of metastatement, *self-talk*, helps. It is possible, for instance, to improve both learning and transfer by doing nothing more than asking problem solvers to state a reason for each move they make as they are thinking (Ericsson & Simon, 1985). Educators and therapists have seen lasting effects from cognitive therapy and self-regulated learning in which hyperactive, impulsive children learn to talk themselves through tasks, talking out their intentions, calmly noticing and recovering from errors, and congratulating themselves for trying. In other studies, college students who saw themselves as uncreative learned to alter their self-defeating stream of self-talk into supportive and strategic self-instruction (Harris & Pressley, 1991; Meichenbaum, 1977; Meichenbaum, 1985). The techniques of *self-instruction* and *self-regulated learning* vary, but the three essential features include (1) modeling a repertoire of strategies, (2) teaching learners to monitor their own thinking through group or self-talk, and (3) motivating this process by helping students recognize the links between outcomes and their own strategies (A. Brown, 1987). The case for statable metacognition, for self-talk, is a strong one and helps explain how process and strategy teaching can intervene in the very act of writing. However, we must maintain our initial skepticism and recognize that this evidence for self-talk does not extrapolate into a mandate for reflection as a literate practice. The form of metacognition this research on self-talk supports is a highly situated, unelaborated, goal-directed, awareness in action.

In the next two chapters, I would like to follow the traces of another, less studied, form of metacognition found in students' observation-based self reflections. This literate practice appears to stand somewhere between the specificity of in-process self-talk (i.e., mentioning and access) and the generalizing sweep of naive theories or retrospections. This form of metacognition is especially relevant to writing because it comes from students' data-based self-observations and subsequent interpretations of their own writing and thinking. It is, on the one hand, a relatively articulated, written, even revised account with a concern for coherence and evidence—a personal theory. It is, however, based on self-observations, tapes, and transcripts of a process in action making it potentially closer to in-process reflections and critical incident accounts (Flanagan, 1954) than to retrospections or students' conventional accounts of their own writing (Rubin, 1983). It is, we might say, a *situated theory* that tries to generate an elaborated understanding or hypothesis about an issue, but it does so on the basis of systematic rather than incidental observation and with the goal of understanding and acting in a specific situation (Flower et al., 1993).

This form of metacognition is a complex, intentional, time-taking act of reflection. For instance, a student writer might review the state of her topic knowledge (e.g., What do I know for an assignment on the meaning of *Moby Dick*, 5 pages, due Tuesday?) and then go on to consider the discourse conventions or even ideology of communities who assign (and apparently like to read) such texts. Facing a new task, reflection might lead her to think about the assumptions, values, goals, and strategies that are informing her present act of composing. She might even pause to monitor how she is managing her own thinking (e.g., I'd like to write a critique of this inane assignment, but since I'm actually coming up with good ideas, I'll keep going) or to note her own strategies (e.g., I'm getting bogged down in perfecting sentences again). To operate at this level of reflective metacognition calls for both a heightened awareness (beyond that needed to regulate cognition) and for a language (beyond self-talk prompts) to talk about, evaluate, and manipulate that knowledge.

Reflection is clearly a constructive process, but the question remains: What sort of knowledge or meaning does such reflection create? And do verbal statements (including our assumptions, insights, fictions, and self-observations) actually reflect, predict, or guide the other business of regulating cognition (e.g., planning, monitoring, managing one's thinking)? We will consider two issues in the vigorous theoretical debate over metacognition that have a special relevance for writers. One is the problematic epistemology of reflection, and the second is the charge that reflection is merely a luxury.

Reflection: An Interpretive Act

The epistemological status of reflection and verbal reports in general has always been problematic. Although reflection has a privileged status in the humanities, it has been treated as an artistic or philosophical form rather than as a significant part of what students do or how they learn. What exactly does metacognitive cognition know? In psychology, self-reports have had a checkered history. The introspectionist enterprise wrecked on the fact that even with hours of training, people were unable to report on elementary mental processes such as perception or memory search. In radical behaviorism, thoughts (and verbal reports) were banished altogether as epiphenomena rather than causal agents in learning or behavior (Skinner, 1963). Because words and actions were seen as separate systems of response, the relationship between them is arbitrary. One's words (interpretation, insight, explanation) are not the product of insight into the real causes of action but the product of whichever verbal response (interpretive scheme, discourse, set of commonplaces) is being reinforced by one's reading, teachers, culture.

In clinical psychology, by contrast, self-awareness claims authority based on its power to change behavior or predict future actions. However, clinical interventions based on awareness of motives located in an unconscious mind have a rather depressing record of success: "It is not entirely surprising that self-insights are often unaccompanied by changes in behavior. It is easier to alter people's beliefs about the causes of their behavior than to change how they behave. Alcoholics, for example, can be more easily persuaded that they drink because of a fixated oral dependency than they can be induced to forsake alcohol" (Bandura, 1986, pp. 4–5). More problematic is the possibility that gaining insight is "more like a belief conversion than a self-discovery process." The therapist's conceptual orientation is a strong indicator, for example, of "whether or not clients will find an unconscious mind and what will be in it. . . . Hence, one can predict better the types of insights and unconscious motivators that persons are apt to discover in themselves . . . from knowledge of the therapists' conceptual belief system than from the clients' actual psychological status." (p. 5)

In contrast to behaviorism and psychoanalytic inquiry, cognitive psychology attempts to open the black box, placing thought at the center of its inquiry into how people learn, structure their knowledge, and solve problems. Because cognitive psychology operationalized thought as the processing of information, it tended until recently to ignore social and emotional aspects of thinking. However, that perspective also led to an explosion of knowledge about thinking as a process of creating and transforming symbolic representations and solving problems. And it led to an intense interest in the relationship between knowing, broadly conceived, and the articulated, structured, and linguistically coded knowledge represented in a verbal report.

We know that access to our own thinking is limited in some predictable ways. Processes that are frequently used may become automated or tacit, slipping underground, out of focal attention, while many perceptual/motor processes, including memory search, are simply not open to introspection (Hayes, 1978). If that were not enough, assumptions, ideology, or suggestion can conspire to create reasonable fictions about cognition, lightly constrained by reality. Retrospections by famous writers, for instance, typically function more as theories or proclamations than observations (Emig, 1971). And then there is an awkward gap between those features of our experience to which we normally and selectively attend, and those that we *could* perceive with a different mind-set. In sum, the relationship between our regulatory metacognitive processes (planning, monitoring, switching strategies, etc.) and our reflective metacognitive statements about those acts of planning, monitoring and about our assumptions, goals, reasons, habits, and so on is neither dependable nor straightforward. As educators, we need to approach metacognition, especially intentional reflection, with our eyes open.

One solution, argued by Paris (1988), is to restrict the discussion of metacognition to reflective statements themselves, to knowledge about mental states and abilities that can be shared so that such knowing can indeed be measured, evaluated, and related to action. Since people's reflective awareness of their own regulative metacognitive processes (such as, monitoring and testing) is normally limited, much of what we now call metacognition would drop out of the picture. Paris's conception narrows the focus to statements about knowledge and strategies that are teachable and measurable. Yet unlike many definitions, his does include attitudinal and motivational perceptions about cognition, such as, "I'm not good at writing." Note that in this approach to metacognition, it would not matter whether such a perception is true of the writer's actual skill. As Paris acknowledges, limiting inquiry to reflective talk does not resolve epistemological problems with the status of such knowledge. Self-perceptions of the sort he describes can be notoriously inaccurate descriptions of cognition even though such beliefs may well dictate a student's behavior.

Another response to this problem is to develop a theory that can account for what people can—and cannot—report about their cognition under what circumstances, that is, to plumb the process of how reflections are being constructed. Ericsson and Simon's (1985) widely cited theory of verbal reports has laid a foundation. It defines two conditions under which people do not have access to their own cognition and so will be forced to draw on memory and, in many cases, to generalize across multiple, dissimilar instances separated in time. One such condition is when people are asked to make predictions about how they *would* think (such as "How would you read this story if paragraph two had been omitted?"). The other is when people are asked to offer retrospections about past performance (such as "How did you [or do you "normally"] deal with conflict?"). Such questions are widely used in research and by teachers, but as Ericsson and Simon's theory predicts, they are not reliable accounts. As many studies and critiques of such verbal reports have documented, it is possible to imagine and report processes one does not, in fact, use and at the same time, to use many strategies of which one has little awareness, such as the fleeting acts of comprehension monitoring seen in experienced readers. This is not to dismiss the potential interest of such statements but to treat them like other generalizations or inferences for which we inquire politely about the evidence and reserve judgment when there is a sizable leap between data and claim.

Ericsson and Simon's third condition exists when people are asked to give a concurrent verbal report of thinking as they are carrying out a task. Such reports allow more direct access to cognition but with some important qualifications. The cognition people can reliably report will be knowledge and processes that are operating in focal attention (i.e., not automated processes or weakly activated knowledge) and secondly, knowledge and processes that are already verbally coded. (Think, for instance, of the nonverbal perceptual processes computer troubleshooters seem to possess as they race through and manipulate a person's files looking for a problem. However, this form of knowledge may require considerable recoding when they are asked for a verbal explanation.) People's access to their own cognition is also compromised when they are asked to report selectively (e.g., to attend to word choice or feelings about authority as they work). Such requests will change the process by literally changing part of the writing task and altering the writer's focus of attention.

Ericsson and Simon's theory shows how verbalizing thinking while in the act of thinking can give us a better window on cognition, but like any window, it also has a frame that blocks out tacit and nonfocal information in some predictable ways. Likewise, retrospective reports based on cued recall and recent experience will be subject to less interpretive distortion than are broad generalizations covering a sweep of events or speculations about causes (of which the writer was unaware at the time). Most importantly, and this is the heart of the Ericsson and Simon argument, the data of verbal reports are still and only that—the data of observation that, like all data, await interpretation. The meaning of the data is not self-evident; it lies in the way that data is used as evidence by students and researchers alike.

In sum, reflection must be recognized as a highly interpretive process, influenced by the prior knowledge we bring and the way it is conducted. The value of observation in this process is its ability to challenge as well as to shape the ways we construct ourselves as writers.

Reflection: A Guide to Action?

A second issue in the metacognition debate is whether metacognition plays an important role in learning: Is it a necessity or a luxury, a deep discovery or an epiphenomen—and if each can be true at times, which is which? We know that some metatalk is just another name for inert knowledge—the party line on paragraph structure or writing that many students could produce on demand along with the names of state capitals. Such declarative knowledge was learned and remains as a self-contained package, unconnected to actions, problems, or situations a student might encounter. Even when relevant, it is useless because it is neither linked to nor cued by situations of use. At the other end of the significance scale, A. Brown (1987) argues that sophisticated, intelligent systems, human and computer alike, are highly dependent on the feedback supplied by metacognitive functions like planning in action, troubleshooting, monitoring, revising, contingency planning. But just how much do learners need to think about thinking to develop these metamoves?

We know that the first steps in acquiring control strategies, such as the comprehension monitoring good readers do at the end of a paragraph, may take place in a collaborative, verbalized social experience (a parent interrupts reading to ask, "What did the wolf think?"). Those steps may also depend on awareness, conscious attention, and declarative knowledge, even though such moves later become automated (Brown & Palincsar, 1989; Dansereau, 1985; Vygotsky, 1986). Likewise, our procedural knowledge for driving a car (Anderson, 1980) goes through an initial period in which learning to operate the clutch, the gear shift, and the accelerator takes full concentration and muttered self-commands. Later, awareness reappears when people encounter conflicts or new, ill-defined problems that invoke a problem-solving process. It is no surprise that problem-solving pedagogies in math, physics, design, reading, and writing focus on both expanding students' repertoire of strategies and increasing their awareness of when to switch among them (Hayes, 1981). But how much is awareness necessary?

For example, Brown and Palincsar's (1989) reciprocal teaching helped children make great gains in reading comprehension by making these control strategies explicit in the form of questions and prompts young readers gave each other in a collaborative effort to comprehend the text. Because the ultimate goal is for learners to internalize and automate these reading strategies, students take turns helping each other to state the gist, predict what will come next, clarify uncertainties, and predict comprehension questions. However, they spend little time at the next "meta" level, reflecting on the strategies or on themselves. This form of "direct instruction" turned four key control strategies into named, articulated actions that readers could model and learners could try out. And when they needed help shaping a good question or a prediction, as many young readers did initially, a more experienced reader could intervene in the process, helping to shape a better question. Such direct instruction stands in contrast to "blind training" in which students are swept up in activities that the teacher assumes will promote learning or performance. Although the teacher may intend that a given activity (e.g., group talk) will elicit certain strategies or reach certain goals, that information is not shared with students. A familiar form of blind training criticized by Applebee is the use of process activities in writing that are not anchored to a goal-directed image of the process—students are not let in on the goals of the activity, including what it is good for (and what it is not). When journal keeping, for instance, was taught as an end and value in itself, students came to see it not as a heuristic that might help them learn material, but as yet another exercise/assignment quite unrelated to the serious business of preparing for the test.

Advocates of cognitive apprenticeship, direct instruction, and strategic teaching make a strong case for teachers who not only engage students in trying out heuristics but who show their hand and let students in on the purpose and the structure of the strategies (Brown & Palincsar, 1989; Collins et al., 1989; Jones, Palincsar, Ogle, & Carr, 1987). They make the case for a first level of metacognitive instruction. However, informed practice is not the same thing as cultivating a more complex reflective awareness of one's own strategic knowledge. And, a skeptic might claim, it seems unlikely that such cultivation would have much effect on normal comprehension or the fluent generation of unproblematic prose. People possess strategies they cannot and do not need to talk about. We cannot assume that heightened, articulate awareness is always necessary beyond the level of metacognitive regulation and control that can be developed through direct instruction. And yet, thinking about thinking—metacognition as reflection—has been treated as a critical step by humanistic educators from Socrates to Dewey to the current rhetorical and critical thinking movements. If reflection is not necessary for the fluent, unproblematic moments of composing, does it have a place in learning to write?

Reflection: A Strategic Act

The metacognitive debate makes it clear that reflection does not hold up the mirror of mimesis; it is a goal-directed, interpretive act that can let people understand, monitor, and guide cognition. However, an undiscriminating embrace of reflection per se makes as little sense as the uncritical, unconditional valorization of collaboration we discussed earlier. Reflection, like collaboration, is not only a powerful constructive process, it is a highly variable one. The educator's question is, What kind of knowledge is being created through reflection (under a given set of conditions), and how is that knowledge going to guide action?

To develop a theory of reflection as a situated, strategic act, one needs to ask:

- How is reflection embedded within its educational situation; what purposes do students perceive their reflection to be serving?
- What is the nature of students' interpretive, constructive process; what is the nature of the knowledge they actually construct?
- How does reflection lead to action?

The next two chapters try to answer these questions in the context of a specific educational experience in which metacognition was built on the foundation of collaborative planning. In the two college classes we will examine, students collected tapes and observations of themselves in order to examine their own planning, writing, and/or collaborative processes. Reflection took the form of articulate, considered, written reflections that were an important part of the course work and discussions.

Just as collaborative planning talk has its own signature as a form of collaboration, reflection based on self-observation will shape the experience in distinctive ways. When reflection is built on collaborative planning, it takes on the character of a problem-posing strategic inquiry quite different from the "how I write" introspections in which writers seek global patterns and speculate on underlying causes. Although such introspective journeys can yield revealing statements of writers' assumptions, they also bring to mind the "key to all mythologies" that Casaubon, the slowly withering scholar of *Middlemarch*, labored so long to create. Introspective thinking about thinking is more likely to satisfy us with its ability to create a comforting sense of coherence than with its power to surprise or guide. The signature of observation-based reflection (like the theory building described in chap. 1) is that it looks at cognition in context in response to a problem the writer poses, aided by an independent observational record that can both support and challenge interpretation.

Observation could—in theory—play two important roles in these reflections. (What it actually does becomes an empirical question.) First, it could help students balance their assumptions, prior knowledge (and the informing concepts presented by the course) with the evidence of experience and the feedback it gives to those expectations. Observation urges the writer out of the comfortable chair of retrospection where insight can be formed with the plastic stuff of memory to fit a schema or tell a coherent story. When, on the other hand, students observe their own learning, their reflections can be forged, tested, and reconstructed in the resistant context of experience.

Secondly, self-observation can also play a decisive role in learning when success in the activity depends on the fidelity, the consistency, and the immediacy of self-monitoring (as when athletes monitor their form, readers monitor their comprehension, or collaborators monitor the coherence of their plan or the escalating signals of a partner's confusion) (Bandura, 1986). Observation, we must be clear, is never independent of interpretation; it is not a pure mimetic act. For example, prior self-conceptions as well as mood will influence what aspects of experience people perceive in themselves, how they are evaluated, how they are linked to other memories, and so on. Moreover, reliable self-monitoring takes sustained, focused effort. Observation is important not because it stands as a simple veridical account but because it functions as a resistant, balancing, mediating force that is capable of surprising us into the unanticipated. Bandura has described this situation in his theory of reciprocal causation in which cognition, context, and ongoing behavior interact. If he is right, then a student's writing is unlikely to be shaped by any single cause. The logic of a given learner must be treated as an open question. If our description of negotiated construction is right, significant writing is likely to emerge out of conflicting goals, contradictory schemas, and multiple unreconciled alternatives. In the face of this complexity, observation can help counter the tendency of memory and introspection to form a good gestalt and achieve the comfort of closure. Observation (based on tapes of planning sessions, process logs, periodic self-interviews, and so forth) can retain the traces of the roads not taken and of the goals and decisions that lie behind the current meaning.

The type of metacognition we will explore, then, is a distinctive construction, shaped by observation and focused on the strategic knowledge students found themselves bringing to some specific rhetorical situations. Their reflections represent what they selected as significant out of those experiences and the working theories they created to interpret them. They also let us address the epistemology and the luxury problems sketched above by asking:

1. When students construct an image of their writing process from observational data, what sort of knowledge are they creating (the issue on which the rest of this chapter will focus)? Does the representation they build differ, for instance, from the images found in their textbooks and in journal articles? Can these writers gain access to their own cognition in a way that might challenge private theories and/or process fictions with which they started?
2. Does the opportunity to observe, to articulate difficulties, to interpret and reflect on one's experience have any affect on what happens next? Does metacognitive awareness bear any relationship to action (the issue on which the next chapter will focus)?

II. Representing a Cognitive, Social, and Affective Process

Placing Reflection in Context

According to the old adage, the best way to learn something is to teach it. Studying one's own learning has some of the same virtues if students begin to examine, appreciate, and question what they know and how they think. However, doing research on thinking is often a slow and uncertain process, while teaching must do the best job possible in 15 weeks. Making observation and reflection part of an educational process poses two problems for teachers. One is to help students collect manageable amounts of high-quality observation (that is, data that is independent enough of their own preconceptions that it has the power to surprise). And the second is to make reflection contribute directly to the course. Over the last few years, I have tried to make observation and reflection a part of my courses and have learned a lot from my mistakes as well as the occasional successes.[1] Let me place this examination of reflection in some of its contexts.

In the Context of Classroom Inquiry

In the next two chapters, I want to examine the role of reflection in the context of two classroom inquiry projects in which both my students and I (with our differing reasons) were looking into what reflection might offer. As the teacher in the middle of these stories, I was not an independent observer but a participant whose interpretation of events on Monday could return to shape the action on Wednesday. Therefore, this account needs to be read with a recognition of how classroom inquiry shapes what people learn. Compared to an experimental design, classroom inquiry is not the best way to test a technique or to more generally validate the success of one's own teaching as a recommendation to others. It is, however, a good place for discovery—to see how students are using or interpreting your teaching, to bravely examine the fate of your hopes and expectations, and to discover something of what your students are in fact doing or learning. In this process of classroom inquiry, I was joined by the other high school and college teachers of the Making Thinking Visible project. Although we were all interested in how to make the practice of collaborative planning work in our classes, our inquiries focused on students and on that mysterious link between our expectations and their experience. As this collaborative inquiry made it clear, teaching is a theory-building process;

> that is, it is a hypothesis-creating, prediction-testing process that leads to the framing and reframing of action. Theory-building is an act of mind by which teachers construct an imagined frame for actual pedagogy. . . . As a teacher, starting to run this complex scenario through my mind, I am spinning out a model of my students, imagining the assumptions, habits, and strategies they bring, predicting a dynamic interaction between these students, the task, the ethos of the course, other students, and projecting the cognitive process and intellectual stance I hope to teach and support. (Flower, 1993c, pp. 3–4)

Classroom inquiry was a place to articulate those dynamic situated theories that guide teaching, to find out where hypotheses were wrong and expectations unmet, and to reframe our situated theories of practice.

Unlike some more independent observations, classroom inquiry also helps create the event it studies. As my class and I discovered what was happening, we often used that knowledge to reshape what would happen next. So from one perspective, the interest of these accounts lies less in our particular conclusions than in the inquiry process they document—the attempt to understand some of the inner voices students were listening to and the strategic knowledge they brought to negotiation in this class.

On the other hand, I have placed these classroom observations at the center of a more general theoretical debate on metacognition because I think these situated accounts can tell us a lot about the kinds of meaning that reflection lets students construct; that is, the particular insights my students "discover" are not independent of my goals for them or my ongoing interpretations of the experience with them. Reflection is not a direct line to broad personal or public truths. But in the case I hope to build here, reflection may be the road to an even more useful, situated meaning making.

In the Context Under Negotiation

The context for any act has many layers, some of which we as observers see, some of which we theorize about. Consider for a moment just a few alternative versions of the "context for writing" in which we could imagine these writers to be situated:

- The sociocultural context of Western society, its macrostructure shaped by economic and power relations, maintained by ideology, and reflected in material realities and practices of daily life, including school (Giroux & McLaren, 1989; Lave, 1988)
- The exclusive context of a discourse community and its set of discursive practices that locate a text within academic discourse and freshman composition (Bartholomae, 1985; Flower et al., 1990)—a community that stands in contrast, for instance, to the 17th-century emerging community of Royal Society scientists or the established expectations of physicists reading each other (Bazerman, 1985), or the hybrid discourse of a graduate student moving between an expressivist and empirical mode of thinking and speaking (Berkenkotter et al., 1988)
- The more explicit context of specific textual and literate practices: record keeping (Scribner & Cole, 1981), the essay (Scollon & Scollon, 1981), the bedtime story (Heath, 1982), the placement essay (Bartholomae, 1985), biologists' proposals (Myers, 1985), and the scientific article (Bazerman, 1988)
- The localized community of people that shapes learning from the historically changing communities of the disciplines (Graff, 1987) to places called school (Goodlad, 1984); to the social, ethnic background that demands a student's allegiance (Fordham, 1988) and goes with a person when he or she leaves (Rose, 1989); to neighborhood groups organized around collaborative literate action (Peck, 1991)
- The even more intimate context of interpersonal relations: conversation (Cazden, 1988; DiPardo & Freedman, 1988; Nystrand, 1986; Sperling, 1990); the collective of classmates that share reading and writing (Dyson, 1986); and the peers and partners in collaborative planning, cooperative learning, and peer editing groups (Freedman, 1987; Gere, 1987)

Each of these versions of "the context for writing" not only draws attention to distinctive features, it brings a language that interprets those features in theoretically loaded ways. The potential context for the metacognition in the following study included all these dimensions postulated by educational theory and more. However, for our inquiry, the most relevant version of context for understanding these reflections is the more limited arena we could call the *context under negotiation*. In contrast to the social and discursive structures outside observers might perceive, these reflections are located in those aspects of the rhetorical situation that are *present* to these writers and actively impinging on what they do. This is not to say that other contexts, other unrecognized forces, cease to exist or cease to have an effect, but the context under negotiation is the operative context for reflection. Let me be clear: this operative, present context, as I read the data, is not a writer's solipistic, self-referential, self-generated fiction, his or her imaginary relation to reality. Nor is it the pattern of events, expectations, and material realities an ethnographer could document or a social theorist might postulate. Instead, the context these reflections help us to understand is created by the *relationship* between a writer's personal representation of the rhetorical situation and the events, situations, and representations of other people that the writer is bumping up against, resisting, responding to, and reshaping. Context is a point of interaction.

The context under negotiation is an interesting place, in part because it allows us to compare the writer's representation of the context with other elements in the drama from the wording of an assignment to the canons and conventions of a discourse that the writer may misread, resist, or reinterpret. We can, for instance, compare the writer's image of the teacher as reader to what the teacher wrote in an assignment, said in an interview, or stated as the assumptions behind a course. We can compare the writer's intended text to the text a reader then constructs as she or he draws inferences, forms gists, departs from the writer's expectations, attempts a sympathetic reciprocity, and succeeds or fails (Haas & Flower, 1988; Nystrand, 1986; Schriver, 1992).

The idea of a negotiable context—as a relationship, a place where representations are in contact and sometimes conflict—is a conceptual tool for understanding learning. It downplays the vast penumbra of contextual forces that might shape learning, to focus on what the writer either cares about, understands, recognizes, or has been forced by circumstances to see.[2] The particular course that shaped these student observations was not "typical," if any course is. What makes these observations worth our attention as images of possibility is not their typicality or uniqueness but the way in which students used them to respond to multiple layers of contex within and beyond this course—to other classes, to the writer's past history as a student and writer, to his or her self-image, and to the relations of authority and agency.

In the Context of a Course

In the course we will look at first, reflection was a tool students used to examine their own writing strategies. The course, Cognition and Rhetoric, focused on ideas from two sources: 1) theoretical articles on "what it meant to be a rhetor from different cognitive and rhetorical perspectives (e.g., Bartholomae, 1985; Bransford, 1985; Farb, 1974; Flower, 1993b; Freire, 1989), and 2) students' self-observations of themselves as "rhetors" based on a variety of process-tracking techniques. It was designed to let students use various cognitive and social perspectives on what readers and writers do as a lens with which to examine their own process and to speak back to the theory. The 12 students, primarily senior and first-semester M.A. students majoring in professional writing, saw themselves as aspiring writers. This discussion draws extensively on work done with Barbara Sitko who joined the class on days devoted to students' observations and reflections and coauthored our analysis of the papers (Sitko & Flower, in press).

Assignments. The first three assignments were two-page papers in which students were asked to read chapters in Farb's book *Word Play*, which offers a readable introduction to sociolinguistic research and to problems in language use, such as linguistic chauvinism, power relations, and discourse strategies. Students were asked to "*interpret* or *apply* this chapter to the task of understanding how academic discourse, as you see it, works, using the chapter to analyze and explain some problem students encounter in using or learning academic discourse." (Many students found the task surprisingly difficult, since it was neither a straight analysis of the readings nor a direct personal response, but a request to apply theory or research to a problem that they had to define.) They were also asked to monitor their own planning process, using strategies that will be described shortly, as a basis for their later observations and writing. The longer midterm paper then asked students to write about their own writing process and the way they used "such strategies to solve your own rhetorical problem or to develop your own purpose." This paper was to be based not on readings but on the self-observations students had been collecting.[3] Instruction, classroom discussion, and writing then focused on three elements: on theory, on students' self-observations, and on the application of both sorts of knowledge to practical writing problems.

Observation. In this class, as students experimented with new writing strategies, they used various process-tracking techniques (logs, self-interviews, collaboration, and private thinking aloud) to observe their own thinking and to evaluate how different writing strategies worked (or did not work) for them as they were writing their papers. Collaborative planning (which was developed with the help of this class) quickly became the strategy of choice and the most useful method of observation.[4] In addition to taping their collaborative sessions, students did a self-interview on their plans before writing and a private wrap-up after the session. Taping the 15- to 20-minute sessions was nonintrusive; the social nature of the collaboration often elicited the writers' best thinking; and the compressed nature of the session revealed the writers' priorities and threw problems into higher relief. When this record was combined with the writers' own knowledge, triggered by listening to the tapes or reading a transcript, students were able to make data-based reflections that were both richly supported and often surprising to the writer and the group.

Reflections: How did it go? Reflection in this class was of two kinds. The first depends on taking an open, experimental stance to the strategies one is teaching and creating a forum that validates students' observations by treating them as part of the knowledge of the course. Each out-of-class collaborative session was followed by time devoted to in-class reflection on what each writer observed. They followed a pattern I have since seen repeated when students are authorized to speak from the data of observation as the authority on their own experience. The initial question is usually, "How did this session/this strategy work for me?" For every student who has discovered new ideas, resolved a problem, or reversed his or her skepticism about collaboration, there will be students who felt little benefit ("I was unprepared"; "I was past planning and didn't want to revise"; "I'm not used to explaining my ideas"; "We used the blackboards as a checklist and found the discussion superficial"; etc.) This can be one of the most useful teaching and turning points in the course: sessions that do not work are as important to understand and talk about as ones that do (even if the teacher advocates the process in principle). Strategies carry no guarantee, so the teacher's role is not to defend her instruction but to ask the writer: How could you design this process so it will work for you? What will you do next time to adapt the session so it achieves your goals and makes the best possible use of your time? How will you take advantage of any potential it holds?

The question here is really one of ownership for learning. As we saw with Vince ("I'm only discussing this"), a strategy perceived as a "teacher's process" is fair game for evasion. Other students may not even realize they have trivialized a potentially powerful strategy or turned it into a mere checklist until they hear other students reflect on their own experience and what it bought them. Observation puts these problems on the table as negotiable questions. The use of valuable class time validates the significance of what students (as opposed to teachers) observe and their independent evaluation of how their learning is going. Perhaps more importantly, these observation-based reflections can make it suddenly clear that the responsibility for learning (for using and adapting a strategy to make it work for you) is in the hands of the student, not the teacher.[5]

Reflections: What did you discover? A second kind of reflection shifts attention to the larger question: What were you able to discover about your writing strategies, your assumptions, and yourself as a writer? The written reflections on which we focus in this chapter were a central part of this course. But one cannot assume that "assigned" reflection on writing will work as a learning process, since it can also sink merely to mirroring and mouthing the party line of the course. These reflections are interesting in light of some of these possibilities. For instance, it would be easy for self-reports to be merely a regurgitation of the readings: students could repeat the claims of theorists and describe their own process in terms of abstractions, conveniently supplied by Bartholomae's talk of stylistic discourse communities, Freire's sociopolitical vision, Bransford's cognitive processing theory, or Flower's problem-solving concepts. Alternatively, students might be less influenced by their readings and rest with a set of truisms untainted by theory and uncorroborated by experience. For other students, the request to reflect might be interpreted as an occasion to generate a stream of consciousness narrative about a writing event—such reflection could be a genuine personal response but an underexamined, undertested representation that ignored underlying assumptions and processes. Perhaps worst of all, students might reduce and shape their planning to fit the instructor's perceived expectations and use their observations to report the dutiful use of a given dialogue or rhetorical planning strategy.

Although one wants students to "try on" new strategies and points of view, what one hopes to see is not a perfect reflection but the refraction and transformation that goes with learning. For instance, these accounts clearly reflect the course's problem-solving stance and emphasis on rhetorical purposes. The Planner's Blackboard prompt almost certainly influenced the features students noticed in their own planning or noted by their absence. However, we also see students taking an experimental, evaluative stance toward these strategies. For me, the most significant feature of these reflections will lie in how they differ, as working theories, from the ways writing is represented in the assigned readings.

Students' Images of Their Writing Processes

At the time of this course in 1988, a growing number of composition theorists might have described writing as a social or a cognitive process, but the literature in the journals (and the students' readings) had little to say about how these mighty forces interact (Flower, 1989a). At best, the literature might have suggested a pervasive but inarticulate relationship, a twilight zone in which context would cue cognition in its silent, inexorable ways while the mind would inevitably construct a rhetorical situation in its own image. In short, the images of writing offered in the course readings had little to say about this relationship and even less to say about how affect (feelings, attitudes, motivation, and attributions) might influence students' writing (McLeod, 1987).

By contrast, the images students constructed of their own writing processes were sites of dilemma-driven action that were marked to a surprising degree by the interaction of cognition, context, and affect. Trying to enter the world of advanced academic discourse, these writers were trying out new strategies required to apply theory to a problem they had to define. As they tried to articulate the process presented to them in the memory-aided data of tapes and transcripts, they described an active, conscious attempt to negotiate a confusing rhetorical situation. The process they constructed involved not only acts of cognition but sharply drawn images of the contexts that were shaping their writing, such as past confrontations with a news editor, projections of their future professional roles, and conversations in the hall. These images also involved clearly articulated statements of affect, including self-doubts and fear of depending on collaboration, balanced by relief at seeing their own needs for social support legitimated but qualified by a nagging assumption that real writers should not need any help. Finally, the multidimensional picture they drew was far more interactive, far more strategic, than their readings (or current textbooks) did justice to.

In order to explore this interaction, Sitko and I used the following, somewhat reductive formalism of figure 8 to help categorize the writers' comments (Sitko & Flower, in press). In reality, many of the comments writers made reflect the way cognition is suffused with affect or defined as a response to a given context or situation. This theoretical separation is merely a tool that helps illuminate the distinctive contribution each way of representing writing was making to the students' images. If one envisions these reflections as a map of someone's writing process, this map recognizes three semioverlapping territories.

Within the category of affect in figure 8, one hears students reflecting on their attitudes, motivation, emotions, self-image, and so on. The process of

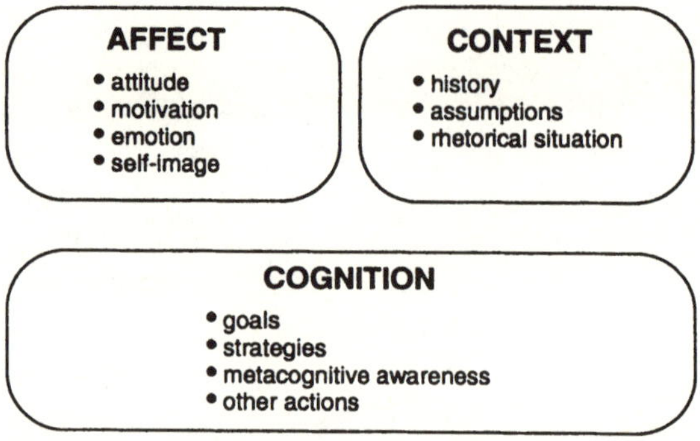

Figure 8. A schematic view of a writer's representation

writing is envisioned as an affectively loaded experience over which writers can often feel little or no control. But affect here also includes aspirations to be a writer, surprise at themselves, and the less conscious patterns of attribution—the ways students attribute their success or failure to luck, time, or ability versus effort, strategies, or experience.

Within the category labeled context, students represent their writing process as an event within their personal histories as students; it is seen as an expression of assumptions or expectations triggered by the situation or carried as unseen baggage from previous experiences. Writing is also represented as a contextually defined act when students focus on their "reading" of the class, the roles they play, or the ones they feel expected to play. In comments like these, the process of writing is represented as an essentially social act, seen at times as an almost unmediated response to past, present, or imagined contexts.

Although all of these observations are obviously acts of cognition, the category of cognition in figure 8 is used when students represent writing in terms of a thinking process subject to their intentions and decisions or as a problem they are wrestling with. In the reflections writers talk about their goals, their strategies, the process they go through, and the choices they make. Such comments portray writing as a tapestry of mental actions. Other comments foreground not just cognition but acts of metacognition when writers stand back to reflect on any or all of these elements—on the context they are in, the feelings they have, and the thinking process they orchestrate.

To explore the nature of these representations, we will look first at four students who built some distinctive, personal maps. The representation that our first student, Janet, constructed was one in which all roads seemed to lead to issues of affect.

Janet: How Do You Motivate Yourself?

From her very first protocol, Janet heard herself struggling with a problem of motivation. This attitude, however, was not mere disinclination; it appeared to reflect an active conflict in her own relation to school. Here was a hardworking, responsible, and quite successful student. But now in her last semester of a M.A. program in professional writing, she saw herself as professional writer, not as a member of an academic community. She represents writing the three Farb papers as both an affective and contextually defined event: "In writing [the three] papers, I had a problem in motivation. I wasn't interested in writing about academic discourse and could see no practical purpose in doing so. . . . I'm more interested in applying what Farb says to the task of writing in a medical community or in the computer industry. . . for which I can see many ties." The links between context and affect stand out even more clearly in the tape she quotes from her collaborative planning session:

> I mean, part of it was a reaction just to the topic of academic discourse, but it was bigger than that really: it was that I didn't want to do these assignments at all because I really couldn't see the purpose. . . . I have a different reason for being here, and some types of writing assignments or whatever that I've had to do since I've been here seem just more as getting in the way of what I'm really here to do.
>
> Even the idea of getting good grades, which used to be a source of motivation, no longer matters much. The problem, she says, is "finding (that) I'm not identifying with this assignment; I'm not identifying myself as being a college student."

Given this emotional and social context for writing, the strategies Janet found herself using come as little surprise. She describes herself as "satisfycing" on the second paper: "I went and did a response paper with no real purpose at all in mind, you know, just to say something." However, the plot thickens. When she received some positive feedback on this paper (despite her limited effort), the context appeared to be sending messages that were out of synch with her personal evaluation of her process. The situation seemed to her "completely contradictory." To top it off, when she mentioned the problem of motivation to the instructor (one of those conversations walking down the hall), she was encouraged to shift the topic to nonacademic discourse because the real point of the assignment was for students to *use* Farb for a purpose of their own. The constraints upon her were in part her own making. Figure 9 captures some of this confusing array of attitudes, expectations, actions, and social interactions.

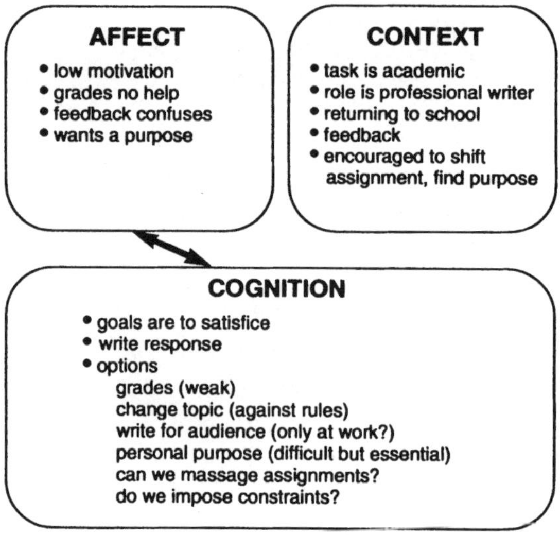

Figure 9. Negotiating affect

This abbreviated sketch of Janet's representation illustrates an interesting complexity. In imposing our interpretive framework of cognition, context, and affect on this story, we inevitably reduced detail to highlight a more general structure. But even this abstract representation does not add up to a set of simple cause and effect relations with school as the boogey man or to a map in which one element single-handedly determines another. Instead, we see a tangled web of intentions and feelings. Despite this writer's feelings of resistance, she does not wish to abandon the situation or her writing: she describes herself caught in a "vicious cycle" created by the problem of motivation followed by frustration at her inability to forge a meaningful purpose for herself.

When Janet presented this view of her writing process to the class, foregrounding the contradictory rhetorical context she perceived, the frustration she felt, and the low-effort path her thinking had taken, her talk evoked sighs of sympathetic recognition in the class. It was a situation everyone had seen before, and the question as they put it was: How do you, as a writer, negotiate such situations when they occur? As Janet and other students put it, "How do you motivate yourself?"

Janet's midterm "reflection" paper and the collaborative planning session that led up to it offer some insight into that negotiation and into this writer's process of constructing metacognitive awareness. In them, she examines both her feelings and some strategies she might have used to break the vicious cycle and motivate her writing. She considers four key options. One was grades, but they simply did not matter enough to work. A second option was to change the topic, and in fact, her voluminous planning notes show she wrestled with this possibility. Why was this option abandoned? Here Janet's observation shows how cognition, the strategies she used, was bound up with her image of the context of school writing:

> Ultimately I didn't feel comfortable changing the assigned topic. I wasn't confident that I could break the rules of the game without penalty and so *I assumed a constraint* [italics added] to write about academic discourse. In retrospect, I believe many of the points Farb was making about speech communities could be generalized to apply to any discourse community and I could have legitimately stated that a particular point in Farb could be applied to technical writing in the same way it could be applied to academic writing.

Alternatively, Janet reflects that she could have tried to take a more personal perspective, to write about something more personally relevant. But as she notes in her paper, "Writing from a personal perspective is difficult to do well and not widely accepted [even though, she feels] it is an essential technique to learn." So that option died, too.

Janet's reflection is the story of opportunities not taken, the sort of story that makes a teacher wince with, "If only I had realized sooner. . . ." But more importantly, perhaps, it is also the story of a writer examining her own role in negotiating this link between affect and cognition. The arrow in figure 9 symbolizes this active negotiation. In the collaborative planning session that preceded her reflection paper, Janet and her partner begin to examine how they deal with motivation in other contexts.[6]

> Janet: I mean, I'm thinking like [about] working and writing things at work that you really don't want to write, but you need to write. In some cases they're easy enough that it's not a big deal. I mean, writing a memo... you just do it... But even, say I'm writing a manual [. . . .] I think there... linking yourself to the audience or reader can help motivate you. Because you can say... "I don't really want to do this. I don't really have any interest.
>
> Supporter: I'm not interested in it. I'll never use it. But somebody else...
>
> Janet: But how can I explain this really well? How can I write a really good manual that, you, that a reader is...
>
> Supporter: It can be a challenge in that sense [. . . .] You know, pride comes into play.

Later in the planning session, Janet's collaborator adds another piece to this picture of negotiation. She begins in a tentative way:

Supporter: How could you if you were given an assigned topic that didn't motivate you in and of itself, is there a way to kind of massage that topic to . . . to try to find a way to approach it that maybe is a personal approach, but still somehow tried to deal with the topic? Um, I guess what I mean is maybe is, are there ways to try um. . . to shape a topic to fit a purpose, somehow? And I'm not [. . . .] I—I haven't really thought about this before.

Janet: Yeah, I think I know what you mean.

Finally, Janet's representation of options expands yet again when she begins to recognize her own place as the interpreter of her context who can, in fact, try to negotiate this link between affect and cognition. "But so, I think that is one thing you can do is write personally. And, in fact, even with that first assignment I toyed with not even addressing academic discourse. I toyed with completely ignoring that and doing something else. And yet, I felt that I really couldn't maybe... which, I don't know, I mean maybe that's just something we impose."

Janet's representation of her writing shows a process in which cognition, context, and affect are linked with multiple, intricate threads but one in which those links can also become the subject of reflective awareness and renegotiation. Terri's representation provides an interesting contrast, for here, the path of negotiation goes between cognition and context.

Terri: I Couldn't Believe It Was Happening to Me

Terri's first paper came back with clear signals that the instructor found it disorganized. It told an interesting story about a childhood experience, but the purpose of the story (and the paper) was not stated. Its point, which was hard to infer, did not appear to link the individual paragraphs together. The paper was not meeting the instructor's expectations for academic discourse. "I realized that I had on my hands a very serious problem that I never had before: I simply could not focus. But what was worse was that I didn't know why I couldn't focus nor did I know what to do to learn to focus again."

For Terri, the fact that she had a problem at all was a source of shock and bewilderment, but if we look at how she represents her own history and the context of writing, we can understand where these feelings came from and why her strategies for organization took the form they did.

> Since I had been taught to write like a journalist since high school, I had integrated this sense of organization . . . into all of my writing without realizing it. In college while my writing and journalism classmates were writing and rewriting stories, I was spewing them out with amazing suc-

cess. . . . I was promoted to an editorial position because I know how to organize a story and could spot another writer's disorganization and easily remedy it. So when I came to [the M.A. program] and acquired a serious writing problem I couldn't believe it was actually happening to me."

Terri's history brought with it not only feelings of confidence but a set of tried-and-true strategies for "spewing out" stories and creating a linear, associative development of ideas. Unfortunately, these strategies, apparently well adapted to one literate practice, were not helping her write analytic papers that required a more explicit rhetorical purpose.

For Terri, as figure 10 shows, reflection led to active negotiation. First, it let her create a far more clearly articulated sense of her own history and assumptions; it let her see how history had translated itself into writing strategies. In creating this reflection, Terri's feelings of insecurity did not magically vanish but were, in fact, foregrounded by the opportunity to express them. However, in taking thought, she translated this problem into a strategic problem, a question of learning a new language and style of writing. Her way of negotiating this situation was to figure out how she could reinvent a strategy. "I started studying the papers from all of my classes [looking for causes, symptoms, and solutions]. . . . I started seeing white space and lots of little paragraphs in the successful papers and darkness and crowded sentences in the others."

Based on this observation, Terri began to experiment with a new strategy of starting with small paragraphs and then trying to connect them rather than trying to maintain the focus of those disastrous long paragraphs. Terri's experiment did not produce miracles. The marvel here is the very fact of

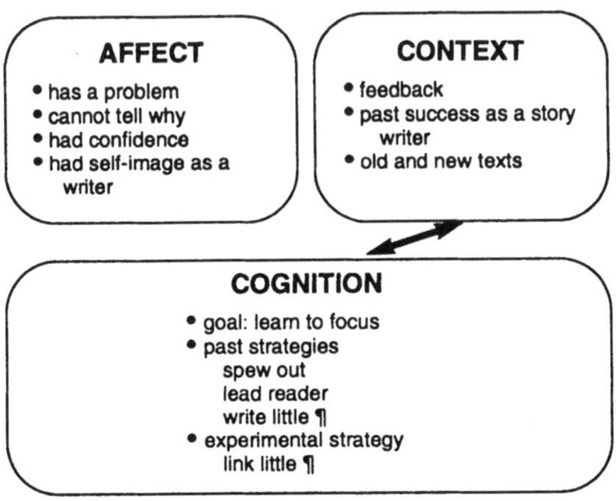

Figure 10. Negotiating context

the experiment. She dealt with the "shock" to her self-image (a significant affective problem writers may often face as they cross the boundaries of new literate practices) by trying to negotiate the relation between her writing strategies and her own history.

In reflecting on her process, she came to see her history in terms of strategies (indicated by a link between context and cognition in fig. 10), and she came to see her own cognition and emotionally laden self-image in terms of the transition into a new discourse community. The concept of changing discourse communities itself offered a new way to think about context that was an alternative to "past success as a writer." The new representation Terri forged created a manageable problem. Her new strategy was not plucked out of a textbook but was a metacognitive invention built on the foundation of reflection.

Responding to Reflections

Reflections unveil difficulties that implicate the teacher as well as the learner. One of my responses to Janet and Terri as a teacher is to assume responsibility for the dilemma—"If only I had realized, been a more sensitive teacher, spelled out more options, softened my criticisms," and so on. The inevitable "if only's." Another response that also takes the dilemma out of the students' hands is to see it as yet another piece of evidence for the oppressive structures of school that make writing an inauthentic act for Janet and that fail to validate the personal narrative voice with which Terri feels most comfortable. With this thought, our gaze shifts from the students to a critique of the system. Both these responses recognize our responsibility to make school a better place, but they do not appreciate the significance of what these students themselves did as critical agents. As Janet and her partner point out to us, the thorny problem of "motivating oneself" is a necessary part of writing in many contexts. And Terri had chosen this program, not journalism, because she wanted capabilities she did not already have. Her problem was managing a rocky transition. In her own way, each of these women was confronting a genuine dilemma. Teachers cannot eliminate the dilemmas that accompany learning even if they can affect them. The real achievement here is that of the students, who not only confronted a genuine issue but used these reflections to engage in a sustained dialogue with it.

Reflections like these underscore that learning and literacy are an encounter with a series of genuine dilemmas. In the face of conflict, reflection can become a form of significant action. In their different ways, Janet and Terri constructed images of a writing process in which the elements signified by the terms *cognition*, *context*, and *affect* are linked by multiple, contradictory, visible, and invisible lines of interaction. For them, observation-based reflection became an attempt to understand these elements of their own experience and to negotiate the lines of influence they saw. Their effort to track their own cognition became an act of strategic metacognition. The tangled webs of feeling, thinking, and social action they constructed did not become untangled. But with awareness seemed to come a sense of options and the opportunity to mediate both context and feelings and to translate understanding into action. In the final two cases, we will see students who cast themselves even more explicitly as problem solvers and used their reflections to sketch plans for strategic action.

Marla: A Great First Sentence

Marla looked on her writing process during the first eight weeks of the course as an experiment designed to alter a habitual strategy that had led to "outstanding first sentences and half-baked ideas." By midterm, she had experimented with three new strategies, evaluated what worked for her and what did not, analyzed the results of her experiments, and formulated a new strategic goal: to develop a personal method of inner dialogue, "the kind of dialogue within myself that Freire talks about."

Tracing the evolution of her new awareness, Marla begins with a description of what she observed as an habitual writing strategy. It is comprised of

> three typical steps, one more inefficient than the other. When assigned a writing task, my first move has been to randomly flip through a text looking for a key point. Then, having had a moment of Eureka I flip through the text or texts in search of topic information, pulling out data that supports my thesis while ignoring everything else. Finally, because my key point usually occurs to me in the form of an introductory sentence, I plunge into writing with nothing more substantial than a great first sentence and a tenacious hold on a vague idea.

Rereading the transcription of her first protocol, Marla observes the precise way in which this strategy failed her, which she represents as a lack of planning:

"At one point, after about ten minutes of trying to pull something out of the chapter, I found a single sentence that looked promising. My reaction to it was 'Here's something interesting; maybe I can use this to talk about a freshman learning to write in college.' But because finding that single sentence was all the planning I could do, writing the paper was really difficult and I got caught in the middle with nothing else to say." The goal Marla sets links the new strategies presented in the course to her own specific needs: "In learning three new strategies, I was looking for a way to solve my problem of substituting an idea for a plan by doing a different kind of thinking before writing."

In effect, she turns the instruction the course provided into a personal experiment. At first, she finds her old habits hard to break, recording that she modifies the strategies to fit her habitual pattern of closing off planning prematurely. Thus, in using the first strategy, dialoguing, she limits herself by working only at a local level, with "two or three sentences rather than the general argument of the chapter." When such a piecemeal approach does not result in "something interesting," she "resorts to old tactics," returns to her habitual method of searching for a key sentence, and turns out what she perceives to be an unsatisfactory paper.

The Planner's Blackboard becomes the object of a second experiment. She finds that the method helps her to reach one of her goals, to produce a lot of ideas. However, she records encountering a new problem, one that she attributes to her inflexible use of the method. Because she permits herself to become "busy filling in one box after the other," she misses opportunities to develop a single major point. In writing about this attempt, Marla sees an alternative—to use the blackboards as a source of direction, letting go when she is on the trail of a good point. At this point in the course, Marla has articulated for herself one of the key dilemmas of learning to write—strategies only become useful when one can use them to fit one's own needs and purposes.

The third strategy in Marla's experimental tale is collaborative planning, which she evaluates as "the most successful way of improving my planning." To begin with, it solves her earlier problem of providing direction. By providing focused questions, her collaborator helps her "to complete and explain my ideas by filling up all of the blackboards. My protocol for the last paper was much more focussed, without the mental wandering characteristic of the first two, because my collaborator was asking me questions and prompting me in ways that helped me direct my thoughts and elaborate on good ideas."

On the basis of this post hoc learner's experiment, Marla sees her midterm paper as a place to "work all three strategies into something of my own." Her method for designing this new personal integration is to begin with the most successful strategy, the collaboration, to examine these sessions (one of which was transcribed) for evidence of what makes the collaboration work and then to use her knowledge to design "something private," a strategy usable in the absence of another person. This private strategy turns out to be a set of questions based on specific moves she observed her collaborator using:

> To get me to focus on a key purpose my collaborator would ask me if she had gotten the gist of what I was talking about by saying, "So what you're saying is. . . ." She helped me make transitions by asking, "Now does that fit into what you were saying before?" Similarly, she eliminated excess baggage by saying, "That's interesting, but I don't see how it fits with the point you're trying to make." She also helped me think more deeply about my audience by offering different ways of interpreting points which I had thought perfectly clear. Finally, my collaborator prevented me from plunging into writing with an incomplete plan by asking me what I was going to do with a idea, or how I was going to tie my thoughts in with the assignment.

To test this construction, Marla actually carried out a kind of experiment. She reasons that if it is, indeed, the questions that help her to solve problems, perhaps she can use them as a kind of "private collaborator." Her evaluation of this variation records her dissatisfaction, however. In attempting to reduce the collaborative method to the content of the questions, she feels that she has created a mere "checklist, helpful, but hardly the imaginary collaborator I expected it to be." The problem is that the list does not of itself suggest alternatives, "coming up with different ways of thinking about a problem or getting rid of dead weight." Marla ends her paper by speculating about a way she might solve this new problem by developing a living inner dialogue.

Marla's plan for an "inner dialogue" is an interesting example of metacognitive awareness, in that it leads her into thinking over not only how to use strategies but how to design, control, and test them. For instance, in assessing her use of the blackboards, she says, "I know I am on the right track if I can see links between them in my plan." What limits her use of these strategies is her own inflexibility that makes them "uncomfortable because I have placed restrictive limits on ways to use them." Marla's inner dialogue is her step toward being a more adaptive planner.

It is hard to say if Marla's new, experimental strategy will do all she hopes. In fact, when Marla and another student presented their plans to become their own "collaborators" to the class, it allowed us to examine assumptions that "good" writers do not depend on others, that they learn to work alone, and that regular collaboration is cheating or at least unprofessional. The success of collaboration had itself created a generative dilemma for some students. Whether Marla's new plan solves the problem or not, the act of developing it called not only for awareness and control but for a critical questioning and a creative stance to the ideas taught in the course.

This writer searches the data she collected in a goal-directed way, trying, first, to discern how she typically goes about writing. Having characterized her habit of "outstanding first sentences and half-baked ideas," she searches for evidence of whether the strategies introduced in the course are working to solve her individual problem. When they work, she specifies what makes them work, such as a collaborator's offering alternative ideas. When they do not work, she analyzes why and catches a glimpse of her own self-imposed inflexibility. It is apparent throughout this appraisal that her purposes are both diagnostic and creative. She wants to analyze "inefficient steps" as well as "work all three strategies into something of my own." Although the prose of problems, experiments, steps, and solutions reduces a complex experience to a manageable story, it also records a student grappling with a significant educational issue realized in the terms of a personal dilemma.

Tanya: Awareness Makes Progress Possible

Like Marla, Tanya reads her protocols and reviews her papers, looking for "patterns and similarities" that would let her define problems and their causes. Unlike Marla, she does not see the patterns in the protocols themselves, perhaps because of feeling "artificial" while recording her planning sessions. Rather, the protocols function to "trigger the memory of what I was thinking during the planning stages of the first three assignments." As she reviews this data her "frustration" at not being able to diagnose the causes of her difficulties turns to surprise: she is "startled" to see that some strategies appear to work for her even when causes are unknown. With this, Tanya decides to turn her attention from unlocking the secret of causes to designing helpful strategies. The following description traces this odyssey.

Tanya's initial goal is to locate writing problems. She finds three. The first is "finding my purpose for writing." In contrast to Marla who believes that she cuts the planning dialogue short, Tanya records that she prolongs dialogue with the material, paraphrasing and interpreting "long after I was fully comfortable with the material." She speculates that she fills up the time dialoguing with the text because she does not have anything of her own to say. In the absence of an alternative strategy, but knowing that she should be doing something, she reiterates Farb's ideas. Tanya's second problem resembles the first. She records that having decided on a purpose, she writes down everything she "knew or thought about my purpose whether or not it was relevant to the assignment." Her problem is that having committed ideas to paper, she finds it difficult to decide what to keep and what to discard. Once she has made these decisions, the next step of outlining comes easily to Tanya, but a new problem arises at the point where she has to "make the jump from an outline of sentence fragments to coherent prose."

Notice here that Tanya and Marla refer to a common problem—finding a focus and purpose—for which it would be easy to prescribe some standard generic solutions. But while one writer needs to produce more ideas before she leaps to text, the other needs to reduce and channel an uncritical, associative invention process. The solutions for the two women are different because they arise out of a distinctive individual matrix of strategies and assumptions, a matrix that only emerges when detailed observations like these take us below the surface of the generic problem of focusing.

Tanya apparently spends a good deal of time attempting to understand the causes of these problems, an exercise that ends in the frustration. During her analytical review of protocols and papers to ferret out causes, however, she notices a puzzling phenomenon: that simply by using the blackboard strategy she appears to solve at least the last of the three problems: "It was while reviewing the tapes and notes that are relevant to my third trouble spot that I realized that this problem was not as severe in the second and third assignments. After we had introduced the blackboard strategies in class, I had an easier time moving from outline form to written prose. This surprised me." Closer examination reveals that using this strategy leads her to write more complete sentences, chunks of text that are easily integrated into the final prose form: "I realize now that using the blackboard strategy allowed me to elaborate on the features of my outline before I felt pressured to compose good text. I began to form complete sentences while filling in the blackboards, so I did not encounter the abrupt transition that I faced in the first assignment." "Re-searching" this surprising result produces a second realization when Tanya concludes that her initial frustration may have been self-imposed:

> Recognizing that the blackboard strategies can minimize one of my writing problems is significant because it illustrates how I imposed the obstacles to progress myself. I had unrealistic expectations of my metacognitive powers, and this prevented my seeing the value of a strategy. In fact, I was doubting that any strategies could be valuable until I reached some imagined higher level of understanding. I realize that my first and second trouble spots are more severe than the third, and effective strategies will not be easy to find or employ. However, I recognize that such strategies could exist—or that I could design them myself—and this awareness makes progress possible where before it was not.

Tanya appears to be aware not only of the power of a particular strategy but also of her ability to control her writing process by designing personal strategies. Further, she knows something of self-imposed limits.

In looking at the representations these writers constructed (i.e., our interpretive analysis of them), the last two illustrate students whose text focused primarily on the cognitive dimension of our map: goals, strategies, intentions, and decisions. Both discover something surprising when reading the transcriptions of their protocols. Both report using, evaluating, and redesigning strategies to suit their needs. Both record insights about self-imposed limitations. Both engage in some theory building, attempting to link data about their processes by making and testing the connections they think they see. Only a longitudinal study could look at the durability of their learning, the long-term effects of their newly designed strategies, but even a cursory reading of their texts shows that these writers are self-reflective and obviously motivated to actively participate in their own learning.

Although they focus on cognition, these writers build representations that include affect and context. Tanya is "discouraged and frustrated" trying to assign causes to her writing problems, while Marla counts on her "Eureka" experience for the momentum needed to begin writing. For both, this affective language is a part of the problem they hope to change. For Marla, the "Eureka" feeling creates an illusion of readiness to write. If she succumbs to its temptation to begin text on the strength of this spurt of energy, she soon discovers that the impetus is a single introductory sentence containing one key point. The problem is not the feeling itself—she has no desire to get rid of her "Eurekas"—but its lack of staying power. Her solution is to design other ways to sustain the energy needed to produce a complete text. Similarly, Tanya's frustration at her inability to attribute causes to her problems does not disappear, but she chooses to focus her attention differently. Instead of concentrating on what she cannot do—assign causes—she concentrates on what she has proved she can do—design strategies that work.

A sense of context is also present in the way students represent writing as a social act and as an event within their personal histories as students. Marla and Tanya use reflection to talk about usual problems, not just the writing in this course. And in trying to understand her own cognition, Marla highlights her collaborator's suggestions, and Tanya uses a discussion with her husband to affirm her insight that one can work on a problem without understanding its cause. While Janet and Terri emphasize the influences of affect and context and Marla and Tanya focus on cognition, all four create representations that link social histories and personal feelings with a sense of new control over their own cognition.

Some Patterns of Strategic Knowledge in the Class

How shall we characterize the knowledge these writers constructed? And how does it differ from the familiar discourse of academic theory and textbooks? The cases of Janet, Terri, Marla, and Tanya were selected to illustrate four representations of writing that focused in differing degrees on affect, context, and cognition, but they also illustrate some ways of thinking and talking about writing that are characteristic of the reflections as a whole.

First, the knowledge that emerges from such reflection is strategic knowledge. Students not only recognized their own *strategies*, maneuvers, techniques, habits, they described them in terms of the *goals* that were driving such strategies. These goals ranged from old and problematic ones, such as quelling anxiety by getting something/anything down fast, to personal goals, such as Ann's skeptical need to test my claim that the role of "intellectual," could apply to her, a forty-year-old returning student. For her, the dialogue strategy was not a homework exercise but a private test of our conversation and of the unlikely notion that she might have something to say back to academic authorities. Unlike the incidental reflection and strategic knowledge we observed in the transcripts of freshmen, there is a striking *awareness* with these junior, senior, and M.A. students of where one's goals come from and why writers cling to them, of whether the instructor's advice really works, and of where new options lie.

Secondly, the strategic knowledge the writers built was clearly driven by dilemmas. It emerged out of a sense of problems and desires. Clearly, some of these were triggered by my critical comments (as on Terri's anecdotal alternative to analysis). But, as I think these excerpts suggest, within this advanced writing class, these writers quickly assumed ownership of their own dilemmas. Their reflections were highly action-oriented, whether the goal was developing personal strategies or simply understanding oneself as a writer.[7] To show how these four case studies both typify and differ from the class as a whole, we analyzed the midterm papers of the group in terms of the features highlighted in the case studies.[8] Table 5 shows a profile of these reflections along three key dimensions that Sitko and I defined as representation, problem awareness, and control. We chose to look for the presence of awareness and control because these two features figure prominently in the literature on metacognition and in the performance of our case study writers.

Representation. How is the writing process represented? In terms of cognition, context, affect, and/or the integration of the three?

Problem Awareness. Does the writer's metacognitive awareness take the form of detecting and defining problems, creating more elaborated images of those problems, and/or making causal attributions that inquire into the source of problems?

Table 5. Representations of Metaknowledge in Midterm Papers

Writer	Representation of the process				Metacognitive elements					
					Awareness			Control		
	Aff	Cog	Cxt	Int	Dect	Attr	Elab	Altr	Stra	Eval
1	X	X	X	X	X		X	X	X	X
2	X	X	X	X	X	X	X	X	X	X
3		X	X		X	X	X	X	X	X
4	X	X	X		X	X	X	X	X	X
5	X	X	X	X	X		X	X	X	X
6	X		X	X	X		X	X		X
7	X	X			X	X	X	X	X	X
8					X		X	X	X	
9		X		X	X		X	X	X	X
10		X			X		X	X	X	
11		X	X		X	X	X	X	X	X

Note. Aff = affect; Cog = cognition; Cxt = context; Int= integrated; Dect = problem detection; Attr = attribution; Elab = elaboration; Altr = alternatives; Stra= strategies; Eval = evaluation.

Control. Is metacognition operating as a source of control in the form of imagining alternatives, mapping out new strategies, or specifying a way to evaluate one's own success?

The following quotations from papers of three writers not previously discussed illustrate statements of each category.

Metacognitive Awareness

Problem detection. Problem detection is signaled by statements such as these:

> I was struck by how often I encounter difficulty in the middle of writing a paper as the result of insufficient planning at the start (Writer 2). This problem is giving a general overview of a topic instead of giving an analysis of an issue that directly relates to my purpose or key point (Writer 3).

Problem elaboration. As we have seen in the research on revision, detecting a problem is a good beginning, but a more elaborated representation offers a stronger basis for action (Flower, Hayes, Carey, Schriver, & Stratman, 1986). The following elaborations come on the heels of detection statements:

> What particularly interested me was discovering that my planning tracker interviews revealed that I was caught by surprise when my initial plan proved so problematic (Writer 2). In the Blackboard Planner paper,

> I had numerous examples of an issue, but I never defined a problem that students have when writing for academic discourse (Writer 4).

Causal Attribution. Some writers extend their understanding of a problem by attributing its cause to some particular force or event:

> When I asked myself why I am not able to give an analysis of one issue that directly relates to my purpose, I knew that my problem began with the fact that I take too many notes on both the text material and on my own thoughts and ideas (Writer 3). I saw that I was so pleased with myself for generating so many ideas, that I ignored that important clue (Writer 4).

Metacognitive Control

Statements indicating awareness are often accompanied by statements indicating control, which in this case took the form of comments about alternatives, strategies, and evaluation.

Alternatives. Alternatives are indicated when a writer juxtaposes several ways of acting:

> These strategies now have names, and just that helps me see what I am doing while I am writing so that I will know what needs to be changed, developed, or defined more clearly (Writer 3). As I originally conceived the paper, its key purpose was to support Farb's contention that the English language discriminates against women. As I considered his statements in their entirety, however, I became aware that they amounted to less than an endorsement of my own positions on the subject of sexist language (Writer 2).

Strategies. Strategies are action plans:

> Eventually I worked out an approach that appeared to satisfy both myself and the terms of the assignment, although it required formulating an entirely different plan for the paper (Writer 2). Working with a collaborator helped me make the connection between my final thesis and the ideas I had generated earlier in my planning (Writer 4).

Evaluation. This is indicated when writers assess the success of a strategy or specify the conditions under which it might be useful:

> Perhaps one way the collaborative technique might work for me in the future would be to spend five or ten minutes with a classmate discussing ideas for a paper. I know this type of thing goes on among professionals in the working environment when they are working on projects (Writer 4). I am not banishing this strategy forever. I know now that it is avail-

> able and how it can be useful to me. I will be able to call on this strategy when I do need additional ideas for something I am writing (Writer 3).

The table records the pattern of how students used these moves in their papers. Although this simple categorization only reflects a significant presence or absence rather than the quality of the comments, it gives us a fuller picture of the kinds of thinking this reflective self-observation encouraged, and it suggests the frequency and distribution of such moves across the group. The table also supports what we saw in the cases—that students used this occasion for reflection in distinctive ways.

Using Reflection to Construct Working Theories

In their concern with dilemmas and strategic knowledge, these reflections address some of the same issues that fill journal pages in rhetoric and education, but they also differ from scholarly discussions in some provocative ways. As we have already noticed, these representations often offer articulate images of writing as an affective process embedded in social contexts past and present, played out as a cognitive act, and guided by the writer's expectations, strategies, decisions, and habits of response. Moreover, unlike the theory students read, these observation-based images often make clear, forceful links between cognition, context, and affect. They describe habits of thinking embedded in students' own history as writers and in their reading of the class and its expectations. They locate turning points in a thinking process driven not by simple reason (much less the instructors' advice) but by attitudes—by a slump in motivation, by the liberation of new awareness, or by the energy of self-efficacy. Finally, these images go beyond commonplaces to articulate problems, such as Janet's attitudes toward school and Terri's feature-writing strategies, which might have remained invisible, and to make connections that seemed surprising and empowering to the writers.

However, in generalizing about these representations, abstracting them to highlight the categories of cognition, context, and affect or to note indications of meta-awareness and control, we also lose their distinctive character. If these representations can be called "theories" of the process, they are deeply grounded and highly individualized theories. More importantly, they are energetically purposeful representations, devoted to solving problems, investigating questions, extending the writer's knowledge and control. Even though we could read these accounts as an instantiation of a broad concern (e.g., the problem of generating and organizing ideas, the issue of authority and motivation within the constraints of school), that would distort their essential character. The goals that drive these inquiries are personal and idiosyncratic, felt difficulties or desires tied to conflicts or aspirations that are (in this situation) unique to a Terri but not particularly relevant to a Marla.

This personalized, purposeful investigation of a supposedly good strategy is essential to being a flexible, strategic thinker. The meaning of instruction is in what the writer makes of it. For instance, one writer, the anxious returning student I mentioned earlier, found the dialogue strategy a liberating option. It contradicted her assumption that she should already "have" or "know" something smart to say about the assigned reading and encouraged her instead to draw on personal experience to generate and evaluate inferences: just the sort of response instructors imagine and desire. For Tanya, by contrast, the dialogue strategy became an accomplice in her flight from purpose. It provided yet another way to generate reams of notes without a central point, notes that then seemed impossible to integrate and use. Although Marla locates a difficulty in her "inflexible use" of dialoging, the problem for these and other students is not really in them or in the strategy per se, but in the way any given strategy, or any instructional advice for that matter, fits into what the students already do or know. The value of dialoguing for the returning student was just such an interaction. It had the power to derail an old process of fruitlessly searching memory (when she needed instead to draw a new inference) and to suggest that the option of making knowledge was under her control.

The most striking feature of these reflections, then, is not in the way they parallel theory or textbook talk but in the way they transform principles into working knowledge. These data-based observations offer, I believe, a level of analysis that is qualitatively different from detailed process tracing or ethnographic accounts of researchers or the observations of teachers. On the one hand, the issues they raise grow out of personal dilemmas in learning or writing. They are expressed in the language of specificity and action, grounded in both immediate experience and the writers' history. Their potent combination of observation, theory, and memory lets writers construct images of their own meaning making that confront issues and principles but do so in the language of action. Issues and principles, in fact, play a large role in these reflections. One does not see in them the commonplaces of process teaching Rubin (1983) observed or the familiar process narratives that recount "when I sit down to write, I always have coffee, pens . . ." and so on. Issues such as finding personal sources of motivation, moving among discourse communities, making the transitions from one literate practice to another, and the relation between cognition, context, and affect are significant matters in anyone's book. But the representations constructed here take the form of working knowledge and personal theories about how to confront and perhaps resolve such dilemmas in terms of the practical decisions that make up the "dorm-room" practice of writing.

I am not suggesting that these personal theories of action are somehow more virtuous or true, that they should replace the more abstract discussions in our journals. They do not aspire to present a generalized or conditionalized account of shared experiences. Nor do they provide an alternative to teachers' and textbooks' explanations of general, transferable strategies. However, for us as educators, these reflections offer a fresh insight into cognition in context, a glimpse into the strategic knowledge these writers are invoking and into their assumptions, expectations, dilemmas, and responses. More importantly, for each writer, the meanings created here constitute a "text" no one else could write; they are the necessary reconstructions of learning that transform abstract ideas into personal working knowledge.

We started this chapter with a hard question: What sort of knowledge can reflections like these construct? Without claiming that reflection made the learning we observed happen, this analysis does argue that observation-based reflections let students create a new, articulated understanding of their experience and a distinctive, theoretically significant representation of the writing process. In the next chapter, we will explore some possible links between reflection and action as another group of writers record changes in their understanding and performance.

9

Reflection and the Reconstruction of a Literate Practice

> When I previously had been asked to apply a theory or a model, it involved relating the material to something practical, either a personal experience or an everyday occurrence. For example, a simplified application of Norman's [learning theory] might involve making connections to . . . one theory of literary criticism, [which] involves a reader accepting a new text by relating it to his or her prior knowledge of that specific culture and . . . cultural repertoire. This is where my old notion [of the assignment "to apply" a theory] would end. . . . It had been enough to make connections, and relate the new material with other knowledge or a practical experience. Now, there was a new question involved concerning *my purpose in making those inferences.* [Italics added]

Gina's experience is not unusual. She is at the beginning of a new writing course, learning the ropes of a new literate practice, wisely drawing on rhetorical moves that succeeded in recent literature classes, and asking what she needs to add to that repertoire. The literate practice in question—the "to apply" paper—asks her to apply her reading of a theorist to a problem she defines. Her first paper was a personally and intellectually engaged response to Norman's learning theory. However, the structure of the paper merely followed the tracks of her reading; it was a rambling series of insightful responses to ideas she found personally relevant. It was a good use of writing to learn, a good paper for another discourse, but in this course, it elicited comments asking for a more sharply defined intellectual purpose and focused structure. For me as instructor, the request to "apply theory" involved *articulating* that purpose, using Norman to explore a problem the writer defines.

But as it turned out, this request was not a feature Gina could simply add on to a personal response text or to her image of the task. "For me, the question of *purpose was greatly tied to affecting an audience.* If I have an outside audience, my goal in writing is clear. . . . Perhaps that notion [of an internal audience] is part of the nature of academic discourse . . . [but] I had never related that to a greater purpose." Then enter the Planner's Blackboard, designed precisely to help students articulate purposes. But the demonstration in class focused on a persuasive task with what Gina saw as an "outside" audience, an experience that did nothing to contradict her assumption that purposes were important in affecting readers but not in guiding personal inquiry. In her own writing, as she later described, Gina was indeed in search of new meanings, "forming new theories for myself, . . . ready to draw new conclusions about the relationships across the discourses of learning and literary theory. But at the time, that did not seem to be a purpose. I was interpreting the question of purpose as the need for a solution." As a result, she read the Blackboard Planner's "purpose" prompts not as a guide to inquiry but as an injunction to structure her text around a grand public purpose: "It was as if the blackboards made me impose a formula to find some sort of solution to a noble, worldly concern [for] the very process of writing." Gina, I'm happy to say, eventually worked out a new reading of the task: "By the time I got to the [next] assignment, I had a more comfortable working definition of purpose. I was trying to identify my purpose with making certain inferences or applications. . . . Instead of trying to create a grand function for the work I was doing, [I was asking] "What have you done with it?". . . . I realized I had a purpose all along with the Norman assignment, but I did not recognize it as such."

This particular story had a happy ending. But why was the process so star-crossed? Past literate strategies did not seem to transfer, and the new feature of purpose resisted being "added on" to the writer's repertoire because it did not fit into the schema she already had. The instruction designed to help only reinforced her confusion and lead her to envision a paper no one wanted, a noble solution to a grand problem structured around the categories of the blackboards. The constructive process Gina describes could have been scripted by a learning theorist; it involves transfer, adapting and extending prior schemas and practices, direct instruction, modeling, practice, and feedback. What we sometimes do not see is the seamy underside to all this—the sustained, often frustrating, creative, interpretive, and reconstructive process a writer goes through, a process that is not just building but rebuilding and revising an image of a literate practice and how to do it. Gina's experience is probably normal—not easy or ideal, but psychologically realistic. The difference is that through her observation and reflection we both came to understand in a new way what it meant to "learn" this new literate practice.

My purpose in this chapter is, like Gina's, to initiate an inquiry rather than to offer solutions. I would like to explore here another dimension to the process of constructing meaning raised by the writers in Gina's class. At issue here is the problem of entering a new discourse and learning a new literate practice when this entry is not a slow initiation via apprenticeship but learning in the hothouse context of a classroom and a semester course. The basis for this inquiry will be detailed accounts and working theories developed in the writers' data-based reflections on their own writing and learning process.

These accounts portray the construction not just of a text but of a literate practice itself. They describe writers in the process of building a personal theory of the task, which in this case was the task of reading and applying theory to a self-defined problem in writing. However, the constructive process they track might be more accurately called a process of *re-construction* in which meaning emerges from a dialectic between the writer's existing schemas and understanding, her or his performance, and the responses to that performance.

I. A Theoretical Case for Working Theories

Before we turn to what actually happened, let us consider some arguments for why the working theories of these students might bear more than a fictive relation to reality and how they might indeed shape action. In essence, why should learners go to the effort of such theory building?

One answer is that their assigned task (i.e., applying theory to a self-defined problem) is not adequately defined by simple text conventions, formats, or features of prose style. Applying theory is a culturally organized, literate practice that involves who you are and how you talk to other writers (Simmons, 1985). It starts with the assertive goal of appropriating information for one's own purpose, the difficult act of finding and defining a problem, and the dangerous move of taking authority within a discourse even as you are still learning it (Greene, 1990b). To apply theory calls for conventions of problem analysis and argument, as well as strategies for rhetorical reading, elaborating, and transforming knowledge (Ackerman, 1991; Haas & Flower, 1988; Stein, 1992). And for most students, to learn a new practice like this will probably demand more than merely adding new information to a repertoire (e.g., a few new text conventions) or fine tuning those that are there; it is likely to require reorganization of what a student already knows (Norman, 1980). It is saying in essence: abandon your well-learned strategies for summary and response and reconsider some of your old relations to source texts and even to authority.

If we look at a student's writing strategies as culturally organized practices, as integrated, working schemas for doing school writing in different contexts, it is not surprising that they resist change. Is it likely that mere suggestion (an assignment), advice (class talk), or initial feedback would penetrate the skin of the schema? Or would such information be absorbed, not seen as a challenge to the writer's underlying theory of the task but rather as an anomaly, easily reinterpreted or replaced by the default values of strong social and cognitive schemas? In this scenario, merely adding conventions and commonplaces or attempting to mimic the discourse is likely to be the low road to learning. Even if there are many students on that road with you, it is the slow and indirect route if what you *need* to do is reorganize your understanding. To return to our initial question, then, building reflective working theories may be a better way to penetrate a cultural practice.

If learning to write sometimes takes us into the troubled waters of reorganizing our understanding of a resistant culturally organized practice, it is also likely to plunge us into active negotiation. The meaning we are trying to construct as we agonize over the text or talk with other writers about what this teacher, that journal, or this new context requires will be an actively negotiated construction pushed and pulled by a crowd of options and constraints. Learning to write effectively means building a theory of the task. In their research on how scientific thinking develops in children and adults, Kuhn, Amsel, and O'Loughlin identified thinking about a theory as a fundamental part of this development.

> First, and most fundamental, is the ability to think *about* a theory, rather than only think *with* it. In the latter case, a person uses theories as a means of organizing and interpreting experience, but is not aware of their existence. . . . If a theory is only used rather than contemplated, the possibility of the theory's being false and of the existence of alternative theories is not conceived. In such a case, the person . . . does not "have" a theory in the sense of knowing that he or she has it or of having any awareness of control of the manner in which that theory guides his or her thinking. (1988, p. 219–220)

Reflection, then, is a tool for negotiating and reconstructing meaning. But working theories are by their very nature provisional and tentative. Like the observation and reflection that helps construct them, they will sometimes be inaccurate, misleading, or downright wrong. What is to say that Janet's theory of motivation or Terri's experimental strategy of linking small paragraphs will work (chap. 8)? Reflecting is an interpretive process with no precision guarantees. And, in fact, its value may lie less in the accuracy of the "insights" it produces, than in the process of reflection/action itself. As we saw with Terri, Martha, and Tanya, when writers rehearse their stories of facing, articulating, and coming to grips with problems, they also come to see themselves as thinkers and problem solvers. Their very inquiry can contribute to a sense of self-efficacy—a kind of self-belief that is not based on certainty or comfort but on confidence in one's ability to meet one's goals through sustained effort.

When Bandura and Wood (1989) describe the situations that demand such self-belief, they sound surprisingly like the contexts that call for epistemic rhetoric: situations in which one must make inferential judgments about conditional relations among events operating in probabilistic environments. To translate that definition to writing, envision Darlene (chap. 1) trying to summarize conflicting authorities or Carter (chap. 6) who had just received his C+ trying to manage the ambiguities and uncertainties of learning. Envision them generating hypotheses, remembering what worked, testing their judgments. In situations like this, self-efficacy actually changes how people perform.

> It requires a strong sense of efficacy to remain task oriented in the face of judgmental failures. Indeed, people who believe strongly in their problem-solving capabilities remain highly efficient in their analytic thinking in complex decision-making situations, whereas those who are plagued by self-doubts are erratic in their analytic thinking (Bandura & Wood, 1989; Wood & Bandura, 1989). Quality of thinking, in turn, affects performance accomplishments. (Bandura, 1989, p. 1176)

Seeing oneself as a problem solver influences what one actually does in another way. "Peoples' perceptions of their efficacy influence the types of anticipatory scenarios they construct and reiterate. Those who have a high sense of efficacy visualize success scenarios that provide positive guides for performance. [This is in contrast to] visualizing failure scenarios that undermine performance by dwelling on how things will go wrong" (p. 1176). Finally, the stronger peoples' beliefs are in their power to achieve something, the more effort they put into the task and the longer they persevere. Perseverance plays such a large role in learning because, as Bandura argues: "ordinary social realities are strewn with difficulties. They are full of impediments, failures, adversities, setbacks, frustrations and inequities. . . . Self-doubts can set in quickly after some failures and reverses. . . . Because the acquisition of knowledge and competencies usually requires sustained effort in the face of difficulties and setbacks, it is resiliency of self-belief that counts" (p. 1176).

The human experiences described by the distanced language of "self efficacy" are loaded with emotion. They are the reasons student writers give up too soon and stay up all night trying; they are the overgeneralized self-criticisms that produce writer's block and the optimism in the face of failure that nurtures learning. Reflection is one place in which writers can acknowledge the affective nature of writing, but because reflection is a step removed from the emotional moment, it allows students to bring some critical distance to problematic feelings and fears and to channel emotional energy into rhetorical action as Terri did. Bandura's arguments are also about the ways affect is transformed into action. They suggest ways that reflection—as an effortful, interpretive, and fallible but strategic process—could motivate a more informed and sustained negotiation with meaning. But let us now look at the links between action and reflection that were in fact forged in this college class.

II. How Writers Acquire a Literate Practice: Students' Working Theories

The working theories we will examine were constructed out of the attempt to understand (and appropriate) a new literate practice. Like the representations of the writing process we saw in chapter 8, these are dilemma-driven accounts. They rise out of problems a writer faces; they are couched in the language of personal experience and specifics; they are directed toward action. Like other "theory," they go beyond narrative to name and confront issues. But in contrast to more formal theory or textbook talk, they represent these issues in the language of strategic knowledge that can reveal something of these students' goals and meta-awareness as well as their strategies and behavior.

The three working theories we will examine closely are also interesting as students' perspective on their own learning—a perspective quite different from what either a teacher or an observer could have constructed. This is not to suggest they offer a truer or more unvarnished reality or that they are insensitive to their readership any more than any published theory is. The insights, like the criticisms these students make, are polite and certain to be censored in ways we will never know. Given the issues they inevitably exclude, what makes them interesting is the sharply drawn portrait of a constructive process they include.

The Context for Theory Building

As the final paper in an advanced writing course (similar to the one described in chap. 8), these observation-based reflections were shaped by a number of forces.[1] To explore the nature of being a rhetor, students read articles and chapters by Bartholomae (on initiation to academic discourse), Freire (on learning as naming and banking), Norman (on learning processes), Anderson (on schema theory), Bazerman (on schemas within a discourse), Flower (on problem solving), and others. The goal of the reading and writing assignments was threefold: to *understand* these theories and to *apply* them to a problem or issue in writing that the writer would need to *define*. This task or literate practice, which became known as the "to apply" schema, was the basis for one oral presentation and three written papers. It was backed up by five short journal-like assignments called observation and response statements in which students noted and commented on interesting features of their own learning, writing, or collaborative planning processes. The final paper for the course was simply an extended occasion to apply reading plus observation to a student-generated problem.

The final papers of three writers (Gina, Cheryl, and Jennifer) focus in different ways on the subject of this chapter: How did writers in this class come to develop a schema for this new literate practice of "applying theory to a larger problem."[2] For each writer this question came up as part of a problem the student was pursuing. For Cheryl as a technical writer, the problem motivating her inquiry was how instructions get interpreted—her difficulty with the "apply schema" instructions became a case in point. Gina, caught up in questions of interpretation and culture, was interested in the reasons why teachers' models "go wrong" and in students as interpreters. But embedded within these texts are some closely realized, observation-based reflections that talk about meaning making from a new perspective.

For example, these reflections draw on a good deal of data collected over the course of the entire term from the writers themselves and other students. In addition to their own observation and response statements and papers, they had access to everyone else's writing in a circulating loose-leaf binder. They reviewed tapes from collaborative planning sessions, and one writer collected reading protocols as an additional window on these schemas.

These reflections also grow out of other sorts of collaboration: class sessions devoted to students informally presenting their observations, collaborative planning sessions, and out-of-class talk. Cheryl and Jennifer were collaborative planning partners and friends. Both were seniors: Cheryl in technical and professional writing and Jennifer in literary and cultural studies (although by the end of the course she had decided to apply for graduate school in rhetoric). They were friends and classmates of Gina, a senior in professional writing. For different reasons, these three also paid special attention to the experience (and written reflections) of Martha, a calm, confident M.A. student in professional writing who had had "a successful nine-year stint in the newspaper business" as reporter, then editor, of a small newspaper, and of the maverick Laura, a senior, self-designed major, and self-styled "hacker" who impatiently endured the traditional English courses on her road to writing about software. In reading and quoting each others' reflections, these five students formed an informal network of ideas and support. In this network, I also appear to be given three roles. One is as a teacher with a relatively focused agenda for assigning and evaluating papers. At other times, I am a fellow researcher as curious and at times as confused about their reading of the situation as they are about mine. Because I felt comfortable with these two roles and the distinction between them, I am sure I encouraged this reading of our relationship. But I was also intrigued to see another role being created for me in these texts, as the audience for this investigation who needs to read carefully, take these discoveries to heart, and get her act together. I must admit to being a little overwhelmed at times at the omniscience into so many different needs that real success would take. But this sort of classroom inquiry always reminds us that teaching only succeeds when individual students succeed in negotiating their own dilemmas and in learning what they need to know.

The Issues at Stake

The "working theories" that the students propose are worth our attention not just as examples of observation-based reflection but because they offer an account of how the meaning of a literate practice is constructed. They trace a path to successful and personally satisfying text that is full of twists and turns not found on the teacher's map. Constructing this image involves negotiation with a teacher's instructions and feedback, with the writer's own history and favored strategies, and with other students' ideas, all of which may foreground different criteria, different advice, different moves. Furthermore, constructing a theory of the task is never done from scratch but is forcefully shaped by the writer's prior knowledge, especially schemas for other sorts of texts. As a well-organized, integrated body of knowledge, a schema for a given practice contains slots for key features and brings with it default values that fill that slot and automatically supply information. Schemas let us go beyond the information given, and once invoked, they can so vigorously supply their own values or default features that they can readily silence explicit information supplied in assignments and lectures.

Because writers do not come to these constructive acts as with a tabula rasa, they often bring with them schemas that overlap with the new task in useful ways—and that actively conflict with it in others. In the face of such conflicts, construction of meaning looks much more like *re-construction.*

Writers must recognize these points of deceptive overlap and distinguish between the reasonable or natural features that their old schema dictates and the features and reader expectations of the new discourse. If locating these sites of conflict seems demanding enough, dealing with conflict can create its own affective hurdle. Schema research makes it clear that people alter or relinquish familiar schemas only when conflict or desire offers a strong motivation to change. Moreover, as we discussed in chapter 3, schemas are not learned as intact templates; they are built up and abstracted from experience. As a way of representing knowledge, a schema then involves both general, prototypical knowledge and specific instances. It is, however, misleading to talk of schemas as if they were repositories of declarative information. The meaning of a schema lies in the way it *functions* as instructions for what to perceive, how to interpret it, and what to do then.

As we will see in the accounts below, to reconstruct a schema in conflict, to rewrite its instructions for perception and action to fit a new situation, depends greatly on students' ability not just to read the instructions or assignment but to read the situation, to draw useful inferences from the context of the class and from the teacher's feedback. Because inferences are just that and because smart guesses are not always accurate, the process of reconstructing meaning when that meaning is represented as a familiar schema is an extended and cumulative act. It extends over the entire course (and one hopes beyond) in a process of recognizing conflict, inferring its meaning, tuning, experimenting, and retuning one's image.

Loaded Language and Rationales for Resistance

Cheryl's working theory of this process locates an important site of conflict in the loaded language of assignments, in which single terms can suggest elaborate strategic agendas for purpose, format, and style, as well as appropriate social roles for the student writer. Beyond that, she portrays this conflict as an emotionally charged event in which learning depends on a personal motivation to embrace change. (Paragraphs are numbered for reference.)

(1) In order to more clearly understand the processes by which people represent a task from written instructions, I decided to analyze my own experiences as well as two other class members, . . . Jenni and Martha. I chose Martha because she is from a different discourse community than Jenni and myself. From class discussions I also realized that Martha had many of the same problems as myself in trying to conceptualize the assignment. For the opposite reasons, I decided to study Jenni's writing

experiences. Jenni seemed to have no problems in representing the task effectively to herself. I found this intriguing since Jenni and I share a common writing background. I wondered why Jenni could easily understand the assignment while I and many others had so many problems.

(2) Below is a relation of my problems defining the writing task [excerpted from an earlier observation and response].

> (3) I have a great deal of trouble trying to write papers for this class. During my collaborative planning sessions and before I sit down to write I become very confused and frustrated. I seem to know what I want to say and what I want to accomplish in my papers, but my expectations are totally different from what Dr. Flower wishes me to accomplish. Our perceptions of the writing task appear to be totally different. I perceive writing a response paper as an informal means of discovering something about yourself in the texts. I think that Dr. Flower views a response statement as an analytic essay applying what you have read to a specific writing problem and resulting in a solution to the problem. Although, I think I understand the nature of our class assignments, I still cannot easily write a paper according to Dr. Flower's specifications. Why?
>
> (4) From my first two years in the Carnegie Mellon English department, I have a concrete idea in my head of what a response statement consists of. I also have a firm perception of what teachers are looking for in a response statement. . . . I seem to have created a formula or a type of pattern in my head for accomplishing this task.
>
> (5) I find it hard to understand and assimilate Dr.Flower's ideas towards papers into my already evolved schema of how to write a good response statement. In the papers I have written for this class, I have tried to draw inferences and tried to relate in an analytic manner the material to my own experiences, but instead I find myself falling back into my response statement schema. I feel compelled to write in a certain manner, and trying to change my writing habits takes an extreme mental effort. It feels unnatural and stressed.

(6) My experience was not unique. Martha also described similar feelings in her Apply Schema paper. [A quotation from Martha's paper follows.]

> (7) The problem I am confronting is putting myself smack dab in the middle of my papers for this Rhetoric and Cognition class. I am not accustomed to writing about myself in academic work. I am not used to applying academic theorists to my own life. It is unsettling.
>
> (8) Thinking about these assignments, it occurred to me at first that my problem really lies in the fact that I have no formula for this new

> kind of writing. I cannot click on "automatic pilot" and breeze through these papers like I can with most kinds of writing. That's one reason why they seem difficult and problematic. . . .
>
> (9) In previous academic writing, sources were the experts, up on pedestals, in books or articles, while my relationship to them was as the lowly, ignorant student. My usual assignment was to examine one or more of them, synthesize what they said, and compare their ideas to those of other sources. What I wrote about was dictated by the assignment imposed by the professor. There was no personal involvement with the sources, and I generally forgot about them as soon as the writing was done.
>
> (10) This new kind of writing demands a different relationship with the sources. It demands not only that I read them, but that I apply them to a personal problem. It also demands that I become a source, since I am the expert on my own problem and on deciphering the reading for my own purpose.
>
> (11) Those demands have several implications for my own reading and writing. Since there's a piece of myself at stake, I must consider the sources differently. I must read them with my own problems in mind. I must interact with the text to a degree that has been the norm for me before only in leisure reading. And it forces my own thinking to overlap with that of the sources, to weigh their ideas, critique them, push them further, perhaps. No longer can I stand idly by beneath the pedestal.

(12) There are many parallels between Martha's and my own experiences. Both of us were still frustrated and confused with the assignments over mid-way into the semester. We each read the assignment descriptions and thought we understood what Linda Flower expected of us, but something got lost in the translation between reading the assignment and writing the assignment. Instead of completing the task according to the outline that Linda Flower gave to us, we insisted on defining the task according to the writing models or prototypes that we were most comfortable with. According to Norman, we were constructing an explanation of the assignment and a framework for completing an assignment according to our prior writing experiences. Because the instructions were explicit, yet abstract, we filled in the abstraction with our own model of writing.

(13) In addition, my writing representation [problem] was compounded by the "commonplaces" or key writing phrases that I am familiar with as an English major at Carnegie Mellon. When I asked Dr. Flower in class questions about the assignment, she responded that it was essentially a re-

sponse to the articles that we read. However, she did not realize that in my discourse community of the literary and cultural studies program that the phrase "response statement" was a loaded term. To me, and other members of the class, a response statement refers to a short, informal essay in which the student is asked to write about what interests him in a piece of literature. The goal is not to validate a specific idea critically. Instead, the response statement is a way of starting with an idea, exploring possibilities about the topic in your mind, and then putting these possibilities into words.

(14) Linda Flower's definition of a response essay was radically different from my literary definition. Linda Flower defined a response statement as an analytic essay applying what you have read to a specific writing problem and resulting in a solution to a problem. As soon as I heard the phrase "response statement," I applied this phrase to my schema of writing, in which writing literary response statements was an integral part. In fact, my definition of response statements was so strong that I could not re-evaluate this definition. I could understand Linda Flower's definition consciously, but I could not transcend it sub-consciously.

(15) More importantly, looking back I do not think that I truly wanted to re-evaluate my writing schemas. My method of writing had always worked well in the past and I was happy with my writing style. I did not see the rationale for changing it. Whereas Martha stated:

> But the idea of writing—and learning—without formulas appeals to me. How interesting! How challenging! To actually be able to use the theories, to interact with them and apply them, seems sensible."

(16) I thought, "What a pain! I do not see the point in these assignments. What is she driving at with these assignments" Anderson believes that "the likelihood of a schema change is maximized when a person recognizes a difficulty in his current position and comes to see that the difficulty can be handled with a different schema." Anderson and Freire also believe that in order for a student to be responsive to a schema change that the student must be persuaded that it is worth his time and effort to change his schema. This can be achieved through a dialectic process between the student and the teacher. The teacher should carefully explain the weaknesses in the students' theory to the student and convince him that a schema change would be beneficial to his way of thinking. . . .

(17) Whereas I fought the rationale behind this type of analytical writing because I found it too constricting and too formal, Martha, familiar with

strict journalistic and academic restrictions on her writing, found the apply approach to be refreshing since it permitted her the freedom to enter into the writing with herself as the source. Unlike myself, Martha did not need to be persuaded to change her schema. Instead, the type of freedom that she began to experience with the apply papers gave her the incentive to try to change her schema! . . .

(18) In my case, I was only willing to change my schema after I talked with Linda Flower personally. She convinced me, through her own personal experiences, that my response statement method of writing would be inadequate in a more professional setting, such as in the corporate sector. Her methods of personally discussing the strength's and weaknesses of each type of writing persuaded me to work on changing my schemas. . . .

(19) One other comparison that I found interesting to note was the time that each of our schema's began to radically change. After we studied the nature of schemas in class, Martha, Jenni, and I all became very conscious of our writing processes. . . . [We] were each relying to an inordinate degree on our past experiences to formulate a representation of the task. This is not an unnatural response. When faced with a new task, individuals have no choice but to rely on their past experiences. . . . Before we changed our writing schema's, we first had to go through the painful process of learning that these schema's had weaknesses that we were not familiar with before and that it would be to our benefit to adopt the new, apply schema.

(20) The confusion and frustration . . . were not a result of Linda Flower's problem definition. The assignment in itself was phrased clearly and coherently, and contained more than enough information to give us an adequate task representation. Now, when I read over the assignment definition, I have a very clear conception of the task at hand. I find it hard to understand why I could not initially perceive what Linda Flower's goal was in formulating the assignments. . . . Before I adopted this new mode of writing it was as if Linda Flower and I were trying to communicate in different languages. We were both assuming that the other person used the same schemas for writing. We did not perceive the differences in communication which result when each party has a different mental representation of the task at mind.

Although Cheryl's reflection was constructed to understand her own process and answer her own questions about the limits of instructional writing, her working theory raises some important issues in how meaning is reconstructed more generally. One of these issues is the limits and negotiable meanings of language. Although "plain language" is a god word in technical writing and "clarity" the standard to which all good English teachers rally, a virtuously clear text becomes a comprehensible text only as the result of the reader's active interpretive process. Of course, assignments and instructions like the ones Cheryl read can always be improved, even though they seem to "contain more than enough information" on second reading. And as a teacher, I will use the loaded word *response* with more care after Cheryl. But the point here is a larger one. As Cheryl herself comments, no class is homogeneous enough for a teacher to predict misreadings; I am sure to err again. And students, given the nature of perception and the wise necessity of drawing on prior experience, will draw on schemas for other literate practices. And these schemas will overlap in many ways (e.g., both response and apply tasks give priority to the writer's own observations and to critical reflection on the implication of them). But when some features of the new literate practices differ, these features will have to buck the system just to get recognized. The power (and virtue) of schemas is, of course, their ability to supply (impose) their own default values in the absence of specific cues, even to the point of actively overriding available information. Even instructions that seem "clear and coherently" phrased in retrospect are a weak voice in competition with the strong schema-driven expectations generated by the "writing models or prototypes that we were most comfortable with." As Fiske and Linville (1980) point out, schema-driven perception is built for speed and designed for efficiency not accuracy.

Cheryl's own two-paragraph discussion of response (¶13–14) is in fact a miniature case in point. In calling the assignment an "observation and response statement," my wording was a conscious (if ineffectual) attempt to avoid the familiar phrase *response statement* and emphasize analytical observation. Cheryl not only assimilated my wording to her expectations, the Norman paper to which she refers was *not* an observation and response but was, in fact, one of the "apply theory" assignments. In the first paragraph of this discussion (¶13), Cheryl maintains the distinction between my real comments, which were about "response" (an action), and the comment that she was hearing, which was about "response statements" (a text type). But in the second paragraph, her terms for the topic in question (an observation and response statement) begin to slip and merge as she attributes to me talk about a *response essay*, then a *response statement*, and finally a *"response statement"* in quotations. Even in this account, done in the afterlight of reflection, Cheryl's expectations seem to be appropriating, translating a classroom discussion even as she reports it. In a similar way, the syllabus asks writers "to apply both theory and observation to a discourse problem of your own choosing," but for Cheryl, like Gina, the request to analyze a problematic situation ("a rhetorical situation, a discourse community, or a problem you, as a speaker or writer, face and want to learn about") seemed to bring with it an unquestioned injunction to find a solvable problem and to solve it. (Note that Cheryl's final paper courageously abandons that assumption and takes on a meaty problem she could not solve.)

The first phase in constructing a new theory of the discourse, then, is even noticing where it differs from what one already knows and does—especially if that other practice has served one well in school, if it is valued in one's home, culture, or in a career culture to which one aspires. Negotiating meaning under these circumstances is a complicated reconstruction that for this writer involved getting feedback, trying to interpret the feedback in a conservative way (making minor adjustments within a familiar schema), getting another round of feedback, and finally facing the conflict directly—actively attempting to figure out what this now inescapably different practice was about. For Cheryl, constructing the meaning of applying theory as a literate practice was a cumulative series of trials and errors, of questioning, tuning, and retuning her notion of the task. As we will see more clearly in Jennifer's account, this image is not a generalized "sense of the text," but it rather carries clear specifications for how sections, such as the introduction and conclusion and even individual paragraphs, are supposed to function; how summary is supposed to interact with one's own ideas and what sort of ideas are valued; whether generality is prized over specificity; and so on. Although Cheryl rightly suggests that more sample texts would have helped in this case, we can predict some of the miscues they will introduce. The larger point of all this is that neither instructions, feedback, nor examples—even our best attempt—will obviate the learner's inevitable task of inferring the principle from the instance. And when such inferencing involves meaningful reconstruction, this process may require a series of encounters extended over time—if the short span of a semester can be seen as extended. What is so impressive is that many students, like Cheryl, do it. What is troubling, even if more understandable, is that others do not.

Conflict, described in terms of schemas that do not match up, misinterpretations, and unrecognized elements of a discourse, is a critical part of the cognition of meaning making. But as Cheryl's working theory makes eloquently clear, conflict can also be an affective event, as the writer confronts the inevitable, unwelcome feelings of uncertainty, the danger of not succeeding on a first or second try, a challenge to one's self-image (as an about-to-graduate "writer," for instance). Although we can make useful distinctions among the cognitive and affective dimensions of this event through the terms we use (e.g., focusing on Cheryl's reasons, her image, her attitudes, and motivation), I would argue that in this case they form inseparable elements of the same experience for the writer. In Cheryl's account, we hear echoes of Piaget's observations that learning and growth emerge out of conflict when old ideas encounter new realities or other people's realities. But we also hear the strong undertones of resistance—to authority, to change, to conflict itself?—and a perceptive account of why conflict does not automatically lead to growth or change even in a supportive environment. As Martha says in one of her early reflections, "Given my background [newspaper reporting], I bristle against these strange new methods in the academic planning process." The problem is that bristling is a reasonable response; it could also prevent a writer from learning a new literate practice he or she might need.

What tips the balance? Is it, as Tanya (in chap. 9) claimed, that awareness makes change possible? Is it, as Cheryl's language suggests, that her instructor's reasons convinced her of the worth of a new practice, or is it, as the tone of her account suggests, the personal encounter, the personal recognition of her struggle, that tipped the balance? The event Cheryl refers to was serendipitous and unsolicited, not even a paper conference, but a walk down the hall after class. In my recollection, I simply turned to Cheryl to "get on her case," to ask her why her two papers took a limited, repertorial stance to her sources when in class she was revealing a person who could make insightful, analytical, and critical statements (the kind we see in the final text). What she does not mention, but which stood out in my intentions, was that my argument was a feminist one—that quiet, docile, compliant women who do not take authority for their actions and speak in their own voices are doomed to be small cogs and eternal little girls doing repetitive jobs in the production-oriented, men's world of technical writing. No doubt we also talked about the value of writing that applies theory; I don't recall. Perhaps the point of these different recollections is that at that moment I as the teacher did not address or even understand the problem Cheryl defines in her final paper. If my intervention seemed to be a turning point, it was because Cheryl made it so. She read this encounter as a motivation to change, to walk outside the boundaries of the response statement and technical report and to speak with a dangerous authority about her sources.

Who knows why this new rhetorical move seemed somehow dangerous: because it was a personal assertion or because it was a discourse practice this successful student was not sure she could handle? Maybe discovering why is not the point. Although her conclusion attributes this change to a dialogue that explains the pros and cons of her schemas, a broader view might put less weight on reasons or the teacher as causal forces and more on Cheryl's own successful negotiation of the conflict. Her working theory of her particular dilemma and its resolution is, I would argue, an example of the dilemmas student writers encounter all the time when schemas collide, when learned literate practices conflict with new ones.

Learning a new literate practice, as Cheryl describes it, is a process of negotiation in which both resistance and motivation play a part. Consider what is involved. Issues of authority are clearly at stake since the teacher both sets the goal of learning a new practice and offers the feedback and evaluation that generates the conflict. At the same time, these new literate practices could help the writer to achieve new authority in a wider set of rhetorical settings. Negotiation here involves not only the delicate adjustment of power in which a learner takes ownership of learning for herself, it calls for negotiation in the other sense I have called path finding—charting a course through rocky waters that still honors multiple purposes. Cheryl's Scylla and Charybdis are both cognitive and affective. In these sites of conflict, when the writer's competence is challenged and her sense of control over the situation momentarily shaken, the outcome may depend strongly on motivation to work through both the intellectual and emotional problem—whether that impetus comes from a dialogue with a teacher or collaborator or whether the writer, like Janet, finds a way to motivate herself.

Motivation, we should remember, is itself a personal construct. It often depends on unseen acts of attribution, that is, on the causal stories students tell themselves. To see this rhetorical situation as a solvable problem, the writer must attribute the dilemma to forces she or he can control in a situation where change is possible (McLeod, 1987; Sitko, 1989; Sitko, 1992). Students whose private stories of causality attribute difficulty to uncontrollable forces like the teacher's whims and to static elements like their own "ability" (or lack of it) have little motivation to keep trying. A climate for growth is one in which change is not only desirable but possible. Teachers obviously help create—or destroy—that climate through dialogue and feedback as well as through explicit instruction in thinking processes themselves. And schools structure a climate that tells students, you are expected to succeed; you to fail. Creating a climate for growth is a weighty responsibility that justifies continued arguments over and research into teaching practices. It demands critical examination of how institutions and individual teachers structure this opportunity to learn.

But at the same time, concentrating solely on what teachers (classrooms or cultures) do can give us a limited vision of how meaning is actually being constructed. We must also recognize that learning ultimately depends on the student's individual negotiation of such dilemmas. The student's own *awareness* of the problem she or he is facing and *working theory* of what she or he needs may be more critical to success than the teacher's ability to guess and respond with the right words at the right time. The teacher/student dialogue Cheryl saw as a turning point was indeed opportune but only because it was an opportunity Cheryl seized in her active engagement with making meaning. In negotiating this dilemma, she constructs in her paper a personal representation of this literate practice as a rhetorical practice that *she* could carry out within the social context of this course, within the context of instruction writing more generally (on which her paper focused), and within the broader, professional context she imagined for herself as a technical writer.

Cheryl's account of conflict, confusion, resistance, and motivation suggests one way the threads of cognition, emotion, attitudes, and social interaction are woven together in the acts of negotiated meaning making. But, as she makes clear, social support, reasonable instruction, and the will to understand are not enough. The more clearly cognitive or intellectual aspects of this constructive process are also part of the complex territory she must traverse. Building an image of a task can be a process of reconstruction as writers abstract general principles from diverse instances. What matters is not just the facts of the situation (my reference to response) but inferences writers draw from those facts. Jennifer's reflective paper, which follows, tracks down a revealing inferential process that led to the remaking of her schema.

Reading the Context, Imagining Action

To an outside observer, the writing in this course posed no dilemmas for Jennifer. Why should it? Jennifer, like Cheryl, was an A student in English; the strongly positive feedback on her "apply Norman" paper seemed to indicate she had read this rhetorical situation with insight and imagination. Best of all, she had been able to apply theory to a meaty problem that really mattered to her. In her work-study job for a research group doing risk analysis, Jennifer was helping to write recommendations whose grim statistics would presumably persuade the public to use seat belts. In Jennifer's hands, Norman's learning theory not only explained why such attempts/such texts had failed so often in the past but suggested that the project's current approach might meet the same fate. However, the reflection on her collaborative session tracks a different and far less certain process.

> I found that in my collaborative planning session I needed continual reassurance that my ideas were relevant and that they fit the assignment. I always have problems while planning a paper [and] put myself through hell while debating with myself, "Am I on the right track or am I wasting my time?" This need for reassurance kept cropping up in my plan-

> ning session. Cheryl and I spent a lot of time discussing just what the assignment was. . . . I then wasn't sure that . . . my risk communication job was relevant because everyone else in the class always seems to apply our readings to their own academic situations. . . . It really helped for Cheryl to tell me to relax. . . . It seemed that I ended up doing a lot of my planning while I was trying to convince Cheryl to reassure me! (Observation and Response, 2, 21 Feb.)

Uncertain which features have priority and relevance in the literate practice she is being asked to do, Jennifer is drawing inferences and imagining alternatives. But even with a reasonable plan, this successful student is in danger of shutting herself down with doubts in the midst of the negotiation. The plot thickens with the next paper. It had, of course, been written with inferences drawn from the "apply Norman" success but received feedback that surprised her and called these inferences into question.

As a result of this experience, Jennifer became interested in why writers often fail to affect readers as they intended. Her final paper explores "a theory I have . . . [that] writers cannot meet the expectations of the reader if their schemas do not match." Interested in writers who "face direct consequences from their reader," she see the placement tests in Bartholomae's (1985) article as illustrating a series of matches and mismatches between the schemas that freshmen and the panel of readers brought to the task. To test this nascent theory, she then decides to track the process by which she, Laura, and Martha developed their schema of apply papers as a literate practice within this particular class. To do this, Jennifer reviewed everyone's texts and planning tapes and conducted interviews with both writers. Then, to let her talk more precisely about possible matches and mismatches between instructor and student, she asked me to think aloud as I did a brief rhetorical reading of a paper by each writer, commenting every few sentences on my unfolding expectations and response to these as apply papers and on my evaluation of their strengths and weaknesses. She then asked the writers to do the same but in their case to predict what I would note and how I would respond.

Her paper describes a dialectical, often dilemma-driven process of constructing and reconstructing an image of this literate practice. In the fast-paced context of a writing course, successful schema formation is a highly inferential, no-guarantees process of making and negotiating possible meanings. For instance, at first look, Laura and the instructor seem to be seeing the same paper but holding different expectations for what is valuable to do. However, as Jennifer begins to follow out the internal contradictions in the story, a more complex picture of Laura's awareness and her developing strategic knowledge begins to emerge.

Linda Flower's Schema

I will begin with Linda Flower's schema for reading the apply papers. She sees the apply papers as a discourse strategy that is the best way to learn theory because it connects the theory to prior knowledge. It forces the student to adapt theories to their own purpose. She goes into each paper looking for certain key ideas from the theorists, but after that she really doesn't have a specific group of expectations. It seems to me that she isn't looking at the papers for "right" answers or applications. She is looking to see how the writer fits the theories to their own experience. This experience must be something that "matters"—an important idea that really is an issue and worth thinking and talking about, not just a trivial application. . . .

Linda doesn't claim to have one set expectation for a particular pattern either. She has a repertoire of the kinds of moves that can be used, and leaves a lot of latitude for different moves as long as the theory is applied to make new knowledge. This seems to be her purpose for the paper. Her schema for a good paper seems to be determined by the paper itself. If it isn't a "bad" paper—and she does have a repertoire for what does not meet her expectations—then she is open to a variety of strategies for the paper.

Laura's Schema

Laura seemed to know that her paper wouldn't match her reader's expectations, and indeed, [it] did not. The textual features that Laura pointed out to me were very similar to how Linda saw the textual features. Laura said that her purpose was to show how Hypercard documentation was structured just like Norman's prototype models, and Linda, too, saw this as the purpose of the paper. However, this purpose did not meet Linda's expectations. Though Laura saw an interesting parallel, she didn't take this observation further. She didn't do anything with the knowledge or apply it to a specific problem. Linda simply saw this paper as using a different type of discourse strategy than the apply discourse strategy. I see this different discourse strategy as a type of observation-response strategy. Laura makes an observation about the relationship between Norman and her own experience, and then she responds to it. . . .

[Here Jennifer expands on what Laura did know.] Despite the fact that [Laura] says she didn't know what was expected, I saw definite parts of the schema she had for this first paper. . . . She felt that she was supposed to have a great revelation, [but] . . . knew the idea of prototyping too well to have any new ideas about it. It seems to me here that she accommodated her [expectations] to fit this dilemma—she . . . simply eliminated this criteria. This elimination is one of the reasons she wasn't satisfied with the paper. . . .

[The next paper] was a much better experience. . . . Laura felt that she had done everything that Linda wanted in the paper—she used the theory in an application to a personal problem and drew inferences from this application. . . . [Here Jennifer does a point by point comparison of how Laura and I saw the paper working, noting the strong agreement.] I think that Laura's predictions and expectations for the first paper influenced her second paper. For example, she knew that she needed a "revelation" (or, in Linda's terms, to make new knowledge) and she did so in the second paper. . . . According to Laura, though she felt she knew what Linda wanted, she was less conscious of writing specifically for Linda. She seemed to be secure enough with her schema that she didn't have to be thinking constantly while writing the paper of what Linda would think. All in all, Laura thought this paper was a great experience for her.

The simple version of Laura's story might focus on the writer's acquisition of new discourse features, a remodeled schema. But Jennifer's story suggests a more complex negotiation by a writer who, feeling uncertain about new expectations, charted a path based on what she knew. At the same time, she still shared the instructor's expectations for what would make a paper "a great experience" and felt disappointed with the choices she made. Jennifer's own experience reveals some different negotiations that include trying to interpret feedback as a guide to action.

Schema

I also seemed to meet Linda's expectations. My purpose was to apply Norman to show why it is difficult for writers to affect readers. . . . [Here she does a point by point comparison of her rhetorical analysis and mine.] After listening to my reflection tape, I can see that I was aware in some respects of what Linda wanted. My predictions of my audience's response were rather accurate. . . . [However,] in some ways she saw more in my paper than I consciously put into it. All through the paper, she found what she called "back and forth inferencing" between Norman, my risk study, and the writing problem I chose. However, I did not do this consciously. In all honesty, I used Norman for my risk study and the writing problem because I wasn't sure which one to focus on to fulfill the assignment. I saw the application of Norman to both, and I didn't know which one was more appropriate for the assignment, so I used both. It wasn't totally a blind move—I saw that there were connections between all three—but I was not aware that I was inferencing anything, or that I would meet Linda's expectations. . . . At the time, I didn't really see why Linda thought that the paper was so good, which is part of the reason I misinterpreted what Linda expected for the second paper. Now I understand the [strategy] I used and why it was effective, but I didn't then. . . .

Interestingly enough, I was not aware of my schema for the first apply paper until now. I thought when I wrote the second paper I was following the same schema as I did for the first; I can see now that I did not. It was very interesting to listen to Linda's [reading aloud] protocol of my Apply Schemas paper because I had thought that this was a good paper; she didn't feel that it was as good as my first. . . . This seems to be an example of metacognition gone wrong! I had an idea of what my schema was and what Linda's expectations were, but they were different than the reality. Consequently, when I tried to use it again, . . . it didn't have the same result because I misinterpreted what I did in the first paper. . . .

[For instance,] when I looked at my first paper then, I did not see the importance of the specificity of my application of Norman to my risk study. I basically ignored it. . . . Linda felt that my conclusion was a good wrap-up [because of its] two specific conclusions for a complex application. I saw [the other features also present in my conclusion] what Linda has termed a "happy ending conclusion" [i.e., a broad, comforting generalization that resolves all]. . . . I started out [the next paper] with a general application of Bazerman . . . [and] wrapped it up with a conventional happy-ending conclusion—what I supposedly saw in my first paper. The paper isn't terrible. I did do some inferencing, which was what I was supposed to do, but my application just was not specific enough.

Jennifer's close analysis gives new specificity to the metaphor of construction. As her simple experiment showed, her three writers are able to build a highly accurate image of a reader's response, predicting what their reader will look for and respond to in the text, even when like Laura, they feel they do not know or cannot meet all the expectations they are aware of. However, early in the course, these theories of the reader and the task are still in draft form, sketches based on past experience and probabilistic reasoning. Moreover, Jennifer's developing image of the task is built not out of simple facts but, in many cases, out of inferences. And these inferences for action are themselves based on an interpretation of the instructor's paper comments. From those comments, she inferred priorities—which features of this discourse were key. And she transformed her own text—read now as a model of a successful paper—into a set of instructions for generating new texts. But this schema-building process that maps out a network of key features, general principles, and their relations is inevitably a reconstructive process. Whereas my enthusiastic comments about the conclusion of her Norman paper were a response to its specificity and surprisingly concrete application to a real problem, those features did not stand out to Jennifer. What did stand out was her shift in focus to a general problem. Her next paper was shaped by "a complex inference" that identified talking about theory with a broadly generalized conclusion, with no mention of the redeeming specificity and new ideas that had marked her first conclusion. Although she calls this "metacognition gone wrong," it is perhaps more a case of business as normal in the process of inferring principles from particulars. Moreover, as Jennifer suggests, this process is a largely tacit one, and the image it constructs is likely to seem normal, to be an obvious reading of the situation. It is only when conflict arises that this custom-made image is called into question.

Negotiations with Convention

Cheryl, Laura, and Jennifer draw us into the train of decisions and revisions, the good guesses, astute inferences, uncertainties, and misfires that make up constructing one's working theory of a new literate practice. They ground their own theories of this process in finely detailed specifics that reassert the active decision making that lies just beneath the surface of the performances we see. Gina, on the other hand, is drawn to some large questions about her status as a "victim of convention" or an "independent thinker" as she uses her paper to trace "one woman's journey through a Rhetoric and Cognition class." Rather than focus on her answer to these weighty questions (which are by design answers *for* Gina), I want to trace the path of a conflict caused by the instruction in the course and raise once again the paradox of instruction as the imposition of authority with the goal of helping the student to develop ways to take authority. Her paper starts with a realization: that her desire for "being Right" has made her a victim of convention far more than she had ever realized.

I could . . . sum up what I've learned in this class with one word. . . . Awareness. It seems as if the whole curriculum was designed around awareness, or maybe that's a personal curriculum I've established for myself. . . .

[As I saw in my reflections on a paper from last term,] I had never realized how much I was a victim of convention and outside influences in my writing (for example, what the professor expected or points brought up in class I hadn't come up with on my own). . . . Even when writing the paper last year, I knew those strategies were in effect. . . . The distinction lies in the fact that back then, I didn't realize how this was affecting my overall writing process.

I've always had the relatively vain notion that my writing was my own, that I was an independent thinker. Now I'm starting to think that after three years of college, I've fallen into a pattern of plugging information into the correct formula, to get a satisfactory piece of writing, or to do the work correctly. I think everyone has a tendency to do that, but I don't like what it tells me about my writing. . . . I've been cheating myself.

Gina goes on to describe how the expectations of collaborative planning—the heavy hand of "outside expectations"—in fact, thwarted both Gina and her partner from writing the paper they wanted to write.

I think my basic problem with the planning was that I'm used to working alone, especially when I write. I've done group projects before, but I've never really had to explain myself the way the blackboard planning requires. Instead of letting it help me, I somehow made it pressure me. I say "let it help me" and "made it pressure me" for a reason. I definitely think the problems I had were my own. . . . I don't think blackboard planning is perfect, and I can think of ways it can be made better, but in the case of applying Norman, it was all me.

The problem, that Gina describes at the beginning of this chapter is that my injunction to consider her purpose called up for her a concept of purpose that would silence most writers: "I thought it had to be a grand conclusion or resounding statement about the world as we know it." And yet, she and her partner persist in trying to do what they think is expected and end up with papers born of this unreconciled tension. My demand for purpose has in fact interfered in Gina's writing, leaving her "distracted from what I really thought and what I really wanted to say, because I felt it wasn't right."

Gina's story seems to have two resolutions. One is in favor of a new commitment not only to being aware of these influences but to resisting external definitions of success.

In writing this paper, I've been wrestling with the ideas of being Right and what really motivates my writing. I've come to the conclusion that more is involved than just impressing a professor. I think it's more personal, [but] I'm bothered by the fact that I seem to be more comfortable with an insincere correctness than being successful. . . . This is where the concept of awareness comes into play for me. . . . Being aware of a habit or influence in your writing, or being able to discuss it, does not necessarily mean that you will use that awareness to make you do better. I think, for me at least, I have a responsibility to myself to use such awareness, to apply it.

In this reading, Gina's reflection leads to awareness that is the basis for resistance and for an assertive independence of mind—a step beyond her naive theories of unchallenged independence. However, there is another layer to this story: such independence seems possible because Gina can also draw on a newly negotiated sense of purpose. It is this new sense of purpose that lets her say:

Maybe being capable [in fulfilling assignments] isn't enough or shouldn't be enough. The question of purpose, which confused me so much before, is now crystal clear. If you don't ask yourself, "so what? What are you going to do with it?" you're doing yourself a disservice. You're cheating yourself.

The paradox of educational authority is with us again. Assigned collaborative planning and its assigned concern with purpose did indeed interfere with fluent writing, but it also pushed this writer into an active negotiation with the concept of purpose and authority structures of school. And by forcing her definitions of purpose to the fore, it led to a reconstruction of the meaning of purpose and a new understanding of how such purpose fits in her own practice. This new meaning (this new notion of a purposeful literate act) was bought at a price. The conflict between my expectations (or her interpretation of them) and her desires led to an extended negotiation—a process of difficulty, of experimentation, and of constructing and reconstructing her own image of success and purpose that went on from February to April.[3] Gina could have found entry into the community of this class by mimicking its conventions, keeping up the pretenses, sidling into the conversation as she has obviously found herself capable of doing before, or she could have resisted convention and outside influence and avoided the demand that interfered with familiar kinds of writing. But instead, she chose to negotiate the meaning of this new practice, and out of that came, ironically, a different way to resist the force of conventional practices.

Negotiation as Balancing Power and as Path Finding

Gina talks about meaning as a site of conflict between competing forces, each of which is aching to create meaning in its own image. In fact, she describes with dismay her own automatic and conventional response to an in-class experiment in which her "old and worn-out schema" for doing a summary took over, even though with a moment's thought she might have called on far more sophisticated maneuvers. Negotiation is working out a balance of power, of creating meaning in the face of competing influences—a process of asserting values, of making choices. It is an act that may call for resistance or for balance among competing demands. It often emerges in situations in which the writer's own values, goals, and ideas are in conflict with those of other kinds of authority, with the intellectual imperialism of other voices, or with rigid rules and old assumptions.

However, to reduce negotiation to this model of toe-to-toe power struggles is to oversimplify the rich interweaving of values that seems to characterize the negotiations in our studies. Even for Gina, negotiation is finding the path through writing that honors and values multiple goals. It leads her, for instance, to keep learning, to accept the engagement with a problematic notion of purpose when she could have easily resisted or subverted the course's request. It leads her to try again, to establish a personal curriculum, and to persist to a new meaning of purpose—a meaning that makes inquiry a purposeful act and encourages risky, independent thinking, while it acknowledges the mixture of discomfort and benefit she feels explaining her purposes to a partner. Her purpose is an interestingly complex concept, that entertains ambiguities. Like Jennifer's image of a conclusion, it tries to find a path that simultaneously fulfills many goals, acknowledges multiple constraints, and avoids as many problems as possible. Perhaps that is why negotiated meaning often remains "under construction."

How Does Reflection Support Action?

The best way to understand the role that reflection plays is through Freire's notion of naming and all that it entails: "To exist, humanly, is to name the world. Once named, the world in its turn reappears to the namers as a problem and demands of them a new solution" (1989, p. 76).

It is, of course, hard to know how much the practices of observation and of written reflection contributed to the learning we saw. Indications from the beginning of the course suggest that the writers were, indeed, attuned to these dilemmas early on; they did not need a program to know they were entering a new discourse. However, even if we want to remain skeptical about causal claims here, there are some reasonable arguments we can make. The writers in chapter 8 showed how reflection creates a distinctive kind of knowledge in the form of situated working theories. These writers show us some ways reflective awareness translated itself into constructive action.

For instance, the working theories of Gina, Jennifer, and Cheryl describe an extended (and ongoing) effort to construct and reconstruct an image of a literate practice. Reflection not only supports such meaning making, it seems to support a certain kind of construction as well. Reflection allows writers to recognize some of the complexity of their rhetorical situations, to acknowledge and to honor multiple and often conflicting goals. It seems to make action more immediately problematic but more ultimately satisfying.

Secondly, if we look at these reflections as the history of a writer's thought, an interesting dialectic seems to emerge. On the one hand, there is a growing, often disconcerting, insight into forces one does not control—into the sources of one's own assumptions and the causes of difficulty. On the other hand, this knowledge seems balanced by a growing meta-awareness of the writer's own power to make and negotiate meaning in the midst of dilemmas.

Jennifer's analysis of Laura is a good example. She chose to discuss Laura, the enthusiastically self-proclaimed "hacker" in the class, because she expected that Laura's immersion in the discourse community of computers and technical writing would influence her writing. What Jennifer saw instead was a reflective attempt to transfer and then transform old knowledge. Laura, she discovered, was working out of a cluster of assumptions, which Jennifer labeled the "general writing schema," that led both women to confront a question that is at the heart of education. Do such general writing schemas exist? Does knowledge transfer? Or does each new literate practice entail a new construction?

Laura had, in fact, raised the issue of transfer in a dramatic way one Monday morning with a story of a weekend ordeal writing a short piece she had expected to toss off. It should have been easy to write a news story about her current reigning passion, the Hypercard project. Here is how she wrote about it a few days later:

> I have never written journalism. For three years now, I had been concentrating on technical writing, and I had become very good at technical writing. I had a very distinct schema for technical writing. When I volunteered to write a news story for a friend of mine, an editor on the *Tartan*, I had thought it would be easy. I am not a bad writer. I had not thought I would have any problems writing the article—writing is writing. The truth was very different and very interesting to me. I spent hours agonizing over an 8-paragraph news story, writing and re-writing, and throwing it out and starting over. When I finally handed in the story, I was so disappointed in my talents as a journalist that I vowed never to write for a newspaper again. (7 Mar.)

In class, Laura spelled out the funny, but painful story of her long weekend starting with her attempts to figure out the genre, reading past news stories, looking for models, and then being shocked at the failure of her general or technical writing strategies. Laura's unexpected encounter with conflicting schemas outside of class put the problem of learning to do an "apply theory" paper in class into a larger perspective. It also led Jennifer to locate the problem not in news stories but in Laura's assumption that "writing is writing" and her naive theory that her general purpose schema would allow untroubled transfer.

Jennifer is not alone in her suspicions. Among other educational theorists, the notion is problematic (Bransford et al., 1986). The essence of transfer in learning is the ability to use old knowledge in new settings.[4] But the proponents of situated cognition, discussed in chapter 3, have called any simple idea of transfer into question. They have argued that learning is embedded within situations, that knowledge is entwined with its use, and that abstract, general principles (for all their power in some settings) do not travel well when students go from class to class or from home to school. Math does not make one logical; Latin does not train the mind; and learning to control one literate practice (such as a traditional English class theme) does not make one literate. The transfer of complex processes is not the automatic event the word implies. Instead, effective transfer of knowledge is possible when people recognize—actually attend to the fact—that features of this situation fit prior situations, and as a result, they adapt old knowledge and strategies to fit these new conditions. And as we have seen, successful transfer happens when people also figure out the misfits. Transfer, at least in the complex tasks like writing, seems to depend not merely on possessing relevant information but on having strategic knowledge—on reading a situation, setting appropriate goals, using appropriate strategies, and being aware of one's own options and assumptions.

Laura's story of reinventing the news story made its way into the theory building of other writers in this class. For one thing, it illustrated the need to cross discourse boundaries and to build negotiated meaning—to deal with conflicts, constraints, and options as a writer. Moreover, this same process was cropping up in an act of self-assigned, personally important, and professionally significant writing—just as it was in school. And once again, this negotiated meaning making was an affectively loaded cognitive event.

Reading these accounts, I, like Jennifer and Cheryl, am also impressed with the affective weight of these events, with writers in "culture shock" who are "bristling" at new strategies and skeptical about the value of new forms of discourse, writers who are (surprisingly) surprised at their own difficulty. At the same time, there is an energetic, assertive tone to these discussions in class and in text. Writers seem to be making radical shifts in attitude as they succeed in the practice and begin to appropriate this new literacy for their own purposes. Negotiated construction provokes satisfaction and engagement; it also documents frustration and turmoil, whether the task is a self-assigned story on a topic near to one's heart or a short paper assigned to support learning and experimentation.

And yet, one wonders, does Laura's level of anxiety have to be this high? Does one have to attribute the source of difficulty to one's hopeless "talents as a journalist"? In this context, Jennifer frames an intriguing hypothesis: perhaps Laura's faith in a general writing schema is itself a part of the problem. If writers come to new discourses with the assumption that "writing is writing" or that they know how to write, what happens when they encounter not only diverse discourse practices but conflict among overlapping schemas? Common sense and experience shows us that much of our writing knowledge does indeed transfer, but successful transfer may not depend on tacit processes. Sometimes it depends on awareness of differences and on strategic adaptation. If Jennifer is right, abandoning the myth of a general writing ability may be part of a whole frame of reference with regard to writing that can prepare a writer for the active negotiation that is required and for the strategic, adaptive transfer that awareness makes possible.

Reflection, especially these observation-based reflections, is a way to name the world and in naming to create new problems. But they are often good problems, and in the reflections themselves, we see writers are taking action as they reconstruct their own understanding and begin to document, even celebrate, their own power to construct negotiated meanings.

10

Coming to Conclusions

At the end of a long book, the writer wants to heave a sigh and stop. The reader wants a conclusion. To be more accurate, most of us (readers and writers) would like the intellectual equivalent of a happy ending: a coherent statement of a manageable argument with some clear implications.

However, the trouble with the observation-based theory building in which we are engaged is that the resistant, obstreperous voice of the observed world always wants to have the last say, to still resist the theory builder's urge to coherence and closure. As a researcher and as a teacher, I have tried to see these freshman collaborators and my students' reflections as a puzzle in which the pieces do not all fit and the truth is not a unified story. And at the same time, I have tried to interpret, to appropriate parts of this data to build a theory of writers constructing negotiated meaning and a framework for studying that process. My own construction, then, was a purposeful, not a mimetic act, motivated by the public debate over literacy and my own investment in the riddle of a social cognitive process. So how, then, should one conclude? The story the data has to tell and its web of meaning is always bigger than the claims and implications to which we can reduce it for one purpose or another. The Victorian insight was to write multiple endings, seen from different vantage points.

Conclusion 1: Teaching A Social Cognitive Process

I come to this discussion as an educator. I have followed this social cognitive controversy—even read most of the book at hand—and I, too, am skeptical about the lines I see drawn: where some see a process of socialization, others see a student thinking. But like the author, I want a more integrated vision of literacy that recognizes that writers need to know discourse conventions as well as strategies, to belong to a community and still take independent journeys of the mind. And even though some of us teach from a rhetorical tradition and some from an expressive one, both seem to offer genuine bedrock on which to build a redefinition of the basics. I see in this social cognitive view a strong, more assertively inclusive alternative to the limited literacies of correctness and convention. On the other hand, this social cognitive position is not a happy valley. Would a more integrated vision ever resolve these conflicts at its own core? Should it try? In this book, as I read it, the point of interest to which our gaze is drawn is not an integrated theory or a ideal pedagogy but a contested space where these possibilities converge—a space we might define as the cultural, social, interpersonal, and private process of a writer constructing meaning.

I must admit, I am not used to thinking of my students and Sir Phillip Sidney in the same frame, much less to thinking of my freshmen doing something quite so exalted as constructing meaning. I guess I am a bit of a conventionalist, brought up on the language of expressive writing. On the other hand, I have had enough student conferences and long nights myself to feel the weight of this argument for negotiation. I think there is a tendency to assume that even though *we*, as writers, always make the task more difficult, always bring too many voices into that internal conversation as we wrestle with our options, *other people* somehow have the right schemas, know what they are doing, and simply join in the conversation. And *our students*—well, it seems they aren't even noticing the voices embedded in the assignment calling for analysis, evidence, detail, and so on, as they happily spin out the text we didn't ask for. And yet I must admit, the hidden logic behind those problematic papers is almost invariably surprising, if you can take the time to find it out.

In fact, like any good teacher, I know enough to know how little we know about the logic of most learners. My own response has been to put most of my effort into constructing a supportive, motivating climate for writing, what this book calls apprenticeship. I am thinking now of how cognitive apprenticeship would alter this picture. So I came to the studies of collaborative planning and student inquiry in the second half of this book with a very particular question in mind: Is it possible to embed explicit strategic instruction (the rhetorical thinking our author is so enthusiastic about) within a collaborative social context designed to motivate students and nurture writing? And I was also asking myself, How might this strategic instruction serve the political and social agendas of my teaching? Are such agendas served only by a pedagogy of critique?

This book argues for a middle ground where the transformation of an individual and a social system are both possible. Using the language of cognitive rhetoric, it locates this transformation in an interesting place—in a process of inquiry in which students work to extend their repertoire at the same time they try to examine and take metacognitive control of their own decisions. There is a hopeful tenor to these final chapters. As I read them, the framework of collaborative planning foregrounded for writers some of the multiple expectations they had to negotiate; the tools of observation let students forge working theories of their own negotiation. I am not sure what kinds of transformations are possible or what it would take to support them for different students, but I see this uncertain ground of negotiation as a good place for us to stand.

On the other hand, this hopefulness seems yoked to a certain skepticism this theory urges. If it is indeed true that construction and negotiation lead to the hidden logics of learners and texts, just how sure can we be of which forces are at work in that hidden logic (whether those forces are a repressive ideology or my own best efforts to teach)? I am not a researcher. I freely admit I skimmed the bit on statistics, and my eyes didn't jump to the tables and graphs. But like the author, I am becoming increasingly skeptical of the simplifying dichotomies that stop at critique and impatient with untested and unconditionalized, if internally coherent, versions of theory. Running through this text is a subtext about how we build theory. It sometimes surfaces as an attempt to step back from the author's own methods to place them in the context of other methods with different strengths or to justify their use. But the large issue, I am convinced, is not how we observe but how we make our theory building more responsible to the evidence of observation, more open to the tests that disconfirm our assumptions or hopes, and more responsive to conditional and situated realities of writing and learning.

But as I said, I am a practical person, and in my professional life, the issue often comes to this: When I design our freshman course next term and prepare to teach the new TAs, where shall I stand? The conventionalists are lined up: some have been teaching comparison/contrast essays for years. The new breed is pulling in two directions. Some want to demystify academic discourse, immersing students in texts that let them imitate the intimate tricks of the trade for writing in English departments. Others who gravitate to the texts of popular culture will use convention not as a model but as the focus of a critique, as evidence of the assumptions that shape a given discourse. And the process educators line up as well with their repertoires of valued strategies: there's the Aristotelian teaching an art of invention for dealing with subject matter, another immersed in journaling and revising techniques for personal writing, another encouraging students to goal-directed, problem-solving strategies for rhetorical situations. But then there is also the student who, unfortunately, needs to manage all these possibilities—to be a member of an academic community who knows not just the conventional moves and is aware of the baggage they carry and the expectations they raise but is a flexible thinker with a repertoire of strategies and the awareness to choose among them. That's what a social cognitive curriculum has to do, not to teach an approach but to teach the student in the midst of negotiating an academic community. The syllabus for a critical, cognitive apprenticeship could be a tall order, but . . .

Conclusion 2: Literate Acts

My colleague is, as he says, a practical man. I am sometimes stirred by the wisdom of the merely possible. I hear his desire to synthesize perspectives and, in fact, see a more integrative curriculum already emerging in the work of some of my colleagues. But the question remains, Will we do justice to a literacy of personal and social action by teaching its strategies if students are not also prepared to embrace or understand its goals? My colleague's reading of this constructive theory will have stopped short if it only leads us to teach that peculiar beast, the "classroom practice." On the positive side, this literate practice, probably an essay of some stripe, achieves life and meaning within the social world of an English or WAC class. And in learning to carry out this special literacy, students do indeed find themselves immersed in a community, learning its mysteries and developing a repertoire of strategies for composing this special creature. We have created a manageable arena for a social cognitive process.

But since responding to a book, as I am, gives one license to imagine the difficult, I want to stand in a different place. On the continuum that starts with limited literacies and moves us into generative, if still classroom-based, literate practices, I want to keep moving. I want a curriculum on the other end that supports not just literate practices, but literate acts.

Looking over the picture of writers developed in these studies, I have begun to construct a story line of what this intellectual experience (that is, the attempt to achieve it) might require of me and my students.

To begin with, a student who opts for literate action can't stop at learning the multiple conventions of community; she will have to orchestrate, even adapt them, she will be making strategic decisions about how to use the repertoires she has learned. Conflict enters this story early on, whether it is the conflict of competing practices and incompatible goals or of merely alternative possibilities springing up in the fertile ground of an ill-defined problem. Past experience, present expectations, old schemas, and new intentions shoulder their way into the negotiation; external forces become internal voices asserting their priority, suggesting how to proceed, or trying to halt the entire process with a critical certainty of what isn't acceptable. Literate acts are constructed out of such negotiations—they demand a willingness to entertain uncertainty and to listen to voices that expand the network of possibilities, and yet in the midst of that, to construct not only a coherently organized text but a coherent rhetorical act.

Secondly, this choice means that as an educator I will have to do more than teach the repertoires of convention, of text, of process activities, or of strategies that I can name, point to in examples, or model. The knowledge my students need to develop is strategic knowledge; that is, in addition to strategies and conventions, they need to understand the goals that spawned the conventions of a given discourse or the goals that drive a strategy. And I must help them develop the metacognitive awareness of those goals and strategies as the basis for informed choice. For instance, it won't be enough to teach a strategy such as collaborative planning without also teaching how to make a strategic use of it, to monitor and adapt the practice, or to recognize the limitations posed by their own assumptions of what the teacher expects. Likewise, it won't be enough to write explicit assignments if I can't help students learn how to interpret those tasks and to gain some self-reflexive distance on the fact that they are interpreting them.

And finally, there is the pragmatic question of how to do this. This book does present some possible models, such as the general outline of cognitive apprenticeship and the more specific practice of collaborative planning, but the studies that support these practices also undercut them. Whatever I do or teach is transformed by the students' interpretation of it, shaped like any other meaning by their prior knowledge, goals, and awareness of options. Like my students, I am negotiating a path among multiple realities. On the one hand, I act as a person committed to the power of pedagogy guided by theory, shaped, tested, and reshaped by formal research and classroom inquiry. I act out the rhetoric of possibility.

But on the other hand, the site of change is not in my hands or in our collective knowledge. It is in the uses an individual student makes of it. Over this we have little control. Positions like cognitive rhetoric assert the generalizing power of principles and argue for practices that can cross boundaries of age and and discourse, that can reinvent themselves in different settings. But they also assert a contradictory truth—at the center of this process stand the constructive acts of individual writers.

If learning occurs in a vortex of negotiation, then the logic that drives students is not merely an attempt to approximate the models of thought and prose we give them. It is the logic of negotiating a complex rhetorical situation, including voices I, the instructor, never hear. As a teacher in this process, it is not enough for me to rest satisfied with providing the right information (whether I think that information is a cultural canon, an anti-establishment gospel, a process pedagogy, or good models). In teaching a constructive process, the action that matters is an interaction. The scene for action has shifted from my teaching to a site of conflict and negotiation in which each writer is constructing not just the meaning of a text and the meaning of my instruction but his or her own working theories of writing. Students are reading, misreading, and rereading the class, its books, their partners, testing out old notions, and constructing new, more complex webs of meaning.

Where does that leave me? Teaching with conviction, working out of theory, testing my expectations with research, but all the time knowing that the learning is not reproduction or mere imitation (though it is at times) and that conversation may shape what is possible but only as it is interpreted by individual agents. Even my best instruction will be but one more voice in the circle of negotiation—I just hope it will emerge as a live option.

My response is to stay in the game and join the circle, but beyond that, teaching begins to take the shape of an inquiry into students' learning. It starts with my own search, focused on three promising places: (1) on students' interpretations (of tasks, of feedback, of situation), (2) on sites of conflict and acts of negotiation, and (3) on the insights of students' own reflection. However, since my observations can only lay a better foundation on which writers do the real construction, the primary inquiry is the one students conduct themselves. The same tools that support my inquiry support theirs, that is, reading other positions, other accounts combined with observation-based reflection of their own. In their inquiry, I see not only a way I might teach strategic knowledge but an opening for students to carry out a literate act, to use writing for their own ends within the structure of school. I see the possibility that their own inquiry could create working theories, self-constructed understandings that situate issues, principles, and dilemmas in the personal experience of writing.

There were other conclusions, but since the Victorians usually stopped at two, so shall we.

APPENDIX
NOTES
REFERENCES
INDEX

Appendix
Carter and Jennie's Planning Session

Transcription Conventions:

Pause	...
Short, abrupt pause	—
Overlapping speech	/inserted word/
Editorial ellipses	[. . .], [. . . .]
Coding (at end of turn)	
Single category code	[*info*]
Consolidation	[*aud/rh pur*]
Double code only	[*aud* and *rh pur*]
Reflection	[*R*]

C: Carter
S: Supporter, Jennie

1 S: Okay, Carter. I listened to your self-interview and... [*off*]

2 C: Did you like it? [*off*]

3 S: Yeah. [*off*]

4 C: Okay. That's good. [*off*]

5 S: Carter, could you just briefly run through it again. What... what is your discourse problem? [*info* (coded as *prompt* only)]

6 C: Okay. My discourse problem is how—how some people have difficulty—or a lot of people probably have difficulty in switching writing styles for different writing assignments. And this is mostly—more common in switching assignments from class to class. I said in my self-interview that you use a totally different kind of writing for writing a paper for Technology and People, as opposed to writing papers for Strategies for Writing. In Technology and People, they give you a problem that you're asked to solve, and you just solve a problem. They don't care even if it's in paragraph form, or—or—you know, you can miss punctuations, spelling and they don't really care. [*key pt*]

7 S: Oh, really? [*off, R*]

8 C: They just want... You know... They just want what your thoughts are and that you solved the problem right. [*info, R*]

9 S: Uh-huh... Right. [*off*]

10 C: But in Strategies for Writing, if you don't use paragraphs and you misspell lots of words wrong... then you're gonna get in big trouble. [*info, R*]

11 S: Yeah, you get in trouble. [*info*]

12 C: So there definitely is different writing for different classes. [*key pt*]

13 S: Yeah. [*off*]

14 C: And the problem that can come out of this is—is trying to decide what style to use for different classes, because when you first start taking the class, you really don't know what to expect, so you might not know what writing style to use for that class. [*key pt*]

15 S: Yeah... Yeah. I definitely see how different classes require different things from you. And I think that in itself can be a problem for writing, just because each class will like kinda put you in a mold of what they want and you have to fill those requirements, and you know they're gonna have limits on you, which will be a problem in writing when you want to express something in a different way, and you just can't do that. So that's gonna be like your main focus and key point, right? [*key pt*]

16 C: Right. [*off*]

17 S: Well, what are some of the main points that you're gonna bring out in this paper? [*prompt*]

18 C: I'm gonna try to—well convince the reader that these differences do exist for a lot of people. I'm sure that they don't exist for everybody, because probably a lot of people write the same way for everything—they don't really have a difference. [*rh pur/aud, R*]

19 S: I don't know. [*aud, R*]

20 C: You don't think? I think some people... You know... They might... [*aud, R*]

21 S: Well, it depends... [*aud, R*]

22 C: They might not care. I mean, they might just write the same way for everything and not really care. I'm sure no students [here] do that, but... [*info, R*]

23 S: Yeah. Yeah. That's what I mean. Well, who's your audience for this? [*prompt*]

24 C: My audience would probably be college students... It would really be of interest probably to freshman because they're switching from high school and starting out college writing. So... [*aud/rh pur, R*]

25 S: So is that gonna be another... [*off*]

26 C: Yeah. It's gonna be one of my /components?/ Yeah. I forgot to mention that. I'm sorry. [*off*]

27 S: I see. Well, Carter, if your audience is gonna be a college student, I think every college student, you know, has to go through this changes... I can see if your paper is to the general public, and some people really don't write too much, and really write for one specific purpose, and which would be the same all the time. But if it's for a college student, I think you should focus that it *does* change, not that it *might* change. [*aud, R*]

28 C: Okay. You're right. I guess. You're always right. [*off*]

29 S: (Laughs) Well... Nah... I'm just kidding. [*off*]

30 C: And my audience... They're probably gonna expect a lot of examples. I'm gonna have to use a lot of examples to prove—to prove it to them that different writing styles exist, and I want my audience to be able to relate

their own experiences to this, and maybe, and see how it affects them. [*aud/tx con/rh pur, R*]

31 S: So, what kind of examples are you gonna use? Can you give me an example? An example... [*tx con*]

32 C: Um... Okay... I'll give you a real big example. Switching from high school writing to college writing. [*info*]

33 S: Uh-huh. [*off*]

34 C: In high school, you could—most of the times for any class you could get away with, you know, BS in a lot of papers. And you'd get good grades, just 'cause it sounded intelligent, even though it really didn't say much. In college they don't go for that stuff. You gotta really, you know, go write, and you can't BS your paper, because they'll know right away that you're doing that. And, another example I could use is, like I said before, the Technology and People and Strategies for Writing... And maybe... I haven't thought of this until now... is maybe ask some people from a different college, maybe like [College of Science] or whatever, if they have any different writing styles that they use for their classes, since I don't have some of their classes. Maybe compare it to like [College of Engineering] writing styles, if I could do that. [*tx con*]

35 S: Yeah, I think you might be better to compare it to like someone more different, like H&SS [Humanities and Social Sciences]... [*tx con, R*]

36 C: CFA: [College of Fine Arts]... [*info, R*]

37 S: Yeah. Or CFA [College of Fine Arts]. Because I think MCS [the college of science] is kind of close. But I think—um... you were kind of... Well... how do I want to say this? So some of your main points are gonna be that from high school to college—in high school, you can get away with saying things that aren't really relevant. In college you can't. But how are you gonna explain that? Are you gonna give a specific example in your life? With like... in high school I did this, in college I can't do that. Like I think it would become more real. [*key pt/tx con, R*]

38 C: Yeah. Okay. I can do this. In high school, in my senior year, we had to write a thesis paper. And we had an entire semester to do it. And, just like me—I waited until like the last three weeks of the semester to start doing it. And I didn't have all the research done that I should have, but I started working on it real hard. And I had a lot of pages. It ended up being 15 pages long... /wow/ with bibliography and... Well, that's what she expected—she said 10 to 15 pages. And it was really long and drawn out, and it didn't really say much of anything, but it sounded like it did. You know what I mean? [*info*]

39 S: Yeah. That's a good example. I really like that. [tx con]

40 C: I got an—I got an A on it... [*info*]

41 S: Oh! Congratulations! [*off*]

42 C: It really didn't say anything, so I was so happy and I got an A in English, and that made my day, and then I graduated, and I was even happier. But, for college... [*off*]

43 S: Yeah. That's a good example. [*tx con*]

44 C: I'm not done yet. [*off*]

45 S: (Laughs) Sorry, Carter. [*off*]

46 C: (Laughs) Okay. And comparing that to the—the first semester of college... I took a class [on culture and history], which is probably the most boring class I've ever taken in my life. But, we had to write... [*info*]

47 S: I hope [name] doesn't listen to this tape (giggle). [*off*]

48 C: Well, I'm done with it, and I got a B in it, or whatever. But anyway... [*off*]

49 S: Whatever. [*off*]

50 C: So, we had to write a 5-page paper on African nationalism, which I had no idea, and I waited like the night before I was due to start that... [*info*]

51 S: You have a bad habit of doing that. [*off*]

52 C: I know. Well, I put all that into my writing-style analysis paper, so that's all there. So, anyway... So I wrote five or six pages on nothing, but I included the words *African nationalism* in there once in a while. I thought, why this is just like high school, I can get away with doing this. I got the paper back, and it was a C-, or a C, or something like that. It said "no content." And I was introduced to the world of college writing. [*info*]

53 S: Great, Carter. Well, that... Well, that's good that that happened to you, and... For two reasons, you know. One, so you can learn from it, and two, so you can use that for an example in your paper. And that's an excellent, excellent example. [*tx con*]

54 C: And three, so I can write about African nationalism. [*info*]

55 S: Yeah. It's excellent. Um... But... Okay, so that's an example for one of your points. What about an example for how writing varies?... Well, I think you already kinda told me that... How writing varies from Tech. and People to Strategies of Writing. Just, you would say, one needs more content than the other... I mean, more facts and details, and not as much style. [*tx con/key pt*]

56 C: Yeah. Well, I can give a specific example for that. For a problem analysis paper in Strategies for Writing, my first draft... It wasn't very well organized, and... Well, you know, we handed the papers in and got them back, and Rebecca commented on them... [*tx con*]

57 S: Hm-hm. [*off*]

58 C: She said my paper wasn't very well organized, and she gave me ideas of how I could structure it better. [*info*]

59 S: Oh, that was nice. [*off*]

60 C: That was very nice of her. I got a B on the paper, so I was real happy. [*info*]

61 S: Oh, great. [*off*]

62 C: But... And she told me how I could structure it better, you know, make it more smoothly flowing, and whatever. And... And so I wrote it like that, as, you know, real paragraph form, everything was ordered, and everything like that. Good spelling. Good grammar. Good punctuation. [*info*]

63 S: Yeah. So that's necessary in an English paper. [*info*]

64 C: Yeah. But in Technology and People, we have papers due almost every Friday, and most of them are... They'll give us a problem, and they'll ask

us to give a possible solution of the problem. You know... in a report form sort of. And my papers for Tech. and People... Usually, they'll have maybe a paragraph. And then maybe a problem, like an equation worked out or something like that. They won't really be structured. I mean, I'll just have like one, problem one, and then all that, you know, so it's really different. [*info*]

65 S: Yeah. Okay. So... Good example. What's some of the other texts you mentioned that you're gonna be using besides examples? [*tx con*]

66 C: I don't really see a lot of places I can fit text conventions in here, other than maybe... [*tx con, R*]

67 S: Well, comparisons, along with examples. [*tx con, R*]

68 C: Yeah. Comparisons, contrasts. [*tx con*]

69 S: Headings? Would you use headings? [*tx con, R*]

70 C: Hm. I don't think so. [*tx con, R*]

71 S: How about a concluding paragraph? [*tx con*]

72 C: Yeah. A concluding paragraph. It'll definitely be in there. That's a necessary in Strategies for Writing paper. I might... [*tx con*]

73 S: Well, let's talk about your conclusion then. [*tx con*]

74 C: Okay. My conclusion... [*tx con*]

75 S: Like, are you gonna try to offer a solution to this problem, or just talk about it? [*gen pur, R*]

76 C: I might give them ideas on how to at least try to give ideas on how to, you know, keep—keep these things straight. [*rh pur/aud*]

77 S: Well, how could you really solve those problems? [*gen pur, R*]

78 C: I don't think you really can solve it. All I said is, I might give ideas to maybe help, you know, nurse along. [*gen pur, R*]

79 S: Help what? [*rh pur*]

80 C: Help people catch on to these—to these differences sooner than I did... I learned the hard way. [*rh pur/aud*]

81 S: Okay. Okay. Yeah. I see that. [*off*]

82 C: You know. If a high school student read this, or a college freshman, like a beginning year freshman, they'd know they couldn't get away with the same stuff that they could in high school. [*aud/rh pur, R*]

83 S: Yeah. That's good. And even for someone who hasn't learned that yet, it would be emphasizing... [*aud/rh pur*]

84 C: Seniors haven't learned that yet. [*aud/rh pur*]

85 S: Yeah. Definitely. Well, by the time you're a senior, that's almost worthless... Okay. So, you're not really using text conventions a whole heck of lot. Well, Carter, what do you think is the most interesting part of your paper? [*aud* and *tx con*]

86 C: I think it's gonna ... be the examples, I guess. [*off*]

87 S: Uh-huh. That's what I was thinking. [*off*]

88 C: I think that'll be pretty interesting. [*off*]

89 S: Yeah. Just to see... Well, just so the reader can learn more about the problem, and so the reader can learn more about you, and some of the experiences you've been through. [*tx con/aud/gen pur, R*]

90 C: Because, I... I don't think people think about this, you know, too often. Like when they sit down to write—"Oh, it's different from like the Strategies paper." [*aud/gen pur, R*]

91 S: Yeah. And by reading your paper they'll sit down and see... [*aud, gen pur, R*]

92 C: Maybe they'll be able to realize their own differences, and everything, realize that they exist. [*rh pur, R*]

93 S: Yeah. I think that's the part of the paper that interests me the most. Just so I can see that, yeah, it's really different. And even though there's nothing you can do about it—even if there are boundaries set on you, and that's a given, and you can't really change that—but if you're aware of that, you can be more aware of what is expected of you, and you can work with that. That's really good. Well, so has this talk helped you change your plan, or reinforce anything... [*rh pur, R*]

94 C: Um... It made me think a little bit more about my examples. [*off*]

95 S: Huh-huh... [*off*]

96 C: Further just kind of general examples. I thought more about the specifics. It made me think about my audience a little bit more. [off]

97 S: Huh-huh. [*off*]

98 C: And definitely my text conventions a little bit more. Because I have little notes here. I have two lines up for text conventions. [*off*] [. . . .]

108 S: Well, do you think you're gonna have a problem with the length? I'm sure you have enough information. But do you think it will get too long? Will you ramble with this, or can you condense it, or... [*tx con, R*]

109 C: It'll be easy. I'm not the best writer in the world, I'll admit to that. But I think I can condense it, and make it short and sweet, you know... [*tx con, R*]

110 S: Yeah. [*off*]

111 C: Two pages. [*tx con*]

112 S: Yeah. You know, with examples. That's great. That's great. [*tx con*]

113 C: I'm going to have an opening paragraph, examples, more examples, then maybe like ideas on how to, you know, realize this paragraph, and maybe a concluding paragraph. [*tx con*]

114 S: Maybe? [*off*]

115 C: Yes. Concluding paragraph. [*tx con*]

116 S: You definitely... You need a concluding... [*tx con*]

117 C: Definitely have a concluding paragraph. [*tx con*]

118 S: Yeah. Is there anything else you want to talk about? [*off*]

119 C: If this is fifteen minutes, no. [*off*]

120 S: (Laughs) Oh. Okay. [*off*]

121 C: Has this been fifteen minutes? [*off*]

122 S: Yeah. Yeah. [*off*]

123 C: Well, I think that's about... I learned about everything there possibly is to learn about my paper... [*off*]

124 S: Good. Good. [*off*]

125 C: So this has been a real great learning experience. [*off*]

126 S: Good. Well, good luck to you, Carter. [*off*]

127 C: Oh, thank you very much, Jennie. [*off*]

128 S: Hope everything comes out okay. [*off*]

Notes

1. Literate Acts

1. At some level, of course, all discourse is personally meaningful. My aim is not to create a categorical distinction between practices and acts where in fact the reality is a continuum. My aim is to draw attention to acts that spill over the boundaries of conventions, in which an account based on the features of a practice would be inadequate and in which looking at the writer's own intentions, transformations of knowledge, and adaptations of conventions could offer us a more satisfying explanatory account.

2. DeCastell and Luke argue that the undoing of the progressive movement in American education was, in fact, its reliance on a vague and ambiguous notion of dialectic as a way to deal with "the apparent contradictions and conflicts in social practice." Its failure to "resolve contradictions (between self and society, individual and institution, science and art, education and socialization)" allowed its progressive ideals to be pared down into the limited goals of social, workplace utility (1988, p. 168).

2. Constructing Negotiated Meaning

1. I do not want to ignore the valid point made by Bloome and Bailey and others that "the meaning or significance of any utterance is not located solely in a person's intent, but rather in the event, in the concerted action of people with each other" (1992, p. 187). However, because I am concerned with how writers construct meaning, my focus is on the representations of meaning that are created and held—not in the eye of a camera or ethnographer recording an event—but in the minds of meaning makers who participate in that event. Acknowledging the reality of both events and individual representations, I intend to study representations as they are embedded within and shaped by events.

2. This discussion, written in a spirit of celebration, has a sad afterword that is important to recognize. On December 1991, Joseph Shabalala was murdered in South Africa under disputed circumstances by a white man who was not charged with the murder. Genuine problems rarely go away. The dilemma-driven but constructive negotiations of individual writers have a parallel in the social process of argument and rhetoric itself as an alternative to violence. The conclusion of Perelman and Olbrechts-Tyteca's *New Rhetoric* states it best for me: "Only the existence of an argumentation that is neither compelling nor arbitrary can give meaning to human freedom. . . . It is because of the possibility of argumentation which provides reasons, but not compelling reasons, that it is possible to escape the dilemma: adherence to an objectively and universally valid truth, or recourse to suggestion and violence to secure acceptance for our opinions and decisions" (1969, p. 514).

3. If such negotiation is a reality for students—and I will argue that it is—some contemporary images of meaning making may be blocking this recognition. We are, for instance, unlikely to see this process if students are characterized (thus perceived) with deficit metaphors—as learners lacking certain basic thinking skills, as mere

initiates trying to imitate discourse patterns, or as unwitting pawns of their culture and ideology. And we are certain to miss much of this constructive performance if we look only at the texts student writers, especially less successful student writers, produce.

4. LeFevre's (1987) analysis of "invention as a social act" cuts the pie somewhat differently than I do by focusing on the social unit involved in invention and evaluation, which she identifies as either an individual, two people interacting, or a social collective. This helpful analysis of who is involved does not, however, speak directly to the nature of construction by an individual writer who participates in a dialogue or collective.

5. For example, in pandemonium models, perception operates through the competition for attentional resources (Lindsay & Norman, 1972). Connectionist theories of memory and learning (discussed in chap. 3) specify elaborate systems for weighting, activating, and suppressing nodes and connections (Bechtel & Abrahamsen, 1991).

6. Some of the reasons for this difference were revealing. In some cases, the judges' standards for synthesis demanded a substantive synthesizing concept (not just a simple generalization that would frame a summary). In others, students described as "intenders" could not always carry out the plans they envisioned. One wonders if such unarticulated differences between students' and teachers' expectations make it difficult for students to interpret teachers' feedback.

3. Construction as a Metaphor for Meaning Making

1. For Sidney, the essential conflict would probably have been framed as "false art" based on courtly Petrarchan conventions versus the "true art" inspired by love. However, "Invention," the creation of ideas through the art and craft of rhetoric, plays a key role in both scenarios (cf. Kalstone, 1967).

2. This discussion draws heavily on Bechtel and Abrahamsen's (1991) balanced account of connectionist theory.

3. In the earlier discussion of connectionist and symbolic architectures, *symbolic* referred to the rule-based forms of representation such as logic and linguistics used to develop the architecture for an artificial intelligence system. In the broader sense intended here, I assume that a complex symbolic representation (a word, a gesture, a concept) is best understood as part of a connectionist network.

4. Construction Sites: Observations of Meaning Making in Learning, Development, and Literacy

1. This tradition of extended periods of menial work before apprentices even touched a clock or watch is documented in histories of the guilds. However, according to older watchmakers trained in Germany, this form or apprenticeship was still being practiced in Germany in the 1920s (Tim Flower, personal communication, Sept. 1990).

5. Collaborative Planning: An Educator's Account of a Constructive Process

1. This growing body of close, systematic studies of writers' planning has begun to sketch some alternative paths writers take to building a representation. See, for instance: Ackerman, 1991; Applebee, 1986; Bereiter & Scardamalia, 1987; Berkenkotter, 1984; Blyler, 1989; Bracewell, Frederiksen, & Frederiksen, 1982; Bransford & McCarrell, 1974; Burtis, Bereiter, Scardamalia, & Tetroe, 1983; Emig, 1977; Flower & Hayes, 1981; Flower et al., 1992; Greene, 1990b; Hayes-Roth &

Hayes-Roth, 1978; Herrington, 1985; Kantz, 1987; Langer, 1984; Myers, 1985; Nelson, 1990; Selzer, 1983; Voss, Tyler, & Yengo, 1983; Witte, 1987.

2. The results of this study are also discussed in Flower and Higgins (1991) and in Higgins (1992). Higgins and Petraglia played central roles both in the data collection and analysis of these transcripts and in thinking through what a constructive process becomes in the context of freshman composition. We want to thank Dave Wallace, Rebecca Burnett, Tim Flower, and Stuart Greene for their close reading of those manuscripts and for many long and fruitful discussions about their ideas.

6. "Welcome to College": Construction and Negotiation in a Freshman Class

1. The classes, part of the university-wide freshman composition course at a research university, were taught by two experienced instructors interested in experimenting with collaborative planning and in seeing how students actually used the strategy. This was their first experience with collaborative planning and the first time it had been used in the course. The 22 university students involved in this analysis (10 from one class, 12 from the other, out of the total of 36) were originally selected because we had a complete set of tapes and papers from three different sessions over the course of the term for this group. Only the second session, which occurred around the middle of the term, is used in this analysis.

2. Carter's conclusions offer an interesting parallel to some more systematic observations of the Reading-to-Write project in which some students saw that college might require a change in the writing strategies they normally used (which are adapted to reciting knowledge, subordinating one's ideas to the authority of the source text, and avoiding conflicts and contradictions). On the other hand, summary and response may still be a sensible move, since in any given course, the rules of the game for integrating one's own knowledge with a source can be difficult to figure out and integration is risky to attempt (Flower et al., 1990).

3. These points were operationally defined as comments that raised a problem or question that an experienced writer would see as calling for goal setting or knowledge transformation, a point that could not be answered with a yes or no or with content information. Using this definition to locate these points avoided any need to infer the supporter's intention and let us distinguish between a cue calling for such planning and the planner's response to it. Reliability on identifying these prompts and on whether planners engaged with or rejected the request was 96% based on pair-wise comparisons.

4. Special rules to deal with fine points of coding will be mentioned in endnotes. Since other categories such as audience and text conventions frequently include or "drift" into a discussion of topic information, an episode was coded as Topic Information (*info*) only when it was the sole focus of the entire turn or (in the occasional cases of double-coding) an independent segment of a turn.

5. Although one would like to see reliability closer to 80%, this rate of agreement seems particularly good given the large number of categories raters had to consider and the frequency of turns that called for double coding.

6. In order to interpret the significance of table 3, we may also need to understand how a comment functions. The low frequency of some kinds of planning, such as an average of only 1.86 rhetorical purpose statements per session, may even make the category seem negligible. However, as we saw in Carter's comment (turn 30) on going beyond proving a thesis to showing other students how conflicting writing styles affect them, a single turn devoted to purpose helped frame a broader conception of the task and opened the door to Jennie's continued prompts to make his examples "more real."

7. A narrowed focus on activities and outcomes carries a cost. Hillocks (1986) and Applebee (1986) have shown how this happens with the *natural process* view of writing. The *natural process* approach has at times popularized itself into a set of approved activities—a sort of process canon that includes "brainstorming, journal writing, focus on students' ideas and experiences, small-group activities, teacher/student conferences, . . . emphasis on multiple drafts, postponement of attention to editing . . . and elimination or deferment of grading" (Applebee, 1986, pp. 95–96). Applebee suggests that in this enthusiasm for activities one can do and teach (and see students perform), teachers may lose sight of the goal-directed nature of writing (and the thinking they cannot see). Instead of presenting writing strategies as means to the writer's own ends, teachers prescribe a set of "naturalized" or even required activities. The students in Applebee's study ended up seeing process activities like journal writing as just another exercise to complete by the rules, instead of a writer's tool to use for certain purposes.

Cognitive rhetoric gives us a different way to analyze students' performance by shifting the focus from activities associated with the natural process to the writer's problem-solving process. It concentrates more directly on a writer's plans and goals and foregrounds the merely probabilistic, heuristic nature of any given technique, whether it is using Aristotle's topoi, drawing an issue tree, or doing collaborative planning. Nevertheless, when it comes to developing explanatory accounts of students' writing processes, the standard approach of cognitive rhetoric (like the expert/novice analysis above) is likely to tell us more about what students do than why they did it. Likewise, the curriculum research Hillocks reviews analyzes the effect of activities teachers conduct or assign. Other studies that seek to contextualize their findings still focus on the external dimensions of a process; they use ethnographic data to describe how knowledge is presented and how students interact within a class (Herrington, 1988) or textual data to infer the discourse knowledge students lack (Bartholomae, 1985). Other studies with a more theoretical/cognitive focus may look for developmental patterns within a large set of general thinking behaviors (Langer, 1986) or use experimental instruction to produce a theoretically revealing change in writers' performance (Bereiter & Scardamalia, 1987). Or they may look for expert/novice patterns and differences that reveal key features of a process such as planning or revision (Flower et al., 1992; Hayes et al., 1987). For all that process research has taught us, its focus has been primarily on the situations and activities into which students are swept or on the definable strategies they exhibit.

8. I want to thank David Wallace for his suggestion and enthusiastic pursuit of this analysis and his insight into the convergence of the statistical and strategic analysis, which points to the revealing patterns of individual difference.

7. Strategic Knowledge and the Logic of a Learner

1. We should be aware that the term *strategic knowledge* has a certain inevitable ambiguity. Are we talking about stored knowledge or current cognition? The word *knowledge* suggests that the possession of appropriate goals, strategies, and awareness (or metaknowledge of options) exists as a body of stored knowledge, as something we learn, recall, and modify. And indeed, there seems little question that writers develop a strategic repertoire: on seeing a familiar rhetorical situation, they then call on a cluster of goals, strategies, and a sense of options evoked on previous occasions. This cluster becomes part of a schema that includes discourse conventions, readers' responses, and so forth. And, of course, we hope that the strategic knowledge we see operating in the structured world of a class is not just a onetime performance but a cluster that is being learned and will be invoked again.

However, we should not assume that the strategic knowledge we observe reflects prior, organized knowledge—a body of stored information. In many cases, what we see students doing is better described as *strategic cognition,* as an action in real time in which we see writers setting goals, invoking strategies, and exercising some level of awareness. We cannot tell what if anything is being learned at that moment nor what clusters of possibly stored strategic knowledge are being called upon. All we can safely say is that we can see evidence of strategic cognition operating and that this knowledge of the writer's goals, strategies, and awareness seen in action helps us understand the logic of the writer's performance. Take, for example, the following exchange in which the goal of using a source becomes linked to a particular text convention:

22 S: How do you like... How are you gonna... This is a paper about the Farbs [sic] book, right?
23 Paul: Yeah. Hm-hm.
24 S: So, how're you gonna use the Farb book into this thing?
25 Paul: Hm. I didn't really think about that.
26 S: Perhaps you should include that in your text convention.
27 Paul: Yeah. Okay. That's a good idea. I forgot all about that Farb was...
28 S: Yeah. In writing about Farbs, you should mention some statement about Farbs.
29 Paul: Yeah. That's true. I should probably... Yeah. That's a good idea. Can I borrow your pencil for a second, just write that down.

When the supporter suggests using the Farb book in the text, it raises a goal Paul apparently had not yet considered. The "mention" strategy (again offered by the supporter) may be a familiar part of Paul's repertoire or an interesting new option that is worth writing down. It is hard to separate what Paul knows about using sources (and will use again) from the goal-directed act of knowing we witness. (Either way, Paul's final text may suggest some limits to this knowing: it begins by quoting a fine generalization from Farb—and neither claim nor source are ever heard from again.) The strategic knowledge/cognition a writer exhibits, then, may reflect a locally triggered, opportunistic, context-specific act (such as deciding to use the source text), or the operation of a well-established, generalized schema (such as the "mention" or "quote" technique for using a source), or a context-specific act in the process of becoming part of a such a schema. One could hope, for instance, that our writer may be developing a repertoire of ways to integrate sources with his own thinking—"mentioning" is certainly a start. Given the inevitable ambiguity of our data, the concept of strategic knowledge/cognition, then, refers both to knowledge one can possess and to the process of using such knowledge—the nature of our evidence will determine which description seems most appropriate.

As a concept, strategic knowledge is primarily an argument for expanding the boundaries of what we recognize as relevant knowledge. It foregrounds the role that goals and awareness, as well as strategies, play in the logic of the writer's process. This means that the term is not an honorific, in the way *strategic* is often used to mean *planful.* It is not a quality one can have or lack. All writers operate with some level of awareness and metaknowledge (including the misleading or limiting assumptions students often have about their own ability). All operate with a repertoire of strategies (including "buggy," error-prone routines and efficient techniques for all-nighters). And all are guided by some set of goals, including unexamined ones, just as instructors suspicious of theory nevertheless operate with tacit theories and assumptions about teaching and learning. In sum, the logic of the learner's process rests on the occasionally irrational, often inconsistent, but always influential body of goals, strategies, and awareness brought to the task.

2. The Hayes-Flower models of the writing process, of revision, and of task representation made some parallel claims when they distinguished among cognitive processes in writing, available knowledge, the task environment, and the text-so-far as elements in a recursive process and when they argued that a writer's image of the task evolves in relation not only to external pressures and internal suggestions but to the developing text itself (Flower & Hayes, 1981; Hayes et al., 1987; Flower et al., 1990).

3. Giroux (1983) might describe this as an instance of *accommodation*, in that the students fail to question how the conventions being learned privilege some forms of knowledge at the expense of others. His focus is on the presence/absence of ideological critique; mine on learning. However, as we saw at the beginning of this chapter, Carter's interpretation of his own writing history suggests that he is quite aware of the differences and trade-offs among alternative ways of constructing meaning in school.

4. For this post hoc analysis, we took a set of papers, including Vince's and Carter's, back to the instructor for a taped commentary on the papers and on how each would have been graded.

8. Metacognition: A Strategic Response to Thinking

1. The Reading-to-Write project began from such a class, and it eventually combined actual dorm-room protocols (transcribed for students over the weekend), self-analysis sheets, focused journal writing, and class presentations. Collaborative planning also began as one of a variety of observation techniques and written responses we tried. It emerged as the minor success story of these classes because it offered both observational data with the power to surprise and immediate help for writing.

2. For example, Rose's *Lives on the Boundary* (1989) gives us a similar, compellingly grounded account of personal, community, social, and educational contexts that influenced his own development and that of the underprepared students he worked with. He shows us contexts under negotiation and the confrontation and confusion that occurs there. But one could argue that his experiential account, like these student reflections, is selective, that it fails to acknowledge ideology, or the influence of poorly written textbooks, or any number of other shaping influences—some of which might have been significant, some of which might have had little or no real influence on the highly literate mind that evolved within those circumstances. To focus on negotiated contexts, then, runs that risk. On the other hand, it avoids the trap of simply replicating our own theories of what the shaping context is. As we all know, notions like discourse community, social matrix, and so on reify a claim. They turn these theoretical constructs into objects, as if they really existed, until they are challenged when other researchers try, for instance, to specify the boundaries of a discourse community in practice. The thrust of observation-based theory, then, is to see these forces insofar as they operate in the minds and actions of writers and in the context of literate events.

This selective focus is, of course, a necessary move in education. One thing both radical, liberal, and conservative educators—from Giroux and Freire, to Graff, Heath, Rose, A. Brown, and Collins, to Hirsch and Bloom—do is try to influence what voices enter the circle of negotiation, which are foregrounded, open to scrutiny, and involved in learning. Most writers grow up within multiple ideologies of repression, of liberation, or of mainstream cultural values found in canonized texts. The goal of many educators is to promote some of these ideological contexts into the arena of a negotiable context, in which writers can forge new relations (including some specific relations the educator usually has in mind).

3. These papers were also influenced by the role they were to serve in the second half of the course, in which the social structure and focus of the class underwent a radical change. Discoveries made in the midterm papers became the basis for a video newsletter about writing that the class scripted and helped produce and direct. With the help of Jeannette Abi-Nader and the media department of the Pittsburgh Public Schools, the scriptwriters tried to turn the key discoveries that had emerged in the midterm papers into illustrative vignettes. The video showed students, playing themselves, thinking aloud as they wrote and faced dilemmas, like getting started or writing for different courses and discourse communities, and ended with interviews with individual writers. Since the immediate audience was juniors at a creative and performing arts high school (who would do their own video in reply), students felt that their discoveries would have to pass muster with viewers who were potentially critical but also worried about the prospect of writing in college. A final paper at the end of the course was a commentary on the video.

4. Prior to paper 1, the instructors modeled a simple dialogue technique for reading-to-write in which (in the privacy of home) a student would "talk back" to a source text and allow the text to reply to them—a strategy that might help writers go beyond simple summary or response to build a more qualified, conditionalized understanding. We had observed this "expert student strategy" in the Reading-to-Write project and presented it as such—a strategy worth trying on the Farb text. To evaluate the strategy and observe something of their own planning, students taped and transcribed themselves thinking aloud during an initial 10-minute planning period and later after a break or at a turning point they selected. Although such a close look at their own thinking was revealing to many students, the technique was too time-consuming to be a practical teaching tool and too brief to count on capturing critical moments. Almost all the students' analyses were based on their collaborative planning sessions. In this early experimental use of collaborative planning, we were able to have one session transcribed but concluded that although transcription was valuable to us, it was not really necessary for the students' reflection.

5. As the Making Thinking Visible project continued this experiment with collaborative planning, we became convinced that the observational, experimental stance of this process and the time spent on critical reflection were as essential as teaching and modeling such thinking. For many students, reflection appears to be a turning point in taking new control of their writing process and doing so with an enlarged awareness of their own assumptions and goals (even when their goals are not those of the instructor). Our group's attempt to present planning and reflection as a necessary pair, however, was often ignored by teachers eager to use collaborative planning. In some cases, this use of reflection appeared to violate teachers' assumptions about their role as information givers and students' powers of insight (Flower et al., 1993).

6. Quotation from transcripts follows the conventions noted at the beginning of the appendix.

7. A word of contextualization is in order here. While this vigorous problem-solving style seems quite reasonable from students who have already identified themselves as writers, when the freshmen in the Reading-To-Write project reflected on their dorm-room protocols, their dilemmas reflected a more general uncertainty about academic writing and their surprise was often at seeing that there was a logic to their own efforts. The dilemmas students define will be shaped by their situations and their needs.

8. The papers of 11 of the 13 students are represented in the table. One student

wrote a video script as her midterm paper, anticipating the upcoming project, and another paper was unavailable for analysis. Interrater reliability on a sample of 30% coded by the authors was 0.90.

9. Reflection and the Reconstruction of a Literate Practice

1. In this version of the Rhetoric and Cognition course described in chapter 8, the video project was replaced with additional reading, more short papers, and a good deal more time given to writing and discussing observation-based reflections. The unifying question asked of each theory was: What does a rhetor/writer do? The two key assignments were described in this way:

Journal. In response to the articles we read, you will be keeping a journal made up of brief but regular "observation and response statements" that ask you to observe some situation or process talked about in the article, to describe what you observed, and to write a brief response to your own observations. Some of these "observations" will involve listening to tapes of your own collaborative planning sessions.

Papers. Your own observations will come into play in the papers as well. In three, 1–2 page papers, you will be asked to apply what you have learned from the reading to a problem in academic discourse or to some other discourse community or context in which you are interested. The goal of these short papers is to use what we are learning for a purpose of your own.

The final project is like the short papers. It will be an opportunity to apply both theory and observation to a discourse problem of your own choosing. Start thinking about this problem early in the term. First, you will need to choose a rhetorical situation, a discourse community, or a problem you, as a speaker or writer, face and want to learn about. This situation could involve academic writing, a professional writing situation, or some more general experience, such as planning or revising. Secondly, describe this rhetorical situation in terms of the rhetorical and cognitive theory we have explored in the course. Create a rich cognitive and theoretical picture of what is involved in your situation. Third, put yourself in the situation and do one or two collaborative planning sessions or another sort of direct data gathering so you can reflect on your own writing process and problem-solving strategies in that context. The paper will then include both a theoretical analysis of a rhetorical situation and a data-based observation of your own process in that situation. Some problematic situations that you might want to explore for this project would include: writing for a specific course, writing for an internship or a professional project, or writing for a rhetorical situation you face in a social organization. Or you may wish to study a situation such as collaborative planning itself by tracking your own process over the term, the problem of writing for Peabody High School students, or the process of coauthorship. The goal of this project is to learn about both a rhetorical situation and yourself as a writer.

2. Although I have used pseudonyms for other students throughout this book, I am, with their permission, citing these former students by name as writers in their own right, since it is their working theories, not mine, that this chapter will consider. The writers are Gina Marsala, Cheryl Montgomery, Jennifer Severa, Martha Vockley, and Laura Ann Lemay, who are all, as of 1992, practicing professional writers.

3. In reviewing this account, two and a half years later, Gina suggests that part of the difficulty here is not just agreement or disagreement but bridging the gap between the formal, structured theories and her own experience. But whatever the source of difficulty, it is clear that such a process takes time: "It wasn't until the end of class, when working on the final project that I really felt comfortable in 'negotiating' the material for myself—working through ideas I may or may not agree

with to construct an understanding that could give me more insight into writing processes" (Gina Marsala, personal communication, 12 January 1993).

4. In her review of this account, two years and a half years later, Jennifer put an interesting twist on transfer:

> I've discovered that in my position [as a technical writer in aerospace software development], I don't necessarily reflect on my own writing, but I do reflect on the writing of my developers and their schemas for writing manual text. I've named these schemas, in a sense, and my knowledge of them affects what I do with their writing. For example, Bob uses what I call a "storybook" schema—lots of descriptive adjectives, a narrative tone, and never the same sentence twice. He's even said to me, "It's boring to repeat the same sentence or phrase." Kevin simply writes what he thinks—he transcribes his thoughts into written words and occasionally adds some punctuation. Craig is "Mr. Formality." It doesn't matter if the text is clear, as long as it "looks nice" and sounds formal.
>
> Quite frankly, these schemas do not match MY schema for appropriate manual text. But unlike a professor who penalizes a student in this situation, I rewrite their text to fit my schema. I anticipate what I am going to receive from them and my awareness shapes the questions I ask: I do not hesitate to ask Bob if he is expressing the same idea in three different sentences and then edit accordingly.

Jennifer goes on to note that these men hate to write (and appreciate her work). But because she is rewriting without challenging their schemas, their writing does not develop—and, she is realizing, this prevents her from expanding into other writing she would like to do (Jennifer Severa, personal communication, 5 Jan. 1993).

References

Ackerman, J. M. (1989). Reading and writing in the academy: A comparison of two disciplines (Doctoral dissertation, Carnegie Mellon University, 1989). *Dissertation Abstracts International*, *51/02A*, p. 464.

Ackerman, J. M. (1991). Reading, writing, and knowing: The role of disciplinary knowledge in comprehension and composing. *Research in the Teaching of English*, *25*(2), 133–178.

Anderson, A. B., & Stokes, S. J. (1984). Social and institutional influences on the development and practice of literacy. In H. Goelman (Ed.), *Awakening to literacy* (pp. 24–37). London: Heinemann Educational Books.

Anderson, J. R. (1980). *Cognitive psychology and its implications.* San Francisco: W. H. Freedman.

Applebee, A. N. (1981). *Writing in the secondary school.* Urbana, IL: National Council of Teachers of English.

Applebee, A. N. (1984). *Contexts for learning to write.* Norwood, NJ: Ablex.

Applebee, A. N. (1986). Problems in process approaches: Toward a reconceptualization of process instruction. In A. R. Petrosky & D. Bartholomae (Eds.), *The teaching of writing* (pp. 95–113). Chicago: National Society for the Study of Education.

Aristotle. (1932). *The rhetoric* (L. Cooper, Trans.). New York: Appleton-Century-Crofts.

Aston, J. (1993). Collaborative planning and the classroom context: Tracking, banking and transformation. In L. Flower, D. L. Wallace, L. Norris, & R. E. Burnett (Eds.), *Making thinking visible: Writing, collaborative planning, and classroom inquiry* (pp. 181–203). Urbana, IL: National Council of Teachers of English.

Baker, L., & Brown, A. L. (1984). Metacognitive skills in reading. In P. D. Pearson, R. Barr, M. L. Kamil, & P. Mosenthal (Eds.), *Handbook of reading research* (pp. 353–394). New York: Longman.

Bakhtin, M. M. (1981). *The dialogic imagination.* (C. Emerson & M. Holquist, Trans.). Austin: University of Texas Press.

Bandura, A. (1986). *Social foundations of thought and action: A social cognitive theory.* Englewood Cliffs, NJ: Prentice Hall.

Bandura, A. (1989). Human agency in social cognitive theory. *American Psychologist*, *44*(9), 1175–1184.

Bandura, A., & Wood, R. E. (1989). Effect of perceived controllability and performance standards on self-regulation of complex decision-making. *Journal of Personality and Social Psychology*, *56*, 805–814.

Baron, D. (1982). *Grammar and good taste.* New Haven: Yale University Press.

Bartholomae, D. (1985). Inventing the university. In M. Rose (Ed.), *When a writer can't write: Studies in writer's block and other composing-process problems* (pp. 134–165). New York: Guilford Press.

Bartlett, F. C. (1932). *Remembering: A study in experimental and social psychology*. Cambridge: Cambridge University Press.

Bazerman, C. (1981). *The informed writer*. Boston: Houghton Mifflin.

Bazerman, C. (1985). Physicists reading physics: Schema-laden purposes and purpose-laden schema. *Written Communication, 2*(1), 3–23.

Bazerman, C. (1988). *Shaping written knowledge: The genre and activity of the experimental article in science*. Madison: University of Wisconsin Press.

Bazerman, C. (1991). How natural philosophers can cooperate: The literary technology of coordinated investigation in Joseph Priestley's History and Present State of Electricity (1767). In C. Bazerman & J. Paradis (Eds.), *Textual dynamics of the professions: Historical and contemporary studies of writing in professional communities* (pp. 12–34). Madison: University of Wisconsin Press.

Beach, R., & Eaton, S. (1984). Factors influencing the self-assessing and revising by college freshmen. In R. Beach & L. Bridwell (Eds.), *New directions in composition research* (pp. 149–170). New York: Guilford Press.

Bechtel, W., & Abrahamsen, A. (1991). *Connectionism and the mind: An introduction to parallel processing in networks*. Cambridge, MA: Basil Blackwell.

Bereiter, C. (1991). Implications of connectionism for thinking about rules. *Educational Researcher, 20*(3), 10–16.

Bereiter, C., & Scardamalia, M. (1982). From conversation to composition: The role of instruction in a developmental process. In R. Glaser (Ed.), *Advances in instructional psychology* (Vol. 2, pp. 1–64). Hillsdale, NJ: Erlbaum.

Bereiter, C., & Scardamalia, M. (1985). Cognitive coping strategies and the problem of "inert knowledge." In S. F. Chipman, J. W. Segal, & R. Glaser (Eds.), *Thinking and learning skills: Vol. 2. Research and open questions* (pp. 65–80). Hillsdale, NJ: Erlbaum.

Bereiter, C., & Scardamalia, M. (1987). *The psychology of written communication*. Hillsdale, NJ: Erlbaum.

Berkenkotter, C. (1984). Decisions and revisions: The planning strategies of a publishing writer. *College Composition and Communication*, 34, 156–169.

Berkenkotter, C., Huckin, T., & Ackerman, J. (1988). Conventions, conversations, and the writer: Case study of a student in a rhetoric Ph.D program. *Research in the Teaching of English*, 22, 9–41.

Berlin, J. (1988). Rhetoric and ideology in the writing class. *College English, 50*(5), 477–494.

Bitzer, L. F. (1968). The rhetorical situation. *Philosophy and Rhetoric*, *1*(1), 1–14.

Bizzell, P. (1989). [Review of *The social construction of written information*]. *College Composition and Communication*, 40(4), 483–486.

Bloome, D., & Bailey, F. M. (1992). Studying language and literacy through events, particularity, and intertextuality. In R. Beach, J. L. Green, M. L. Kamil, & T. Shanahan (Eds.), *Multidisciplinary perspectives on literacy research* (pp. 181–210). Urbana, IL: National Council of Teachers of English.

Blyler, N. R. (1989). Purpose and composition theory: Issues in the research. *Journal of Advanced Composition*, 9, 97–111.

Bracewell, R. J., Frederiksen, C. H., & Frederiksen, J. D. (1982). Cognitive processes in composing and comprehending discourse. *Educational Psychologist*, 17(3), 146–164.

Brandt, D. (1990). *Literacy as involvement: The acts of writers, readers, and texts*. Carbondale, IL: Southern Illinois University Press.

Brandt, D. (1992). The cognitive as the social: An ethnomethodological approach to writing process research. *Written Communication*, 9(3), 315–335.

Bransford, J. D. (1985). *Human cognition: Learning, understanding and remembering*. Belmont, CA: Wadsworth Publishing.

Bransford, J. D. (1990). Anchored instruction and its relationship to situated cognition. *Educational Research*, 19(5), 2–10.

Bransford, J. D., & McCarrell, N. S. (1974). A sketch of a cognitive approach to comprehension: Some thoughts about understanding what it means to com prehend. In W. B. Weimer & D. S. Palermo (Eds.), *Cognition and the symbolic processes* (pp. 189–229). Hillsdale, NJ: Erlbaum.

Bransford, J., Sherwood, R., Vye, N., & Reiser, J. (1986). Teaching thinking and problem solving: Research foundations. *American Psychologist*, 41(10), 1078–1089.

Britton, J., Burgess, T., Martin, N., McLeod, A., & Rosen, H. (1975). *The development of writing abilities*. London: Macmillan.

Brown, A. (1987). Metacognition, executive control, self-regulation, and other more mysterious mechanisms. In F. Weinert & R. Kluwe (Eds.), *Metacognition, motivation, and understanding* (pp. 65–116). Hillsdale, NJ: Erlbaum.

Brown, A. L. (1980). Metacognitive development and reading. In R. J. Spiro, B. Bruce, & W. F. Brewer (Eds.), *Theoretical issues in reading comprehension : Perspectives from cognitive psychology, linguistics, artificial intelligence, and education* (pp. 453–481). Hillsdale, NJ: Erlbaum.

Brown, A. L., & Palincsar, A. S. (1989). Guided, cooperative learning and individual knowledge acquisition. In L. B. Resnick (Ed.), *Knowing, learning, and instruction: Essays in honor of Robert Glaser* (pp. 393–451). Hillsdale, NJ: Erlbaum.

Brown, J. S., Collins, A., & Duguid, P. (1989). Situated cognition and the culture of learning. *Educational Researcher*, 18(1), 32–42.

Bruffee, K. A. (1984). Collaborative learning and the "conversation of mankind." *College English*, 46, 635–652.

Bruner, J. (1983). *Child's talk: Learning to use language*. London: Oxford University Press.

Burnett, R. E. (1991). Conflict in the collaborative planning of co-authors: How substantive conflict, representation of task, and dominance relate to high-quality documents (Doctoral dissertation, Carnegie Mellon University, 1991). *Dissertation Abstracts International*, 52/04A, p. 1236.

Burtis, P. J., Bereiter, C., Scardamalia, M., & Tetroe, J. (1983). The development of planning in writing. In B. M. Kroll & G. Wells (Eds.), *Explorations in the development of writing* (pp. 153–174). Chicester, England: Wiley.

Carbaugh, D. (Ed.). (1990). *Cultural communication and intercultural contact*. Hillsdale, NJ: Erlbaum.

Carey, L., & Flower, L. (1989). Foundations for creativity in the writing process: Rhetorical representations of ill-defined problems. In J. A. Glover, R. R. Ronning, & C. R. Reynolds (Eds.), *Handbook of creativity* (pp. 283–303). New York: Plenum Press.

Carter, M. (1988). Problem solving reconsidered: A pluralistic theory of problems. *College English, 50*(5), 551–565.

Cazden, C. B. (1988). *Classroom discourse: The language of teaching and learning*. Portsmouth, NH: Heinemann.

Chase, G. (1988). Accommodation, resistance and the politics of student writing. *College Composition and Communication, 39*(1), 13–22.

Clark, G. (1990). *Dialogue, dialectic, and conversation: A social perspective on the function of writing* (Studies in Writing and Rhetoric Series). Carbondale, IL: Southern Illinois University Press.

Clifford, J. (1983). On ethnograhic authority. *Representations, 1*(2), 118–146.

Collins, A., Brown, J. S., & Newman, S. E. (1989). Cognitive apprenticeship: Teaching the craft of reading, writing, and mathematics. In L. B. Resnick (Ed.), *Knowing, earning, and instruction: Essays in honor of Robert Glaser* (pp. 453–494). Hillsdale, NJ: Erlbaum.

Cooper, M., & & Holzman, M. (1989). *Writing as social action*. Portsmouth, NH: Boynton/Cook.

Crowley, S. (1990). *The methodical memory: Invention in current-traditional rhetoric*. Carbondale, IL: Southern Illinois University Press.

Crowley, S. (1992, March). *Audience as party spirit*. Paper presented at the Conference on College Composition and Communication Annual Convention, Cincinnati, OH.

Dansereau, D. F. (1985). Learning strategy research. In S. F. Chipman, J. W. Segal, & R. Glaser (Eds.), *Thinking and learning skills: Vol. 2. Research and open questions* (pp. 209–239). Hillsdale, NJ: Erlbaum.

DeAngelo, F. J. (1975). *A conceptual theory of rhetoric*. Cambridge, MA: Winthrop Publishers.

deBeaugrande, R. (1984). *Text production*. Norwood, NJ: Ablex.

deCastell, S., & Luke, A. (1988). Defining "literacy" in North American schools: Social and historical conditions and consequences. In E. R. Kintgen, B. M. Kroll, & M. Rose (Eds.), *Perspectives on literacy* (pp. 159–174). Carbondale, IL: Southern Illinois University Press.

Delpit, L. D. (1986). Skills and other dilemmas of a progressive Black educator. *Harvard Educational Review, 56*(4), 379–385.

Delpit, L. D. (1988). The silenced dialogue: Power and pedagogy in educating other people's children. *Harvard Educational Review, 58*(3), 280–298.

DiPardo, A., & Freedman, S. W. (1988). Peer response groups in the writing classroom: Theoretic foundations and new directions. *Review of Educational Research, 58*(2), 119–149.

Durst, R. K. (1987). Cognitive and linguistic demands of analytic writing. *Research in the Teaching of English, 21*(4), 347–376.

Durst, R. K. (1989). Monitoring processes in analytic and summary writing. *Written Communication, 6*(3), 340–363.

Dyson, A. H. (1986). Transitions and tensions: Interrelationships between the

drawing, talking, and dictating of young children. *Research in the Teaching of English, 20*(4), 379–409.
Elbow, P. (1981). *Writing without teachers.* New York: Oxford University Press.
Elbow, P. (1991). Reflections on academic discourse: How it relates to freshmen and colleagues. *College English, 53*(2), 135–155.
Emig, J. (1971). The composing processes of twelfth graders (NCTE Research Report No. 13). Urbana, IL: National Council of Teachers of English.
Emig, J. (1977). Writing as a mode of learning. *College Composition and Communication, 28*, 122–128.
Erickson, F. (1988). School literacy, reasoning, and civility: An anthropologist's perspective. In E. R. Kintgen, B. M. Kroll, & M. Rose (Eds.), *Perspectives on literacy* (pp. 205–226). Carbondale, IL: Southern Illinois University Press.
Ericsson, K. A., & Simon, H. A. (1985). *Protocol analysis: Verbal reports as data.* Cambridge: MIT Press.
Erlmann, V. (1987). Liner notes on music album, *Mbube roots: Zulu choral music from South Africa, 1930–1960.* Cambridge, MA: Rounder Records.
Farb, P. (1974). *Word play: What happens when people talk.* New York: Knopf.
Feltovich, P. J., Spiro, R. J., & Coulson, R. J. (1989). The nature of conceptual understanding in biomedicine: The deep structure of complex ideas and the development of misconceptions. In D. Evans & V. Patel (Eds.), *The cognitive sciences in medicine.* Cambridge: MIT Press (Bradford Books).
Fisher, R., & Ury, W. (1983). *Getting to yes: Negotiating agreement without giving in.* New York: Penguin Books.
Fiske, S. T., & Linville, P. W. (1980). What does the schema concept buy us? *Personality and Social Psychology Bulletin, 6*(4), 543–557.
Flanagan, J. C. (1954). The critical incident. *Psychological Bulletin, 51*(4), 327–358.
Flavell, J. H., & Wellman, H. M. (1977). In J. R. V. Kail & W. Hagen (Eds.), *Perspectives on the development of memory and cognition* Hillsdale, NJ: Erlbaum.
Flecker, S. A. (1990). Writing in deep water. *Pitt Magazine, 5*(3), 16–19.
Florio-Ruane, S. (1991). Conversation and narrative in collaborative research: An ethnography of the written literacy forum. In C. Witherell & N. Noddings (Eds.), *Stories lives tell: Narrative and dialogue in education* (pp. 234–255). New York: Teachers College Press.
Flower, L. (1987). Interpretive acts: Cognition and the construction of discourse *Poetics, 16* (Special issue: The New Rhetoric and the New Literacy Theory), 109–130.
Flower, L. (1988). The construction of purpose in writing and reading. *College English, 50*(5), 528–550.
Flower, L. (1989a). Cognition, context, and theory building. *College Composition and Communication, 40*(3), 282–311.
Flower, L. (1989b). Taking thought: The role of conscious processing in the making of meaning. In E. Maimon, B. Nodine, F. W. O'Connor (Eds.), *Thinking, reasoning and writing* (pp. 185–212). New York: Longman.
Flower, L. (1993a). Cognitive rhetoric: Inquiry into the art of inquiry. In T.

Enos & S. C. Brown (Eds.), *Defining the new rhetorics* (pp. 171–190). Newbury Park, CA: Sage.

Flower, L. (1993b). *Problem-solving strategies for writing* (4th ed.). New York: Harcourt Brace Jovanovich.

Flower, L. (1993c). Teachers are theory builders. In L. Flower, D. L. Wallace, L. Norris, & R. Burnett (Eds.), *Making thinking visible: Writing, collaborative planning, and classroom inquiry* (pp. 3–22). Urbana, IL: National Council of Teachers of English.

Flower, L., & Ackerman, J. (1994). *Writers at work: Strategies for communicating in business and professional settings.* New York: Harcourt Brace Jovanovich.

Flower, L., & Hayes, J. R.. (1981). A cognitive process theory of writing. *College Composition and Communication, 32*(1), 365–387.

Flower, L., & Hayes, J. R. (1984). Images, plans, and prose: The representation of meaning in writing. *Written Communication, 1*(1), 120–160.

Flower, L., Hayes, J. R., Carey, L., Schriver, K. A., & Stratman, J. (1986). Detection, diagnosis, and the strategies of revision. *College Composition and Communication, 37*(1), 16–55.

Flower, L., & Higgins, L. (1991). *Collaboration and the construction of meaning* (Tech. Rep. No. 56). Berkeley: University of California, Berkeley and Carnegie Mellon University, National Center for the Study of Writing and Literacy.

Flower, L., Schriver, K. A., Carey, L., Haas, C., & Hayes, J. R. (1992). Planning in writing: The cognition of a constructive process. In S. P. Witte, N. Nakadate, & R. D. Cherry (Eds.), *A rhetoric of doing: Essays on written discourse in honor of James L. Kinneavy* (pp. 181–243). Carbondale, IL: Southern Illinois University Press.

Flower, L., Stein, V., Ackerman, J., Kantz, M. J., McCormick, K., & Peck, W. C. (1990). *Reading-to-write: Exploring a cognitive and social process.* New York: Oxford University Press.

Flower, L., Wallace, D. L., Norris, L., & Burnett, R. E. (1993). *Making thinking visible: Writing, collaborative planning, and classroom inquiry.* Urbana, IL: National Council of Teachers of English.

Fordham, S. (1988). Racelessness as a factor in black students' school success: Pragmatic strategy or pyrrhic victory? *Harvard Educational Review, 58*(1), 54–84.

Fordham, S. (1991). Peer-proofing academic competition among black adolescents: "Acting white" Black American style. In C. Sleeter (Ed.), *Empowerment through multicultural education* (pp. 69–93). Albany, NY: State University of New York Press.

Foucault, M. (1977). What is an 'author'? In D. F. Bouchard (Ed.), *Language, counter-memory, practice: Selected essays and interviews.* Ithaca, NY: Cornell University Press.

Freedman, S. W. (1987). *Response to student writing.* Urbana, IL: National Council of Teachers of English.

Freedman, S. W. (1992, April). *The teaching and learning of writing in Great Britain and the United States: Comparing social contexts.* Paper presented at the American Educational Research Association, San Francisco, CA.

Freire, P. (1989). *Pedagogy of the oppressed* (M. Bergman Ramos, Trans.). New York: Continuum.
Gardner, H. (1985). *The mind's new science: A history of the cognitive revolution*. New York: Basic Books.
Garrison, J. W., & Macmillan, C. J. B. (1984). A philosophical critique of process-product research on teaching. *Educational Theory*, 34(3), 255–274.
Gee, J. P. (1989). Literacy, discourse, and linguistics. *Journal of Education*, 171(1), 5–17.
Gere, A. R. (1987). *Writing groups: History, theory and implications*. Carbondale, IL: Southern Illinois University Press.
Gere, A. R., & Stevens, R. S. (1985). The language of writing groups: How oral response shapes revision. In S. W. Freedman (Ed.), *The acquisition of written language* (pp. 85–105). Norwood, NJ: Ablex.
Giroux, H. A. (1983). *Theory and resistance in education: A pedagogy for the opposition*. South Hadley, MA: Bergin Garvey.
Giroux, H. A., & McLaren, P. (1989). *Critical pedagogy, the state, and cultural struggle*. Albany, NY: State University of New York Press.
Goodlad, J. (1984). *A place called school*. New York: McGraw-Hill.
Goodnow, J. J. (1976). The nature of intelligent behavior. Questions raised by cross-cultural studies. In L. B. Resnick (Ed.), *New approaches to intelligence* (pp. 168–188). Potomac, MD: Erlbaum.
Goody, J. (1977). *The domestication of the savage mind*. Cambridge: Cambridge University Press.
Graff, G. (1985). The university and the prevention of culture. In G. Graff & R. Gibbons (Eds.), *Criticism in the university* (pp. 62–82). Evanston, IL: Northwestern University Press.
Graff, G. (1987). *Professing literature*. Chicago: University of Chicago Press.
Greene, S. (1990a). Toward a dialectical theory of composition. *Rhetoric Review*, 9(1), 149–172.
Greene, S. (1990b). Writing from sources: Authority in text and task (Doctoral dissertation, Carnegie Mellon University, 1990). *Dissertation Abstracts International*, 52/02A, p. 450.
Greene, S. (1992). Mining texts in reading to write. *Journal of Advanced Composition*, 12(1), 151–170.
Greene, S. (1993). The role of task in the development of academic thinking through reading and writing in a college history course. *Research in the Teaching of English*, 27(1), 46–75.
Greene, S. (in press). Students as authors in the study of history. In G. Leinhardt & I. Beck (Eds.), *Teaching and learning in history*. Hillsdale, NJ: Erlbaum.
Haas, C., & Flower, L. (1988). Rhetorical reading strategies and the construction of meaning. *College Composition and Communication*, 39 (2), 167–183.
Hall, S. (1980). Encoding/decoding. In The Centre for Contemporary Cultural Studies, University of Birmingham, England (Ed.), *Culture, media, language: Working papers in cultural studies, 1972–79* (pp. 128–138). Boston: Unwin Hyman.
Hall, S. (1986, Summer). On postmodernism and articulation: An interview

with Stuart Hall, by L. Grossberg (Ed.). *Journal of Communication Inquiry*, 45–60.

Harris, K. R., & Pressley, M. (1991). The nature of cognitive strategy instruction: Interactive strategy construction. *Exceptional Children, 57*(5), 392–404.

Hayes, J. R. (1978). *Cognitive psychology: Thinking and creating*. Homewood, IL: Dorsey Press.

Hayes, J. R. (1981). *The complete problem solver*. Philadelphia: Franklin Institute Press.

Hayes, J. R., Flower, L., Schriver, K. A., Stratman, J. F., & Carey, L. (1987). Cognitive processes in revision. In S. Rosenberg (Ed.), *Advances in applied psycholinguistics: Vol. 2: Reading, writing, and language learning* (pp. 176–240). Cambridge: Cambridge University Press.

Hayes-Roth, B., & Hayes-Roth, F. (1978). A cognitive model of planning. *Cognitive Science, 3*, 275–310.

Heath, S. B. (1982). What no bedtime story means: Narrative skills at home and in school. *Language in Society, 11*(2), 49–76.

Heath, S. B. (1983). *Ways with words: Language, life, and work in communities*. Cambridge: Cambridge University Press.

Herrington, A. (1985). Writing in academic settings: A study of the contexts for writing in two college chemical engineering courses. *Research in the Teaching of English, 19*, 331–361.

Herrington, A. (1988). Teaching, writing and learning: A naturalistic study of writing in an undergraduate literature course. In D. Jolliffe (Ed.), *Advances in writing research: Vol. 2. Writing in academic disciplines* (pp. 133–166). Norwood, NJ: Ablex.

Higgins, L. (1992). *Argument as construction: A framework and method*. Unpublished doctoral dissertation, Carnegie Mellon University, Pittsburgh, PA.

Higgins, L., Flower, L., & Petraglia, J. (1992). Planning text together: The role of critical reflection in student collaboration. *Written Communication, 9*(1), 48–84.

Hillocks, G. (1986). *Research on written composition*. Urbana, IL: National Council of Teachers of English.

Hull, G. (1991). *Hearing other voices: A critical assessment of popular views on literacy and work*. Berkeley: University of California, National Center for Research in Vocational Education.

Hull, G., & Rose, M. (1989). Rethinking remediation: Toward a social-cognitive understanding of problematic reading and writing. *Written Communication, 6*(2), 139–154.

Hull, G., & Rose, M. (1991). *Reconceiving remediation*. A Research Proposal to the Spencer Foundation.

Hull, G., Rose, M., Fraser, K., & Castellano, M. (1991). Remediation as social construct: Perspectives from an analysis of classroom discourse. *College Composition and Communication, 42*(3), 299–329.

Hunt, R. A., & Vipond, D. (1986). Evaluations in literary reading. *TEXT, 6*, 53–71.

Jones, B. F., Palincsar, A. S., Ogle, D. S., & Carr, E. G. (Eds.). (1987). *Strategic teaching and learning: Cognitive instruction in the content areas*. Alexandria, VA: Association for Supervision and Curriculum Development (in cooperation with the North Central Regional Educational Laboratory).

Kaestle, C. F. (1988). The history of literacy and the history of readers. In E. R. Kintgen, B. M. Kroll, & M. Rose (Eds.), *Perspectives on literacy* (pp. 95–126). Carbondale, IL: Southern Illinois University Press.

Kalstone, D. (1967). *Sidney's poetry: Context and interpretation.* Cambridge: Harvard University Press.

Kantz, M. J. (1987). Composing from textual sources: Rhetorical stances for writing syntheses (Doctoral dissertation, Carnegie Mellon University, 1987). *Dissertation Abstracts International,* 48/09A, p. 2344.

Kaufer, D., & Carley, K. (1993). *Reading and writing arguments in a community: An issues-centered approach.* Hillsdale, NJ: Erlbaum.

Kiniry, M., & M. Rose. (1990). *Critical strategies for academic writing: Cases, assignments, and readings.* New York: St. Martin's Press.

Kintsch, W. (1988). The role of knowledge in discourse comprehension: A construction-integration model. *Psychological Review,* 95(2), 163–182.

Kuhn, D., Amsel, E., & O'Loughlin, M. (1988). *The development of scientific thinking skills.* New York: Academic Press.

Kuhn, T. S. (1970). *The structure of scientific revolution* (2nd Ed.). Chicago: University of Chicago Press.

Labov, W. (1972). *Language in the inner city.* Philadelphia: University of Pennsylvania Press.

Langer, J. (1984). The effects of available information on responses to school writing tasks. *Research in the Teaching of English,* *18*(1), 27–44.

Langer, J. A. (1986). Reading, writing, and understanding: An analysis of the construction of meaning. *Written Communication,* 3, 219–267.

Larkin, J. (1983). The role of problem representation in physics. In D. Gertner & A. Stevens (Eds.), *Mental models* (pp. 75–98). Hillsdale, NJ: Erlbaum.

Latour, B. (1987). *Science in action.* Cambridge: Harvard University Press.

Lave, J. (1988). *Cognition in practice: Mind, mathematics and culture in everyday life.* New York: Cambridge University Press.

LeFevre, K. B. (1987). *Invention as a social act.* Carbondale, IL: Southern Illinois University Press.

Lindsay, P. H., & Norman, D. A. (1972). *Human information processing: An introduction to psychology.* New York: Academic Press.

Lunsford, A. A., Moglen, H., & Slevin, J. (1990). *The right to literacy.* New York: Modern Language Association of America.

Macrorie, K. (1970). *Uptaught.* New York: Hayden Book.

Making Thinking Visible Project Series: ERIC No. ED 334593, December, 1991; ERIC No. ED 334594, December, 1991; ERIC No. ED 335682, January, 1992; Eric No. ED 348670, January, 1993.

Mandel, B. (1980). The writer writing is not at home. *College Composition and Communication,* *31*(4), 370–377.

McClelland, J. L., Rumelhart, D. E., & P. D. P. Research Group. (1986). *Parallel distributed processing: Explorations in the microstructure of cognition: Vol. 2. Psychological and biological models.* Cambridge: MIT Press/Bradford Books.

McLeod, S. (1987). Some thoughts about feelings: The affective domain and the writing process. *College Composition and Communication, 38*, 426–435.

Meichenbaum, D. (1977). *Cognitive behavior modification: An integrative approach*. New York: Plenum Press.

Meichenbaum, D. (1985). Teaching thinking: A cognitive-behavioral perspective. In S. F. Chipman, J. W. Segal, & R. Glaser (Eds.), *Thinking and learning skills: Vol. 2. Research and open questions* (pp. 407–426). Hillsdale, NJ: Erlbaum.

Meyer, B. J. F. (1982). Reading research and the composition teacher: The importance of plans. *College Composition and Communication, 33*, 34–49.

Myers, G. (1985). The social construction of two biologists' proposals. *Written Communication, 2*(3), 219–245.

National Assessment of Educational Progress. (1981). *Reading, thinking and writing: Results from the 1979–80 National Assessment of Reading and Literature*. Denver: National Assessment of Educational Progress.

Nelson, J. (1990). This was an easy assignment: Examining how students interpret academic writing tasks. *Research in the Teaching of English, 24*(4), 362–396.

Newkirk, T. (1984). How students read student papers: An exploratory study. *Written Communication, 1*, 283–305.

Nisbett, R. E., & Wilson, T. D. (1977). Telling more than we know: Verbal reports on mental processes. *Psychology Review, 84*, 231–257.

Norman, D. A. (1980). What goes on in the mind of the learner. In W. J. McKeachie (Ed.), *Learning, cognition and college teaching: Vol . 2. New directions for learning and teaching* (pp. 37–63). San Francisco: Jossey-Bass.

Nystrand, M. (1986). *The structure of written communication: Studies in reciprocity between writers and readers*. New York: Academic Press.

Nystrand, M. (1990). Sharing words: The effects of readers on developing writers. *Written Communication, 7*(1), 3–24.

Odell, L. & Goswami, D. (1985). *Writing in nonacademic settings*. New York: Guilford Press.

Olson, David R. (1988). From utterance to text: The bias of language in speech and writing. In E. R. Kintgen, B. M. Kroll, & M. Rose (Eds.), *Perspectives on literacy* (pp. 175–189). Carbondale, IL: Southern Illinois University Press.

Palincsar, A., & Brown, A. L. (1984). Reciprocal teaching of comprehension-fostering and comprehension-monitoring activities. *Cognition and Instruction, 1*, 117–175.

Palincsar, A., & Wineburg, S. (1989). Response to situated cognition and the culture of learning. *Educational Researcher, 18*(4), 5–8.

Paris, S. (1988, April). *Fusing skill and will in children's learning and schooling*. Paper presented at the annual meeting of the American Educational Researchers Association, New Orleans, LA.

Paris, S., & Winograd, P. (1990). How metacognition can promote academic learning and instruction. In B. F. Jones & L. Idol (Eds.), *Dimensions of thinking and cognitive instruction* (pp. 15–52). Hillsdale, NJ: Erlbaum.

Peck, W. C. (1991). Community advocacy: Composing for action (Doctoral dissertation, Carnegie Mellon University, 1991). *Dissertation Abstracts International, 53/02A*, p. 431.

Perelman, Ch., & Olbrechts-Tyteca, L. (1969). *The new rhetoric: A treatise on argumentation* (J. Wilkinson & P. Weaver, Trans.). Notre Dame, IN: University of Notre Dame Press.

Petraglia, J. (1991). Interrupting the conversation: The constructionist dialogue. *Journal of Advanced Composition, 11*(1), 37–55.

Phelps, L. W. (1990, May). *The discourse of controversy in composition studies.* Presented at the conference on "The Rhetoric of Controversies in Literary Criticism," University of Waterloo, Ontario.

Philips, S. U. (1990). Epilogue to "Some sources of cultural variability in the regulation of talk". In D. Carbaugh (Ed.), *Cultural communication and intercultural contact* (pp. 345–348). Hillsdale, NJ: Erlbaum.

Piaget, J. (1932). *The language and thought of the child.* (M. Gabin, Trans.). New York: Harcourt, Brace.

Poovey, M. (1990). Cultural criticism: Past and present. *College English, 52*(6), 615–625.

Prawat, R. S. (1989). Promoting access to knowledge, strategy, and disposition in students: A research synthesis. *Review of Educational Research, 59*(1), 1–41.

Pressley, M., Harris, K. R., & Marks, M. B. (1992). But good strategy instructors are constructivists!! *Educational Psychology Review, 4*, 3–31.

Resnick, D. P., & Resnick, L. B. (1988). The nature of literacy: A historical exploration. In E. R. Kintgen, B. M. Kroll, & M. Rose (Eds.), *Perspectives on literacy* (pp. 190–202). Carbondale, IL: Southern Illinois University Press.

Resnick, D. P., & Resnick, L. B. (1989). Varieties of literacy. In A. B. Barnes & P. N. Stearns (Eds.), *Social history and issues in human consciousness: Some interdisciplinary connections* (pp. 171–196). New York: New York University Press.

Rogoff, B. (1990). *Apprenticeship in thinking: Cognitive development in social context.* New York: Oxford University Press.

Rosaldo, M. Z. (1990). The things we do with words: Ilongot speech acts and speech act theory in philosophy. In D. Carbaugh (Ed.), *Cultural communication and intercultural contact* (pp. 373–407). Hillsdale, NJ: Erlbaum.

Rose, M. (1985). The language of exclusion: Writing instruction at the university. *College English, 47*(4), 341–359.

Rose, M. (1988). Narrowing the mind and page: Remedial writers and cognitive reductionism. *College Composition and Communication, 39*, 267–301.

Rose, M. (1989). *Lives on the boundary: The struggles and achievements of America's underprepared.* New York: Free Press.

Rubin, L. (1983). Exploration of the writing experience: A way to improve composing. *College Composition and Communication*, 34, 349–355.

Saxe, G. B. (1991). *Culture and cognitive development: Studies in mathematical understanding.* Hillsdale, NJ: Erlbaum.

Schank, R. C., & Abelson, R. P. (1977). *Scripts, plans, goals and understanding: An inquiry into human knowledge structures.* Hillsdale, NJ: Erlbaum.

Schriver, K. A. (1992). Teaching writers to anticipate readers' needs. *Written Communication* , 9(2), 179–208.

Scollon, R., & Scollon, S. (1981). *Narrative, literacy, and race in interethnic communication*. Norwood, NJ: Ablex.

Scribner, S., & Cole, M. (1981). *The psychology of literacy*. Cambridge: Harvard University Press.

Selzer, J. (1983). The composing processes of an engineer. *College Composition and Communication*, 34(2), 178–187.

Simmons, W. (1985). Social class and ethnic differences in cognition: A cultural practice perspective. In S. F. Chipman, J. W. Segal, & R. Glaser (Eds.), *Thinking and learning skills: Vol. 2. Research and open questions* (pp. 519–536). Hillsdale, NJ: Erlbaum.

Simon, P., & Shabalala, J. (Composers: Words and music). (1986). Homeless (Song on *Graceland* music album). Burbank, CA: Warner Bros.

Sitko, B. M. (1989). Writers' cognitive and decision processes: Revising after feedback (Doctoral dissertation, Carnegie Mellon University, 1989). *Dissertation Abstracts International*, *51/02A*, p. 439.

Sitko, B. M. (1992). Writers meet their readers in the classroom: Revising after feedback. In M. Secore & D. Charney (Eds.), *Constructing rhetorical education* (pp. 278–294). Carbondale, IL: Southern Illinois University Press.

Sitko, B. M., & Flower, L. (in press). *Metaknowledge in writing: The fruits of observation-based reflection* (Tech. Rep.). Berkeley: University of California and Carnegie Mellon University, National Center for the Study of Writing and Literacy.

Skinner, B. F. (1963). Operant behavior. *American Psychologist, 18*, 503–515.

Sloane, T. O. (1989). Reinventing *inventio*. *College English, 51*(5), 461–473.

Sperling, M. (1990). I want to talk to each of you: Collaboration and the teacher-student writing conference. *Research in the Teaching of English*, 24(3), 279–321.

Spivey, N. N. (1984). *Discourse synthesis: Constructing texts in reading and writing* (Outstanding Dissertation Monograph Series). Newark, DE: International Reading Association.

Spivey, N. N. (1987). Construing constructivism: Reading research in the United States. *Poetics, 16*,169–192.

Spivey, N. N. (1990). Transforming texts: Constructive processes in reading and writing. *Written Communication*, 7(2), 256–287.

Stein, V. (1992). *How we begin to remember: Elaboration, task, and the transformation of knowledge*. Unpublished doctoral dissertation, Carnegie Mellon University, Pittsburgh, PA.

Swales, J. (1984). Research into the structure of introductions to journal articles and its application to the teaching of academic writing. In R. Williams, J. Swales, & J. Kirkman (Eds.), *Common ground: Shared interests in ESP and communications studies* (pp. 77–86). Oxford: Pergamon.

Trimbur, J. (1989). Consensus and difference in collaborative learning. *College English, 51*(6), 602–616.

Tulving, E. (1972). Episodic and semantic memory. In E. Tulving & W. Donaldson (Eds.), *The organization of memory*. New York: Academic Press.

Turner, G. (1990). Text and contexts. In *British cultural studies: An introduction*

(Media and popular culture [ed. David Thorburn]: 7) (pp. 87–130). Boston: Unwin Hyman.

Voss, J., Tyler, S., & Yengo, L. (1983). Individual differences in the solving of social science problems. In R. F. Dillon & R. R. Schmeck (Eds.), *Individual differences in cognition* (pp. 205–232). New York: Academic Press.

Vygotsky, L. (1986). *Thought and language* (Rev. ed.). Cambridge: MIT Press.

Vygotsky, L. S. (1987). *Mind in society.* Cambridge: Harvard University Press.

Wallace, D. (1991). From intention to text: Developing, implementing, and judging intentions in writing (Doctoral dissertation, Carnegie Mellon University, 1991). *Dissertation Abstracts International,* 52/04A, p. 1242.

Walvoord, B. E., & McCarthy, L. P. (1990). *Thinking and writing in college: A naturalistic study of students in four disciplines.* Urbana, IL: National Council of Teachers of English.

Watt, I. (1967). *The rise of the novel.* Berkeley: University of California Press.

Willinsky, J. (1990). *The new literacy: Redefining reading and writing in the schools.* New York: Routledge.

Witte, S. (1987). Pre-text and composing. *College Composition and Communication, 38,* 397–425.

Witte, S. P. (1992). Context, text, intertext: Toward a constructivist semiotic of writing. *Written Communication,* 9(2), 237–308.

Wood, R. E., & Bandura, A. (1989). Impact of conceptions of ability on self-regulatory mechanisms and complex decision-making. *Journal of Personality and Social Psychology, 56,* 407–415.

Young, R. E. (1974). Paradigms and problems: Needed research in rhetorical invention. In C. Cooper & L. Odell (Eds.), *Research on composing*(pp. 29–47). Urbana, IL: National Council of Teachers of English.

Young, R. E., Becker, A. L., & Pike, K. L. (1970). *Rhetoric: Discovery and change.* New York: Harcourt, Brace & World.

Index

Linda Flower is a professor of rhetoric at Carnegie Mellon University and a codirector of the National Center for the Study of Writing and Literacy at the University of California, Berkeley and Carnegie Mellon. Helping to define the new field of cognitive rhetoric, her work with John R. Hayes offered models of basic cognitive processes in writing and revision. In a second generation of studies (including *Reading-to-Write: Exploring a Cognitive and Social Process*), her research turned to the situated cognition of students entering a new discourse and argued for a more integrated social cognitive theory. Flower's research has been grounded in teaching. She is the author of *Problem-Solving Strategies for Writing*. Her interest in collaborative planning as a tool for teaching and reflection grew into a 5-year classroom inquiry project with local school and college teachers, whose observations appear in *Making Thinking Visible: Writing, Collaborative Planning, and Classroom Inquiry*. With coauthor John Ackerman, she has attempted to bring this collaborative, social cognitive perspective to nonacademic writing in *Writers at Work: Strategies for Communicating in Business and Professional Settings*. Flower's current work with Wayne Peck has led to the founding of Pittsburgh's Community Literacy Center focused on action research with inner city teenagers as they use writing to take literate action and with college mentors as they learn to enter this intercultural conversation.